SIMONE WEIL'S APOLOGETIC USE OF LITERATURE

OXFORD MODERN LANGUAGES AND LITERATURE MONOGRAPHS

Editorial Committee

C. H. GRIFFIN   E. M. JEFFREYS   A. KAHN
K. M. KOHL   M. L. MCLAUGHLIN
I. W. F. MACLEAN   R. A. G. PEARSON

Simone Weil's Apologetic Use of Literature

Her Christological Interpretations of Ancient Greek Texts

MARIE CABAUD MEANEY

OXFORD
UNIVERSITY PRESS

Great Clarendon Street, Oxford OX2 6DP

Oxford University Press is a department of the University of Oxford.
It furthers the University's objective of excellence in research, scholarship,
and education by publishing worldwide in

Oxford New York

Auckland Cape Town Dar es Salaam Hong Kong Karachi
Kuala Lumpur Madrid Melbourne Mexico City Nairobi
New Delhi Shanghai Taipei Toronto

With offices in

Argentina Austria Brazil Chile Czech Republic France Greece
Guatemala Hungary Italy Japan Poland Portugal Singapore
South Korea Switzerland Thailand Turkey Ukraine Vietnam

Oxford is a registered trade mark of Oxford University Press
in the UK and in certain other countries

Published in the United States
by Oxford University Press Inc., New York

© Marie Cabaud Meaney 2007

The moral rights of the author have been asserted
Database right Oxford University Press (maker)

First published 2007

All rights reserved. No part of this publication may be reproduced,
stored in a retrieval system, or transmitted, in any form or by any means,
without the prior permission in writing of Oxford University Press,
or as expressly permitted by law, or under terms agreed with the appropriate
reprographics rights organization. Enquiries concerning reproduction
outside the scope of the above should be sent to the Rights Department,
Oxford University Press, at the address above

You must not circulate this book in any other binding or cover
and you must impose the same condition on any acquirer

British Library Cataloguing in Publication Data

Data available

Library of Congress Cataloging in Publication Data

Data available

Typeset by Laserwords Private Limited, Chennai, India
Printed in Great Britain
on acid-free paper by
Biddles Ltd., King's Lynn, Norfolk

ISBN 978–0–19–921245–3

1 3 5 7 9 10 8 6 4 2

To my parents, especially to my father, Jacques Cabaud, who inspired me with his love for Simone Weil

Preface

This book aims to address an important aspect of Simone Weil's thought that has not been covered so far, namely her original interpretations of ancient Greek texts. Though her article 'L'*Iliade* ou le poème de la force' is highly regarded among classicists, her interpretations of Greek tragedy are hardly known. On the one hand, this is due to the fact that they are mostly fragmentary, consisting of notes taken for talks and in view of a book she wished to write together with the Dominican priest, Father Perrin. On the other hand, the reason for this lacuna may lie with the Christological nature of her readings. Though her article on the *Iliad* ends with a comparison of the epic to the Gospel, its focus on Christianity is not obvious since a redeemer figure is precisely missing in the Homeric text. This, in Weil's eyes, is not the case in the Sophoclean *Antigone* and *Electra*, or in Aeschylus' *Prometheus Bound*. Antigone becomes a Christ-figure, dying out of a folly of love, and undergoing a Passion in which she feels forsaken by gods and men. Electra stands for someone going through a dark night of the soul, but not abandoning hope and thus being rewarded with a mystical experience, symbolized by the revelation of Orestes to his sister. Prometheus, on the other hand, is not really in conflict with Zeus, but is experiencing the dereliction of Christ on the cross. For Weil, these tragedies as well as Homer's epic reveal the presence of the supernatural in the world, be it in the form of the moral law, of a supernatural perspective overruling all ideology, or of God's presence in suffering and in mystical encounters.

Since first reading Weil, I have been intrigued by her Christological and imaginative approach to ancient Greek literature. This compelled me to analyse her hermeneutics, explore her motivations, and see whether her misreadings could also contribute something to the field of Classics. Her approach made sense once I came to realize that her intentions were apologetic, at least in part. If the agnostic intellectuals of her day came to see that these texts which they cherish so much could only be fully understood in the light of Christ, then they might be more open to Christianity. On the other hand, Weil thought that if Catholics came to the same conclusion, then they would have to admit that Catholicism is much more universal than generally accepted and that Christianity had existed before the incarnation of Christ. Thus, they too would be led to display greater openness and dialogue. In paradigmatic form the Greek classics would convey to both groups the existence of the supernatural.

Though proficient in Latin and Greek Weil did not care to consult or use the classical scholarship of her day, at least not in depth. She preferred to read the texts directly and closely—something she had been trained to do by her famous teacher, the philosopher Alain. Therefore, I chose to disregard in great part the secondary literature of her time, and instead focus on what her interpretations could contribute to modern scholarship. In consequence, I compared her readings to those of modern classicists, situating her approach and pointing out the ways in which they were sometimes extravagant and sometimes insightful.

Weil is a 'strong' reader, casting these familiar texts into new shapes. Her thought, her personality, and her manner of expressing herself have the power to attract, but also the tendency to repel. No matter what our reactions to Weil are, her interpretations startle and will make us think about these classics in new ways. This book attempts to analyse and explain her approach, and perhaps make it compelling. Thus I start in Ch. 1 with an investigation of Weil's love for and perspective on ancient Greek texts before looking, in Ch. 2 at her ideas on apologetics and at her as an apologist, prior to comparing her to other apologists in Ch. 3. Only then do I give a close reading of Weil's interpretations of *Antigone, Iliad, Prometheus Bound*, and *Electra* in Chs. 4–7. In order to do this I often had to piece together her fragmentary readings of these texts and draw on a whole number of her writings to explain in depth some of the concepts she used.

By definition any book on Weil will have to be interdisciplinary. Weil herself moved seamlessly between the fields of philosophy, literature, theology, Classics, history, politics, and mathematics. Therefore this book should be of interest to specialists and amateurs in different fields: obviously to Weil-specialists, but also to classicists, theologians, and French linguists, as well as to the wider audience of Weil-lovers or to those who are encountering her for the first time. Though it cannot pretend to give a complete overview of Weil's thought, it offers an important key to many of its aspects since a significant number of her central ideas are contained in her interpretations. Finally, her existential readings of Greek texts reveal something of her own personality, of her ideals and her approach to all matters intellectual: her intransigent search for the truth, her desire to put it into practice immediately no matter what the consequences are, and her desire to share with others this treasure that she felt had been given her. These attitudes are not just reflected in her interpretations but are embodied by the very figures she interprets with such admiration—thus offering us a further key to Weil.

To make the book accessible to a wider audience, English translations of the French quotes have been included. When no published translation existed or when I disagreed with it, I provided the translation myself. In order to avoid the text becoming too convoluted, however, I chose to give the references only to the French editions of Weil's texts—except in the case of a quotation, when I give the references to the editions in both languages. At the beginning of Chs. 4–7 in which I analyse Weil's interpretations of individual Greek texts, I start off with an overview of the passages Weil quotes and the history of her interest in the tragedy or epic. This may be of greater interest to the Weil-specialist or classicist than to others and can easily be skipped by the reader. Furthermore, for those who simply want learn about Weil's interpretation of a specific Greek text these chapters can be read separately without the need to peruse the first three chapters.

M.C.M

Acknowledgements

My first thanks go to my parents, Jacques and Rosemarie Cabaud, who made my studies possible and who supported me in every way. My father, who wrote the first major biography on Weil, initiated me into the thought of this great thinker and sparked my love for her. I also wish to thank my husband Joseph, who encouraged me all along with his cheerful spirit. Dr Toby Garfitt (Magdalen College, Oxford) has done everything one could wish from a thesis supervisor, from detailed corrections and helpful suggestions to general encouragement. My special thanks go to him. Dr Nicholas Richardson (Merton College and Greyfriars, Oxford) has very kindly followed my work on Weil from its beginnings, and has made valuable suggestions from a classicist's perspective. Florence de Lussy from the Bibliothèque Nationale in Paris generously gave me access to the Weil archives, pointing out relevant texts, as well as sending me photocopies when needed. With his enthusiasm and erudition the late Prof. Malcolm Bowie (All Souls, Oxford and Magdalen College, Cambridge) was of significant help as adviser in my first year. Prof. Oliver Taplin (Magdalen College, Oxford) kindly commented on parts of my chapter on the *Iliad*. I am also grateful to Dr Josef Seifert, rector of the International Academy of Philosophy, Liechtenstein, who gave me the philosophical training necessary to deal with such a thinker as Weil. Similarly my thanks go to Dr Rocco Buttiglione and Dr John White. Furthermore, I would like to thank Tom Perridge and other editors at Oxford University Press who have been very helpful. Finally, I would like to express my gratitude to all my friends who consistently encouraged me, in particular Dr Maria Fedoryka, Dr Kateryna Cuddeback, Dr Helena Saward, Clothilde Morhan, Bruce Griffin, and many more. Dr Dan Varholy made helpful suggestions of how to downsize the original thesis. My thanks also go to the ISI which granted me the Western Civilization Scholarship.

I would like to thank Fayard for allowing me to use quotes from Simone Weil's *Attente de Dieu* (© Librairie Arthème Fayard, 1966) and from *Intuitions Pré-chrétiennes* (© Librairie Arthème Fayard, 1951). Penguin kindly allowed me to use excerpts from Simone Weil's *Waiting for God* (© G. P. Putnam's Sons, 1951, renewed 1979, trans. Emma

Crauford). Furthermore, I wish to thank Sylvie Weil for providing me with and allowing me to use for the front cover the famous photograph of the 12-year-old Simone Weil.

Contents

Abbreviations	xv
1. Simone Weil and the Classics	1
2. Simone Weil and Apologetics	29
3. Simone Weil as Apologist	58
4. Antigone and the Moral Law: Glimpses of the Supernatural	77
5. *Tableau de l'absence de Dieu*—A Modern Interpretation of the *Iliad*	115
6. *Prometheus Bound*—An Apologetics of the Cross	143
7. *Electra*—Waiting on God	178
8. Conclusion: Simone Weil—An Apologist of the Supernatural	207
Appendix: References to Ancient Greek Texts in the Works of Simone Weil	216
Bibliography	223
Index	241

Abbreviations

WORKS BY SIMONE WEIL

AD	*Attente de Dieu* ([Paris]: Fayard, 1966).
CO	*La Condition ouvrière* ([Paris]: Gallimard, 1951).
CS	*La Connaissance surnaturelle* ([Paris]: Gallimard, 1950).
CSW	*Cahiers Simone Weil.* For a complete list of articles, see Bibliography.
E	*L'Enracinement* ([Paris]: Gallimard, 1949).
EHP	*Écrits historiques et politiques* ([Paris]: Gallimard, 1960).
EL	*Écrits de Londres et dernières lettres* ([Paris]: Gallimard, 1957).
FLN	*First and Last Notebooks* (London: Oxford University Press, 1970).
IPC	*Intuitions pré-chrétiennes* (1951; repr. [Paris]: Fayard, 1985).
IC	*Intimations of Christianity among the Ancient Greeks* (1957; repr. London: Routledge, 1998).
IOPF	*Simone Weil's The Iliad or the Poem of Force: A Critical Edition*, ed. and trans. James P. Holoka (New York: Lang, 2003).
LOP	*Lectures on Philosophy*, ed. Anne Reynaud-Guérithault, trans. Hugh Price (Cambridge: Cambridge University Press, 1978).
LP	*Leçons de philosophie*, ed. Anne Reynaud-Guérithault ([Paris]: Plon, 1959).
LR	*Lettre à un religieux* (1951; repr. Paris: Gallimard [1974]).
LTP	*Letter to a Priest*, trans. Arthur Wills (1954; New York: Penguin, 2003).
ML	'Morale et littérature', *CSW* 10/4 (1987), 349–53.
NR	*The Need for Roots*, trans. Arthur Wills (1952; repr. London: Routledge, 2002).
NB	*The Notebooks of Simone Weil*, trans. Arthur Wills (1956; London: Routledge, 2004).
OAL	*Oppression and Liberty*, trans. Arthur Wills and John Petrie (1958; repr. London: Routledge, 2001)
OC	*Œuvres complètes*, ed. André Devaux and Florence de Lussy ([Paris]: Gallimard, 1988–2002).
i	*Premiers écrits philosophiques*, ed. Gilbert Kahn and Rolf Kühn (1988).
ii/1	*Écrits historiques et politiques: l'engagement syndical (1927–juillet 1934)*, ed. Géraldi Leroy (1988).

ii/2	*Écrits historiques et politiques: l'expérience ouvrière et l'adieu à la révolution (juillet 1934–juin 1937)*, ed. Géraldi Leroy and Anne Roche (1991).
ii/3	*Écrits historiques et politiques: vers la guerre (1937–1940)*, ed. Simone Fraisse (1989).
vi/1	*Cahiers (1933–septembre 1941)*, ed. Alyette Degrâces *et al.* (1994).
vi/2	*Cahiers (septembre 1941–février 1942)*, ed. Alyette Degrâces *et al.* (1997).
vi/3	*Cahiers (février 1942–juin 1942): la porte du transcendant*, ed. Alyette Degrâces *et al.* (2002).
Œ	*Simone Weil: œuvres*, ed. Florence de Lussy ([Paris]: Quarto Gallimard, 1999).
OL	*Oppression et liberté* ([Paris]: Gallimard, 1955).
P	*Poèmes, suivis de 'Venise sauvée'* ([Paris]: Gallimard, 1968).
PG	*La Pesanteur et la grâce* (Paris: Plon, 1948).
PSO	*Pensées sans ordre concernant l'amour de Dieu* ([Paris]: Gallimard, 1962).
RL	'Lettre aux *Cahiers du Sud* sur les responsabilités de la littérature', *CSW* 10/4 (1987), 354–7.
S	*Sur la science* ([Paris]: Gallimard, 1966).
SE	*Selected Essays 1934–43*, ed. and trans. Richard Rees (London: Oxford University Press, 1962).
SG	*La Source grecque* ([Paris]: Gallimard, 1953).
SL	*Seventy Letters*, ed. and trans. Richard Rees (Oxford: Oxford University Press, 1965).
SNL	*On Science, Necessity, and the Love of God*, ed. and trans. Richard Rees (London: Oxford University Press, 1968).
SW	*Simone Weil*, ed. and trans. Eric O. Springsted (New York: Orbis, 1998).
SWC	*Simone Weil on Colonialism: An Ethic of the Other*, ed. and trans. Janet Patricia Little (Lanham, Md.: Rowman & Littlefield, 2003).
VS	*Venise sauvée: tragédie en trois actes* ([Paris]: Gallimard, 1955).
WG	*Waiting for God*, trans. Emma Craufurd (New York: Putnam, 1951; repr. New York: HarperCollins, 2001).
WOG	*Waiting on God*, trans. Emma Craufurd (Routledge, 1951; repr. Glasgow: Fount, 1983).

OTHER ABBREVIATIONS

Ant.   Sophocles, *Antigone*, ed. and trans. Hugh Lloyd-Jones, Loeb 21 (1994; repr. with corrections, Cambridge, Mass.: Harvard University Press, 1998).

El.   Sophocles, *Electra*, ed. and trans. Hugh Lloyd-Jones, Loeb 20 (1994; repr. with corrections, Cambridge, Mass.: Harvard University Press, 1997).

Il.   Homer, *Iliad*, trans. A. T. Murray, rev. William F. Wyatt, Loeb 170, 171; 2 vols. (1924; 2nd edn., Cambridge, Mass.: Harvard University Press, 1999).

Prom.   Aeschylus, *Prometheus Bound*, trans. Herbert Weir Smyth, Loeb 145 (1921; repr. Cambridge, Mass.: Harvard University Press, 1996).

BN   Archives Simone Weil (if not otherwise indicated), Bibliothèque Nationale de Paris.

SP   Simone Pétrement, *La Vie de Simone Weil*, 2 vols. ([Paris]: Fayard, 1973).

For Weil's own works, I have adopted the abbreviations currently used among Weil scholars, inserting them directly into the text for the sake of convenience. For the Greek tragedies, I also cite them in the main text with parenthetical references indicating the line numbers. Otherwise I have adopted the author–date system, giving the last name of the author followed by the date of publication of the work in question, which I put into footnotes. For certain standard texts, such as those of Plato and Aristotle, I cite only author and work.

1
Simone Weil and the Classics

Hantée par cette distance [infinie entre Dieu et l'homme], la Grèce n'a travaillé qu'à construire des ponts. Toute sa civilisation en est faite. [...] nous avons hérité de tous ces ponts. Nous en avons beaucoup surélevé l'architecture. Mais nous croyons maintenant qu'ils sont faits pour y habiter. Nous ne savons pas qu'ils sont là pour qu'on y passe; nous ignorons, si l'on y passait, qui l'on trouverait de l'autre côté.[1]

(*EHP* 77)

Simone Weil (1909–43) is mainly identified as a political thinker and a religious author. Her interpretations of ancient Greek texts are less well known except for her article on the *Iliad* which has elicited some recognition among classicists.[2] Her readings of the Sophoclean *Antigone* and *Electra*, of Aeschylus' *Prometheus Bound*, of Plato and of the Pythagoreans are not usually included in the bibliographies of secondary works on the Greek classics. The reason is obvious: her anachronistic and Christological readings are shocking to those who wish to analyse texts with a critical-historical approach. Antigone, in her eyes, is a Christ-figure, giving her life out of a folly of love, adopting a supernatural perspective while Creon has embraced worldly reasoning. The recognition scene between Electra and her brother Orestes symbolizes for her a mystical encounter between the soul and God. Prometheus, on the other hand, is not really punished by Zeus, she believes, but simply experiences the same abandonment as Christ

---

[1] 'Haunted by this distance [between God and man], Greece worked solely to bridge it. This was what made her whole civilization. [...] [W]e have inherited all of the[se bridges]. We have built them up much higher. But we believe now that they were made to live in. We are unaware that they are only there to be passed across; we do not know, if we crossed over, whom we should find on the other side' (*SE* 46).
[2] This article is part of the recommended reading-list for undergraduate students in Classics in Oxford, for example.

on the cross. It is perhaps no wonder therefore that Weil's unorthodox readings have not found a wide hearing in the field of Classics. Yet P. Savinel gave a talk to the well-known Budé Association in 1958, later published in the *Bulletin de l'association Guillaume Budé*, saying that Weil is to be listed 'parmi les grands hellénistes français'. 'Helléniste', he explains, must be understood here in the wider sense of 'lecteur génial des œuvres grecques'.[3]

Weil's interest in ancient Greek texts dates back to her youth. But it was only after her first mystical experience in November 1938 that she started looking at antiquity in the light of Christianity, as she explains to Père Joseph-Marie Perrin in 1942: 'C'est après cela [l'expérience mystique] que j'ai senti que Platon est un mystique, que toute l'*Iliade* est baignée de lumière chrétienne, et que Dionysos et Osiris sont d'une certaine manière le Christ lui-même' (*AD* 46).[4] Born into an agnostic Jewish family, Weil had adopted a form of practical atheism in her teens, thinking the question of God irresolvable. It came as an absolute surprise to her when, as she writes, 'le Christ lui-même est descendu et m'a prise', while she was reciting George Herbert's poem 'Love' (ibid. 45).[5] Within a year she was writing her article on the *Iliad*. In Marseille, where she fled with her parents after the German occupation of Paris, she wrote her Christocentric interpretations of Greek tragedies. At a time when civilization seemed in grave danger, when the new barbarism of the Nazis seemed victorious, Weil significantly turned to the classics. Rather than interpreting this as an escape into an ivory tower, it should be understood as one of her ways of contributing to the raging spiritual battle.[6] For her, Nazism was a pseudo-religion, presenting itself as an absolute, and inspiring fanaticism in its adherents. It must be treated as such, Weil thought, and combated not only with material weapons, but also with spiritual ones. Only a true religion, for Europe only Christianity, could be this weapon. People must be reconverted and live the virtue of charity radically, for this alone can

---

[3] 'among the great French Hellenists' 'brilliant reader of Greek works', Savinel 1960: 123.

[4] 'After this I came to feel that Plato was a mystic, that all the *Iliad* is bathed in Christian light, and that Dionysus and Osiris are in a certain sense Christ himself' (*WG* 28).

[5] 'Christ himself came down and took possession of me' (ibid. 27).

[6] One cannot accuse Weil of an ivory tower mentality, given that she was engaged in the Resistance, distributed the clandestine paper *Témoignage chrétien*, and obtained false papers for those escaping the Nazis, among whom were Jews (Blum-David 1979: 181–2; id. and Rabi 1981: 79).

change the world. Surprisingly, Weil used the Greek classics to this end. For her Christological readings not only shed new light on the texts themselves, but also present Christianity anew. That Weil had an apologetic intention in mind when writing them is my claim and the main point I will argue in this book. As she wrote to Perrin, she thought it of the utmost urgency: 'de nouveau [d']élever le serpent d'airain [c'est-à-dire la croix] pour que quiconque jette les yeux sur lui soit sauvé' (ibid. 53).[7] Weil's interpretations are thus anything but mere academic exercises. They lack the characteristics of scholarship while making room for ideas that Weil thought more significant. Thus one needs to examine her general approach to ancient Greek texts, which I will do in this chapter, before turning to a thorough analysis of her individual interpretations. Here I will also give a brief introduction to her life, together with an overview of her writings and of the relevant secondary literature.

BIOGRAPHY

Simone Weil was born in Paris on 3 February 1909, three years after her brother André. Her parents were Jewish agnostics, but she only learnt about her Jewish background in 1919.[8] Her brother was a mathematical genius who became a famous mathematician. Simone Weil always felt inferior to him. She went through a crisis at 14, despairing of ever having access to the realm of truth because of 'la médiocrité de mes facultés naturelles' (*AD* 38).[9] However, after months of darkness, she reached the certainty that whoever desires to know the truth will do so. This inspired her search for truth throughout her life.

Her father, a medical doctor, served in World War I. After the war Simone went to the Lycée Fénelon, but at different periods was taught at home for health reasons. She attended the lessons of the idealist philosopher René Le Senne in 1924–5 at the Lycée Victor-Duruy, but he probably had little influence on her.[10] After completing her *baccalauréat de philosophie* in 1925 (a certificate taken at the end of high school with a focus on philosophy), she entered the prestigious Lycée

---

[7] 'The bronze serpent [i.e. the cross] must be lifted up again so that whoever raises his eyes to it may be saved' (*WG* 32).
[8] *Œ* 40; SP i. 48.   [9] 'the mediocrity of my natural faculties' (*WG* 23).
[10] SP i. 57, 63.

Henri IV and studied for three years under the famous philosopher Alain who made a significant impact on her. In 1928 she entered the École Normale Supérieure where she wrote her thesis on 'Science et perception dans Descartes'. In 1931 she was ranked seventh in the *agrégation* (a very competitive examination for the recruitment of teachers), and was sent to teach philosophy at the girls' *lycée* in le Puy. There she got involved in the syndicalist movement and fought to improve the working conditions of the proletariat. She wrote articles on the question and joined demonstrations. Problems with the authorities followed at various points, which did not disturb her in the least. She was then sent to teach in Auxerre and afterwards in Roanne. In the summer of 1932 she travelled to Germany to study the political situation there. She wrote some articles on the question for the revolutionary syndicalist journal *La Révolution prolétarienne*, for Alain's paper *Libres Propos*, and for the left-wing teachers' journal *L'École émancipée*. Throughout her life she wrote articles and signed petitions on questions dear to her heart. In November 1932 she met the dissident communist intellectual Boris Souvarine who became a friend and the editor of *La Critique sociale*, in which she often published. She obtained a sabbatical year in 1934–5 during which she worked in different factories in order to experience the working conditions of the local proletariat. She first completed, however, her *grande œuvre*, the 120-page long 'Réflexions sur les causes de la liberté et de l'oppression sociale' (*Reflections Concerning the Causes of Liberty and Social Oppression*), originally planned as an article for *La Critique sociale*; therein she criticizes Marx, asks why oppression is still so prevalent, and suggests that it is due to the nature of industrial production rather than to capitalism. She worked for Alsthom, Renault, and other companies, with periods of sick-leave and unemployment. Her health deteriorated greatly, and the headaches she had suffered since 1930 grew worse: 'J'avais l'âme et le corps en quelque sorte en morceaux' (*AD* 41).[11] In order to recover, she travelled with her parents to Spain and Portugal. In the poor Portuguese fishing village of Povoa do Varzim she witnessed a religious procession on 15 September, the feast of Our Lady of Sorrows, and came to see Christianity as the religion of the poor and of slaves, among whom she counted herself since her industrial experience.[12] In October 1935 she started a new teaching

---

[11] 'I was, as it were, in pieces, soul and body' (*WG* 25).

[12] 'J'ai reçu là [en usine] pour toujours la marque de l'esclavage, comme la marque au fer rouge que les Romains mettaient au front de leurs esclaves les plus méprisés. Depuis

position in Bourges. In August 1936, she volunteered for service in the Spanish Civil War on the side of the anarchists. However, after only two weeks she burnt herself badly by stepping accidentally into a cooking-pan filled with boiling oil. This meant a year of sick-leave in 1936–7. Aware of the danger of war, she wrote many articles in defence of pacifism. She last taught in Saint-Quentin in 1937, but had to stop in January 1938 because of her headaches. Though she asked for a teaching post in August 1940, after the occupation of Paris, she never received the answer from the Ministry of Education assigning her a post in Constantine, Algeria.[13]

She travelled to Italy in spring 1937, and in Assisi in the church of Santa Maria degli Angeli 'quelque chose de plus fort que moi m'a obligée, pour la première fois de ma vie, à me mettre à genoux' (*AD* 43).[14] In April 1938 she went to the Benedictine Abbey of Solesmes with her mother for Holy Week while suffering from terrible headaches: 'il va de soi qu'au cours de ces offices la pensée de la Passion du Christ est entrée en moi une fois pour toutes' (ibid.).[15] There she met a young Englishman, John Vernon, whose angelic expression after receiving communion touched her. She also encountered the American Charles Bell who, according to his own account, introduced her to the English metaphysical poets.[16] George Herbert's poem 'Love' struck her particularly, and she liked to recite it to herself during her headaches. It was probably in November 1938 that 'je croyais le réciter seulement comme un beau poème, mais à mon insu cette récitation avait la vertu d'une prière'. She continues: 'C'est au cours d'une de ces récitations que, comme je vous l'ai écrit, le Christ lui-même est descendu et m'a prise' (ibid. 44–5).[17]

---

je me suis toujours regardée comme une esclave' (*AD* 42) ('There I received forever the mark of a slave, like the branding of the red-hot iron the Romans put on the foreheads of their most despised slaves. Since then I have always regarded myself as a slave') (*WG* 25). Perrin 1983: 135; Canciani 2000: 26 n. 1.

[13] Little 1988*a*: 39; Canciani 2000: 29 n. 1.

[14] 'something stronger than I was compelled me for the first time in my life to go down on my knees' (*WG* 26).

[15] 'It goes without saying that in the course of these services the thought of the Passion of Christ entered into my being once and for all' (ibid.).

[16] Lemarchand 1983: 168, 177; SP ii. 192. Weil, in contrast, thought that the young Englishman John Vernon had introduced her to these poets (*AD* 43–4).

[17] 'I used to think I was merely reciting it as a beautiful poem, but without knowing it the recitation had the virtue of a prayer. It was during one of these recitations that, as I told you, Christ himself came down and took possession of me' (*WG* 27).

Though she abandoned her pacifism in March 1939 when Hitler annexed Bohemia-Moravia, she continued to write anti-colonialist articles. On 13 June 1940 the Weils left Paris (now declared an open city), went to Vichy, then Toulouse, and finally settled in Marseille. There Simone Weil got to know the journal, *Cahiers du Sud*, directed by Jean Ballard, for which she wrote many articles. At this point she was taught Sanskrit by René Daumal, an old friend from Henri IV, whereupon she started reading the *Bhagavadgītā* and the Upanishads in their original language. Daumal also introduced her to the Dominican priest Joseph-Marie Perrin who spoke with her frequently about Catholicism. She worked for the Resistance helping to distribute the clandestine journal *Témoignage Chrétien*. Through Perrin, she met Gustave Thibon, a Catholic writer and farmer, who became a good friend. Thibon later edited one of her more famous works, *La Pesanteur et la grace* (*Gravity and Grace*), a selection from the eleven *Cahiers* ('Notebooks') she left with him before going into exile. She also did farm work, harvesting grapes in autumn 1941. On 27 March 1942 she met the writer Joë Bousquet, paralysed since World War I, and talked to him for one evening. Bousquet and Perrin were the only people to whom she related her mystical experiences, in letters sent before departing for New York. On 14 May the Weils left Marseille, and after a stop in Casablanca, arrived in New York on 6 July. Simone Weil tried to join the Free French Government in England immediately, and almost despaired of succeeding. She had only left France for the sake of her parents who would not have gone without her, and with the hope of joining the Free French in England. Finally she managed through Maurice Schumann, a former fellow-student from Henri IV who was now the spokesperson for the Free French, to get admission to England where she arrived at the end of November 1942. She wanted to be sent on missions to France. Instead, she was assigned the task of examining texts analysing the current situation in France and presenting ideas on the reconstruction of France after the war, sent by different groups of the Resistance to the Free French. She responded with essays later published in *Écrits de Londres*. She analysed the problems in France and developed her own vision of how they could be resolved in her unfinished book *L'Enracinement* (*The Need for Roots*). During these few very productive months, she wrote the equivalent of 800 pages of printed material.[18] However, her hopes of being sent on a mission to France were shattered,

---

[18] McLellan 1990: 245.

which made her despair and regret ever having left Marseille. In April, she was found unconscious in her room, exhausted from her work, suffering from malnutrition and tuberculosis, and was taken to hospital. She sent a letter of resignation to the Free French at the end of July since she disagreed with the Gaullists' policies.[19] On 17 August she was transferred to a sanatorium in Ashford, Kent, and died there on 24 August from heart failure due to her poor condition. She was buried in Ashford cemetery, in the Catholic section, on 30 August.

WEIL'S WRITINGS

Though Weil's more substantial comments on ancient Greek texts are contained in *Intuitions pré-chrétiennes* and *La Source grecque*, other references are widely scattered throughout her writings. It should be kept in mind that Weil's interpretations are fragmentary and that some of the key concepts used in them are often explained in other parts of her work.

Seven of the sixteen volumes of the complete edition of Weil's works with extremely useful commentaries have already been published by Gallimard under the direction of André Devaux and Florence de Lussy. *Intuitions pré-chrétiennes*, one of my main sources, has not yet appeared in this edition. The texts contained in this book were written during Weil's exile in Marseille during 1941–2 and in Casablanca, and were left to the care of Père Perrin, who published them in 1951 with Fayard under this title chosen by him.[20] Having met him in June 1941, she often went to discuss religious matters with him, for he was the first to raise with her the question of baptism. Perrin organized a series of lectures in the crypt of his convent in the winter of 1941–2 for which Weil prepared some of the talks on texts which she deemed 'les plus beaux et les plus révélateurs de la pensée grecque'.[21] These

---

[19] Ibid. 264; SP 510–11.
[20] Perrin entitled the book *Intuitions pré-chrétiennes* because he first thought it expressed best 'l'idée centrale du livre' ('the main idea of the book') (*IPC* 7). Later on he regretted this choice, since the term *pre*-Christian does not really make sense in Weilian thought, for she believed Christianity was present from the beginning of the world in some form or other (Canciani 2000: 146). For the sake of simplicity, however, I will continue using the term 'pre-Christian'.
[21] SP ii. 380; 'the most beautiful and revelatory in Greek thought' (Pétrement 1988: 445).

are now part of the *Intuitions*. She planned to assemble with Perrin the most poignant Christian and non-Christian texts on the love of God.[22] But this was, according to Simone Pétrement—her friend and biographer—a distant project, and what we have is by no means the final product.[23]

In 1953 Perrin also published *Attente de Dieu* (*Waiting for God*) which contains Weil's letters to him together with some of the most striking texts she had bequeathed to him, namely 'L'Amour de Dieu et le malheur' (*The Love of God and Affliction*), 'Formes de l'amour implicite de Dieu' (*Forms of the Implicit Love of God*), 'Réflexions sur le bon usage des études scolaires en vue de l'amour de Dieu' (*Reflections on the Right Use of School Studies with a View to the Love of God*), 'A propos du "Pater"' (*Concerning the Our Father*), and 'Les Trois fils de Noé et l'histoire de la civilisation méditerranéenne' (*The Three Sons of Noah and the History of Mediterranean Civilization*).[24] *La Source grecque* contains texts relevant to Weil's interpretation of Greek thought, some of which have already appeared in the complete edition. This book was first published under the direction of Albert Camus for Gallimard's collection 'Espoir' in 1953. As early as 1949 Camus had published *L'Enracinement*. Only Thibon's publication in 1947 of *La Pesanteur et la grâce* preceded it.

Weil's *Cahiers* or *Notebooks* are a complex genre, made up of meditations on different subjects, quotations, personal reflections, and calculations. They do not contain prolonged continuous texts, but as Florence de Lussy writes in her introduction to the first volume of the *Cahiers* for the complete edition: 'La pensée de Simone Weil procède par éclats' (*OC* vi/1, 16).[25] However, these seeming ruptures should not disguise the sometimes barely visible connections between the different sections. Though Weil wrote these *Cahiers* principally for her own use, they are central to an understanding of her thought. In *Simone Weil: Thinking Poetically*, Joan Dargan claims that they 'are in many ways the nervous centre of her œuvre, a record of a mind's astonishing range and unassuageable restlessness'.[26] Started in 1933, only Weil's first *Cahier* predates the war, but has entries from probably as late as 1938. It is often difficult to determine the exact date when Weil wrote

---

[22] Perrin 1984: 79; Canciani 2000: 146.   [23] SP ii. 380.
[24] These essays are contained in the Penguin edition, *Waiting for God* (*WG*), which I used, except the one on Noah's sons which can be found in the Fount edition (*WOG*).
[25] 'the thought of Simone Weil progresses by flashes'.   [26] Dargan 1999: 19.

a *Cahier*. The date written on its front cover can be misleading, since she sometimes used the notebook again later to write on its spare pages. Thus the introductions to each *Cahier* in the complete edition are very helpful, with good chronological indications. Weil only returned to her *Cahiers* again in Marseille when she began with *Cahier* number 2. According to her own numbering there are eleven *Cahiers*, which precede her departure for the USA in May 1942. However, this does not include notebooks she used on the side (called 'carnets de travail' ('working notebooks') by de Lussy), which have been published in the complete edition when deemed of interest (Œ 808). After Weil's departure from Marseille she started a new series of *Cahiers*, seven of which were written in New York and an eighth in London where she arrived in December 1942 (she only remained four months in the USA). These are assembled in the volume *La Connaissance surnaturelle* (Supernatural Knowledge).[27] *Pensées sans ordre concernant l'amour de Dieu* (Haphazard Thoughts Concerning the Love of God) contains various writings from Marseille and London. *Écrits de Londres et dernières lettres* (Writings from London and Last Letters) includes the essays Weil wrote for the Free French Government, her letters to Maurice Schumann, some fragments and her last letters to her family from England. Her political and historical writings up to 1940 occupy three volumes in the complete edition. Included are her 'Réflexions sur les causes de la liberté et de l'oppression sociale', as well as her better known 'Journal d'usine' (Factory Diary). Some of the later texts not yet published in the complete edition are contained in the earlier publication, *Écrits historiques et politiques*, such as her articles on the Cathars. Weil's early philosophical writings, some of the essays written for Alain as well as her thesis for her diplôme d'études supérieures, are assembled in the first volume of the complete edition. An interesting perspective on Weil as a teacher is given in Anne Reynaud's lecture notes from Weil's philosophy classes at the girls' *lycée* in Roanne in 1933–4, published by Plon as *Leçons de philosophie* in 1959. A selection of notes from her classes in Saint-Quentin appeared as an annexe in the *Œuvres complètes* (ii/2. 526 ff.). *Oppression et liberté* contains among other things Weil's articles criticizing Marxism, also present in the complete edition. While

---

[27] Weil started the twelfth *Cahier* in Marseille in order to copy the most important elements from the eleven *Cahiers* she was going to leave with Thibon. She continued to write in it on her trip to the US (*OC* vi/3, 375). It extends to the bottom of p. 38 of the *Connaissance* and also appears in *Œuvres Complètes*, vi/3.

in the USA, Weil wrote a letter to Père Couturier, a French Dominican, who was also in America and who had been recommended to her by Jacques Maritain. She asks Couturier whether she could be baptized with or in spite of the opinions she holds, which she then lists. This letter was later published under the title *Lettre à un religieux* (*Letter to a Priest*). *Poèmes, suivis de 'Venise sauvée'* contains Weil's poetry as well as her unfinished tragedy. In *Sur la science* one finds essays, letters, and fragments with Weil's reflections on science, a subject that intrigued her throughout her life.

Weil's complete letters have not yet been published. Apart from those mentioned in *Écrits de Londres, Attente de Dieu*, etc., some have appeared in the *Cahiers Simone Weil* (a quarterly journal published by the *Association Simone Weil*), some in *Seventy Letters*, edited by Richard Rees, and a few others in the recently published *Œuvres*.[28] In this volume in the Gallimard Quarto collection, Florence de Lussy has assembled some of the best and most fundamental texts by Weil to make them accessible to a wider public. It also contains some of Weil's unpublished translations of the *Iliad, Antigone, Prometheus*, etc. Weil, whose Greek was excellent, translated her favourite texts for her friends. Most of these translations are in the Simone Weil archives in the Bibliothèque Nationale in Paris, and confirm Weil's predilection for certain authors and for specific passages from their works.

Many of Weil's writings have been translated into English, though unfortunately they are often assembled differently which makes matters difficult for the reader. *Intimations of Christianity among the Ancient Greeks* (1957) contains essays from *Intuitions pré-chrétiennes* as well as from *La Source grecque*. Some of her key-texts are contained in *Selected Essays 1934–1943* and *On Science, Necessity, and the Love of God*, edited by Richard Rees, but come from different French sources. *The Need for Roots* and *Oppression and Liberty*, on the other hand, coincide with the French choice of texts. The English readers must therefore solve some puzzles to find their way around.[29] It is to be hoped that an English translation of the complete Gallimard edition will eventually be envisaged.

---

[28] See Bibliography for a list of letters and texts by Weil that have as yet only been published in the *Cahiers*.

[29] To make matters easier I will indicate in which English volume a text is to be found when it is unclear from the context.

BIBLIOGRAPHY

There has been a trend in recent years to look at Weil's interpretations of literature, to trace her influence on writers, and to compare her to other authors. In this respect Katherine T. Brueck in *The Redemption of Tragedy: The Literary Vision of Simone Weil* (1995), investigates Weil's interpretation of tragedy. Interestingly, Brueck picks only one of the plays Weil writes about in greater detail, namely the Sophoclean *Antigone*. Otherwise Brueck analyses Sophocles' *Oedipus Rex*, Shakespeare's *King Lear*, and Racine's *Phèdre*—plays Weil only comments on briefly—in the light of the latter's literary approach and philosophical concepts. Brueck does not concentrate on Weil's interpretations of ancient Greek texts, as I do, nor does she seem aware of their apologetic dimension.

A number of studies have been written in the same vein. To mention just a few, Brueck's essay 'Simone Weil et Dostoïevsky' (1985) looks at *Crime and Punishment* through a Weilian lens, and in 'The Mysticism of Simone Weil and François Mauriac's *Viper's Tangle*' (1989), Weil's concept of 'affliction' is applied to Mauriac's novel. Ann Loades in 'Simone Weil and Antigone: Innocence and Affliction' (1993), stresses the link between the Sophoclean figure and Weil's own life. Paul Croc (1995) pinpoints Weil's influence on Mauriac, thus giving a key for the interpretation of Mauriac's work. Similarly Jacques Cabaud (1985) shows the impact Weil had on Camus.[30] Sophie Ollivier (1995) compares Dostoevski's and Weil's conception of evil and the meaning of suffering. Comparative studies exist between Weil and Valéry, whom she admired (Lussy 1994; Lanfranchi 1983), Marie Noël, whom she did not seem to know (Bonnardot 1979), and Péguy, whose appreciation of Roman civilization she did not share (Fraisse 1989). William Bush (1985) parallels Weil's and Bernanos's understanding of divine love and human suffering. Several articles have appeared on Weil's reading of the *Iliad*, and will be discussed in Ch. 5. Weil's poems, and especially her unfinished tragedy, *Venise sauvée*, have been analysed by Little (1970*a*), Birou (1991), Herling-Grudzinski (1990), and Mansau (1988) among others.

---

[30] Recently, two issues of the *Cahiers Simone Weil* appeared focusing on the two thinkers (*CSW* 28/4 (Dec. 2005) and 29/1 (Mar. 2006)).

Weil's particular approach to antiquity has been investigated by a number of scholars. I have already mentioned P. Savinel's article, which summarizes Weil's ideas on Greek culture (1960). Simone Fraisse has published a number of articles on the question, namely 'Simone Weil et le monde antique' (1978), 'Simone Weil contre les Romains' (1980), and 'Simone Weil et la tragédie grecque' (1982a).[31] Others have researched Plato's influence on Weil, such as Eric Springsted in *Christus Mediator* (1983) and different Weil specialists in *The Christian Platonism of Simone Weil*, edited by E. Jane Doering and Springsted (2004). A very thorough comparison between Heidegger's and Weil's approach to Greek culture has been made recently by Maria Villela-Petit in her article 'Simone Weil, Martin Heidegger et la Grèce' (2003).

Nothing is published as yet on Weil's apologetic purposes. However, in *Audience, Intention, and Rhetoric in Pascal and Simone Weil* Thomas Stokes analyses Weil's use of language, her intended audience, and her intentions, and even speaks of an *apologia* that she had in view (1996). However, he does not pursue further the idea of an apologetic dimension to Weil's thought.

Weil's aesthetics have received some attention in recent years in a series of articles and books, most prominently in *The Beauty that Saves: Essays on Aesthetics and Language in Simone Weil*, edited by John Dunaway and Eric Springsted, which focuses on the central position beauty occupies in Weil's thought (1996). This is significant since beauty plays an important part in her apologetics. Others, such as Little (1993b), Marchetti (1989), Dargan (1987), and Klein (1987) have studied Weil's ideas on poetic creation. In 1999 Joan Dargan published the afore-mentioned book, *Simone Weil: Thinking Poetically*, on Weil's style, which will be helpful when tracing Weil's apologetic intentions. Richard Bell's *Simone Weil's Philosophy of Culture: Readings toward a Divine Humanity* (1993) assembles articles on the different ways in which she attempted to transform her culture as a moral philosopher, political thinker, classicist, mystic, etc. Weil wanted to Christianize society, and her interpretations of the classics were just one way of achieving her goal.

The literature on Weil is vast, and I do not intend to compile a complete bibliography on the subject. However, I have tried to

---

[31] For a comparison of Weil's and Hannah Arendt's views on ancient Greece, Rome, and the Jewish people, see Courtine-Denamy (2001).

assemble everything relevant to this particular topic. In 1973 J. P. Little put together a bibliography, followed by a supplement in 1979 which is now outdated, due to the exponential growth of Weil studies. The *Cahiers Simone Weil*, a quarterly journal since 1978, is a goldmine of information for all Weil scholars, and accounts for many of the references in this book. Jacques Cabaud's biography of Weil in French (1957) and English (1964) remains a standard reference work. Simone Pétrement's *La Vie de Simone Weil* from 1973 yields more information, since she was a close friend of Weil. Perrin's books on Weil remain a 'must', starting with *Simone Weil telle que nous l'avons connue* (1967), co-authored with Gustave Thibon, and later *Mon dialogue avec Simone Weil* (1984). Many biographies have appeared since then looking at Weil from different perspectives, ranging from a political emphasis in McLellan's *Utopian Pessimist: The Life and Thought of Simone Weil* (1990), a psychological one with Oxenhandler's *Looking for Heroes in Postwar France: Albert Camus, Max Jacob, Simone Weil* (1995), a focus on Weil's Jewish background in Giniewski's visceral attack in *Simone Weil ou la haine de soi* (1978) or Nevin's more balanced outlook on the question in *Simone Weil: Portrait of a Self-Exiled Jew* (1991). Miklos Vetö's *La Métaphysique religieuse de Simone Weil* from 1971 is still helpful in its presentation of Weil's philosophy and has been translated by Joan Dargan (1994). However, Emmanuel Gabellieri gives a much more comprehensive and substantial overview of Weil's philosophy in his recently published book *Être et don* (2003b). Canciani's *L'Intelligence et l'amour: réflexion religieuse et expérience mystique chez Simone Weil*, assembles much valuable information and historical data, as well as including a whole section on Perrin's view of Weil fifty years later, gathered in interviews with the priest (2000).

During her lifetime, as in the writings about her, Weil tended to provoke either love and admiration, or irritation. Weil, in any case, neither courted approval nor shunned criticism, since she wanted neither herself nor her thought, but truth alone to be the object of attention.[32] Thus, she expressed regret that her intelligence had become an object of admiration, and a pretext for not looking at the truth of her statements (*EL* 256). She did not seek followers. Rather, the greatest favour one could do her was to engage in critical debate, which I shall try to do concerning her interpretation of the classics.

[32] Little 1988a: 156.

WEIL AND THE CLASSICS

Simone Weil probably started learning Greek with a private teacher in 1922 when she was 13 years old.[33] Though she and her brother would recite entire scenes from Racine and Corneille at an early age, the Greek classics do not seem to have been part of their repertoire.[34] From her writings and the fragments left from her time at Henri IV and at the École Normale, one could conclude that Greek tragedy was not of great importance to her then. No single piece is dedicated to a Greek play. Yet when she wrote a fragment on Freud and the significance of sexuality, while at the École Normale, she began with a Greek quotation from the famous hymn to Eros in the *Antigone*: 'Amour invincible au combat [. . .] et quiconque te possède est fou' (*OC* i. 278, vi/1. 261–2) (*Ant.* 781, 790).[35] It is astonishing, however, that she does not refer more to these plays, which were to become so important for her at a later period. In any case, she did not keep any *topo* referring to these (*topos* were essays written for Alain's classes on topics chosen by the students themselves)—something which is significant enough.[36]

Alain would select a philosopher and a writer at the beginning of the academic year, and each would be studied for an hour a week. No Greek dramatist seems to have been among these during Weil's time, though the *Iliad* and most of Plato's dialogues were read.[37] However, Weil adopted Alain's approach to texts. She neglected commentaries, and preferred to read the texts carefully and closely (*CSW* 1/3: 3–4).[38] As the classicist Michel Narcy points out in his introduction, 'Le Domaine

---

[33] SP i. 53.   [34] Ibid. 35.
[35] 'Love invincible in battle [. . .] and he who has you is mad.' When not indicated otherwise, the translations from Greek into French are by Weil. The English translations are from the Loeb Classical Library Series (except when taken from the English translations of Weil's works): *Antigone* and *Electra* are translated by Hugh Lloyd-Jones, *Prometheus Bound* by Herbert Weir Smyth, and *The Iliad* by A. T. Murray.
[36] SP i. 78.   [37] Ibid. 79.
[38] For example, she wrote in a letter to Déodat Roché of 21 Feb. 1941: 'Pour moi, en toute matière, rien ne vaut les textes originaux, nus et sans commentaires. Seuls ils me procurent le contact avec ce que je désire connaître. Peu m'importe si je ne les comprends que partiellement. Ensuite seulement j'ai recours aux études et commentaires, s'il y en a qui m'inspirent confiance, puis je reviens aux textes' (*CSW* 25/2: 143) ('For me, in any case, nothing equals the original texts, naked and without commentaries. They alone give me the kind of contact with what I desire to know. I do not mind if I only understand them partially. Only later do I have recourse to studies and commentaries, if there are some that I trust; then I return to the texts')

grec', to volume vi pt. 1 of the complete edition of Weil's works, her approach to ancient writings was not scholarly. She indiscriminately used different editions of unequal value though she was very careful about the translations given, which she sometimes corrected. Weil's own library was in fact rather unexceptional, as Narcy points out, as are the quotations in her *Cahiers*. It is her use of them, and the manner in which she invests them with new meaning, which make them interesting (*OC* vi/1. 20–3).[39]

At the beginning of each *Cahier*, Weil wrote on the front and back cover (inside and outside), the quotations which appealed to her. Thus one can see which texts were close to her heart at different times. As early as her first *Cahier*, on the inside and outside front cover, Weil refers to seven ancient Greek plays (*Antigone, Electra, Philoctetes,* and *Ajax* by Sophocles, *Agamemnon* and *Prometheus Bound* by Aeschylus, and *Medea* by Euripides), three times to the *Iliad* and once to the *Odyssey*. She gives eight quotations from Goethe and four from Marcus Aurelius and Horace, and also quotes Virgil, Juvenal, Terence, Lucretius, Dante, Baudelaire, Verlaine, and Mallarmé. In her later *Cahiers* the French authors disappear from the covers and make room almost exclusively for ancient Greek and Latin authors, for the New Testament, and especially for the *Bhagavadgītā* and the Upanishads from the third *Cahier* onwards.

Already Weil's first *Cahier* indicates her growing interest in the Greek tragedians and the *Iliad*, since she writes about them and quotes from them. As Narcy points out, these references belong to the part of the *Cahier* written before 1935 and show signs of a systematic reading of those texts (*OC* vi/1. 23). In 1936 she was pleased to be able to fulfil a long-standing ambition to introduce workers to the world of Greek literature. She published an article on *Antigone* in *Entre Nous*, the journal of the workers at the foundry of Rosières, close to Bourges. She wrote another on *Electra*, and started one on *Philoctetes*, but since her contact with the person in charge of the journal broke off, they were not published. Weil thought the particular form of hardship the workers were experiencing—what she calls *malheur* ('affliction')—should enable them to understand and appreciate Greek tragedy. According to her, the Greeks had a certain insight into *malheur*, which is so extreme a form of affliction that it crushes the person, takes away all sense of self-worth, and cannot be understood by anyone who has not experienced

---

[39] Simone Fraisse (1978: 198–9) makes a similar point in her article 'Simone Weil et le monde antique'.

it. The Greeks portrayed this in their tragedies. In 1938 she had the time to reread the dramas of Aeschylus and of Sophocles as well as the *Iliad*, together with many other texts in the original, when she was on sick-leave.[40] These works were therefore fresh in her mind at the time of her first mystical encounter in 1938. This might explain why she immediately saw these texts in a Christological light (*AD* 46).

A clear distinction must be made between Weil's interpretation of these works before her mystical experience in November 1938 and afterwards. Her encounter with Christ concretely changed her understanding of literature and of the world in general, though she maintained the unscholarly and lively approach that she had learnt from Alain. She now looks at these texts through a Christological lens, and through her close reading 'discovers' Christian elements. This Christological interpretation of Greek literature probably predates her knowledge of the Church Fathers to whose approach her own could perhaps be compared. In any case, her references to the early apologists occur only after her mystical experience, and thus seem to have been afterthoughts, rather than sources of inspiration.

Weil does not really refer to any secondary literature on Greek texts. However, the possibility cannot be excluded that Père André-Jean Festugière's work might have inspired her, as Canciani points out.[41] She mentions his name in her *Connaissance* in a list of writers, many of whom were looking at Greek thought and Christianity together (*CS* 22; *OC* vi/3. 393).[42] She might well have read Festugière's *L'Idéal religieux des grecs et l'évangile*, published in 1932, where he tries to show how far Greek culture, religion, and philosophy were a preparation for Christianity. However, he claims the Greeks were lacking elements that only Christianity could give them. He believes the Greeks were open to the Gospel not because of their similarities, as Weil would have thought, but because so many people from the lower classes could not live according to the Greek ideals, reserved for the noble and rich. Christianity, however, was accessible to the underprivileged, and offered a much more promising afterlife than the shadow-like existence Greek religion foretold. Weil would also disagree with Festugière's claim that in Plato's thought no relationship is established between God and man. God does not come to man according to Greek understanding, as

---

[40] SP ii. 216–17.   [41] Canciani 2000: 146 n. 1.
[42] Weil had extracted these names and titles from Maurice de Gandillac's *La Philosophie de Nicolas de Cues* (*OC* vi/3. 531 nn. 71, 72) (Gandillac 1941).

Festugière points out, since he is neither his creature nor his child. Nor do the mystery religions lead to union with God for their purpose is not redemption, but to save from suffering.[43] However, both Festugière and Weil agree that Greek wisdom has its source in suffering.[44]

The two thinkers who had the greatest impact on Simone Weil are without doubt Alain and Plato.[45] Yet—as has been claimed in both cases—though they may serve as an introduction to her thought, they cannot explain it.[46] Alain himself says in his journal: 'Je ne crois pas qu'elle m'ait jamais appelé maître—mais bien plutôt elle m'a toujours échappé; elle courait devant par des moyens à moi inconnus' (*OC* vi/1. 13).[47] Plato is transformed through Weil's interpretation, as Narcy points out in his article 'Ce qu'il y a de platonicien chez Simone Weil'. Rather than discovering Plato through Weil's writings, one finds a Weilian dimension in Plato's thought as he becomes her disciple, as Narcy and Heidsieck put it.[48] Little points out in her biography of Weil that she is unclassifiable and has affiliations with but few of the major intellectual currents in France. She does not belong to any school, and is 'both fully in touch and profoundly out of tune with much of the first half of the twentieth century'.[49]

WEIL'S CHRISTOLOGICAL INTERPRETATIONS

Weil's approach to antiquity is original and imaginative for her times though she uses well-known texts to trace the existence of pre-Christian

---

[43] Festugière 1932: 13–14, 32 ff., 52–3, 133–4.

[44] Canciani thinks Weil might have read some of Festugière's lectures, for example 'L'Héritage moral de l'antiquité' (1942), where he defends this idea (Canciani 2000: 146, n. 1). Narcy on the other hand thinks it probable that Weil might have read Festugière's *Contemplation et vie contemplative chez Platon*, published in 1936 (Narcy 1982: 254–5). The difference between the two thinkers becomes more pronounced later on. For example in *De l'essence de la tragédie grecque*, published in 1969, Festugière shows in ch. 1 how far removed Greek tragedy is from Christianity.

[45] Other philosophers have also had significant influence on Weil. For the influence of Kant, see Vetö 1971: 143 and 1985: 43; for Descartes's impact see Sourisse 1985, Devaux 1995, Narcy 1995; concerning Spinoza's influence on Alain and Weil, see Comte-Sponville 1991 and Goldschläger 1982.

[46] Davy 1966: 11.

[47] 'I don't think that she ever called me master—but rather, she always escaped me; she ran before me by some means which were unknown to me.' For Alain's influence on Weil see Gilbert Kahn's article 'Simone Weil et Alain' (1991), as well as Pétrement's comments on the question (SP i. 71 ff.).

[48] Narcy 1985: 373; Heidsieck 1982: 242.   [49] Little 1988*a*: 151.

intuitions. As Cardinal Daniélou points out in his article 'Hellénisme, Judaïsme, Christianisme', these texts had already been singled out by Christians from the early days onwards because of their Christian resonance.[50] But Weil uses Christology as the hermeneutic key to these mythological texts at a time when people such as Durkheim had reduced religion to a sociological phenomenon, when Bultmann was demythologizing the Gospels, and after Higher Criticism had been looking at the Bible through a positivistic lens since the previous century.[51] Weil, on the contrary, chooses a method opposed in every way to these trends, for she not only denies a mythological character to the Gospel, she even reads myth from a Christian perspective (*IPC* 106).[52] Myth does not mean for her 'human fiction' or 'lie', which should be eliminated in order to discover the 'historical Jesus'. Rather, myth is already an epiphany of Christ taking place before his historical incarnation, or may even be the sign of other incarnations. Weil's approach is at the polar opposite of positivism: rather than reducing reality to the empirical data gathered through sense perception, she sees the sacred in the form of the Logos present everywhere.

Just as for Max Scheler and Rudolf Otto, the Holy is for Weil something *sui generis*, which cannot be understood simply in sociological terms.[53] It is a given, the existence of which must be acknowledged and which cannot be reduced to anything else. For Weil, Durkheim's approach has its validity, however, in order to distinguish between the supernatural as such and mere pseudo-religious phenomena such as group hysteria (*OC* vi/2. 324, 132; *AD* 16).

Weil was familiar with Frazer's work *The Golden Bough*, as her quotations and references in the *Connaissance* and her other *Cahiers* show (*CS* 143 ff., 146; *OC* vi/3. 477 n. 354).[54] Frazer defended a naturalistic interpretation of religion, namely that it was the result of an evolutionary development starting with magic, which would eventually be replaced by science.[55] But Weil turns Frazer's methodology on its head. Rather than interpreting the gestures in rituals in primitive

---

[50] Daniélou 1964: 21–2.   [51] Macquarrie 1988: 156–7; Latourelle 1994: 88 ff.
[52] For Weil's approach to the Bible, see Villela-Petit 2002, Müller 2002, Broc-Lapeyre 2002, and Gabellieri 2003*a*.
[53] Macquarrie 1988: 213 ff., 220–1. In her essay 'La Personne et le sacré' Weil writes of the respect due to the human person, revealing her acknowledgement that some things exist *sui generis* and cannot be explained or defined through anything else (*EL* 12).
[54] The first time Weil explicitly mentions his name is in her *Cahier* 7, written at the beginning of 1942 (*OC* vi/2. 471, 649 n. 230).
[55] Macquarrie 1988: 101 ff.

societies as the imitation of natural phenomena in order to gain power over them, Weil sees in these movements a religious desire for union with Christ (*OC* vi/3. 113). Furthermore, Weil questions Frazer's idea that the portrayal of ritual deaths imitates former human sacrifices. What if those human sacrifices are simply the corruption of earlier ritual gestures rather than vice versa (*CS* 259–60)? Whether one agrees with Weil or not, at least she shows that Frazer's approach is not self-evident, that other interpretations are possible, and that one can infer the opposite from the same data.

Though Weil does not criticize Frazer in the *Connaissance*, she makes in the same pages a statement that underlies her methodology and stands in contradiction to his. She writes: 'Le fondement de la mythologie, c'est que l'univers est une métaphore des vérités divines' (ibid. 145).[56] Mythology thus conveys truths, which the universe already reveals in a metaphorical way. For 'Dieu est le suprême poète', and has created a universe which expresses eternal truths (ibid. 150).[57] According to this Neoplatonic position, fiction is not a lie, or at least need not be, but can become the medium for truth.

At the core of these truths lies the Christological character of the universe, which was created in the shape of the cross: 'l'univers entier dans la totalité de l'espace et du temps a été créé comme la Croix du Christ' (*IPC* 167).[58] For: 'Une anecdote historique dont le personnage central est Dieu ne peut pas ne pas être réfractée dans l'éternité' (ibid. 106).[59] Thus Christ, in a certain sense, has been crucified since the beginning of time (*OC* vi/3. 249, 279). How could this not have been sensed and put into words by great artists, even before the advent of Christ? Thus because of the structure of the universe and because of the nature of artistic creation, ancient Greek literary masterpieces captured some pre-Christian intuitions.[60]

But Weil has more reasons for believing in the existence of pre-Christian intuitions. God's justice requires it, for: 'Comment peut-on sans accuser Dieu supporter la pensée d'un seul esclave crucifié il y a

---

[56] 'The foundation of mythology is that the universe is a metaphor of the divine truths' (*FLN* 191).
[57] 'God is the supreme poet' (ibid. 194).
[58] 'the whole universe, in the totality of space and of time, has been created as the Cross of Christ' (*IC* 198).
[59] 'An historical anecdote whose central character is God cannot [but] be refracted into eternity' (ibid. 70).
[60] As will be seen in Ch. 6, Weil believed that artistic creation is divinely inspired (*IPC* 22 ff.; *OC* vi/3. 278; *E* 241).

vingt-deux siècles, si on pense qu'à cette époque le Christ était absent et toute espèce de sacrement inconnue?' (*AD* 188; *LR* 20).[61] There were prophecies and revelations announcing Christ's coming other than those of the Old Testament, and Weil tries to demonstrate this through her interpretations. Scripture itself, she believes, shows that there were revelations other than those of Israel.[62] In the fragment of a letter to Perrin, she points out that Melchisedek must have received such a special revelation (*AD* 250–1; *LR* 21–2; *OC* vi/2. 345). Each culture in antiquity has received insights into different aspects of God, as she writes in her article 'En quoi consiste l'inspiration occitanienne?' (*The Romanesque Renaissance*) which appeared in a special issue of the *Cahiers du Sud* in February 1943:

Chaque pays de l'antiquité pré-romaine a eu sa vocation, sa révélation orientée non pas exclusivement, mais principalement vers un aspect de la vérité surnaturelle. Pour Israël ce fut l'unité de Dieu, obsédante jusqu'à l'idée fixe. [...] Pour la Perse, ce fut l'opposition et la lutte du bien et du mal. Pour l'Inde, l'identification, grâce à l'union mystique, de Dieu et de l'âme arrivée à l'état de perfection. [...] Pour l'Egypte, ce fut la charité du prochain, exprimée avec une pureté qui n'a jamais été dépassée; ce fut surtout la félicité immortelle des âmes sauvées après une vie juste, et le salut par l'assimilation à un Dieu qui avait vécu, avait souffert, avait péri de mort violente, était devenu dans l'autre monde le juge et le sauveur des âmes. La Grèce reçut le message de l'Egypte, et elle eut aussi sa révélation propre: ce fut la révélation de la misère humaine, de la transcendance de Dieu, de la distance infinie entre Dieu et l'homme.   (*EHP* 76–7; *OC* vi/2. 366)[63]

Since Greece had a particular intuition about the wretchedness of human beings, the transcendence of God, and the distance between the

---

[61] 'How can we bear the thought of a single crucified slave twenty-two centuries ago, how can we help accusing God, if we think that at that time Christ was absent and every kind of sacrament unknown?' (*WG* 125).

[62] In the following chapter her rather eccentric interpretation of Ham will be presented.

[63] 'Every country of pre-Roman antiquity had its vocation, its revelation referring, not exclusively but mainly, to one aspect of supernatural truth. For Israel, it was the oneness of God, which became a fixed obsession. [...] For Persia, it was the opposition and struggle between good and evil. For India, the identification, through mystic union, of God and the soul when it has reached the stage of perfection. [...] For Egypt, it was charity to one's neighbour, expressed with a never-surpassed purity; above all, it was the immortal bliss of saved souls after a just life, and salvation by assimilation to a God who had lived, suffered, died a violent death, and become, in the other world, the judge and saviour of souls. Greece both received Egypt's message and had a revelation of her own: it was the revelation of human misery, of God's transcendence, of the infinite distance between God and man' (*SE* 45–6).

two, it attempted to look for ways of bridging that gulf by means of religion, philosophy, art, and science. Except for their religion, we have inherited these bridges from the Greeks, Weil claims.[64] Yet: 'Nous en avons beaucoup surélevé l'architecture [de ces ponts]. Mais nous croyons maintenant qu'ils sont faits pour y habiter. Nous ne savons pas qu'ils sont là pour qu'on y passe' (*EHP* 77).[65] And Weil adds mysteriously: 'nous ignorons, si l'on y passait, qui l'on trouverait de l'autre côté' (ibid.; *OC* vi/3. 46).[66] Is this not what Weil tries to do through her interpretations of the Greek classics: to show anew that they are bridges to God and to entice her readers to walk over them?

Weil was obviously aware of some of the different ways of interpreting Greek myth and culture. She was critical of Nietzsche who, she thought, wrongly contrasted Dionysus and Apollo. Why, she asks in the sketch of a letter to her brother written between January and April 1940, does he separate these figures, which the Greeks sometimes seemed to identify or at least to mix? She calls Nietzsche's idea 'de la pure fantaisie'. While for Nietzsche Dionysus embodies the Antichrist, Weil sees in him a Christ-figure, since he suffered, died, and was resurrected. He participated in the human condition, and human beings in their turn can share in his perfection and felicity. Really, '[l]a démesure, l'ivresse cosmique et Wagner n'ont rien à voir là-dedans' (*S* 232).[67] Nietzsche called himself an 'homme dionysiaque', but 's'il avait vu juste, la Grèce aurait sombré comme lui' (ibid.).[68] The Greeks, Weil believes, did not have a special taste for suffering and anguish as modern figures, such as Nietzsche, do. For anguish only produces more anguish, and cannot bring about the serenity the Greeks possessed.[69] Though Weil is critical

---

[64] In his article 'Métaphysique de la transcendance et théorie des *metaxu* chez Simone Weil', Springsted analyses the *ponts* or μεταξύ which are not only bridges towards the transcendent, but come from the transcendent, draw our attention towards the good, and pull us up (Springsted 1982: 288, 289, 291).

[65] 'We have built [these bridges] up much higher. But we believe now that they were made to live in. We are unaware that they are only there to be passed across' (*SE* 46).

[66] 'we do not know, if we crossed over, whom we should find on the other side' (ibid.).

[67] 'excesses, cosmic intoxication and Wagner have nothing to do with this'.

[68] 'Dionysian man'; 'if he had been correct, then Greece would have sunk into madness like him'. See also another variant of the letter (*S* 247–8).

[69] On a more personal level, Weil questions how somebody who loves wisdom could have ended like Nietzsche. Even if some physical factors were involved, 'un peu d'humilité sied au malheureux, non un orgueil sans mesure' (a bit of humility is becoming to the afflicted and not a measureless pride) (*S* 231). If Nietzsche needed to compensate for his suffering with pride, then this does not deserve admiration, but pity. In 'Simone Weil

of Nietzsche, she had the same creative approach to the classics, at least formally, if not materially.

At first glance it seems that Weil was not set against interpreting myths euhemeristically (meaning that the gods and mythical heroes were in reality human beings of the past, whose actions were later exaggerated and who were eventually divinized) or in terms of forces of nature: 'Les différentes interprétations de la mythologie: évhémérisme, mythes solaires, forces de la nature, peuvent en certains cas être vraies toutes à la fois' (*OC* vi/3. 188).[70] As Seznec points out in *La Survivance des dieux antiques*, there were three ways of explaining myths in antiquity for those who had lost their pagan beliefs: namely as depicting historical figures (euhemerism), as expressing the struggle of elementary forces, or as philosophical and moral truths clad in allegories.[71] However, Weil turns these approaches on their head, and what seems like agreement at first sight turns out to be the opposite (ibid.). She only accepts euhemerism when it records real incarnations, though this contradicts its very definition—which means that she does not accept it at all. Thus tragedy would not reflect a past event happening to a human being who is then divinized, but would in reality be the report of an incarnation—a Hellenistic gospel, so to speak. Weil reverses the trend, already present within antiquity, of secularizing myths; instead, she sees in myths the sacred story of a god, of a Christological incarnation.[72]

Weil is adamant. Some Greek tragedies are more Christian than any literary piece since Christ's incarnation: 'Sophocle est le poète grec où la qualité chrétienne de l'inspiration est la plus visible et peut-être la plus pure. (Il est beaucoup plus chrétien que n'importe quel poète tragique des vingt derniers siècles, à ma connaissance)' (*IPC* 18).[73] This, for Weil, becomes particularly clear in his *Antigone*, since this tragedy shows it is more important to obey God than men. Furthermore, Plato

---

et l'histoire' Broc-Lapeyre criticizes Weil for her harsh condemnation of Nietzsche's end (Broc-Lapeyre 1978a: 175). However, Weil condemns less his madness than his pride.

[70] 'The various interpretations of mythology—Euhemerus' interpretation, solar myths, forces of Nature—can in certain cases all be true at the same time' (*NB* 489).

[71] Seznec 1940: 8.

[72] Similarly, instead of reducing myth to the representation of elementary forces, Weil thinks that myth and nature can be used as parables for spiritual truths (*CS* 231). Christ, for example, took a natural event in order to represent a spiritual reality, when he said 'si le grain ne meurt' ('unless a grain of wheat falls into the earth and dies') (*PSO* 24; John 12: 24).

[73] 'Among the Greek poets, Sophocles is the one whose quality of inspiration is the most visibly Christian and perhaps the most pure (he is to my knowledge much more Christian than any tragic poet of the last twenty centuries)' (*IC* 8).

is a mystic, and the Greeks possessed unseen depths of spirituality (*SG* 77). One must immerse oneself in the spiritual life these texts propose, and exercise a kind of divination to understand what they were meant to convey (*IPC* 111). Analogously, the classicist Pierre Hadot highlights the religious aspect of Greek philosophy. Because we read Greek philosophical texts in terms of their conceptual data, we fail to see that they were often written as spiritual exercises in which the author wanted to engage his readers: 'Elles [ces textes] sont destinées à former les âmes. Elles ont une valeur psychagogique.'[74] Hadot compares philosophy to conversion. Philosophizing, especially with Socrates and Plato, presupposed a readiness to change, the wish to know oneself, and openness to truth.[75] This is the attitude Weil desired from her readers, particularly when reading Greek tragedy.

Weil is an original and provocative reader, and often shocks through her imaginative approach. Historical accuracy was not her focus, as Perrin points out: 'Elle avait un tel don de fabriquer des rapprochements sans tenir compte des lieux ou des dates, d'élaborer les hypothèses en esquivant les données gênantes, qu'on en était parfois déconcerté.'[76] But her interpretation of Greek tragedy must be seen in terms of her understanding of myth: 'Il ne faut pas regarder ces mythes et tous ceux qui leur ressemblent comme des récits mais comme des symboles, de sorte que des mythes différents peuvent correspondre à la même vérité vue sous telle et telle face' (*IPC* 49).[77] To reveal the truths contained in myth was her goal, though she was aware of the difficulty of making these truths 'sensibles au cœur' (*E* 64).[78]

WEIL AND LITERATURE

I have chosen to analyse Weil's interpretations of the Sophoclean *Antigone* and *Electra*, Homer's *Iliad*, and Aeschylus' *Prometheus* since

---

[74] Hadot 1981: 9. 'These [texts] are destined to shape souls. They have a psychagogical value.'

[75] Ibid. 30 ff.

[76] Perrin and Thibon 1967: 64. 'She had such a gift for inventing likenesses without taking into account either places or dates, and of elaborating hypotheses while evading all the data which interfered with them that it was quite disconcerting at times' (Perrin 2003: 52–3).

[77] 'For the rest one must not regard these myths and all those which bear a resemblance to them as factual accounts but as symbols, in such a way that different myths may correspond to the same truth seen from different angles' (*IC* 113).

[78] 'perceptible to the heart' (*NR* 67)

they are the most substantial ones she gives. But these are not the only Greek literary texts Weil mentions; for example, she often refers to Euripides' *Hippolytus* or to Aeschylus' *Suppliants* and *Agamemnon*. But her comments on the latter texts are so short they can hardly be called interpretations. In her *Cahier* 6 she seems to make a list of the Greek tragedies she considers to be the best (*OC* vi/2. 389). Apart from the tragedies already mentioned, she also lists Sophocles' *Philoctetes* and Euripides' *Bacchae*.[79] In her first *Cahier*, Weil jots down some thoughts on six of Sophocles' seven extant plays, leaving out only the *Ajax* from which she quoted earlier on the *Cahier*'s inside cover (*OC* vi/1. 101–2, 69).

She admires the *Hippolytus*, because it shows the link between chastity and love of God, and because it depicts the redemptive suffering of an innocent being (*IPC* 34; *OC* vi/2. 328). The *Suppliants* reflects the non-interventionist attitude of God who lets necessity reign (*IPC* 31) (*Suppl.* 95 ff.). In the *Agamemnon* there are some lines on the impossibility of naming and therefore of grasping Zeus (whom Weil in consequence sees as God), as well as the famous reference to 'knowledge through suffering', passages Weil admires and quotes (*IPC* 20–1; *SG* 43) (*Ag.* 160). She started an article on the *Philoctetes* in 1936 for *Entre Nous* where she tried to bring home Philoctetes' suffering, especially his abandonment—something the workers can empathize with (*OC* ii/2. 557). The *Bacchae* is of interest to her since the play reveals something about Dionysus in whom Weil saw a Christ figure (*OC* vi/2. 343 ff.; *LR* 24; *PSO* 61; *IPC* 56–7).

One might have expected Weil to refer to further texts, which would have offered themselves for a Christological reading, and were used for this purpose in the past. Daniélou is astonished that Weil does not appropriate Euripides' *Heracles*. Justin Martyr and Clement of Alexandria, for example, already compared Heracles to Christ in his efforts to deliver humanity from the monsters oppressing it. Ulysses bound to the mast was construed as being tied to the cross.[80] Furthermore, Virgil's fourth *Eclogue*, often interpreted in a Messianic fashion because it announces the birth of a child bringing about a new era, was known to Weil, yet she did not use it to prove the existence of pre-Christian intuitions (*OC* vi/2. 474, vi/3. 311–12, 519

---

[79] In the same *Cahier* she quotes earlier from Euripides' *Hecuba* without commenting on the lines (*OC* vi/2. 323) (*Hec.* 345, 348, 356, 362–6, 375–6). She briefly refers to Aeschylus' *Choephoroe* a few times (see Appendix).
[80] Daniélou 1964: 20–1; Rahner 1945: 467 ff.

n. 359). One reason for this might be that Weil thought very little of Roman literature, which she believed was for the most part infected by nationalism and the spirit of *grandeur*. Furthermore, she disliked Virgil, as her critical comments on the *Aeneid* show (*OC* ii/3. 199; *E* 198–9).

Weil's predilection for Plato is not directly treated in this book. However, Weil's readings of her favourite Platonic texts will sometimes be referred to since they shed light on her interpretation of the Greek tragedies.[81] Weil's approach to Platonic myths may also say something about her own approach to myth in Greek tragedy: 'Platon ne dit jamais tout dans ses mythes. Il n'est pas arbitraire de les prolonger. Il serait bien plutôt arbitraire de ne pas les prolonger' (*IPC* 48).[82] Thus when she makes claims which are not based on the texts, she does not believe she is projecting something onto them. Rather, she prolongs them according to what she believes to be their spirit.

But Weil's love for literature does not stop at ancient literature. She has a whole canon of writers whom she appreciates, and others whom she despises. For example, she makes a list of her favourites at the end of her article 'L'*Iliade* ou le poème de la force', naming Villon, Shakespeare, Cervantes, Molière's *L'École des Femmes*, and Racine's *Phèdre* (*OC* ii/3. 253). In *L'Enracinement* she gives another list of authors whose writings she admires since they embody in her eyes a certain purity, adding to the aforementioned selection Racine's *Cantiques spirituels*, Maurice Scève, d'Aubigné, Théophile de Viau, perhaps Lamartine and Vigny, and certainly Mallarmé.[83] Among the prose writers that are included in her canon are Rabelais, Montaigne, La Boétie, Descartes, Retz, the authors of Port-Royal, Molière, Montesquieu, and Rousseau (*E* 201). Among the poems which she deems perfect since they have 'une durée

---

[81] Daniélou puts together a list of Weil's favourite passages in Plato: the myth of *Phaedrus* (*Phaedrus* 246e ff.; *IPC* 91–3) and of the cave, the Eros of the *Symposium* (*Symposium* 186b ff.; *IPC* 41 ff.), the just man who suffers unjustly in the *Republic* (*Republic* 360e ff.; *IPC* 79 ff.), as well as the soul of the world tracing a *chi* over the universe (*Timaeus* 34b ff.; *IPC* 26 ff.), and human beings who are compared to heavenly plants (*Timaeus* 90a ff.; *IPC* 32 ff.) (Daniélou 1964: 21). Narcy enumerates the Platonic dialogues Weil refers to most, and adds to those just mentioned the *Theaetetus, Gorgias, Phaedo*, and *Philebus* (Narcy 1982: 253).

[82] 'Plato never tells all in these myths. It is not arbitrary to extend them. It would be much more arbitrary not to extend them' (*IC* 112).

[83] Weil was so taken by Théophile that she wrote some unfinished letters to André Gide (probably from 1938 or 1939 as noted by the archivist), suggesting that Théophile's work should be re-edited (BN Lettres à Gide, XII, 136). Weil also wrote a letter to her brother in March 1940 singing the praises of the poet (BN Cart. I, 27–8).

qui soit image de l'éternité' are Sappho's 'Ode à Aphrodite',[84] the first two strophes of the hymn to Eros in the *Antigone* (*Ant.* 781–2), George Herbert's 'Love', perhaps Marlowe's 'Come live with me and be my love', and Shakespeare's 'Come away, come away, death', and especially 'Take, oh take your lips away' (*OC* vi/1. 224–5).[85] Other favourites are Dante and Valéry. She mentions many other writers, from Goethe to Rimbaud, Anouilh, Wilde, Pearl Buck, Proust, Lanza del Vasto, Tolstoy, Dostoevsky, Stendhal, Balzac, Hugo, Verlaine, Baudelaire, Jules Romains, Mauriac, Claudel, etc. In her article 'La Création artistique chez Simone Weil' J. P. Little claims that Weil mentions about sixty-seven writers who wrote before the twentieth century, but only nineteen who are of the twentieth century.[86]

Weil collected poems and songs she liked, sometimes just for herself and sometimes in order to send to others. For example, she wrote down sailors' and soldiers' songs, as well as *coplas* and Negro spirituals.[87] During her trip to the USA, she copied into her *Cahiers* poems by Estienne Jodelle, Jean Grévin, and Jean de La Ceppède (*OC* vi/3. 412 ff., 377). In other unpublished *Cahiers* she quotes Scottish poems such as 'Lily', 'Edward', and 'Sir Patrick Spens'.[88] On some loose pages, she collected among others Donne's 'Sweetest love, I do not go for weariness of thee', two sonnets by Michelangelo, the aforementioned poem by Marlowe as well as a passage from his *Faust*, St Francis's hymn to the sun, Verhaeren's poem 'L'Effort', and Rupert Brooke's 'These hearts were woven of human joys and cares'.[89]

The artists Weil is most critical of are mainly Corneille, Gide, and the Surrealists. She dislikes Corneille because he thinks only in terms of *gloire*, an attitude which Weil believes to be fundamentally unchristian (*E* 125–6; *OC* ii/3. 213). Gide is her *bête noire*, since he advocates the *acte gratuit* (gratuitous act). He thereby undermines morality, and yet withdraws from all responsibility behind the motto of *l'art pour l'art* (*E* 28). The Surrealists fall into a similar category as Gide since they deny the very basis of morality, namely the fundamental and metaphysical difference between good and evil (*RL* 355–6). This, as will be shown in the chapter on *Antigone*, is alarming and dangerous in Weil's eyes since

---

[84] 'a duration which is an image of eternity' (*NB* 5).
[85] As the editorial note points out, Weil made a list at the end of her volume of George Herbert's poetry of those poems which caught her attention (*OC* vi/2. 636 n. 485).
[86] Little 1993*b*: 19.
[87] *Annexe* VIII of *OC* vi/1. 427–36; *Annexes* IX and X in *OC* vi/1. 437–45, 446–51.
[88] BN Cahiers inédits II (5), MS 12 ff.   [89] BN Boite de carton 2, IV. 23.

morality is at the very root of human life. Conversion, good actions, sanctity are required for the renewal of culture so badly needed from her point of view, and would be impossible without the acknowledgement of an objective moral law.

Already early in her life Weil used literature to make philosophical points, following the example of Alain who read literature with his students in class, for example Balzac in 1925/6.[90] Weil's first *topo* for Alain in November 1925 was 'Le Conte des six cygnes dans Grimm' (*The Six Swans*). She tries to show that the abstention from action (the knitting of six shirts out of anemones which prevents any other kind of action), this purity of non-action, is more powerful than the kind of deeds human beings tend to perform every day (*OC* i. 58). Probably in 1926 Weil wrote a paper on Stendhal, analysing Balzac's comment that Stendhal belongs to a literature of ideas rather than of images (ibid. 99–106). In her essay 'Le Sentiment de la nature chez Vigny', probably written between 1927 and 1928, she looks at Vigny's understanding of nature from a philosophical point of view. Significantly the professor who corrected this piece of work, J. R. Chevaillier, praised Weil's text, which would have been 'hors de pair',[91] if the topic had been the *philosophy* and the poetry of nature in Vigny, instead of simply the latter (ibid. 107–14, 407 n. 30). Weil also made use of literature in her own philosophy classes. For example at Saint-Quentin in 1937, she discussed Saint-Exupéry's *Vol de nuit*, Pierre Hamp's *Glück Auf!*, and Émile Guillaumin's *La Vie d'un simple*. Her own notes on these works and the notes a student took are included in the volume on Weil's experience as an industrial worker in the *Œuvres complètes*, since her interpretations of these texts focus on the working conditions depicted. She looks at the dynamics between subordinate and superior, showing how fear and obedience rule this relationship, and ultimately weigh upon both (*OC* ii/2. 531). In all three books the hard world of work is portrayed, be it in aviation, in the mines, or for tenant farmers. But Weil did not only try to open the eyes of her students to the situation of the oppressed lower classes. She also addressed the workers themselves and tried to articulate for them feelings they found difficult to express on their own. As already mentioned, she wrote two complete articles on the *Antigone* and the *Electra*, a fragment on the *Philoctetes* and on Johan Boyer's *Le Dernier Viking* for *Entre Nous* (ibid. 558–9). Boyer's novel on Scandinavian fishermen shows the harshness of their working

[90] SP i. 78–9.   [91] 'out of the common'.

conditions. Weil emphasizes the heroism of these men who daily face danger without receiving any recognition from society.

As this short survey shows, Weil uses literature for her own purposes, rather than studying it as an end in itself. She was not a docile reader, but provocatively misread the texts for her own ends. Through this indirect approach she could better illustrate the points she had in mind, and her later interpretations of ancient Greek texts are no exception to this. Martha Nussbaum in *Love's Knowledge: Essays on Philosophy and Literature* makes the point that literature captures certain truths, which other forms of language cannot express.[92] Thus, Nussbaum looks at a range of literary texts to pinpoint philosophical insights, which would have been hard to articulate in purely philosophical terms. Paradoxically, through the medium of literature these truths not only become suddenly more manifest, but can now be conveyed through another medium such as philosophy. Similarly, Greek tragedy and epic allowed Weil to explicate Christian truths and the realities of the human condition in a way otherwise perhaps impossible. Let us presently turn to Weil's more general thoughts on apologetics before looking at her interpretation of specific texts.

---

[92] Nussbaum 1990: 23.

2

Simone Weil and Apologetics

> Dieu seul vaut qu'on s'intéresse à lui, et absolument rien d'autre.[1]
>
> (CS 74)

One does not think of Simone Weil as an apologist. How could someone who was probably never baptized be an apologist for Christianity? Nor did she proselytize for Judaism, of which she was very critical. Yet for someone such as Weil whose personal and intellectual life were always tightly linked, her encounter with Christ left an indelible impact, and changed the nature of her writings. She wrote to Perrin that: 'Depuis cet instant [de l'expérience mystique] le nom de Dieu et celui du Christ se sont mêlés de plus en plus irrésistiblement à mes pensées' (*PSO* 81).[2] God became the centre of her writings, explicitly and implicitly. Furthermore as a Platonist Weil could not be satisfied with contemplating the Good outside the cave, but was going to return to proclaim its existence. What else could one expect from someone who wrote that 'Dieu seul vaut qu'on s'intéresse à lui, et absolument rien d'autre' (*CS* 74)?[3]

Weil worked on her interpretations of ancient Greek texts just before and mainly during the war. In this time of crisis many people were experiencing great anguish, suffering, and death. It was a time of despair and destruction, when the forces of evil seemed to prevail. This made Weil's project more urgent, for then was the time to turn to Christ, before the hope of salvation was extinguished by the hell of hopelessness and evil: 'Jamais, dans toute l'histoire actuellement connue, il n'y a eu d'époque où les âmes aient été tellement en péril qu'aujourd'hui à

---

[1] 'God alone is worthy of interest, and absolutely nothing else' (*FLN* 126).
[2] 'Since that moment, the name of God and the name of Christ have been more and more irresistibly mingled with my thoughts' (*SW* 39).
[3] See n. 1.

travers tout le globe terrestre' (*AD* 53).⁴ Thus it was imperative to present Christianity again in a new light: 'Je pense, et vous aussi, que l'obligation des deux ou trois prochaines années, obligation tellement stricte qu'on ne peut presque y manquer sans trahison, est de faire apparaître au public la possibilité d'un christianisme vraiment incarné' (ibid.).⁵ If Weil felt that treason was the penalty for failing to Christianize society, she would not hold back. Though not a baptized Catholic, she none the less felt that she could draw people closer to Christ. As Perrin puts it, she was like a bell, calling people into Church without entering herself.⁶

Perrin himself seems to imply that their common project, of which the *Intuitions* was the result on Weil's part, had an apologetic function: 'Je crois qu'elle avait conscience d'avoir un vrai message à transmettre et qu'une partie de ce message c'était pour elle d'attirer les hommes au Christ. Ce projet que nous avons formé ensemble, par exemple, ce livre de témoignages sur les mystiques du monde entier, devait montrer qu'ils se retrouvent tous pour proclamer que Dieu est Amour.'⁷

In this chapter I will therefore present Weil's thoughts on apologetics, investigate her personal situation, determine her intended audience, and analyse her ideas on conversion. I will assemble her criticism of certain apologetic arguments. Furthermore, I will compare her to apologists, such as the Church Fathers, Pascal, and Blondel.

APOLOGETIC PRELIMINARIES

In hindsight, after her mystical experience, Weil saw how Greek culture could lead to Christianity. There was no incongruity between the two for, on the contrary, the former already embodied the Christian spirit, perhaps more than the Catholic Church ever had. Thus Christianity became for Weil the key to understanding ancient Greek texts, just as for the Early Church it had been the key to interpreting the Old Testament.

---

⁴ 'In all the history now known there has never been a period in which souls have been in such peril as they are today in every part of the globe' (*WG* 32).

⁵ 'I think, and so do you, that our obligation for the next two or three years, an obligation so strict that we can scarcely fail in it without treason, is to show the public the possibility of a truly incarnated Christianity' (ibid.).

⁶ Perrin and Thibon 1967: 92.

⁷ Canciani 2000: 154. 'I think she was conscious of having a real message to deliver and that part of this message was to draw people to Christ. For example, this project that we had planned together of a book of testimonies on the mystics from the whole world was to show that they all join in proclaiming that God is Love.'

Weil's Own Situation

Traditionally speaking, apologetics is defined as a defence of Christianity against unbelievers, with the purpose of converting them. It also has a pastoral dimension, namely to strengthen the faith of believers against the criticisms of sceptics.[8] Thus if Weil is to be considered an apologist, she remains an unorthodox one. First of all she was not baptized even though she considered herself, at least culturally, to have been Christian long before she converted: 'Je suis pour ainsi dire née, j'ai grandi, je suis toujours demeurée dans l'inspiration chrétienne' (*AD* 37).[9] After her mystical experience, however, through her love for Christ and for the sacraments, she felt she could claim to be more than just a cultural Christian, at least one 'en droit' ('by right') even if not 'en fait' ('in fact') (ibid. 53/*WG* 32). At the time she was working on her *Intuitions*, the question of baptism had been raised by Perrin, but Weil could not make the step. She had problems with the Catholic Church as a social organization, because of the way it dealt with heretics and error, no less than because of its Jewish heritage and its links with the Old Testament. Furthermore, she found fault with the Catholic understanding of dogma which she felt threatened intellectual freedom. Therefore she intended to remain 'au seuil de l'Eglise, sans bouger, immobile, $\dot{\epsilon}\nu$ $\dot{\upsilon}\pi o\mu o\nu\eta$', even though her heart had been transported 'pour toujours, j'espère, dans le Saint-Sacrement exposé sur l'autel' (*AD* 54).[10] She did not close the door to the Church, but adopted her famous attitude of *attente*: to wait and look at a problem or mystery with the utmost attention, until it clarified itself. Whether this question ever resolved itself for Weil is unclear. One of the doctors treating her at the sanatorium where she was brought a week before her death stated that Weil refused to tell the nurses her religion; but she did say to another doctor there that she was Jewish, desired to be Catholic, but still had problems concerning one

---

[8] Dulles 1971: 23, 45.

[9] 'I might say that I was born, I grew up, and I always remained within the Christian inspiration' (*WG* 22). Most of her explanations concerning her relationship to the Catholic Church and the reason why she does not ask for baptism are to be found in her letters to Perrin from which I am mainly quoting here. See also her letter to Maritain, 27 July 1942 (*CSW* 3/2: 68 ff.).

[10] 'on the threshold of the Church, without moving, quite still, $\dot{\epsilon}\nu$ $\dot{\upsilon}\pi o\mu o\nu\eta$', 'forever, I hope, into the Blessed Sacrament exposed on the altar' (*WG* 32–3). Many editions of Weil's works wrongly say *en hupomene* instead of *en hupomone*. I have therefore corrected the term whenever it was spelt wrongly.

point.[11] However, her friend Simone Deitz, who has been considered unreliable by some, claims to have baptized her on her deathbed.[12] Weil supposedly said that if one day she was in a coma, she wanted to be baptized.[13] Whatever the final outcome, the point is that when Weil wrote her *Intuitions*, the question was on her mind. She never concealed her problems with the Catholic Church. As Perrin points out: 'Néanmoins nous ne devons pas perdre de vue que jamais Simone Weil n'a prétendu être arrivée. D'un bout à l'autre, elle est restée dans la conscience de l'inachèvement.'[14]

Yet one may wonder how a non-baptized person can be a convincing witness to Christianity.[15] Instead of seeing this as a handicap, Weil thought it was an asset, given that she thus shared the plight of unbelievers.[16] But on the other hand, she knew that this made her more vulnerable since she was in the situation: 'Où on est aux yeux des incroyants un cas pathologique, parce qu'on adhère à des dogmes absurdes sans avoir l'excuse de subir une emprise sociale, et où on inspire aux catholiques la bienveillance protectrice,

---

[11] SP ii. 517.

[12] In the chapter 'The Baptism of Simone Weil' in *Spirit, Nature, and Community*, Eric Springsted (1994) discusses the question and finds Deitz's account credible as does Wladimir Rabi who wrote an article on the question in 1971. Jacques Cabaud had hinted at the story as early as 1967 (J.Cabaud 1967: 76 ff.; see also id. 1993: 309). Deitz claims that she had baptized Weil at the Middlesex Hospital in London (Springsted 1994: 5; Hourdin 1989: 223–31). However, this raises the problem of why Weil said she was not a Catholic when brought to the Ashford Sanatorium, adding that there was still a point she was unclear on and which hindered her from becoming a Catholic. When asked by Cabaud when she had baptized Weil (whether at the Middlesex Hospital in London, or upon her last visit at Ashford), Deitz said she could not remember, the wartime stress having rendered her memories of those events uncertain in this respect (verbal account) (see also Rabi 1971: 60–1). It is at the least astonishing that Deitz could forget something so important. However, by 1988 in a letter to Birou she claims to be perfectly certain that she baptized Weil at Middlesex hospital three or four weeks before her death (Devaux 1999: 319).

[13] J. Cabaud 1957: 378.

[14] Kahn 1978: 56. 'Nonetheless, we should not forget that Simone Weil never claimed to have reached her destination. From beginning to end she remained conscious of not having completed her journey.'

[15] Weil was never attracted by Protestantism and seems to have approved of the Church's condemnation of Luther (*AD* 58).

[16] She understands her vocation to be 'de rester en quelque sorte anonyme, apte à se mélanger à n'importe quel moment avec la pâte de l'humanité commune' ('to remain in a sense anonymous, ever ready to be mixed into the paste of common humanity') (ibid. 20/*WG* 7).

un peu dédaigneuse, de celui qui est arrivé pour celui qui est en marche' (*PSO* 151).[17]

Her Audience

But whom does Weil want to convert and to what exactly? What are the specific obstacles to conversion she perceives in her day? She identifies secularism, rationalism, and materialism as the ills of her time, though she does not necessarily call them by these names:[18] 'Les erreurs de notre époque sont du christianisme sans surnaturel. Le "laïcisme" en est la cause, et d'abord l'humanisme' (*OC* vi/3. 201).[19] The Renaissance, she thought, had separated human culture from God, and had adopted Protagoras' maxim that man is the measure of all things (*EHP* 78; *SG* 92). In a secular society which excludes the supernatural human beings look at everything in terms of themselves by means of their reason alone and no longer acknowledge the existence of mysteries, which can only be understood by means of *attente*, faith, and supernatural knowledge. Ultimately, this spirit of scepticism leads to an uprooting of whole cultures, to what Weil calls *déracinement*, since the supernatural is the basis of every human being and society. However, Weil stresses the significance and uniqueness of every culture which, if destroyed, is irreplaceable and stunts the individual. But the supernatural is more fundamental. It is as vital for human beings as is light for a plant, as Weil writes in 'La Personne et le sacré': 'Seule la lumière qui tombe continuellement du ciel fournit à un arbre l'énergie qui enfonce profondément dans la terre les puissantes racines. L'arbre est en vérité enraciné dans le ciel' (*EL* 29–30; *IPC* 31 ff.).[20]

---

[17] 'Where one is in the eyes of the unbelievers a pathological case because one adheres to absurd dogmas without having the excuse of submitting to social pressure, and where one inspires in Catholics the protective, slightly disdainful benevolence of those who have arrived towards those who are on their way.'
[18] In his *Classical Apologetics* Sproul points to secularism as the main problem of modern times, of which rationalism is just one expression (Sproul 1984: 3 ff.). In response, apologists between 1910 and 1950—among them Henri de Lubac—were intent on refuting rationalism and reintroducing the supernatural, as Avery Dulles points out in his excellent book *A History of Apologetics* (Dulles 1971: 212 ff.).
[19] 'The errors of our time are the result of Christianity minus the supernatural element. This is due to "laïcisme" (secularization), and in the first place, to humanism' (*NB* 502). She also speaks about the present as 'ces temps où une si grande partie de l'humanité est submergée de matérialisme' ('these days when so large a proportion of humanity is submerged in materialism') (*AD* 19/*WG* 6).
[20] 'It is the light falling continually from heaven which alone gives a tree the energy to send powerful roots deep into the earth. The tree is really rooted in the sky' (*SE* 23).

Whom is Weil addressing with her apologetic zeal? It seems she tries to appeal to, and 'convert', different categories of people through different means, namely Catholics, intellectuals, and the working classes.[21] Weil wants to make Catholics aware of what she thinks Catholicism really means.[22] The word originally derives from the Greek *katholikos*, signifying 'universal' which for the Catholic Church means that Christ is fully present in the Church, which has received the fullness of the means of salvation, and therefore has a mission to the whole human race.[23] In contrast, for Weil the term 'universal' applies to Christianity rather than to the Catholic Church *de facto* (*AD* 52). For she believes there were already Christian revelations preceding the incarnation of Christ and the founding of the Church. Weil's understanding of the universe and of salvation is Christological. Christ is the mediator between God and humanity, but he may—she speculates tentatively—have become incarnate a number of times, in the shape of Osiris, Dionysus, or Apollo (*LR* 22, 24).[24] These earlier revelations are necessary to account for the justice of God. For how could he have allowed atrocious suffering for those who, without this supernatural consolation, would curse God and be damned (ibid. 20; *AD* 188)? The Catholic Church should become aware of this continuing link between ancient civilizations and itself, and realize how radically universal it is. This is important not only for the sake of truth, but also for the Christianization of society, as Weil writes in *Lettre à un religieux* as well as in her fourth letter to Perrin. Our society, claims, is heavily determined by pre-Christian societies, but little by Christianity. In order to create a link between the two, one needs to show how Christian in spirit these ancient cultures were, and how the modern secular approach is a degradation of these high civilizations (*LR* 22–3, 96; *OC* vi/3. 163, 250).[25] In order to be available to Europe

---

[21] Stokes also believes the intellectuals or well-read bourgeoisie as well as the working class to be her intended audience, but he does not mention Catholics (Stokes 1996: 21–2, 24). Though I use the word 'convert' for the sake of simplicity, Weil would have been opposed to the idea that she or anybody else could convert another human being. All she wishes for—as will be shown later on—is to prepare the ground for the descent of grace (*SG* 97).

[22] However, as Perrin points out, Weil did not really have contact with the Catholic intellectual world (Canciani 2000: 13–14, 163). Thus her severe judgements on Catholics should not be taken at face value.

[23] *Catechism of the Catholic Church*, nos. 830–1.

[24] See Eric Springsted's *Christus Mediator* for a better understanding of the centrality of Christ in Weil's thought (1983).

[25] It must be kept in mind that *Lettre à un religieux* was not meant for publication. Weil was voicing her questions to see whether she could become a Catholic while holding

with its diverse cultures, Catholicism must contain everything, except for falsehood, of course (*AD* 53–4, 80, 81). More radically speaking, Weil writes in *La Connaissance surnaturelle* that there is no such thing as a Christian point of view and other points of view, but only truth and error: 'Non pas: ce qui n'est pas chrétien est faux, mais: tout ce qui est vrai est chrétien' (*CS* 24/*OC* vi/3. 395; *E* 112).[26] Did not the apologist St Justin Martyr already say that 'whatever things were rightly said among all people are the property of us Christians'?[27] Weil wants to avoid the excluding attitude of 'we are right and the others are wrong', and take advantage of the unifying nature of truth. Before the gulf separating Christianity and secular society in people's minds can be overcome, it must be bridged in the hearts of Catholics themselves, otherwise they cannot convey the Christian message convincingly. Even Perrin, whom Weil admired and loved greatly, does not live up to her ideals, as she told him. In her last letter to him, written in Casablanca on 26 May 1942, she accuses him of partiality and of denying *in concreto* the possibility of implicit faith (*AD* 77).

Towards agnostic intellectuals she uses a different apologetic approach. The classics they so love and have been brought up with, are not something to prefer to or to find superior to Catholicism. There is no 'either/or', for the one cannot be understood without the other. If ancient culture really is Christian in spirit, then one will miss its true meaning by viewing it from a secular perspective. In a way, Weil is doing something similar to what G. K. Chesterton describes in *The Everlasting Man*, strange as a comparison between such different writers may sound. Familiarity breeds contempt, and people often turn away from Christianity by thinking wrongly that they know what it is. Only the attraction of novelty, Chesterton suggests, can contribute to an impartial outlook on Christianity.[28] Similarly, Weil thinks of ways '[de] donner aux intelligences d'aujourd'hui ce choc dont elles ont besoin pour porter

---

certain opinions. Some of her statements are therefore mere hypotheses, but 'au cas où il serait de foi stricte de les estimer fausses, elles sont pour moi un obstacle aussi sérieux que les autres, car j'ai la conviction qu'elles sont douteuses, c'est-à-dire qu'il n'est pas légitime de les nier catégoriquement' ('were it a strict article of the faith to esteem them false, I should regard them as being as serious an obstacle as the others, for I am firmly convinced that they are held in doubt by me, that is to say, that it is not legitimate to deny them categorically') (*LR* 13/*LTP* 10).

[26] 'There is not a Christian point of view and other points of view; there is truth and error. It is not that anything which isn't Christian is false, but everything which is true is Christian' (*FLN* 80).
[27] St Justin 1997: 2. 13, p. 84.   [28] Chesterton 1993: 13 ff.

à la foi chrétienne une attention neuve' (*IPC* 57).²⁹ The intellectuals need to be shown that the source of Greek culture, its art, science, and politics is generated through the thirst for Christ: 'c'est la soif prolongée pendant des siècles de cette source qui finalement a jailli et vers laquelle aujourd'hui vous ne tournez même pas les yeux' (ibid.).³⁰ By looking at the classics through a Christian lens, she can present Christianity in a new light. At the same time, she is showing us the classics from a new angle, as the following chapters will illustrate.

Finally, Weil is concerned about the evangelization of the working classes. I have already mentioned Weil's attempt in her pre-mystical days to educate the hearts and minds of the industrial workers at Rosières by introducing them to ancient Greek tragedies. After her mystical experience, Weil's concern takes on a religious dimension. *L'Enracinement* is filled with ideas of how to re-Christianize the world of the farmer and worker. Her text 'Le Christianisme et la vie des champs' ('Christianity and Agricultural Life'), written in Marseille, focuses on this question as well. One needs to make the Gospel meaningful to farmers through its images and parables which are often related to the world of agriculture. For example, the allegory about the grain of wheat falling to the ground and dying should be read in church and meditated upon during the sowing season (*E* 85). Weil was very conscious of the power of words, as will be shown in her article from 1937 'Ne recommençons pas la guerre de Troie' (*The Power of Words/SE*).³¹ Later on she was to say that certain words such as God or justice 'sont vivants', and cut like a sword (*EL* 58).³² Therefore those that suffer (often in practice the lower classes) should be nurtured with words 'dont le séjour propre se trouve au ciel, par-dessus le ciel, dans l'autre monde', according to the expression used in 'La Personne et le sacré' (*EL* 30).³³ She, as an intellectual and writer, can attain this result to a certain extent, when she writes for their journals, or perhaps even better, by talking with them, which she liked to do at all times, but especially when she was sharing their life during her industrial and agricultural experiences. However, she stresses the importance of parish priests in conveying the Christian message to farmers by pointing out its relevance

---

²⁹ '[to] give contemporary intelligences that shock which they need to bring a new attention to the Christian faith' (*JC* 119).
³⁰ 'all this was produced by the thirst, prolonged during centuries, for that source which finally sprang up and toward which today you do not even turn your eyes' (ibid.).
³¹ See Ch. 5.   ³² 'are living words'.
³³ 'whose rightful abode is in heaven, beyond heaven, in the other world' (*SE* 23).

in their sermons. Furthermore, as she writes in 'Le Christianisme et la vie des champs', the Eucharist must become the focus of daily life in areas where wheat and grapes are grown. Thus, workers can think of their toil as a sacrifice similar to that of the Eucharist, giving their own energy and body for the sake of others (*PSO* 25).[34] However, after her mystical experience, her interpretations of ancient Greek texts were no longer specifically addressed to the working classes.

The Purpose of Weil's Apologetics

Given that Weil was not baptized, at least when she was still writing, one may wonder about the purpose of her apologetics. It is unusual for somebody to write in favour of a religion with the intention of converting her readers without herself belonging to it. Apparently Weil did not think that her objections to the Catholic faith were compelling enough to prevent other people from receiving baptism. For example, she even advised her brother to baptize his daughter.[35] The utilitarian reasons she gave, namely that it will make marriage with a Christian easier, that this child will not be confronted with the difficulty of choosing whether to become a Christian or not, and that it represents no obstacle to changing religion, might have been determined by the fact that her brother was more open to this reasoning than to spiritual arguments or that she wanted to hide her own spiritual development. On the other hand, all religions are to a certain extent the same to Weil in as far as they express the secret presence of God in the world: 'ces religions sont la religion vraie, la traduction en langages différents de la grande Révélation', as she writes in 'Formes de l'amour implicite de Dieu' (*AD* 132).[36] For Europe and America, the religion that translates this best is Catholicism, but in other cultures such as India this may not be so (ibid. 180).

According to Weil it is difficult to compare religions. As she writes in her 'Formes de l'amour implicite de Dieu', one needs to be inside a religion to understand it. A religion is a food for the soul whose flavour and nutritional value can only be appreciated if one has eaten it. Furthermore, one needs a certain gift of sympathy to view a religion

---

[34] The situation of the industrial workers is more difficult since they have been uprooted more than the farmers (*E* 73). See Weil's discussion of the problem in *E* 46 ff.
[35] SP ii. 435; A. Weil 1990: 18.
[36] 'these religions are true religion, the translation into different languages of the great Revelation' (*WG* 89).

from the inside. Basically, Weil claims, one needs to embrace its faith for a while, to do it justice, and to grasp all the explicit and implicit truths it contains (ibid. 177–9). It is difficult to imagine how Weil wants to achieve this, given that faith is a whole-hearted assent, which is impossible to give, if one knows that one is adhering to it only for a limited period. Though she claims to be using the term 'faith' 'au sens le plus fort du mot', she is using it in her particular sense, really meaning attention, love, and sympathy towards the religion under study (ibid. 178).[37] Given the difficulty of comparing religions, Weil suggests that one keep one's religion, if it is 'pas trop impropre à la prononciation du nom du Seigneur' (ibid. 179).[38] Only if God himself through a direct contact tells the soul to convert, or if the religion is too imperfect or at least appears to be so, or if one has no love for it or has not been raised with any religious practice, may one embrace a new faith (ibid. 179–80). Weil would in fact have considered most of these grounds as applying to herself. She grew up without any knowledge or practice of Judaism. What she learnt about it by merely reading the Old Testament, she did not like. She thought it was a nationalistic religion, seeing God in terms of his power rather than in terms of his love, and thus it falls into the category of being 'impropre à la prononciation du nom du Seigneur'. Finally, Christ 'lui-même est descendu'[39] to her, which means that God directly touched her soul, transforming her from a cultural into a religious Christian.

The conditions Weil sets for conversion are not very conducive to the practice of apologetics. There is no reason to convert to another religion, unless one is called to do so by divine intervention, or because one's religion is too imperfect, or because of special circumstances. The pastoral dimension of apologetics to strengthen believers in their faith ultimately becomes unnecessary. For if many religions are more or less equal, it does not seem to matter whether one keeps one's own or changes to another. But for Weil conversion is 'une décision extrêmement grave', a radical change, a *déracinement* (*AD* 180).[40] For the soul to change

---

[37] 'in its strongest sense' (*WG* 119). One may wonder why the Jewish religion is such a blind spot in Weil, for she never gave it much sympathy and attention. Though she read the Old Testament, she was not interested in its Jewish interpretations, which might have resolved some of her difficulties, nor in the religious practices of the Jews. For example in the camp near Casablanca, she was astonished to witness for the first time the ritual gestures of some Polish Jews during their prayers (*SP* ii. 417).

[38] 'not too unsuitable for pronouncing the name of the Lord' (*WG* 120)

[39] 'himself came down'.   [40] 'a very serious decision' (*WG* 120).

religion is similar to changing languages for a writer—and only a writer knows what this really means (ibid. 177). Yet her pastoral concern for Europe remains unabated, since its religion is culturally Christianity, not only after, but also before the historical incarnation of Christ. Furthermore, secularism is threatening the whole of Europe. What needs to take place is a reconversion. The 'laïcisation' of French culture brought about by the French Revolution needs to be counteracted by a new period of faith. This has happened to some extent, for Weil writes in her essay of 1943 'Cette guerre est une guerre de religions' (*A War of Religions*): 'notre époque est une période d'idolâtrie et de foi, non de simple croyance' (*EL* 106–7).[41] If Europe is not re-Christianized, ideologies, such as fascism or communism, will supersede religion.

So what does Weil mean by conversion, or 'retournement' (reversal) as she also calls it (*OC* vi/3. 229/*NB* 528)?[42] It does not necessarily mean baptism though it implies becoming Christian in some sense, at least for Europeans. Weil likes to use Plato's myth of the cave in her writings as an image of the human condition, not only of human cognition (*IPC* 73–4). The prisoners in the cave are tied to their places and all they can see are shadows reflected on the opposite wall. When they are untied, it is painful for them to get up and move about. They need to turn around to the fire lit behind their backs, before they can realize that all they have been seeing were shadows. This symbolizes for Weil the process of renunciation of *prestige*, which falsifies one's perception of reality. Unfortunately, one often wrongly believes that this is an easy undertaking, or that one has achieved it even when this is not the case (ibid. 77). But why is this operation necessary in the first place? Weil claims that original sin has made it necessary, for sin caused the split between appearance and reality, otherwise: 'Si nous étions innocents, l'apparence serait la couleur même du réel et non pas un voile à déchirer' (ibid. 85).[43] The cause for this breach is not merely an epistemological one, nor is the solution merely cognitive. This distance between appearance and reality will remain, Weil maintains, until our conversion is complete. Before that has taken place, we are at the mercy

---

[41] 'ours is an age of idolatry and faith, not of mere belief' (*SE* 217).

[42] In his article 'L'Impossible conversion' Daniel Boitier points out that Weil prefers to use the term 'vocation' to that of 'conversion'. She speaks about changing religion rather than converting to another religion, since conversion for her means to embrace the virtues of humility, love, and attention (Boitier 1994*b*: 366, 370–1).

[43] 'If we were innocent, the appearance would be of the same colour as the real and have no veil to be torn away' (*IC* 143).

of illusion and of *pesanteur*, as Weil calls the force of gravity within the moral realm, which makes one do what is evil, but pleasant, rather than what is good and difficult.

Moral conversion is the first step towards the fulfilment of the human vocation of which Christ is the model: 'Le Christ comme *idée* (εἶδος) de l'homme' (*OC* vi/2. 394).[44] Human beings cannot be understood except in the light of Christ, nor can they achieve their perfection without him as their implicit or explicit model. Thus conversion not only means leading a morally better life, but is primarily a turning towards and a conforming to God. As the metaphor of the tree rooted in the sky has already shown, human beings need to be rooted in the supernatural in order to flourish.

APOLOGETIC ARGUMENTS

Though human beings may be essentially religious and may, as Saint Augustine said, only find rest in God, it is not through their need for religion that one ought to convince them of the existence of God.[45] For, according to Weil, this pragmatic approach is not only incapable of proving the truth of Christianity, it is also unworthy of the believer since 'le besoin n'est pas un lien légitime de l'homme à Dieu' (*E* 211).[46] God needs to be sought for his own sake otherwise he is instrumentalized. Though Christ is the only bread that can really nourish the soul, he should be approached as Truth in the first place: 'Il faut le désirer d'abord comme vérité, ensuite seulement comme nourriture' (ibid.).[47]

Henri Bergson turned this order of things around, according to Weil, and therefore cannot be thought of as a Christian philosopher. He sees sanctity as the perfection of his famous *élan vital*, instead of realizing that saints do not necessarily have more vitality. Rather, in Weil's eyes, truth has become life in them (ibid.). Truth needs to come first, otherwise one's faith is illusory, and one's religious experiences are fake: 'Or pour que le sentiment religieux procède de l'esprit de vérité, il faut être totalement prêt à abandonner sa religion, dût-on perdre ainsi toute raison de vivre, au cas où elle serait autre chose que la vérité' (ibid.

---

[44] 'Christ as *idea* (εἶδος, of man' (*NB* 284).   [45] St Augustine, *Confessions* 1. 1. 1.
[46] 'need is not a legitimate bond between Man and God' (*NR* 246).
[47] He 'must first of all be desired as truth, only afterwards as food' (ibid.).

212).⁴⁸ Paradoxically atheism can become an apologetic tool as long as it is held to for the right reasons, namely for love of truth: '*Entre deux hommes qui n'ont pas "l'expérience" de Dieu, celui qui le nie en est peut-être le plus près*' (*OC* vi/2. 511).⁴⁹ Atheism can be purifying when one drops the comforts of an easy, but unfounded faith for the love of truth. Why not make use of it? '*puisque nous sommes en fait dans un âge d'incrédulité, pourquoi négliger l'usage purificateur de l'incrédulité?*' (ibid. 339; italic indicates a single underline by Weil, small capitals a double).⁵⁰

Though Weil is critical of the pragmatic approach, she does not completely exclude the apologetic weight that the satisfaction of the desire for God can have as long as one does not argue from man's need to God's existence or seek him merely for the satisfaction he gives. She writes in 'Réflexions sans ordre sur l'amour de Dieu' ('Some Reflections on the Love of God'): 'Il faut seulement attendre et appeler. [. . .] Crier qu'on a faim, et qu'on veut du pain. On criera plus ou moins longtemps, mais finalement on sera nourri, et alors on ne croira pas, on saura qu'il existe vraiment du pain. Quand on en a mangé, quelle preuve plus sûre pourrait-on vouloir?' (*PSO* 44–5).⁵¹ Once God has revealed himself and nourished the soul, there is no room for doubt. In spite of her fears of autosuggestion, Weil could not question, after her experience in November 1938, that Christ had come to her. Thus the satisfaction God provides is an experiential proof of his existence though one's need for him is not.

Weil is generally quite critical of the Church's apologetic arguments. She criticizes not only the 'need-argument', but also the historical argument and the argument from miracles and prophecies. The historical line of reasoning claims that with Christ's arrival, humanity enjoyed a radical improvement. Not only is this difficult to prove, but Weil thinks it is fallacious, probably because of her ahistorical understanding

---

⁴⁸ 'But for religious feeling to emanate from the spirit of truth, one should be absolutely prepared to abandon one's religion, even if that should mean losing all motive for living, if it should turn out to be anything other than the truth' (ibid. 247).

⁴⁹ 'Between two men who have not "experienced" God, he who denies him is perhaps closer to him.'

⁵⁰ 'Since we are, in fact, in an age of incredulity, why neglect the purificatory use of incredulity? I have had experimental knowledge of its use' (*NB* 239).

⁵¹ 'We must only wait and call out. [. . .] cry out that we are hungry and want bread. Whether we cry for a long time or a short time, in the end we shall be fed, and then we shall not believe but we shall *know* that there really is bread. What surer proof could one ask for than to have eaten it?' (*SNL* 159).

of Christianity and her conviction that some ancient cultures were more Christian than the Catholic Church ever has been. Instead, she turns the argument around, asking how humanity could have improved after the murder of a perfect being, namely Christ (*LR* 53). Furthermore, Weil claims, this kind of reasoning falls into the sin of pragmatism for it reduces Christianity 'au niveau des réclames pour spécialités pharmaceutiques, qui décrivent le malade avant et après' (*E* 213).[52] However, one might want to argue that even though humanity as a whole has not bettered itself and that the idea of constant progress has been proved false, especially by the events of the twentieth century, the witness of the saints can be a strong argument in favour of Christianity. The 'transformation in Christ', the virtue of humility and the spirit of forgiveness this brings about in individual Christians, seem to be something specifically, if not exclusively, Christian.

The miracles and prophecies used from the Early Church onwards to authenticate Christianity, are arguments which Weil calls 'misérables' (ibid. 212). She writes a short section about the nature of miracles in *L'Enracinement*, and brings up this theme in various texts (ibid. 225 ff.; *IPC* 152–3). Miracles occur in other religions as well, she argues, and therefore cannot prove in and of themselves the truth of Christianity (*E* 227; *LR* 55 ff.). Furthermore, miracles are the 'natural' consequence of giving one's soul either to good or to evil: 'Car à chaque manière d'être de l'âme humaine correspond quelque chose de physique. A la tristesse correspond de l'eau salée dans les yeux; pourquoi pas à certains états d'extase mystique, comme on raconte, un certain soulèvement du corps au-dessus du sol?' (*E* 226).[53] Thus miracles do not go against the laws of science; they are simply the physiological expression of a certain state of affairs in the spiritual realm.[54] Science and religion are not opposed, therefore the former cannot be used against the latter. Normally the significance of miracles is thought to lie in the fact that

---

[52] 'to the level of advertisements for pharmaceutical products, which describe the state of the patient before and after' (*NR* 248).

[53] 'For every attitude of the human soul is accompanied by a certain particular physical state. Sorrow is accompanied by salt water in the eyes; then why not in certain states of mystical ecstasy, as is averred, a certain lifting up of the body above the ground?' (ibid. 264).

[54] Furthermore, it is absurd to believe that a miracle is the result of God's will, Weil adds. Instead, God lets necessity reign (for the similarity between Weil and Spinoza on this issue, see Goldschläger 1982: 192 ff.) (*E* 225 ff.). This is part of his self-abnegating act of creation during which he had to withdraw in order to leave room to other beings (*EL* 48).

they cannot be explained by science, but for Weil this very feature constitutes an obstacle to conversion. Since miracles are a scandal to the mind, could one not argue that they point to a different reality and break through the narrow limits of a rationalistic worldview? But, as Weil rightly points out, they do not indicate whether their author is good or evil. Regarding Christ, the discernment is easy, Weil claims, since his perfection was made manifest by the purity of his life, the beauty of his words, and because he used his power only to perform deeds of charity (ibid. 227). But the devil and some of his followers also have the power to perform miracles. What is truly miraculous is sanctity rather than unusual phenomena, for sanctity goes against the laws of *pesanteur* (ibid. 226; *OC* vi/2. 386, 442–3). Whether this state is combined with walking on water or healing the sick does not matter.

The resurrection therefore is not important for Weil. This does not mean that she disbelieved it, but that, in terms of her faith, she deemed it unnecessary (*LR* 62–3; *CS* 154; *AD* 37). Christ's absolute kenosis on the cross was enough for her: 'La Croix seule me suffit' (*LR* 62).[55] Belief in the resurrection, Weil thinks, corrupted the faith of the early Christians to a certain extent, and devalued their martyrdom. When Christ died on the cross, he died as a common criminal without the prestige that surrounds those who are killed for political ideals, for example. The early Christians, on the other hand, could glory in the resurrection of Christ, their hope in God's kingdom preventing them from experiencing the abandonment which Christ felt on the cross (*OC* vi/2. 192). This, for Weil, could explain why they felt joy at being martyred instead of experiencing a dark night of the soul (*AD* 108; *IPC* 78).

That the resurrection and an afterlife are superfluous in Weil's eyes deprives her of another significant apologetic argument (*AD* 37). For as St Paul wrote in his first letter to the Corinthians 'if Christ has not been raised, your faith is pointless and you have not, after all, been released from your sins' (1 Cor. 15: 17).[56] Without the resurrection, the promise of eternal life would not have been fulfilled, and Christ's death on the cross would not have been redemptive. Without the resurrection, it would be difficult to proclaim Christianity as the good news. However,

---

[55] 'The Cross by itself suffices me' (*LTP* 55).

[56] As Birou points out in his article, 'Le Christ médiateur et rédempteur selon Simone Weil', Weil quotes this passage without denying its validity. However, she sees the crucifixion as being more important than the resurrection (*IPC* 84) (Birou 1992: 347).

Weil is afraid that the hope of the resurrection might undermine the purifying power of death (*OC* vi/3. 192). God may well grant it, but it is not for us to be thinking about it (*CS* 86, 154).[57] She radicalizes the demands of Christianity, for she asks for death to self, adherence to truth at whatever cost, even martyrdom, but without the promise of eternal life.

Weil and the Church Fathers

The only traditional apologetic argument Weil calls upon in some form is the one which argues that Christ fulfilled the prophecies in the Old Testament. However, she is very critical of the Old Testament which—except for a few books—does not depict in her eyes the true and loving God, but only the God of hosts.[58] In Weil's eyes, the Jews misunderstood God, and turned him into an idol seeking power and defending their national greatness. Other cultures and peoples may have been more capable of receiving the announcements of Christ's coming incarnation. For example: 'La mythologie grecque est pleine de prophéties' (*LR* 23–4).[59] Also: 'On commente couramment certains actes, certaines paroles du Christ en disant: "Il fallait que les prophéties fussent accomplies." Il s'agit des prophéties hébraïques. Mais d'autres actes, d'autres paroles pourraient être commentés de même par rapport aux prophéties non hébraïques' (ibid. 24).[60]

Though Weil does not interpret the Old Testament in the traditional Christian manner, her Christianizing approach to Greek literature and philosophy is in some respects similar to that of the early apologists, the Church Fathers. However, the early apologists were hesitant to delineate the presence of pre-Christian intuitions in Greek culture. They

[57] Birou 1992: 348–9.
[58] The only books of the Old Testament that Weil appreciates are the beginning of Genesis, Job, most of the Psalms, the Wisdom Books, the Song of Songs, Isaiah, a part of Ezekiel, Daniel, and Tobit (*LR* 71, 17; *CSW* 10/1: 4; *CS* 221).
[59] 'Greek mythology is full of prophecies' (*LTP* 209).
[60] 'Certain actions performed by Christ, certain words of his are constantly commented upon as follows: "The prophecies must needs be fulfilled." This refers to the Hebrew prophecies. But there are other actions, other words which might be commented upon in the same way in connection with the non-Hebrew prophecies' (ibid. 21). Weil sees in the dying and resurrecting Greek or Egyptian gods Christological figures and fails to acknowledge that they do not die for the sake of redemption—though André Boulanger points this out in his book *Orphée: rapports de l'orphisme et du christianisme*, which was in Weil's personal library (*LR* 22) (Boulanger 1925: 102; Rahner 1945: 46; Little 1988*a*: 142; Œ 634).

were afraid this might undermine the singularity of Christianity and could lead to syncretism.[61] They preferred the euhemeristic approach of believing that the Greek gods in mythology were in reality human beings who had performed heroic deeds.[62] Or they liked to claim that the Greeks stole elements from the Hebrew tradition, which would account for the similarities between the two, as Arthur Droge points out in *Homer or Moses? Early Christian Interpretations of the History of Culture*.[63] Or they criticized Greek mythology for its anthropomorphism, the immorality of the gods—such as their adulteries, their incest, their fights, or their cannibalism.[64] However, Justin Martyr, Clement of Alexandria, and Origen saw the seminal Logos at work in those elements in Greek thought, which were similar to Christianity.[65] Justin adopts two lines of argument, namely that Greek culture plagiarized from the Old Testament, while the eternal Logos kept some people informed since the beginning of time.[66] In his first Apology, Justin writes that 'there seem to be seeds of truth among all people; but they are proved not to have understood them accurately when they contradict each other'.[67] However, he also thinks that demons invented myths before the incarnation of Christ to imitate certain aspects of his life so as to confuse future generations.[68]

Weil refers to Justin a few times in her work (*LR* 31; *CS* 22, 55, 118, 240, 280; *OC* vi/3. 393). She is aware of his more positive outlook on Greek thought since she writes in her *Connaissance*: 'Justin martyr, milieu du IIe, alliance du christianisme et de la philosophie grecque' (*CS* 55).[69] She refers directly to nos. 59 and 60 of his *First Apology* which talk about the similarity between the accounts of creation in Genesis and in Plato, as well as Plato's reference to the *Chi* laid across the universe in his *Timaeus*.[70] Justin assumes that Plato must have taken this idea from Moses' bronze serpent, which healed everybody who looked to it from snakebites (Num. 21: 6–9). For him, this piece of bronze prefigured the cross.[71] Weil herself uses this passage from Plato to indicate the presence

---

[61] Trousson 1976: 61, 66–7.   [62] Seznec 1940: 15.
[63] Droge 1989: 1, 9 ff.   [64] Dorival 1998: 443–4.
[65] Ibid. 427–8. Weil refers to Origen in the following places: *LR* 47, 74, 85; *CS* 43, 134, 196–7, 200, 245, 332; *OC* vi/3. 410.
[66] Droge 1989: 66 ff.   [67] St Justin 1997: 1. 44, pp. 53–4.
[68] Ibid. 1. 23, p. 39; 54, p. 61.
[69] 'Justin Martyr, middle of the 2nd century, alliance of Christianity and Greek philosophy' (*FLN* 109).
[70] Plato, *Timaeus* 36bc; *IPC* 26; *SG* 135.
[71] St Justin 1997: 1. 60, pp. 65–6, 169–70 n. 358.

of pre-Christian intuitions in ancient Greece: 'Si on lisait Platon avec le même état d'esprit que l'Ancien Testament, on verrait peut-être dans ces lignes une prophétie' (*IPC* 27–8).[72]

Clement of Alexandria, like Justin, thought that the truth of Greek philosophy was derived from the Old Testament and that the Logos illuminated and enlightened the Greeks. For example, he claims that 'philosophy was to the Greek world what the Law was to the Hebrews, a tutor escorting them to Christ'.[73] He also believed that the Greek poets were sometimes inspired by God, as he mentions in ch. 7 of 'Exhortation to the Heathen'.[74] But since the Greeks did not know the Word himself, they were 'unable to follow through on their best insights', as Avery Dulles summarizes Clement in *A History of Apologetics*.[75] Without indicating the reference, Weil quotes in the *Connaissance* from Clement's *Stromata* the passage where he claims that Pythagoras and his followers, Plato, and many other philosophers seized 'the truth in portions and aspect' 'by a happy utterance of divination, not without divine help, concurring in certain prophetic declarations' (*CS* 115/*FLN* 162).[76] This shows that she was aware at least in part of his Logos-theory.[77]

But though Clement was probably an Athenian by birth and a convert to Christianity, the second head of the catechetical school in Alexandria, and an erudite who should have been well qualified to speak about Greek culture and its relation to Christianity, Weil judges him severely: 'A côté des niaiseries de Clément d'Alexandrie—qui ne savait même plus quels liens étroits unissent la philosophie grecque classique et la religion des Mystères—il a bien dû y avoir des hommes qui ont vu dans la Bonne Nouvelle le couronnement de cette religion. Que sont devenues leurs œuvres?' (*LR* 84–5).[78]

---

[72] 'If people read Plato in the same state of mind as they read the Old Testament, they would perhaps see a prophecy in these lines' (*IC* 94).
[73] Clement 1991: 1. 5. 28 (3), p. 42.   [74] Clement 1867: 73 ff.
[75] Dulles 1971: 3.
[76] The exact reference in Clement is Clement 1981: 5. 14. 134, p. 239. Weil quotes this passage in English, as she was in New York at the time and was probably using an English translation or a history of the Fathers, probably from the public library in New York.
[77] Weil's references to Clement: *LR* 33, 47, 84, 89; *CS* 115, 126, 129, 133, 196 ff., 240; *OC* vi/3. 175, 343, 352, 411; *SG* 163.
[78] 'Beside the silly nonsense talked by Clement of Alexandria—who was no longer even aware of the close bonds uniting Greek classical philosophy to the religion of the Mysteries—there must have been men who saw in the Glad Tidings the crowning touch to that religion. What became of their works?' (*LTP* 75–6).

Clement dedicated several chapters to the mystery cults, to Greek mythology, and to the excesses of idolatry in his *Protrepticus*. As Dulles points out, Clement concludes that the true atheists are the pagans who worship unworthy objects.[79] Rather than trusting Clement's analysis which might after all be biased, Weil holds on to her own Christian understanding of Greek culture. However, she allows for an excuse in her criticism of Clement. The mysteries of Eleusis might have been so watered down in their transmission because of the Roman conquest, perhaps becoming by that point only a mediocre reconstruction put together by the lower initiates, that this would explain the contempt with which Clement talks about them though he may once have been an initiate himself (ibid. 89; *AD* 239–40).[80]

Arthur Droge shows in *Homer or Moses?* the role age and tradition played in the ancient world. The Jews, for example, tried to show the antiquity of the Jewish religion over against the Greeks and other pagan religions. At least one pagan philosopher, namely the Pythagorean Platonist Numenius of Apamea, accepted the claim of the Jews, for he said: 'What is Plato but Moses speaking Attic Greek?'[81] The early apologists were simply following a literary tradition, when they were trying to prove that Christianity, through its Jewish roots, was older than the pagan religions. What seems a weak point in their arguments was an acceptable procedure at the time. The older something was, the more likely it was to be true, was the customary reasoning.[82] That is why Christianity was presented as rooted in antiquity, with a long history. The Old Testament not only prepared the advent of Christ and was older than any other texts, but, as Justin argued, the Logos informed the people of all times.[83] A widespread tradition maintained that Plato visited Egypt where, according to Justin, he read Moses who supposedly left a copy of the Pentateuch behind.[84]

Weil uses a similar approach. However, she does not try to prove the antiquity of Christianity with the help of the Old Testament, but traces it back to ancient non-Judaic traditions. She explains this recurring idea of hers at greater length in her eccentric 1942 essay 'Les trois fils de Noé et l'histoire de la civilisation méditerranéenne', a text left with Perrin at her departure for New York. Ham, who saw his father

---

[79] Dulles 1971: 32.

[80] That Christianity is not seen as the continuation of the mystery religions is due to an early conspiracy of the Church in Weil's eyes, but this is pure speculation on Weil's part (*LR* 84–5, 94–5).

[81] Droge 1989: 2. [82] Ibid. 9. [83] Ibid. 65 ff. [84] Ibid. 63–4.

Noah in the state of drunken nudity, whilst his brothers covered their father, was the one who transmitted the primeval mystical tradition. Noah's inebriation symbolizes a spiritual experience, according to Weil, since he was intoxicated with the love of God. He had drunk wine, which was forbidden to priests but had taken on spiritual significance since Melchisedek and would do so even more with Christ. Once drunk with divine love, Noah stripped himself of all social prestige and worldly considerations. This is the condition of spiritual nudity, which St Francis and St John of the Cross also embraced (*AD* 231–2). Ham's brothers, Japheth and Shem, were unwilling to adopt this spiritual poverty, and transmitted to their heirs a desire for power and national recognition (ibid. 241–2). Shem's descendants were the Semites, Hebrews, Arabs, Assyrians, and others, while Japheth's were the Indo-Europeans. Ham's on the other hand were the Phoenicians, Philistines, Sumerians, Hittites, and Egyptians, basically all those who contributed to the Mediterranean civilization (ibid. 229–30; *IPC* 110). In order to find the real forerunners of Christianity, one should not look to the Jews who are the descendants of Shem, but to the heirs of Ham, whether by blood or spirit. The Hellenes, for example, who descend from Japheth, were barbarians when they arrived in Greece, but embraced the spiritual culture they found there (*AD* 236). Thus the Greeks are Ham's spiritual children, and created a Christian culture predating Christ's incarnation.[85] Ham, Weil believes, was a reference-point, a source for spiritual knowledge in ancient times (*LR* 47; *OC* vi/3. 352; *CS* 209).

Thus what seems a wild genealogical construction concerning Noah's descendants by Weil, was common practice among the early apologists.[86] Her knowledge of that practice may explain why she employs a line of argumentation which was going to raise eyebrows in her own days. She refers, for example, to a passage in Justin's *First Apology* where he claims that Plato was influenced by Moses (*CS* 22/*OC* vi/3. 393).[87] Furthermore she writes in her essay 'Israël et les Gentils':

Les premiers chrétiens ont cherché à expliquer sur ce point la ressemblance entre l'enseignement de Moïse et celui de Platon par une influence du premier sur le second, à travers l'Égypte. Personne ne défend cette explication aujourd'hui, mais on n'en propose aucune autre.

---

[85] See also Gabellieri 2003*a*: 40–1. [86] See e.g. *CS* 215
[87] St Justin 1997: 1. 59, pp. 64–5.

Or, la véritable explication crève les yeux: c'est que Platon et Moïse étaient l'un et l'autre 'instruits dans la sagesse égyptienne', ou sinon Platon, en tout cas Pythagore. (*PSO* 48; *CS* 280; *SG* 79–80)[88]

Thus Israel learnt its religious wisdom from other cultures, primarily from the Egyptians (*LR* 17). When the Jews accused other cultures of being idolatrous and polytheistic, they were wrong, for 'tous les peuples de tous les temps ont toujours été monothéistes' (ibid.).[89] It is Israel that was idolatrous, for it put its nation first and adored in God's power before his goodness, at least until the Babylonian exile (*PSO* 48 ff.; *LR* 17; *IPC* 110). That is why other cultures were more receptive to Christ's message than was Israel. Christ needed to instruct his disciples for three years until their formation was complete, Weil points out, while the Ethiopian eunuch only took a few minutes to grasp the message of the Gospel, which Philip had explained to him (*PSO* 52) (Acts 8: 26–40). What Weil fails to mention is that the eunuch was reading Isaiah, and that Philip explained to him the Old Testament in the light of Christ, rather than giving a Christological interpretation of the eunuch's own religion.

Weil and Pascal

We have seen that Weil's approach bears some similarity to the early apologists, but what about more modern ones? Because of her paradoxical style and the fragmentary nature of her notebooks Weil has been compared to Pascal.[90] However, she is very critical of his apologetic method. In his excellent article 'Simone Weil et Blaise Pascal', André Devaux analyses the differences and similarities between the two thinkers, as well as the ways in which Weil, though influenced by Pascal, found fault with him. Weil is, for example, very critical of the fact that Pascal seems to advocate a search for God by the soul, rather than to understand that it is God who comes to the soul (*AD* 192).[91] In the Gospel parables, the bride must wait for the bridegroom, the slave for his master, and it is the bridegroom who issues the invitations to the guests, as Weil writes in 'Réflexions sans ordre': 'Celui qui cherche gêne

---

[88] 'The first Christians tried to explain the similarity between the teaching of Moses and that of Plato by an influence of the first on the second via Egypt. No one holds this position today, but no one proposes another one. However, the true explanation is obvious: both Plato and Moses were "instructed in Egyptian wisdom", or if not Plato, then in any case Pythagoras.'
[89] 'All peoples at all times have always been monotheistic' (*LTP* 14–15).
[90] Dargan 1999: 16.   [91] Devaux 1990: 80–1.

l'opération de Dieu plus qu'il ne la facilite. Celui que Dieu a pris ne cherche plus du tout Dieu au sens où Pascal semble employer le mot de chercher' (*PSO* 44).[92] The soul must wait in an attitude of *hupomone*, of *attente*, which is 'l'immobilité attentive et fidèle qui dure indéfiniment et que ne peut ébranler aucun choc' (*AD* 193).[93] It is anything but passive, and 'quelque chose de plus intense que toute recherche' (ibid. 194).[94] This is consistent with Weil's own mystical experience during which Christ himself came down and took her. It is absurd to try to find God, for: 'Comment pourrions-nous chercher Dieu, puisqu'il est en haut, dans la dimension que nous ne pouvons pas parcourir? Nous ne pouvons marcher qu'horizontalement' (*PSO* 44).[95] The risk is that we construct instead a God of our own making. Pascal commits this error, Weil believes, for he posits the existence of God in order to prove it. He knows in advance what results he wants to obtain, and argues accordingly: 'Pascal déjà avait commis le crime du manque de probité dans la recherche de Dieu. [...] Il a entrepris une recherche intellectuelle en décidant à l'avance où elle devait le mener. Pour éviter tout risque d'aboutir ailleurs, il s'est soumis à une suggestion consciente et voulue. Après quoi il a cherché des preuves' (*E* 212).[96] He lacks intellectual honesty and fears the emptiness which the non-existence of God would leave. But Weil does not do justice to Pascal, as Devaux rightly points out. After Pascal's mystical experience as described in the *Mémorial*, he would have said, like Weil, that 'celui que Dieu a pris ne cherche plus du tout Dieu' (*PSO* 44).[97] Furthermore, Pascal is not describing his own spiritual journey, but has an apologetic purpose in mind. Therefore he cannot help but give the impression that he already knows what he wants to prove.[98]

---

[92] 'To search is to impede rather than to facilitate God's operation. The man of whom God has taken possession no longer searches at all in the sense in which Pascal seems to use the word search' (*SNL* 159).
[93] 'the waiting or attentive and faithful immobility that lasts indefinitely and cannot be shaken' (*WG* 128).
[94] 'something more intense than any searching' (ibid.).
[95] 'How could we search for God, since he is above, in a dimension not open to us? We can only advance horizontally' (*SNL* 159).
[96] 'Pascal had already been guilty of lack of probity in his search for God. [...] So he undertook an intellectual research having decided beforehand where it was to lead him. To avoid all possible risk of landing himself elsewhere, he allowed his mind to be dominated by a conscious and deliberately entertained suggestion. After which, he sought for proofs' (*NR* 247).
[97] 'The man of whom God has taken possession no longer searches at all' (*SNL* 159).
[98] Devaux 1990: 89.

Though Weil admits that Pascal 'a aperçu des choses très fortes' 'dans le domaine des probabilités, des indications', his actual proofs such as the arguments of the wager, of prophecies, and of miracles are 'misérables (*E* 212).[99] We already know Weil's criticisms of miracles and prophecies. What were Weil's thoughts on the *pari* 'wager'? According to Devaux, Weil herself uses a line of reasoning in her *Connaissance* which resembles Pascal's wager:[100]

> Si on subordonne toutes choses à l'obéissance à Dieu sans aucune restriction, avec cette pensée: Si Dieu est réel on gagne ainsi tout—quand même l'instant de la mort apporterait le néant; si ce mot ne correspond à rien qu'à des illusions, on n'a rien perdu, car alors il n'y a absolument aucun bien, et par suite rien à perdre; on a même gagné d'être dans la vérité, car on a laissé des biens illusoires, qui existent, mais qui ne sont pas des biens, pour une chose qui (dans cette supposition), n'existe pas, mais qui, si elle existait, serait encore l'unique bien. . . . Si on gouverne ainsi sa vie, aucune révélation au moment de la mort ne peut causer de regret; car quand le hasard ou le démon gouverneraient tous les mondes, on n'aurait pas à regretter d'avoir vécu ainsi.   (*CS* 109)[101]

Yet she quickly adds: 'Cela est bien préférable au pari de Pascal.'[102] What is the difference between the two 'wagers'? For Pascal the alternatives are either eternal happiness with God or nothingness with the advantage of not having spent one's time on vanities. For Weil, however, both options lead to happiness. For in both cases one desires the good whether it exists or not, which is in itself already the highest good: 'Quand une fois tout mon désir est dirigé vers le bien, quel autre bien ai-je à attendre? Je possède alors tout le bien. C'est cela, posséder tout le bien. Quelle absurdité d'imaginer une autre félicité?' (ibid.).[103] Weil does not wish

---

[99] 'he discovered some very weighty things', 'in the sphere of probability, significant indication[s]' (*NR* 247).

[100] Devaux 1990: 87.

[101] 'If we put obedience to God above everything else, unreservedly, with the following thought: Suppose God is real, then our gain is total—even though we fall into nothingness at the moment of death; suppose the word "God" stands only for illusions, then we have still lost nothing because on this assumption there is absolutely nothing good, and consequently nothing to lose; we have even gained, through being in accord with truth, because we have left aside the illusory goods which exist but are not good for the sake of something which (on this assumption) does not exist but which, if it did exist, would be the only good. . . . If one follows this rule of life, then no revelation at the moment of death can cause any regrets; because if chance or the devil govern all worlds we would still have no regrets for having lived in this way' (*FLN* 157).

[102] 'That is greatly preferable to Pascal's wager' (ibid.).

[103] 'When once all my desire is directed towards the good, what other good have I to expect? I now possess all the good. That is what it is to possess all the good. How absurd to imagine any other happiness!' (ibid.).

for any other happiness. Her desire is primarily to be in the truth as Christ was when hanging on the cross: 'pour ce privilège, je renoncerais volontiers à tout ce qu'on nomme le Paradis' (ibid.).[104] Devaux wonders whether the difference between Pascal and Weil does not lie in the fact that Pascal puts forward an ontological alternative (concerning the existence or non-existence of God), whilst Weil's alternative is of a logical nature (at least the desire for the good is possible whether this good exists or not).[105] Weil's alternative is less attractive, but also more challenging. She offers the unbeliever the good, whether it exists really or only hypothetically, for the mere possibility of its existence already gives the sort of joy that the mere pleasures of the world never can.[106]

Pascal's method, Weil believes, does not provoke real faith, but is merely a form of autosuggestion (*AD* 47, 192; *LR* 68). Yet Pascal does not think that consenting to a wager already means believing, but simply that it could lead to a greater receptivity to grace.[107] Weil's criticism of Pascal is revelatory of her own apologetic approach, just as her disagreements with the early apologists were. By explaining these criticisms, I hope to make her ideas clearer. She does not want to give unbelievers a ready-made faith, nor even encourage them to search for God. Rather, what she wishes to arouse in them is an attitude of complete intellectual honesty, even if this leads temporarily to atheism (*OC* vi/2. 125, 337, 338). Wait, embrace truth, and hope for the good to manifest itself, is what Weil suggests.

Weil and Modern Apologetics

However, Pascal was not her only *bête noire*. She also had a low opinion of the apologetics of her own day, for:

Aucun dialogue de sourds ne peut approcher en force comique le débat de l'esprit moderne et de l'Église. Les incroyants choisissent pour en faire des arguments contre la foi chrétienne, au nom de l'esprit scientifique, des vérités qui constituent indirectement ou même directement des preuves manifestes de la foi. Les chrétiens ne s'en aperçoivent jamais, et ils s'efforcent faiblement, avec une mauvaise conscience, avec un manque affligeant de probité intellectuelle,

---

[104] 'for that privilege I would willingly renounce everything that is called Paradise' (ibid.).
[105] Devaux 1990: 88.
[106] On the question of the existence or non-existence of the good, see Little 1988*a*: 56–7.
[107] Devaux 1990: 88.

de nier ces vérités. Leur aveuglement est le châtiment du crime d'idolâtrie. (*E* 220)[108]

What idol are the Christians adoring? Science, though it is no longer the pursuit of truth, as it should be, but has become fashion-bound and is the result of a whole number of extrinsic factors. Scientists form a little world of their own, dominated by ambition, sympathies, and antipathies. Those scientific theories which make it into a wider forum have achieved this position more by good luck than because of their truth (ibid. 218 ff.).

The reason why the Church puts forward weak arguments when contradicting science is not because it is objectively in a weaker position, but because of an inferiority complex (ibid. 203). It is hypnotized by the prestige of science. This has terrible consequences. For this is why religion has become 'une chose du dimanche matin' while science reigns during the rest of the week (ibid. 209).[109] Because of this and because of the Church's inability to develop a satisfactory doctrine of miracles, 'la foi chrétienne ne mord pas, ne se propage pas d'âme en âme comme un incendie' as it should be doing (*LR* 64).[110]

Weil's answer to the problem is twofold: science must be renewed, and the Church needs to change its attitude towards it. She wants to renovate science by reintroducing the Greeks' understanding of it. Search for truth should be its defining characteristic, rather than the modern pragmatic approach that thinks only in terms of hypotheses. Weil wrote a series of texts on the question, from letters to her brother to articles, unfinished essays, and her *thèse de diplôme d'études supérieures*, mostly assembled in *Sur la science*.[111] The Church, on the other hand, must abstain from following the world in its idol-worship of science, must open itself to the fullness of reality and resist falling into the trap of narrow-mindedness.

---

[108] 'No deaf men's dialogue could possibly equal in comical force the polemic between the modern spirit and the Church. The unbelievers select, in the name of the scientific spirit, and to use them as arguments against the Christian faith, truths which constitute indirectly, or even directly manifest proofs of that faith. The Christians never notice this, and make feeble attempts, with a bad conscience and a distressing lack of intellectual honesty, to deny such truths. Their blindness is their punishment for the crime of idolatry' (*NR* 256).
[109] 'something we relegate to Sunday morning' (ibid. 243).
[110] 'the Christian faith does not "catch on", does not spread from soul to soul like a prairie fire' (*LTP* 57).
[111] I will not delve into this aspect of Weil's thought though it was one of her significant apologetic concerns.

In the Church a debate started at the end of the nineteenth century around the question of apologetics, triggered by Blondel's *L'Action*.[112] At the time when this work was published in 1893, apologetics was generally done in a textbook fashion, which Dulles describes as 'a defensive type [of apologetics] that seeks to argue unbelievers into submission to the faith as traditionally understood'.[113] Blondel wanted to renew the apologetics of his day by addressing himself primarily to apologists and theologians who would set the tone.[114] France was at the time 'the most vital center of apologetical thought at the turn of the century', as Dulles puts it.[115]

In *L'Action*, Blondel poses the question of the supernatural within contemporary philosophy. Though philosophy cannot prove or disprove the existence of the supernatural, the nature of action shows that one cannot avoid the choice for or against the transcendent. Whether one knows God or not, one cannot help but decide between one's egoism and a hidden God.[116] For action raises the question about the meaning of life, and points to something beyond, since it becomes clear that nothing in the world can fulfil one's deepest aspirations. One can 'try out action', like the dilettante who seeks pleasure in many different things without ever committing himself. But 'to try to enjoy everything, without willing anything [...] is to will oneself', as Latourelle synthesizes Blondel's point.[117] To will absolute nothingness instead, is merely caused by one's disappointment with the world, from which one wrongly expected something absolute.[118] To feel the inadequacy of the natural world ever to satisfy the human heart is a crisis immanent to the human condition.[119] Blondel then presents proofs for the existence of God, which should lead to a recognition of the emerging presence of God in ourselves, rather than to a merely rational acknowledgement of his existence.[120] Blondel does not try to prove the truth of Christianity, but

---

[112] For a good summary of the question, see Dulles 1971: 202 ff. and the introduction to the English translation of Blondel's *Letter on Apologetics* (Dru 1995: 13 ff.). Furthermore, Gabriel Daly in his book *Transcendence and Immanence: A Study in Catholic Modernism and Integralism* (1980), gives a good idea of the modernist conflict at the turn of the century.
[113] Dulles 1971: 202.   [114] Dru 1995: 15.   [115] Dulles 1971: 202.
[116] Something he will repeat in his *Lettre sur les exigences de la pensée contemporaine en matière d'apologétique* (Blondel 1956: II no. 3, p. 44). For a good summary of *L'Action*, see Latourelle's article on Blondel in the *Dictionary of Fundamental Theology* (Latourelle 1994: 78 ff.), as well as Dulles's short summary (Dulles 1971: 203–4).
[117] Latourelle 1994: 79; Blondel 1995: I ch.1, no. 2, p. 42.
[118] Blondel 1995: II ch. 2 no. 3, pp. 72–3.
[119] Ibid. IV p. 358; Latourelle 1994: 80.
[120] Blondel 1995: IV ch. 2 no. 3, pp. 374–5.

wants to show that it fulfils the demands of the will, and that a true religion would have dogmas and forms of practice similar to those of Christianity. But only a lived Christianity can show whether it allows for free action and the fulfilment of the human heart.[121] Thus Blondel's 'philosophical apologetics' is different from an apology for Christianity. It is addressed to all people who are willing to follow a philosophical argument to its conclusion.

When Blondel was accused of rejecting metaphysics in *L'Action* in favour of a psychological approach, he answered in 1896 with his *Lettre sur les exigences de la pensée contemporaine en matière d'apologétique*.[122] Before proposing his own method in part II of the *Lettre* along the lines of *L'Action*, he criticizes different apologetic methods. In contrast to the textbook approach, Blondel wants to take into account the fact that mentalities change: what was appealing and convincing in earlier times, is not any more so. If the modern mentality refuses to listen to older apologetic arguments, then they are of no use. There is no sense in accusing dissenters of having 'intelligences faussées' ['perverted minds'] or of suffering from 'maladies de la raison' ['jaundiced outlooks'].[123] Rather, one must start 'du fait d'une incrédulité théorique et pratique' of the people.[124] To argue along the lines of scholasticism is not apologetically successful any longer. Thus Blondel criticizes Thomism:

Mais dès à présent ne comprend-on pas que poser d'emblée les mêmes affirmations initiales et doctrinales qu'au XIIIe siècle, c'est non seulement se fermer tout accès auprès des esprits qui vivent des pensées de notre temps, mais encore vainement chercher à retrouver pour soi-même un équilibre qui a été définitivement rompu, parce qu'il n'était stable qu'avant certaines distinctions faites, avant certains problèmes soulevés? Penser littéralement aujourd'hui comme il y a cinq cents ans, c'est inévitablement penser dans un autre esprit qu'alors.[125]

---

[121] Latourelle 1994: 82–3; Blondel 1995: V ch. 2, pp. 440–1 and V pp. 525–6.
[122] Dulles 1971: 204.   [123] Blondel 1956: I no. 6, p. 28; Dru 1995: 147.
[124] Blondel 1956: I no. 4, p. 20; 'start from the fact of a theoretical and practical incredulity' (Dru 1995: 140). For a good description of the textbook approach, see Blondel 1956: I no. 6, pp. 26–7 and ch. 1 of Daly's *Transcendence and Immanence* (Daly 1980: 14 ff.).
[125] Blondel 1956: I no. 6, pp. 30–1. 'But it should be obvious already that to lay down without more ado the basic doctrinal affirmations of the thirteenth century is not only to stop up all access to those who think in terms of our own time but also to make a hopeless attempt to recover for one's own mind an equilibrium which has been irremediably lost, which could remain stable only because certain distinctions had not yet been made and certain problems had not yet appeared. To think in our day in precisely the same terms as five centuries ago is inevitably to think in a different spirit' (Dru 1995: 148–9).

This is similar to the criticism Weil voices briefly in her article 'En quoi consiste l'inspiration occitanienne?' This kind of return to the Middle Ages is not desirable and is furthermore 'chimérique': 'car nous ne pouvons pas faire que nous n'ayons été élevés dans un milieu constitué presque exclusivement de valeurs profanes' (*EHP* 83).[126]

Though Weil is critical of an unmitigated return to the past, she wants her contemporaries to find inspiration in those ancient cultures that embraced the good. She writes in *L'Enracinement* concerning the desperate situation in which the West finds itself (desperate, since large numbers of its populations are uprooted): 'on ne peut trouver ici-bas de secours que dans les îlots de passé demeurés vivants sur la surface de la terre' (*E* 51).[127] Yet she does not indicate how to apply concretely the inspiration of the past to the present conditions. By contemplating the beauty of that time 'avec attention et amour, dans cette mesure son inspiration descendra en nous et rendra peu à peu impossible une partie au moins des bassesses qui constituent l'air que nous respirons' (*EHP* 84).[128] The good, once let into one's life, starts eating away all evil in oneself. Weil's presentation of ancient Greek texts to the public is meant to inspire her readers and to renew the culture. Since this renewal is supposed to be a Graeco-Christianization of Western civilization, could one not call the purpose of these texts apologetic?

Both Blondel and Weil are critical of the scholastic/traditionalist approach.[129] They also agree in other points of criticism of current apologetic methods. Blondel, for example, disapproves of Pascal's wager, because he considers it to be a human calculation which therefore cannot lead to the supernatural grace of faith.[130] Furthermore, Blondel is critical of the reasoning that Christianity is right because it coincides with the

---

[126] 'since it is impossible for us to undo the fact that we have been brought up in an environment almost exclusively composed of profane values' (*SE* 53).

[127] 'all we can look to for encouragement here below is in those historical atolls of the living past left upon the surface of the earth' (*NR* 51). Birou 1995: 63–4.

[128] 'with attention and love, in that same measure its inspiration will come to us and will gradually make impossible at least some of the ignominies which constitute the air we breathe today' (*SE* 54). See also: 'D'où nous viendra la renaissance, à nous qui avons vidé et souillé tout le globe terrestre? Du passé seul, si nous l'aimons' (*OC* vi/3. 133) ('Whence will *our* renaissance come to us, who have emptied and defiled the entire globe? From the past alone, if we love it') (*NB* 445).

[129] While Blondel is critical of the scholastic approach in apologetics strictly speaking, Weil is sceptical of it in her interpretations of the past (which also have an apologetic dimension).

[130] Blondel 1956: I no. 4, pp. 19–20.

Weil and Apologetics

laws of life.¹³¹ This is a line of argument which Weil attributes to Bergson and severely censures, as we have seen. But what about Blondel's own argumentation? What would Weil have thought of it?

Weil does not give us any direct criticism of Blondel. Though she surely knew about *L'Action*, she does not give any indication of having read it or his *Lettre*.¹³² In her criticisms of apologetic methods, she does not refer to him, nor indicate whether she agrees or disagrees with his approach. But is his line of reasoning not similar to the 'need' argument, which Weil condemns so strongly? Blondel's method is different in a number of ways: first of all he does not try to show that Christianity is true, for he is aware that one cannot do so from the philosophical point of departure he has chosen. Furthermore, he does not argue for the supernatural from a pragmatic point of view, which would be at the heart of Weil's criticism. Rather, he tries to show that the choice for or against the supernatural is inevitable and inscribed in the very nature of human action. This is comparable to Weil's idea that in every human life there must be a choice for or against God, whether implicitly or explicitly. For 'il n'y a que la foi, implicite ou explicite, ou bien la trahison' (*IPC* 165).¹³³

Having looked at Weil's reaction to the Church Fathers, Pascal, and Blondel, and having compared their methods, has given us a better idea of Weil's own approach. I will now turn to an analysis of Weil as an apologist by considering her methods, her self-understanding, and her style.

---

¹³¹ Ibid. I no. 5, pp. 22–6.
¹³² As Gabellieri points out in his article 'Une convergence inattendue: Maurice Blondel et Simone Weil', Blondel read at least Weil's 'Essai sur la notion de lecture' (Gabellieri 1994: 35–6). Gabellieri describes well the apparent differences and real convergences between the two thinkers, without focusing on a comparison of their apologetic ideas.
¹³³ 'There is only faith, implicit or explicit, or else betrayal' (*IC* 196). Gabellieri (1998: 55) also points this out in his excellent article 'Blondel, S. Weil et la panchristisme: vers une *métaxologie*'. He shows how central Christ, the incarnation, and the Eucharist are for the metaphysics, anthropology, and ethics of these two thinkers.

3

Simone Weil as Apologist

Dans mes raisonnements sur l'insolubilité du problème de Dieu, je n'avais pas prévu la possibilité de cela, d'un contact réel, de personne à personne, ici-bas, entre un être humain et Dieu.[1]

(*AD* 45)

Je n'ai besoin d'aucune espérance, d'aucune promesse pour croire que Dieu est riche en miséricorde. Je connais cette richesse avec la certitude de l'expérience, je l'ai touchée.[2]

(ibid. 68–9)

It is striking that Weil did not make use of one obvious apologetic genre at her disposal, namely a personal testimony of her encounter with Christ. As a mystic, Weil could have told her story, and might have convinced others of the existence of God and of his personal love. Yet she chose not to do so. Why?

Given Weil's personality and her situation from her mystical experience onwards, it would, on the contrary, have been astonishing if she had made this intimate experience known to a wider public. She wrote only to Perrin and Joë Bousquet about it, when leaving France, anticipating that she would never see them again.[3] She starts her fourth letter to Perrin by saying that she wants to explain more fully to him

---

[1] 'In my arguments about the insolubility of the problem of God I had never foreseen the possibility of that, of a real contact, person to person, here below, between a human being and God' (*WG* 27).
[2] 'I do not need any hope or any promise in order to believe that God is rich in mercy. I know this wealth of his with the certainty of experience; I have touched it' (ibid. 43).
[3] However, she also mentioned it to the Canon F. Vidal whom she visited in Carcassonne at the end of March 1942. To show him that she had experienced grace herself, she said that ' "le Christ l'avait saisie un jour et s'était révélé en elle" ("Christ had possessed her one day and had revealed himself in her") '. Vidal did not want to intrude on her secret, and it only later became clear to him what she meant (SP ii. 400; Pétrement 1988: 457).

her spiritual state so that 'vous n'auriez aucun chagrin de ne pas m'avoir amenée au baptême' (*AD* 36).[4] For if God came to her in person, does she not need to wait for his explicit command to enter the Church before doing so, especially when she sees so many valid reasons not to (ibid. 53)? Paradoxically she tells Perrin about her mysticism to console him for not having asked him for baptism.

But she also thinks that her mystical encounter might be relevant to others: 'Et comme je pars avec plus ou moins la pensée d'une mort probable, il me semble que je n'ai pas le droit de taire ces choses. Car après tout, dans tout cela il ne s'agit pas de moi. Il ne s'agit que de Dieu' (ibid. 49).[5] She cannot let these expressions of God's love remain forever unknown. Though she is not willing to make them public herself, at least Perrin should know about them and use them however he deems right. They are important in so far as they shed light on God. This reveals an apologetic concern. Weil sees herself as an unworthy instrument of God: 'Si on pouvait supposer des erreurs en Dieu, je penserais que tout cela est tombé sur moi par erreur' (ibid.).[6] But perhaps God likes to use 'les déchets, les pièces loupées, les objets de rebut' (ibid. 49, 75).[7]

She writes to Bousquet because she has the feeling that God 'par amour pour vous, dirige tout cela vers vous à travers moi' (*PSO* 79).[8] Weil had gone to visit Bousquet at the end of March 1942, and had talked to him long into the night—an encounter which turned into a friendship.[9] She writes to him about suffering, because of his paralysis caused by a bullet breaking his spine in World War I. Was it not during a moment of intense suffering, that God made himself known to her (ibid. 81)? Therefore, suffering does not logically preclude the existence of a good God nor one's experience of him. But conversely, the experience of God does not eliminate suffering: 'Cet amour divin qu'on touche tout au fond du malheur [. . .] laisse la douleur tout à fait intacte' (ibid. 83).[10] Weil tries to make Bousquet understand that

---

[4] 'you would not be at all sorry that you did not lead me to baptism' (*WG* 21).
[5] 'And as I am going more or less with the idea of probable death, I do not believe that I have the right to keep it to myself. For after all, the whole of this matter is not a question concerning me myself. It concerns God' (ibid. 29–30).
[6] 'If one could imagine any possibility of error in God, I should think that it had all happened to me by mistake' (ibid. 30).
[7] 'castaway objects, waste, rejects' (ibid.).
[8] 'is addressing all this to you, for love of you, through me' (*SL* 139).
[9] SP ii. 398.
[10] 'That divine love which one touches in the depth of affliction [. . .] leaves pain completely intact' (*SL* 142).

suffering opens up a whole new dimension of reality and of truth which is otherwise hidden.[11]

These are the only indications we have of an apologetic use of her own mystical experience. In the one instance she tells about it in view of a possible later dissemination, and in the other she discloses it to reveal to her correspondent the presence of God within suffering.

However, Weil is not under the impression that she can bring God to others. She cannot give them the grace of faith, nor does she suggest, like Pascal, that one has only to pray and that faith will follow. For: 'Tant qu'un être humain n'a pas été pris par Dieu, il ne peut pas avoir la foi, mais seulement une simple croyance; et qu'il ait ou non une telle croyance n'importe guère, car il arrivera aussi bien à la foi par l'incrédulité' (ibid. 44).[12]

All she can do is the following, as she writes in 'Dieu dans Platon' (*God in Plato*): 'Ce que l'homme peut faire pour l'homme, ce n'est pas lui ajouter quelque chose, mais le tourner vers la lumière qui vient d'ailleurs, d'en haut' (*SG* 97).[13] How she tries to do this will be the focus of this chapter. Beauty will be shown to be central to her apologetic purpose. Proofs for the existence of God are normally essential to any apologetic endeavour. Yet Weil's ideas as to their nature and usefulness will again be unusual. After looking at Weil's self-understanding as an apologist and at the nature of literature as apologetic tool, the chapter will end with an analysis of Weil's style.

BEAUTY

How can one induce people to turn towards the light? Weil thinks that there are three mysteries in human life, which are known more or less to everybody and which are '[les] trois ouvertures qui donnent directement accès à la porte centrale qui est le Christ' (*IPC* 165).[14] The first is

---

[11] Further ways in which Weil analyses suffering for apologetic purposes will be shown in the chapter on *Prometheus*.

[12] 'Until God has taken possession of him, no human being can have faith, but only simple belief; and it hardly matters whether or not he has such a belief because he will arrive at faith equally well through incredulity' (*SNL* 18).

[13] 'What a man can do for another man is not to add something to him, but to turn him towards the light that comes from elsewhere, from above' (ibid. 105).

[14] '[the] three openings which give direct access to the central door which is the Christ' (*IC* 196).

beauty. The second is the contemplation of theoretical necessity in the world and its application within the realm of technology and of work. The last opening consists of these glimpses of justice, compassion, and gratitude—to be discussed in the next two chapters—'qui surgissent parfois au milieu de la dureté et de la froideur métallique des rapports humains' (ibid.).[15] Weil concentrates on beauty which she uses herself for apologetic purposes. Beauty is pedagogically essential for salvation. Those who do not have a sense of beauty 'ne peuvent peut-être être amenés à Dieu par aucune voie' (ibid. 23).[16] This is a very unusual understanding of the conditions of salvation, to say the least. In 'Formes de l'amour implicite de Dieu', beauty is one of the three or four means of access to God, the others being love of religious ceremonies, love for one's neighbour, and the right use of suffering (*AD* 122–3, 151–2).[17] Among these, beauty is the most accessible, common and natural means for modern man (ibid. 151–2). Aesthetes, however, have misunderstood the importance of beauty, for: 'Le point de vue des esthètes est sacrilège, non seulement en matière de religion, mais même en matière d'art. Il consiste à s'amuser avec la beauté en la manipulant et en la regardant' (*E* 85).[18] Aesthetes do not understand the ultimate significance of beauty. They divert it from its real purpose, which is perhaps even worse than being blind to its existence.

For beauty leads to God. Beauty comes from a reality beyond this world, yet is visible here, as Weil believes Plato already saw in his *Phaedrus*. More so, 'en tout ce qui suscite chez nous le sentiment pur et authentique du beau, il y a présence réelle de Dieu' (*OC* vi/3. 126,

---

[15] 'which rise up sometimes in human relationships in the midst of harshness and metallic coldness' (ibid.).

[16] 'cannot perhaps be brought to God by any path' (ibid. 90).

[17] In her *Intuitions*, Weil also mentions pure mathematics as 'un des trous par où peut pénétrer le souffle et la lumière de Dieu' ('is one of the openings through which the breath and the light of God may penetrate') (*IPC* 127/*IC* 166). Later on she writes: 'On donne aux tout jeunes enfants, pour les aider, des objets de forme régulière et faciles à manier, à explorer, à reconnaître, comme des balles et des cubes. De même Dieu facilite l'apprentissage des hommes en leur donnant, dans la vie sociale, les pratiques religieuses et les sacrements, et dans l'univers inanimé la beauté' (*IPC* 170) ('We give to very young children, to help them, objects of a regular form and easy to handle, to explore, to recognize, such as balls and cubes. So, too, God facilitates men's apprenticeship by giving them, in social life, religious practices and the sacraments, and in the inanimate universe, beauty') (*IC* 200–1).

[18] 'The aesthetes' point of view is sacrilegious, not only in matters of religion but even in those of art. It consists in amusing oneself with beauty by handling it and looking at it' (*NR* 93).

118; *EL* 74; *SG* 139; *IPC* 87).[19] Hence, 'tout art de premier ordre est par essence religieux' (*OC* vi/3. 127).[20] Thus through the Greek classics, which Weil considers to be masterpieces, she introduces her readers to something sacred in which God himself is present. Art of this kind is a witness to God's incarnation 'autant que la mort d'un martyr' (ibid.).[21]

God himself uses beauty as 'le piège le plus fréquent [...] pour [...] ouvrir [l'âme] au souffle d'en haut', as Weil writes in 'Formes de l'amour implicite de Dieu' (*AD* 152).[22] Weil likes to interpret the myth of Core or Persephone along these lines. When Core picks the narcissus flower, which according to Weil symbolically represents beauty, she is trapped: 'Elle était tombée aux mains du Dieu vivant' (ibid. 153).[23] When she comes back from Hades, she has eaten the pomegranate seed which perpetually binds her to God (*IPC* 9 ff.; *OC* vi/3. 58–9). Weil distinguishes between two stages of a divine encounter (*IPC* 12). When the soul is first trapped, this is an 'act of violence' on the part of God. But she then has to agree to eat the pomegranate seed for salvation to happen.

Weil interprets in a similar way the myth of the Minotaur: 'La beauté du monde est l'orifice du labyrinthe. L'imprudent qui, étant entré, fait quelques pas, est après quelque temps hors d'état de retrouver l'orifice' (*AD* 153; *IPC* 12–13).[24] After straying around for a long time, hungry and tired, having lost all hope, the wanderer might give up his search, but this would be his most dangerous temptation. If he goes on walking, he will certainly reach the centre of the labyrinth, and there: 'Dieu l'attend pour le manger' (*AD* 153).[25] When he comes out later on, he will be changed. Then Weil adds the significant sentence, revealing her apologetic concern: 'Il se tiendra alors auprès de l'orifice pour y pousser doucement ceux qui s'approchent' (ibid.).[26] Finally, Weil uses

---

[19] 'In everything which rouses in us a pure and genuine feeling for beauty, God is really and truly present' (*NB* 440).
[20] 'all art of the first order is, in essence, religious' (ibid.).
[21] 'as much as does the death of a martyr' (ibid.)
[22] 'the trap God most frequently uses in order to win it and open it to the breath from on high' (*WG* 103).
[23] 'She fell into the hands of the living God' (ibid.).
[24] 'The beauty of the world is the mouth of a labyrinth. The unwary individual who on entering takes a few steps is soon unable to find the opening' (ibid.).
[25] 'God is waiting to eat him' (ibid.).
[26] 'Afterward he will stay near the entrance so that he can gently push all those who come near to the opening' (ibid.).

the Scottish tale, the 'Duc de Norvège', to describe God's search for the soul, but this will be presented in Chapter seven (*IPC* 13–15; *OC* vi/2. 442, vi/3. 45).

What is the nature of beauty, which plays such a significant apologetic role for Weil? Beauty is something *sui generis*: it can only be known through itself.[27] Weil can merely try to disclose the beauty of the Greek classics to her readers, but they have to see it for themselves. It has its origin beyond this world and manifests God.[28] Because it is the only transcendental accessible to the senses, it is the only one which, once inside the cave of Plato's myth, can tempt the prisoners to break their chains and eventually discover the good outside.[29] In this apologetic function, it is irreplaceable. Though Plato does not mention beauty in this context, Weil thinks that one can insert it into this allegory, since it fulfils that self-same purpose in some of his other dialogues (*OC* vi/3. 60–1, vi/2. 446; *SG* 119).

Beauty seems to promise us something, yet it can only give itself (*AD* 157). It is both a challenge and an irritation: 'Nous voudrions aller derrière la beauté, mais elle n'est que surface. Elle est comme un miroir qui nous renvoie notre propre désir du bien. Elle est un sphinx, un mystère douloureusement irritant. Nous voudrions nous en nourrir, mais elle n'est qu'objet de regard, elle n'apparaît qu'à une certaine distance' (ibid. 156).[30] Though beauty can feed the soul, as seen earlier on, it can paradoxically only do so, when seen from a distance: 'L'union

---

[27] 'Car le beau est la seule source du sentiment de beauté' ('for the beautiful is the only source of the sense of beauty') (*IPC* 23/*IC* 90). Or: 'Il n'y a rien au-delà du beau' ('There is nothing beyond Beauty') (*OC* vi/3. 332/*NB* 605).

[28] Thus one also must start with God in order to understand what beauty is: 'Toutes les fois qu'on réfléchit au beau, on est arrêté par un mur. Tout ce qui a été écrit là-dessus est misérablement et évidemment insuffisant, parce que cette étude-là doit être commencée à partir de Dieu' (*CS* 312). 'Whenever one reflects upon the beautiful one is brought up against a blank wall. Everything that has been written upon the subject is miserably and obviously inadequate, because it is a study which must take God as its starting point' (*FLN* 341).

[29] 'La beauté, seul être du monde intelligible qui apparaît aux sens' (*OC* vi/2. 444) ('Beauty—sole form of being of the intelligible world that is apparent to the senses') (*NB* 319–20). 'Ce choc du beau est cette chose non nommée dans la *République* qui fait tomber les chaînes et force à marcher' (*SG* 119) ('The thing which makes the chains fall off and the prisoner begin to walk is not named in the *Republic*; it is the shock received from beauty') (*SNL* 123).

[30] 'We want to get behind beauty, but it is only a surface. It is like a mirror that sends us back our own desire for goodness. It is a sphinx, an enigma, a mystery which is painfully tantalizing. We should like to feed upon it but it is merely something to look at; it appears only from a certain distance' (*WG* 105). See also *EL* 37.

par-dessus la distance est le ressort du beau' (*OC* vi/3. 343).[31] For to nourish the soul, it has to be approached for its own sake and not for the sake of pleasure.[32] Death of self is required.[33]

However, human motivations are often mixed, as the myth of the good and the bad horse in Plato's *Phaedrus* shows.[34] In this allegory the charioteer (reason) tries to keep in check the bad horse (desire), which might bring the chariot to a fall. For the charioteer drives on the arch, which supports heaven, to look through the sky towards the realm of Ideas. But he can only do so if his chariot drives evenly, and if both horses pull in the same direction. Surprisingly, the bad horse is not all bad: 'Il est précieux, car c'est lui qui tire vers le beau. La beauté l'a pris au piège' (*OC* vi/2. 481).[35] This bad horse must be held in check to prevent him from getting out of control. However, without his upward pull the charioteer would not be able to see the heavenly Ideas at all (*SG* 123–4).

Similarly in Diotima's speech in the *Symposium*, the love for a beautiful body is transformed into a love for higher things. What starts with physical attraction generated by bodily beauty leads on to the purer love of a higher beauty.[36] This beauty, meant to serve as a steppingstone to God, can also turn into an obstacle: 'Toutes ces beautés secondaires [c'est-à-dire, ce qui n'est pas la beauté de l'univers en entier] sont d'un prix infini comme ouvertures sur la beauté universelle. Mais si on s'arrête à elles, elles sont au contraire des voiles; elles sont alors corruptrices' (*AD* 155).[37] Hence, beauty is an offer, but also a temptation. It is a challenge, for it purifies as God does 'la souillure que nous jetons en elle, elle la brûle et n'en est pas souillée [. . .] étant présence réelle de Dieu' (*OC* vi/3. 201).[38] Some flee from beauty into mere pleasure of the senses, for:

---

[31] 'The rôle of beauty is to accomplish the union bridging the distance' (*NB* 615).
[32] See analogously *CS* 249–50.
[33] 'Il y a de la mort dans toute beauté' ('In all beauty there is an element of death') (*OC* vi/3. 251/*NB* 541). Vetö 1971: 92, 98.
[34] Plato, *Phaedrus* 254a–e; *SG* 122 ff.
[35] 'He is valuable, for it is he that pulls toward the beautiful. Beauty has trapped him' (*NB* 356).
[36] 'Quelque chose attire la chair vers le divin; autrement comment pourrions-nous jamais être sauvés? L'amour charnel est cette attirance' (*OC* vi/3. 101) ('Something attracts the flesh toward the divine; otherwise how should we ever be able to be saved? Carnal love constitutes this attraction') (*NB* 416).
[37] 'All these secondary kinds of beauty [which are not the beauty of the universe as a whole] are of infinite value as openings to universal beauty. But, if we stop short at them, they are, on the contrary, veils; then they corrupt' (*WG* 104).
[38] 'it burns up whatever defilement we cast into it, and remains uncontaminated being [. . .] the veritable presence of God' (*NB* 501).

'Tout ce qui est médiocre fuit la lumière [...] [La] partie [médiocre de l'âme] est prise de panique toutes les fois qu'apparaît un peu de beau pur, de bien pur; elle se cache derrière la chair' (*AD* 166).[39] In spite of these dangers, beauty must still be used as a central apologetic tool. For the sense of beauty 'quoique mutilé, déformé et souillé, demeure irréductiblement dans le cœur de l'homme comme un puissant mobile', and is therefore present in all aspects of secular life.[40] If one could purify it, 'il transporterait d'un bloc toute la vie profane aux pieds de Dieu, il rendrait possible l'incarnation totale de la foi' (ibid. 152).[41] Therefore aesthetics is of central importance being 'la clef des vérités surnaturelles' (*OC* vi/3. 356).[42]

PROOFS FOR GOD'S EXISTENCE

It is also beauty which gives Weil the starting point for one of the few proofs of God's existence she finds convincing. Normally, proofs for the existence of God are an essential part of apologetics. Weil, however, as a result of her own personal experience, seems sceptical of this practice. As far as reason is concerned, Weil had thought, since her adolescence 'que le problème de Dieu est un problème dont les données manquent ici-bas' (*AD* 36).[43] It is God who comes to the soul and not vice versa, and the soul can only prepare for this encounter by waiting and *attention*.

However, Weil seems to accept three proofs of the existence of God, namely the ontological argument, an argument from beauty, and an

---

[39] 'All mediocrity flies from the light [...] This [mediocre] part [of the soul] is seized with panic every time that a little pure beauty or pure goodness appears; it hides behind the flesh, it uses it as a veil' (*WG* 111–12).
[40] 'although mutilated, distorted, and soiled, remains rooted in the heart of man as a powerful incentive' (ibid. 102).
[41] 'it would sweep all secular life in a body to the feet of God; it would make the total incarnation of the faith possible' (ibid. 103).
[42] 'the key to supernatural truths' (*NB* 627).
[43] '[that] the problem of God [is] [...] a problem the data of which could not be obtained here below' (*WG* 22). In her notes taken in Weil's classes in Roanne in 1933–4, Anne Reynaud-Guérithault writes: '*Par définition*, en tant qu'il est la suprême valeur, *Dieu est indémontrable*. Dieu ne peut pas être senti. "*Vere, tu es Deus absconditus*". On peut dire que Dieu a voulu se cacher précisément pour qu'on ait la notion de lui' (*LP* 219) ('By definition, in so far as he is the highest value, God is indemonstrable. God cannot be felt. "Truly, thou art a hidden God." One can say that the very reason why God has decided to hide himself is that we might have an idea of what he is like') (*LOP* 171–2).

argument from suffering. I will talk about the latter in my chapter on *Prometheus*. The argument by beauty is the only proof Weil admits that takes as its starting point the order of creation. She calls the teleological argument, arguing from watch to watchmaker, from a design in nature to a designer, 'misérable et ridicule' (*SG* 129). In another passage, Weil doubts that one could ever find in nature as much finality as in a humanly produced object. This makes it impossible to conclude from a design in creation to a creator who created with a purpose (*IPC* 23). Instead, God's act of creation should be compared to an artistic creation, as Plato did in his *Timaeus*, rather than to watch-making 'ce qui entraîne dans des absurdités'.[44] What these absurdities are, becomes clearer further down the page, where she points out the advantages of the analogy of artistic creation. For a work of art is not created for a certain purpose. It is essentially gratuitous. The means used are adjusted to the work of art, so 'il y a évidemment finalité, mais [...] on ne peut concevoir aucune fin' (ibid.).[45] Similarly the world was created gratuitously without the mechanistic purpose of a watch, yet not therefore without design. In return, the beauty of a work of art inspires a love which goes, for example, beyond the mere stone of which a sculpture is made. Analogously, the beauty of the universe inspires in the spectator a love going beyond the mere matter out of which the world is made. This love, Weil concludes, must have been kindled by love of God. She calls it the proof of God by love, for: 'Comme par la vue on ne reconnaît pas les sons, de même nulle autre faculté que l'amour ne peut reconnaître Dieu' (*SG* 129).[46] Weil does not propose a proof that goes logically from premise to conclusion. Rather, she suggests a setting where one can more easily be led, through the beauty of the world, to a frame of mind, namely love, conducive to perceiving the existence and love of the Creator.

Weil interprets the ontological argument similarly as an argument of love (*IPC* 131–2; *SG* 148). This proof was first introduced by Anselm of Canterbury, and has been further developed as well as much criticized in the history of philosophy. It starts from the premise that God is *essentially* a being greater than which nothing can be conceived (*id quo maius cogitari non potest*). It is greater to exist in reality than to exist only

---

[44] 'which leads into absurdities' (*IC* 90).
[45] 'obviously there is [finality] [...], but where one cannot conceive of an end' (ibid.).
[46] 'Just as we cannot recognize sound with our eyes, so there is no faculty except love for recognizing God' (*SNL* 131).

in the mind. Therefore God must exist in reality, otherwise he would not be the greatest being possible.[47] For Weil, as we have already seen, the possible existence of the good suffices to make her happy. But this is so because its very possibility already *implies* its existence (*CS* 285) This is confirmed by what she writes later in her *Cahier* 10: 'L'IRRÉALITÉ ÔTE ENTIÈREMENT AU BIEN LA VALEUR, C'EST-À-DIRE LE BIEN. D'OÙ LA PREUVE ONTOLOGIQUE MÊME POUR L'INCARNATION' (*OC* vi/3. 278; *PSO* 136).[48] Thus Weil applies the ontological argument not only to God, but to the existence of the good, and to the incarnation itself (*OC* vi/3. 278). It needs to be kept in mind that for Weil God's existence had become indubitable through her mystical experience which was an experience stronger than any sense perception, yielding: 'une présence plus personnelle, plus certaine, plus réelle que celle d'un être humain' (*PSO* 81).[49] Therefore: 'Le doute concernant la réalité de Dieu est un doute abstrait et verbal pour quiconque a été saisi par Dieu, bien plus abstrait et verbal encore que le doute concernant la réalité des choses sensibles' (ibid. 43).[50] Any proof of the existence of God will seem ultimately unsatisfactory, for it cannot equal a personal contact with him. When she contemplates God, his existence for her is more unquestionable than that of a spouse, child, or friend.[51]

In *Cahier* 8, Weil proposes an experimental form of the ontological argument: since I do not have the means to pull myself up, because of the law of *pesanteur*, I can only direct my thoughts up to something better than myself. If I am pulled up by that to which I am directing my thoughts, this means that what is pulling me really exists. For no imaginary perfection can draw me up 'même d'un millimètre'.[52] This is different from autosuggestion, Weil believes,

---

[47] For the different variations of the ontological arguments and its criticisms see Geisler 1999: 554 ff. and Seifert's book *Gott als Gottesbeweis* (1996), which is a systematic, philosophical discussion of the argument.
[48] 'Unreality entirely takes away the value from good, that is to say, good itself. Whence the ontological proof, even in the matter of the Incarnation' (*NB* 63).
[49] 'a presence more personal, more certain, and more real than that of a human being' (*SL* 140).
[50] 'For any man of whom God has taken possession the doubt concerning the reality of God is purely abstract and verbal, much more abstract and verbal than the doubt concerning the reality of the things of sense' (*SNL* 158).
[51] Weil believes that the existence of God is not a matter of faith: 'Que Dieu, d'une certaine manière—que j'ignore—soit réalité, cela même est une certitude. Cela n'est pas matière de foi' (*CS* 275) ('And it is even certain that God—in some way that I do not know—is reality. This is certain, and not a matter of faith') (*FLN* 307).
[52] 'even by a millimetre'.

since that would only improve me up to the point of the imperfect ideal which I had set for myself. If I try to tell to myself every morning that I am courageous, for example, I might become more courageous, but only imperfectly so, according to the imperfect idea I had formed of courage (*OC* vi/3. 121; *CS* 278, 313). Weil's implicit conclusion is that God pulls one up to levels one never imagined existed, which shows that he is more, or greater, than one could ever imagine.[53]

THE RESPONSIBILITY OF WRITERS

Literature and the Responsibility of Writers

It has become clear that beauty is key to Weil's apologetic endeavour, since beauty ultimately leads to God, if it is not perverted for selfish purposes. Thus literature, as a bearer of beauty, is an important medium. But if literature is potentially a powerful apologetic tool because of its aesthetic values and its content, it can also become a means of seduction, an instrument of propaganda. Thus writers could and should be held responsible for their writings, according to Weil.

Yet Weil was against didacticism, whether in ancient or modern literature. As she writes in her 'Lettre aux *Cahiers du Sud* sur les responsabilités de la littérature' (*The Responsibility of Writers*) in 1941: 'Les écrivains n'ont pas à être des professeurs de morale, mais ils ont à exprimer la condition humaine.' 'Or', she continues, 'rien n'est si essentiel à la vie humaine, pour tous les hommes et à tous les instants, que le bien et le mal' (*RL* 356–7).[54] However, it is not easy to depict good and evil in literature without either falling into the trap of didacticism or portraying good as bland and evil as fascinating. For as she writes in her article 'Morale et Littérature', published in the *Cahiers du Sud* posthumously in January 1944:

> Rien n'est beau, merveilleux, perpétuellement nouveau, perpétuellement surprenant, chargé d'une douce et continuelle ivresse, comme le bien. Rien n'est

---

[53] Though Weil did not develop a systematic theory on apologetics, a consistent position can be developed from her fragmentary notes which indicates that Weil grappled with the question.

[54] 'Writers do not have to be professors of morals, but they do have to express the human condition. And nothing concerns human life so essentially, for every man at every moment, as good and evil' (*SNL* 168–9).

désertique, morne, monotone, ennuyeux comme le mal. Il en est ainsi du bien et du mal authentiques. Le bien et le mal fictifs ont le rapport contraire. Le bien fictif est ennuyeux et plat. Le mal fictif est varié, intéressant, attachant, profond, plein de séductions. (ML 349)[55]

Thus fiction seems inevitably immoral. Those authors who try to avoid this by introducing didactic purposes will fail, for the goodness they portray will appear just as bland, and their writing will be the worse for it. However, those who claim that literature is beyond morality have to prove their point, Weil holds, since every other realm in human life is subject to moral laws. Furthermore, they are proved wrong by the fact that writers have palpably influenced generations of readers for better or for worse (*E* 28, 192–3; RL 354 ff.; ML 350). Besides, reversing the appearance of good and evil is not restricted to literature. People weave webs of lies around themselves. Only when reality hits them hard enough—either through the experience of great suffering, of extreme evil or by encountering a saint—do they wake up from their dream world. Within literature, it is only geniuses who are able to reverse this phenomenon and depict 'l'épaisseur même de la réalité' (ML 351).[56] They portray evil in all its horror, its monotony, but also its complexity within human action. Thus they do not give a simplistic view of reality, but show their readers the multilayered 'architecture de l'abîme'[57] without letting them walk down the slope themselves or allowing them to feel the attraction of the void.

Great writers, such as Sophocles, are able to write in such a way that 'plusieurs pentes [du bien et du mal] simultanément sont visibles et sensibles, situées selon leurs vrais rapports', thus becoming true educators of their readers (ibid.).[58] The contemplation of works of art, such as theirs: 'est la source inépuisable d'une inspiration qui peut légitimement nous diriger. Car cette inspiration, pour qui sait la recevoir, tend, selon

---

[55] 'Nothing is so beautiful and wonderful, nothing is so continually fresh and surprising, so full of sweet and perpetual ecstasy, as the good. No desert is so dreary, monotonous, and boring as evil. This is the truth about authentic good and evil. With fictional good and evil it is the other way round. Fictional good is boring and flat, while fictional evil is varied and intriguing, attractive, profound, and full of charm' (ibid. 160).
[56] 'the actual density of the real' (ibid. 162).
[57] 'architecture of the abyss' (ibid.).
[58] 'several slopes are simultaneously visible and perceptible, placed in their true relations' (ibid.).

le mot de Platon à faire pousser des ailes contre la pesanteur' (ibid.).[59] On the other hand, literature of minor value can have disastrous effects on its readers and on culture in general. Since the eighteenth century and the period of romanticism, writers have usurped the position of spiritual authorities, which has given to art 'une enflure messianique'[60] contrary to its purity (ibid. 352/*SNL* 163; *E* 28; *EL* 16). In former times this responsibility was exercised by priests, sometimes very badly, but with more legitimacy than by writers. For how are authors qualified to speak about matters of spirituality, moral conduct or other existential matters? Their opinions 'ne peuvent avoir aucune espèce d'intérêt' 'à moins qu'une vocation philosophique n'habite en eux en plus de la vocation littéraire' (ML 352).[61]

Though the common people may not read their works, they will read the periodicals which popularize their ideas (RL 355). In contrast, Weil wants the working classes to receive only the best education, bringing to them truth, goodness, and beauty, which alone can nourish their souls (*EL* 30). It is no solution to give them a watered-down higher education, as was happening in Weil's times (ibid. 65). It is wrong to degrade truths; instead they need to be expressed in a language addressing the specific sensibility of the readers. But this is difficult, for: 'L'art de transposer les vérités est un des plus essentiels et des moins connus. Ce qui le rend difficile, c'est que, pour le pratiquer, il faut s'être placé au centre d'une vérité, l'avoir possédée dans sa *nudité*, derrière la forme particulière sous laquelle elle se trouve par hasard exposée' (*E* 64; my italics).[62]

The task of an educator of the public and of an apologist is not easy. One of the qualifications needed is a philosophical vocation, which writers normally lack (ML 352). Weil fulfils the requirements, according to her own criteria (*CSW* 3/2: 70). She speaks as a philosopher and religious thinker on literature and other matters. This leads us to the question of her self-understanding as a writer.

[59] 'is the ever-flowing source of an inspiration which may legitimately guide us. For this inspiration, if we know how to receive it, tends—as Plato said—to make us grow wings to overcome gravity' (*SNL* 165).
[60] 'a Messianic afflatus'.
[61] 'can have no interest at all', 'unless they have a philosophic bent in addition to a literary one' (ibid. 163).
[62] 'The art of transposing truths is one of the most essential and the least known. What makes it difficult is that, in order to practise it, one has to have placed oneself at the centre of a truth and possessed it in all its nakedness, behind the particular form in which it happens to have found expression' (*NR* 67–8).

Simone Weil's Self-Understanding as a Writer and Apologist

Weil has a sense of mission though at the same time she feels unworthy, that she can have been chosen only by mistake. Yet: 'Des idées viennent se poser en moi par erreur, puis, reconnaissant leur erreur, veulent absolument sortir. Je ne sais pas d'où elles viennent ni ce qu'elles valent, mais à tout hasard je ne me crois pas le droit d'empêcher cette opération' (*AD* 61).[63] She is simply an intermediary between God and other people: 'Que mon âme soit seulement au corps et à Dieu ce qu'est ce porte-plume à ma main et au papier—un intermédiaire' (*CS* 81; *EL* 202; *AD* 75).[64] She feels the obligation to let the truth speak through her—or at least what seems the truth to her—even though she believes her natural talents have been destroyed by bad health and other factors (*EL* 202–3). But: 'C'est une grande douleur pour moi de craindre que les pensées qui sont descendues en moi ne soient condamnées à mort par la contagion de mon insuffisance et de ma misère. Je ne lis jamais sans frémir l'histoire du figuier stérile. Je pense qu'il est mon portrait [. . .]. Le Christ l'a maudit' (*AD* 83).[65] Therefore she asks Perrin to use her thoughts and writings for any good they could produce, for his charity will see beyond her failings.

She does not want to stand out—an unrealistic wish given her genius and her original dress and behaviour—but wants to mingle with all human beings, to suffer with them, and help them, if she can: 'J'ai le besoin essentiel, et je crois pouvoir dire la vocation, de passer parmi les hommes et les différents milieux humains en me confondant avec eux, en prenant la même couleur, dans toute la mesure du moins où la conscience ne s'y oppose pas, en disparaissant parmi eux, cela afin qu'ils se montrent tels qu'ils sont et sans se déguiser pour moi' (ibid. 19).[66]

---

[63] 'Ideas come and settle in my mind by mistake, then, realizing their mistake, they absolutely insist on coming out. I do not know where they come from, or what they are worth, but, whatever the risk, I do not think I have the right to prevent this operation' (*WG* 37).
[64] 'May my soul be for the body and for God only what this penholder is for my hand and the paper—an intermediary' (*FLN* 132).
[65] 'It is a great sorrow for me to fear that the thoughts that have descended into me should be condemned to death through the contagion of my inadequacy and wretchedness. I never read the story of the barren fig tree without trembling. I think that it is a portrait of me. [. . .] Christ cursed it' (*WG* 52).
[66] 'I have the essential need, and I think I can say the vocation, to move among men of every class and complexion, mixing with them and sharing their life and outlook, so far that is to say as conscience allows, merging into the crowd and disappearing among

This is one of the reasons why she does not accept baptism: it would separate her from all the non-baptized.[67] Furthermore, she is afraid of losing her intellectual freedom, which would be contrary to her specific vocation, namely to be working 'pour le service de Dieu et de la foi chrétienne dans le domaine de l'intelligence' (ibid. 65).[68] She thinks that her personal vocation is to wait on truth: 'pour moi personnellement la vie n'a pas d'autre sens, et n'a jamais eu au fond d'autre sens, que l'attente de la vérité' (*EL* 213; *PSO* 150).[69]

To impart this truth to others is her specific call. Does this not turn her into a prophet, if not yet into an apologist? She has a sense of mission, apparently divinely inspired. When she writes, it is out of obedience: 'Les œuvres. Celles auxquelles on est poussé par une inspiration, on ne peut pas, quand on le voudrait, s'empêcher de les accomplir, aussi longtemps qu'on est orienté vers l'obéissance' (*OC* vi/3. 123).[70] To write carefully is a condition for being inhabited by the spirit of truth, as Weil continues, interestingly using the example of writing

them, so that they show themselves as they are, putting off all disguises with me' (*WG* 6–7).

[67] For her reasons for remaining outside the Church, see *AD* 17, 52, 53–4, 65–6; *EL* 205.

[68] '[for the service of] God and the Christian faith in the realm of the intelligence' (*WG* 40).

[69] 'life for me means nothing, and never has meant anything, really, except as a threshold to the revelation of truth' (*SL* 178). From early on Weil had a great sense of responsibility and purpose. She wrote to one of her students in 1934 that she avoided any romantic commitments until she was mature enough to know what she wanted to do with her life. For, 'Ce qui importe, c'est de ne pas rater sa vie. Or pour ça, il faut se discipliner' ('What matters is not to bungle one's life. And for that, one must discipline oneself') (*CO* 27/*SL* 14). And in a letter to her friend Albertine Thévenon at about the same period, she wrote of her desire to orient her life in a certain direction (*CO* 18). With hindsight she believed she had already obeyed God's orders during her atheistic phase without knowing it: 'Comment se fait-il que j[. . .]'aie reçu [les ordres de Dieu] dans l'adolescence, pendant que je professais l'athéisme?' ('How did it happen that I received [. . .] [His commands] in adolescence, while I was professing atheism?') (*CS* 87/*FLN* 137). In her fourth letter to Perrin, she also writes about her sense of vocation before her conversion: 'Je pensais que la vie qui mène à ce bien [où la vérité pure entre dans l'âme] n'est pas définie seulement par la morale commune, mais que pour chacun elle consiste en une succession d'actes et d'événements qui lui est rigoureusement personnelle, et tellement obligatoire que celui qui passe à côté manque le but. Telle était pour moi la notion de vocation' ('I thought that the life leading to this good is not only defined by a code of morals common to all, but that for each one it consists of a succession of acts and events strictly personal to him, and so essential that he who leaves them on one side never reaches the goal. The notion of vocation was like this for me') (*AD* 37–8/*WG* 22–3).

[70] 'Works. One cannot,—even if one should wish it,—prevent oneself from accomplishing those works to which one is driven by which inspiration, so long as one lets oneself be guided by obedience'.

an apologetic work: 'Un homme qui écrirait un livre d'apologétique plein de fausses citations, par simple négligence et paresse de les vérifier, l'Esprit de vérité ne le visitera pas' (ibid.).[71] Thus attention to detail is part of the intellectual vocation and a condition for the search for truth.

Similarly Weil reads out of obedience: 'Dans les lectures aussi je me suis toujours efforcée de pratiquer l'obéissance.'[72] Nothing is better for intellectual progress, Weil continues, 'car je ne lis autant que possible que ce dont j'ai faim, au moment où j'en ai faim, et alors je ne lis pas, je mange' (*AD* 45).[73] This is probably what she is expecting from her readers. They are not supposed to read in a detached manner, disconnected from the question of truth, but should come to the text with an existential approach: 'Un repas ne se compare pas, il se mange. De même des paroles, écrites ou prononcées, se mangent dans la mesure où elles sont comestibles, c'est-à-dire pour autant qu'elles contiennent de la vérité' (*EL* 202).[74] Not only does Weil want her writings to be eaten or the truth contained therein, but ultimately she also wants to become a eucharistic host herself, giving herself to others to eat (*CS* 41–2, 205). Through her labour, her writings have become the product of her self-immolation and thus they participate in a way in the sacramental nature of the Eucharist. Ultimately she wants to complete this oblation by her own death.[75]

WEIL'S STYLE

But for her works to have this apologetic and redemptive impact, her readers first need to be drawn in before they can be convinced by arguments—thus the importance of style for apologetics. Weil, however,

---

[71] 'Any one who was to write a book of apologetics full of misquotations, as a result of pure carelessness and laziness in taking the necessary steps to verify his sources, would not be visited by the Spirit of truth' (ibid. 436–7).

[72] 'In reading as in other things I have always striven to practice obedience' (*WG* 27).

[73] 'for as far as possible I only read what I am hungry for at the moment when I have an appetite for it, and then I do not read, I *eat*' (ibid.).

[74] 'A meal is not for comparison, it is for eating. In the same way words, whether written or spoken, are absorbed in so far as they are nourishing, that is to say in so far as they contain truth. That is their only use' (*SL* 169).

[75] See 'Simone Weil as Antigone' in Ch. 4.

does not try to flatter the ear. Her style has often been described as extremely unadorned.[76] There is nothing superfluous in the way she writes. Weil, who has a referential understanding of language, attempts to make her language completely transparent to the reality she is trying to describe. At the same time, she wishes to disappear and make room for that transcendent reality.[77] Her desire is that her writings be in the same category as all great works of art, which are in a certain sense anonymous in that they reveal little about their authors (*EL* 16–17; *E* 240–1).[78] She is aware of the limitations of language, that certain realities cannot be encompassed but only indicated. Those who do not perceive this will remain within the 'prison of language' and live in error.[79] However, some words, such as 'God', 'truth', 'beauty', and 'the good', have in and of themselves a sacramental power: 'La vertu d'illumination et de traction vers le haut réside dans ces mots eux-mêmes, dans ces mots comme tels' (*EL* 42).[80] To speak about God, truth, beauty, the good, already makes them present. No wonder she frequently uses these words, about which Broc-Lapeyre says that 'ce sont des mots vivants, des mots habités'.[81]

As Joan Dargan rightly points out in *Thinking Poetically*, Weil does not try to engage in a dialogue with her readers, as Pascal does, but speaks to them from an impersonal plane. While Pascal starts with the common natural experience of man and goes from there to the religious, Weil immediately refers to the religious with certainty, expecting her readers to understand.[82] Thus Weil speaks from above, 'ex cathedra' as Dargan puts it, relying on her inner conviction and especially on the nature of the things talked of.[83] Dargan thinks that Weil shuts her readers out, leaves no room for arguments, in short says that her texts are 'uninhabitable'.[84] However, though Weil speaks with the authority of somebody who has felt, touched, and seen these realities, it seems to me that she wants her readers to get a sense of them for themselves. She tries to lift the lid off the natural world to give

---

[76] Lussy 1988: 119.   [77] Dargan 1999: 2.
[78] Broc-Lapeyre 1987: 358–9; Marchetti 1990: 66.
[79] 'Même en mettant les choses au mieux, un esprit enfermé dans le langage est en prison. [...] Si un esprit captif ignore sa propre captivité, il vit dans l'erreur' (*EL* 33) ('At the very best, a mind enclosed in language is in prison. [...] If a captive mind is unaware of being in prison, it is living in error') (*SE* 26).
[80] 'it is in the words themselves, as words, that the power to enlighten and draw upwards resides' (*SE* 33).
[81] Broc-Lapeyre 1987: 366. 'these are living words, words which are inhabited'.
[82] Dargan 1999: 25–6, 33, 35.   [83] Ibid. 35.   [84] Ibid. 35, 51.

them access to the supernatural. For if they pronounce these words 'intérieurement avec désir, sans être joints à aucune conception', with the utmost attention, then these will 'élever l'âme et [...] l'inonder de lumière' (ibid. 139).[85] Thus Weil destroys the little rooms of language and security that people construct around themselves. For in reality, 'La différence entre hommes plus ou moins intelligents est comme la différence entre des criminels condamnés pour la vie à l'emprisonnement cellulaire et dont les cellules seraient plus ou moins grandes' (ibid. 33).[86] Instead of simply giving her readers bigger cells, she offers them the secret 'qui fait tomber tous les murs', which is something 'au-delà de ce que les hommes nomment l'intelligence [...] là où commence la sagesse' (ibid. 34).[87] To write with such a tone of certainty means to be 'audacious, stunning, willing to risk offense', as Dargan rightly puts it.[88] But though this authority may startle, it also renders her readers attentive, and challenges their prejudices and comfortable world-views.

Like Pascal, Weil captures her readers' attention through paradoxes. In her article 'Contribution à une étude de l'usage du paradoxe chez Simone Weil' Little points out that in Weil's writings paradox makes one pause, perceive the limits of one's intelligence, and ascend to a higher plane to resolve the problem.[89] For we often are confronted with paradoxes, which Weil believes can only be resolved by looking at them in the context of a higher order of things, from a supernatural perspective. One of the elements of the paradox already pertains to that higher reality, and helps one rise: 'alors la notion de mystère, comme un levier, transporte la pensée de l'autre côté de l'impasse, de l'autre côté de la porte impossible à ouvrir, au-delà du domaine de l'intelligence, au-dessus' (*CS* 79).[90]

---

[85] 'interiorly, with desire, without trying to fit them into any concept', 'elevate the soul [...] and inundate it with light'.
[86] 'The difference between more or less intelligent men is like the difference between criminals condemned to life imprisonment in smaller or larger cells' (*SE* 26).
[87] 'which breaks down every wall', 'beyond what men call intelligence [...] the beginning of wisdom' (ibid.).
[88] Dargan 1999: 2.
[89] Weil mostly uses paradoxes in her *Cahiers*, especially in nos. 2 and 3 (Little 1988*b*: 106, 109).
[90] 'Then, like a lever, the notion of mystery carries thought beyond the impasse, to the other side of the unopenable door, beyond the domain of the intelligence and above it' (*FLN* 131). However, in the case of contradiction, as Little points out, the two contradicting elements are on the same plane, which makes it more difficult to reach the higher plane (Little 1988*b*: 112).

Weil also likes to give words new meanings or simply to join concepts in an oxymoronic fashion. For example, she calls Sophocles the greatest Christian author of the last twenty centuries; she sees in the Greek concept of fate the result of sin, which, by definition is the result of a free act; she perceives nothing but 'liberté dans ce drame [du *Prométhée*] fait de chaînes et de clous' (*IPC* 18, 20, 104).[91] She uses terms from the natural world, such as *pesanteur*, to express spiritual realities, for 'il y a analogie entre les rapports mécaniques qui constituent l'ordre du monde sensible et les vérités divines' (*PSO* 17).[92] The world is like a metaphor, which she tries to explain. By using these kinds of expressions, as Little points out in her article 'Simone Weil, ou la pensée analogique', Weil is not using imagery for the sake of it, but expressing something about reality itself.[93]

Weil wants to incite her readers to walk over the bridges contained in the Greek classics towards that other reality 'hors du monde, c'est-à-dire hors de l'espace et du temps', which is a person, namely God, 'qui depuis l'origine nous a dans ses bras' (*EL* 74; *PSO* 75).[94] How she intends to achieve this will become clearer in the subsequent chapters.

[91] 'freedom in this drama built of chains and of nails' (*IC* 69).
[92] 'There is indeed an analogy between the divine truths and the mechanical relations which constitute the order of the world of sense' (*SNL* 151).
[93] Little 1990: 60.
[94] 'outside the world, that is to say, outside space and time' (*SE* 219); 'who holds us in his arms from the beginning' (*SL* 137).

4
Antigone and the Moral Law: Glimpses of the Supernatural

> What is good is also divine. Queer as it sounds, that sums up my ethics. Only something supernatural can express the Supernatural.
> (Ludwig Wittgenstein, 1929)[1]

'Dans tous les problèmes poignants de l'existence humaine, il y a le choix seulement entre le bien surnaturel et le mal', Weil writes in 'La Personne et le sacré' (*Human Personality*) (*EL* 29).[2] Thus when she says four pages earlier that Antigone follows a supernatural law whilst Creon sees things from a purely natural perspective, it is clear what she is driving at. In applying a purely natural justice by punishing his nephew Polynices even beyond death for being a traitor, Creon is ultimately committing evil. Antigone, on the other hand, dies because she obeys the divine law by burying her brother. What Weil wrote for the Free French Government, applies to everyone. As the *Antigone* indicates, Weil believes there is no compromise possible. Human beings have to make a radical choice between evil and the heroic challenges the good poses to them—the good which is 'situé [...] hors du monde'[3]—between God and idolatry, between a Christian society in some sense and disaster in one form or another (ibid. 74). Weil's times manifested this truth as perhaps no other epoch has. Those who avoided a difficult choice and closed their eyes often became collaborators with totalitarian systems, while others, who refused to

---

Faith and Reason and Peter Lang have kindly allowed me to reprint sections of an article and an essay published with them (Cabaud Meaney 2003*b* and Cabaud 2001*b*).

[1] Quoted in Winch 1989: 206; Wittgenstein 1980: 3e.
[2] 'In all the crucial problems of human existence the only choice is between supernatural good on the one hand and evil on the other' (*SE* 23).
[3] 'outside the world' (ibid. 219).

avert their eyes, frequently had to die as witnesses to truth, justice, and God. Adopting a purely natural point of view could not guarantee the clarity of vision needed to see through the lies of power and ideology. At first glance Creon seems to be in the right. One could add that according to Attic law he was justified in leaving a traitor unburied outside the city. Yet he does not heed divine warnings, and even blasphemes his own gods. Similarly the Free French will make unjust decisions, Weil predicts, even though they are fighting on the right side, if they do not embrace the virtue of justice for its own sake and adopt a supernatural perspective. For the supernatural becomes indispensable, in Weil's eyes, for the possession of true justice, for an adequate understanding of reality, and consequently also for an adequate interpretation of literature.

The crucial role of the supernatural is one of the important apologetic points Weil tries to make in her interpretation of the *Antigone*. She also wants to show the significance of the moral choice between supernatural good and evil, in general and in particular for her contemporaries. Antigone, in her eyes, is a Christological character who suffers for her choice of truth and justice over deceit and *Realpolitik*. These are the points examined in this chapter as well as Weil's self-understanding as a figure like Antigone. One needs to realize, however, that Weil's interpretation of *Antigone* is fragmentary. Her dense analysis as well as her discreet apologetic intentions can frequently only be unfolded fully by reference to other texts she wrote concerning concepts such as the moral law.

CHRONOLOGY AND QUOTATIONS

The *Antigone* seems to have been one of Weil's favourite plays. It is the first Greek tragedy she refers to in her writings in an early fragment on Freud, which she begins with a Greek quotation from the Eros-hymn (*OC* i. 278) (*Ant.* 781, 790).[4] Weil seems to love this hymn, sung by the Chorus after Haemon's heated discussion with his father Creon, for she quotes lines 781–800 in her article in the periodical *Entre Nous* as well as in her translations for Bousquet, and in her *Cahiers*, though she does not mention it in the *Intuitions* (*OC* i. 278, ii/2. 337, vi/1.

---

[4] For a complete overview of Weil's quotes from and references to the *Antigone* as well as to all other texts investigated, see Appendix.

123, 261–2, 368–9; *Œ* 664).[5] She does not use this passage to make a point, but was probably simply struck by its beauty.[6] On the front covers of her first two *Cahiers* she quotes in Greek Antigone's famous line that she was not born to hate, but to love (*OC* vi/1. 68, 219) (*Ant.* 523).[7] As early as 1933–4, Weil wrote a few paragraphs on Sophocles' plays in her first *Cahier* which are significant as a point of comparison to her later Christological interpretations (*OC* vi/1. 74, 101–2).[8]

In summer 1934 Weil saw her friend Simone Pétrement in Paris and talked about Sophocles, 'dont elle admirait dès lors passionnément certaines pièces'.[9] On 16 May 1936 she published her first article in *Entre Nous* on the *Antigone*. In her *Intuitions*, she devotes two dense pages to the drama. Surprisingly, among the texts she translated for her friends before her departure to New York, the *Antigone* is scarcely present—only the hymn to Eros for Bousquet (*Œ* 664) (*Ant.* 781–800). In contrast, the *Iliad* is well represented, and she quotes passages from Aeschylus' *Agamemnon* as from his *Prometheus Bound*, from Sophocles' *Electra* as well as from many other texts (*Œ* 648, 664 ff.).[10] The *Antigone*

---

[5] She also refers briefly to it in *OC* vi/1. 196, 224. Furthermore, she translated the hymn as a dedication to Jean Ballard, his wife and daughter (*CSW* 5/2. 155–6, 25/2. 120).

[6] For the translation error she makes in lines 791–2, see comment of the editor in *OC* vi/1. 512 n. 337, as well as n. 115 on page 482. See also Narcy's account in *OC* vi/1. 22–3.

[7] She also quoted this line in: *OC* vi/1. 379, ii/2. 336; *IPC* 19; *EL* 26; *Œ* 655.

[8] In the first reference, Weil contrasts Sophocles and Homer to Racine. The writings of the Greek authors are set in a time of political unrest in which passions are strong, but simple, where joy and misery are intense, and where there is little place for inner torments. Racine's tragedies, on the contrary, were written during a time of political stability, during which love became an instrument of power (*OC* vi/1. 74). In the second reference, Weil claims that Sophocles' tragedies depict the drama of loneliness and weakness of the heroes—despite their apparent energy (*OC* vi/1. 102). In contrast, necessity is only a political, not a physical phenomenon in Racine's tragedies, for the characters do not experience hunger or abject poverty. Love between siblings as in the *Electra* or *Antigone* does not exist, since Racine's political universe is merely inhabited by passionate forms of love. Corneille is no better, since his plays do not express real *malheur*. None of his characters regret their tragic destiny, for they are rendered immune to real affliction by their sense of the sublime. In 1935 after her industrial experience, Weil writes in the same *Cahier* that Sophocles shows how nothing can destroy the heroes' interior liberty (*OC* vi/1. 120).

[9] *SP* i. 419; 'of whom she passionately admired certain plays' from then on.

[10] BN 'Textes préparés, mais non envoyés à Posternak', 'Textes adressés au Père Perrin', 'Textes destinés à Gustave Thibon'. Weil prepared these texts for Bousquet, Thibon, and Perrin before leaving France with the thought of a probable death. Thus her selection of texts is significant, and almost takes on the value of a testament (*Œ* 662). Her translations for Posternak (a medical student and himself a patient at the Swiss

continues to be mentioned by Weil, from her time in New York and in London to the last letters she wrote from the sanatorium in Ashford (*CS* 17, 222, 291, 306; *EL* 218, 243; *OC* vi/3. 386). For example in her 34-page article 'La Personne et le sacré' she devotes over a page to the *Antigone* (*EL* 25–6). Though she does not mention Antigone and Creon in another essay entitled 'Luttons-nous pour la justice?' (*Are we Struggling for Justice?/SW*), these figures seem to have been in her thoughts, as I will show later on. Despite the fact that Weil makes only some very brief comments on Creon, her analysis of the nature of idolatry and of totalitarian states will shed light on the tyrant who fell prey to the temptation of idolatry.

Apart from the quotes already discussed, Weil mentions various parts of Antigone's *kommos*, her death-song. Later this passage would depict, in her eyes, Antigone's 'Passion', since she experiences an abandonment similar to that of Christ on the cross; but she already quotes from it in her *Entre Nous* article since it so poignantly expresses *malheur* (*OC* ii/2. 337–8) (*Ant.* 806–10, 916–28).[11] When Antigone wonders (in lines 916 to 928) what crime she committed against the gods to be punished thus, Weil translates in her *Entre Nous* article 'God' instead of 'the gods'. Though Weil was not yet interested in proving the identity of the Christian God and of the ancient divinities, her translation is understandable in terms of wanting to make the ancient text as accessible as possible to the modern sensibilities of the workers. In her analysis of the *Prometheus* in the *Intuitions*, Weil refers to lines 942–3 where Antigone claims that she is suffering impiety for having acted piously, again underlining thereby her Christlikeness (*IPC* 99).

The few citations Weil gives in the *Intuitions* are almost all taken from the dialogue between Creon and Antigone in the second act, allowing her to focus on their clashing world-views (ibid. 18–19) (*Ant.* 512–23).[12] Interestingly, Weil was indifferent to the gender tension between the two characters, for she never refers to line 525 where Creon cries out that no woman will ever rule over him.

---

hospital of Moubra where she had gone for treatment of her headaches) were written in 1937. She wanted to introduce him to the Greek classics, and since he did not know ancient Greek, she prepared many translations for him, of which she sent only some.

[11] She also quotes lines 806–16 and 876–82 as well as 897–9 in her *Cahiers* (*OC* vi/1. 261, 268, vi/3. 87).

[12] She quotes parts of this dialogue in her *Entre Nous* article, in her London writings, and in her *Cahiers* (*OC* ii/2. 336; *EL* 25–6; *OC* vi/1. 380, vi/3. 316). Concerning l. 523 see n. 7 or Appendix.

Weil seems to have a predilection for the hymn to the sun, sung at the entrance of the Chorus, though she does not use it for her interpretation (*OC* ii/2. 335, vi/1. 260–1) (*Ant.* 100–9). Twice she quotes some lines concerning the unwritten laws which Antigone claims to be following: the famous lines 453–4 about the unwritten laws of the gods and lines 505–7 are mentioned in her *Entre Nous* article, and lines 450–2 in 'La Personne et le sacré' (*OC* ii/2. 335; *EL* 25). Finally, Weil only once cites some lines from the discussion between Haemon and his father (*OC* ii/2. 336) (*Ant.* 736–9). She gives one line from Antigone's encounter with Ismene at the beginning of the play in her *Intuitions*, where Ismene calls her mad though a true friend (*IPC* 20) (*Ant.* 99). In *Entre Nous* she mentions a few more lines from the first and second meeting of the two sisters (*OC* ii/2. 335–6) (*Ant.* 63–4, 67, 79, 555, 559). Finally, Weil also refers a few times to the hymn to Dionysus which is the fifth and final *stasimon* of the Chorus (*OC* vi/3. 226–7, 231, 236; *IPC* 88–9) (*Ant.* 1146–52).

Weil gives these quotes either in Greek or gives her own translation on which she often spent much time which did not prevent her from sometimes making mistakes.[13] Weil used the Masqueray edition (from the Budé collection) of Sophocles' plays, which she owned. But when she arrived in Marseille, she used the older Dindorf edition, which she borrowed from the town library, before her own copy was sent to her.[14]

THE ANTIGONE OF ROSIÈRES—THE *MALHEUR* OF THE PROLETARIAT

When visiting the foundry of Rosières in winter 1935 and on hearing about the workers' periodical *Entre Nous*, Simone Weil decided to write an article. She started with a text entitled 'Un appel aux ouvriers de R[osières]' ('An Appeal to the Workers at R[osières]'/*SL*), which was refused by Victor Bernard, the technical director of the factory who was also in charge of the journal. He was afraid it would rouse the spirit of class struggle among the workers. In this open letter to the workers, Weil asked them to write what they felt about their work, to describe their sufferings, their joys, the things they might want to change.

[13] See n. 6.   [14] See Narcy's explanation in *OC* vi/1. 22, 466 n. 190.

Weil and Bernard continued their correspondence, and in spring 1936 Weil wrote an article on *Antigone*. She wanted to reach everyone from the directors to the workers, she said, but in the final analysis the article was addressed to the latter (*CO* 154). As Narcy points out, it is obviously of a political nature.[15] But Weil knew her text would be subject to censorship: 'car il s'agit évidemment de vous faire de la prose bien sage, autant que j'en suis capable' (ibid.).[16] This is not easy, since the story itself is problematic: '*Antigone* n'a rien d'une histoire morale pour enfants sages; j'espère cependant que vous n'irez pas jusqu'à trouver Sophocle subversif.'[17]

She starts off the article by saying that ancient Greek literature is of interest to everybody since it is so human. Though read mostly by intellectuals, it should touch those more who know what it is to suffer and to fight, for this is its main theme.[18] The protagonist in Sophocles' tragedies 'lutte tout seul contre une situation *intolérablement douloureuse*' (*OC* ii/2. 334; my italics).[19] Though weighed down by solitude, misery, injustice, and humiliation, 'il tient bon et ne se laisse jamais dégrader par le malheur'.[20] Serenity, not sadness, is the feeling with which the reader is left. Weil indirectly presents the Sophoclean hero as a model to the workers: they too should remain imperturbable in the face of adversity, and maintain their inner liberty in spite of oppression. She writes this despite or perhaps because of the hardships she herself bore during her industrial experience. In her *Cahiers*, probably around 1935, she says: 'Sophocle a choisi les légendes les plus horribles (Œdipe, Oreste) pour y porter la sérénité. La leçon de ses tragédies c'est: il n'est point

---

[15] *OC* vi/1. 25.
[16] 'for clearly I must offer you only the best-behaved prose, so far as I am able' (*SL* 49).
[17] 'Antigone is by no means a moral tale for model children; but all the same I hope you won't go so far as to find Sophocles subversive' (ibid. 49).
[18] 'Par exemple, quelle intensité de compréhension pourrait naître d'un contact entre le peuple et la poésie grecque, qui a pour objet presque unique le malheur! Seulement il faudrait savoir la traduire et la présenter' (*E* 67) ('For example, what an intensity of understanding could spring up from contact between the people and Greek poetry, the almost unique theme of which is misfortune! Only, one would have to know how to translate and present it') (*NR* 70). One of the two main services one can render those suffering is 'de trouver des mots qui expriment la vérité de leur malheur' ('to find the words which express the truth of their affliction') (*EL* 30/*SE* 24). This, she claims, has been done by writers such as Homer, Aeschylus, Sophocles, and Shakespeare.
[19] 'wrestles alone against an intolerably painful situation' (*IC* 19).
[20] 'he holds on and never lets himself be corrupted by misfortune' (ibid.).

de ravisseur de la liberté intérieure' (*OC* vi/1. 120).[21] This would also apply to *Antigone*. Yet how can the worker acquire this stoic composure? Weil wants to let the play speak for itself.

In the first lines of her summary, Weil emphasizes the opposition Antigone offers to her own country, to its laws, and to the head of the state—in consequence of which she dies. It is only three paragraphs after making this point and six paragraphs into the article that Weil mentions that Antigone dies out of love for her brother. In contrast, Weil stresses in her later Christological interpretation that Antigone dies because she obeys God, out of a *folie d'amour* antagonistic to Creon's *raison d'état* (*IPC* 18–20; *EL* 26). But in this article, her main focus is on the opposition of Antigone to the state.

Antigone has a 'cœur aimant' and 'un courage héroïque'.[22] On the other hand Ismene is only 'une enfant douce et timide'[23] who does not have the courage to act against the law though fidelity to her brother would require it (*OC* ii/2. 334). Her character predisposes her to obey rather than to rebel (ibid. 335) (*Ant.* 63–4, 67, 79). Ismene's attitude is familiar to the workers, since they often have to adopt it themselves. How could they stand up against their employers when they are in the weaker position, and are in danger of losing their livelihood? Yet in the eyes of Antigone, this position is 'une lâcheté' ('cowardice') (ibid. 335/*IC* 20). Antigone, Weil implies, is the model to follow.

Antigone and Creon's conflict is not resolvable since each adopts a contradictory point of view. If seen analogously in terms of the relationship between employers and employees (though Weil does not draw attention to that), their confrontation stands paradigmatically for the inability of each to understand the other's perspective. Comprehension is one of the key virtues Weil tried to foster in her first rejected article 'Un appel aux ouvriers': 'Les hommes ne savent jamais se mettre à la place les uns des autres'; 'on ne comprend jamais tout à fait ceux à qui on donne des ordres' (*OC* ii/2. 326, 327).[24] It is interesting to compare Weil's conclusion concerning the first Creon–Antigone scene to the analysis in her later mystical interpretation. There she interprets their conflict in terms of a clash between the natural perspective and the

---

[21] 'Sophocles chose the most horrible legends (Oedipus, Orestes), to imbue them with serenity. His tragedies teach that nothing can destroy the inner freedom' (*FLN* 49).
[22] 'loving heart and heroic courage' (*IC* 20).   [23] 'a shy, sweet girl' (ibid.).
[24] 'Men never know how to see things from one another's point of view' (*SL* 28). 'One never fully understands the people one gives orders to' (ibid. 30).

supernatural point of view. In her article she merely writes: 'Lui juge tout du point de vue de l'État; elle se place toujours à un autre point de vue, qui lui paraît supérieur' (ibid. 335–6).[25] This is as close as Weil gets to her later notion of the supernatural perspective: Antigone *places* herself at a point of view which *seems* superior to her. This is still a point within the natural world, for she can adopt it on her own, rather than being lifted into it, such as the supernatural perspective would require.[26] After citing Antigone's response of being born to love and not to hate, Weil just says: 'Á cette parole touchante, le roi répond par une condamnation à mort' (ibid. 336).[27] In her *Intuitions*, she was to write much more strongly about Creon's answer to Antigone (that, if she needs to love, she should go and stay with the dead), for it shows that: 'Ceux qui ont part seulement à l'amour et non à la haine appartiennent *à un autre monde* et n'ont à attendre de celui-ci que la mort violente' (*IPC* 19; my italics).[28] When writing the article for *Entre Nous*, Weil did not yet see their conflict in such extreme terms.

Weil's interpretations are intended to have an a-temporal as well as a temporal significance.[29] In a fragment of a letter to Bernard, Weil says that the constraints which he believes his editorial control must have put on her were practically non-existent. She thought it more beautiful 'd'exposer le drame dans sa nudité' (*CO* 155).[30] But, of course, even her 'naked' manner of presenting the play reveals the lens through which she is looking at the text. She is addressing her article mainly to the workers: this expresses itself not only in the simple style, the linear manner in which she recounts the story, but also in the emphasis placed on Antigone's integrity despite her disobedience. Furthermore, Weil

---

[25] 'He judges everything from the point of view of the State; she holds to another view which seems to her superior' (*IC* 21).

[26] To accede to the supernatural is not simply a question of will-power: 'Au sommet d'une montagne, on est plus près du ciel que dans la plaine. Mais on n'est pas plus près de voler. On en est exactement aussi loin. [. . .] Le bien commence au delà de la volonté, comme la vérité commence au delà de l'intelligence' (*CS* 224) ('One is nearer the sky at the top of a mountain than in the plain. But one is no nearer to flying. One is exactly as far away as before. [. . .] The good begins at a point beyond the reach of will, as truth begins at a point beyond the reach of intelligence') (*FLN* 262).

[27] 'To this touching declaration the king answers with a death sentence.'

[28] 'those who share only in love and not in hate belong *to another world* and have nothing to expect from this world but a violent death' (*IC* 9; my italics).

[29] 'Car ces vieux poèmes sont tellement humains qu'ils sont encore très proches de nous et peuvent intéresser tout le monde' ('because these old poems are so truly human that they are still very close to us and can interest everyone') (*OC* ii/2. 333/*IC* 19).

[30] 'to expose the drama in its nakedness' (*SL* 50).

thought that simply introducing the workers to the tragedy's beauty was going to improve their situation, for they live in an ugly world (*E* 66–7). Therefore Weil quotes passages from the Eros-hymn or the entrance hymn though they cannot be considered central to the storyline or to understanding Antigone's affliction (*OC* ii/2. 335, 337) (*Ant.* 100–4, 781–90). Ultimately Weil wants the play to speak for itself.

Weil's article ends anti-climactically. She relates the disasters befalling Creon in their chronological order, only saying about him: 'Cet homme qui savait si bien parler en chef s'effondre anéanti par le chagrin' (*OC* ii/2. 338).[31] She lets the Chorus conclude in her stead: 'Les paroles hautaines des hommes orgueilleux se paient par de terribles malheurs; c'est comme cela qu'en vieillissant ils apprennent la modération' (ibid.) (*Ant.* 1350–3).[32] She does not emphasize that Creon gets punished for his pride, a fact that might almost be lost on the reader; for her focus is on the misery of the protagonist in the hold of a superior, rather than on the punishment of the latter.

Weil successfully describes the play in its starkness. Her lucid style, reduced to utter simplicity for this occasion, allowed her to make this tragedy understandable to readers who lacked a formal education; but she did not use a colloquial style as in her first rejected article.

THE MORAL LAW

At no point in her interpretation does Weil dwell on a conflict of contradictory obligations. Ultimately there is no conflict in her eyes, since Antigone obeys the moral law while Creon does not. In her *Entre Nous* article she does not explain what that law is, though she quotes the passage on the unwritten laws of 'God' (*OC* ii/2. 335) (*Ant.* 453–4). In 'La Personne et le sacré' Weil is more explicit: 'C'est par une singulière confusion qu'on a pu assimiler la loi non écrite d'Antigone au droit naturel. Aux yeux de Créon, il n'y avait dans ce que faisait Antigone absolument rien de naturel. Il la jugeait folle' (*EL* 25).[33] Antigone obeys

---

[31] 'this man who knew so well how to speak as a master breaks down, mastered by sorrow' (*IC* 23).
[32] 'The haughty words of arrogant men are paid for by terrible disasters, | From which in old age they learn moderation.'
[33] 'It is extraordinary that Antigone's unwritten law should have been confused with the idea of natural right. In Creon's eyes there was absolutely nothing that was natural in Antigone's behaviour. He thought she was mad' (*SE* 20).

a supernatural moral law while Creon simply follows the narrow logic of a natural justice. Weil does not deny that Creon pursues a certain kind of justice, but it is not true justice.[34] Though Weil rejects the Aristotelian interpretation of the play, which sees Antigone's and Creon's conflict in terms of a clash between the natural ('the unwritten laws') and the positive law (the legally binding laws), she simply radicalizes the conflict by substituting the supernatural moral law for the natural law (ibid. 25–6, 29).[35] An obligation towards other human beings is absolute and unconditional in Weil's eyes. Even if it were not recognized by anyone, not even by the person concerned, this would remove none of its validity (*E* 9). It is eternal, since its authority is not derived from customs or tradition, as she writes in *L'Enracinement* (ibid. 10). Though its absoluteness is not founded on anything in this world, it is confirmed by the universal consensus of moral consciences. For certain obligations towards the human person are universally recognized when there is no conflict of interests. The dignity of the human person—or the sacredness, as Weil calls it—is more or less well reflected in positive law which derives its legitimacy from it (ibid. 11).

Weil calls the moral law, which consists of such obligations, supernatural in four ways without differentiating between those meanings herself. First of all, the moral law is supernatural in requiring us to go against our own sinful nature, against the law of *pesanteur*. It takes a counter-force to oppose that pull, namely grace. How, except by grace, could Antigone have sacrificed herself? But, one might want to object, is it not natural to defend a family member, even at the expense of one's life? However, 'même l'amour d'une mère s'épuise si aucune des conditions de son renouvellement n'existe' (*CS* 75).[36] Love must be unconditional to stand firm in trials, and 'un amour inconditionné est une folie' (ibid.).[37] In her fragmentary interpretation Weil fails to address some elements in the tragedy that might contradict her reading. For example, in a famous passage of her death-song, Antigone says she would not have given her life for a child or a husband, since she could have replaced them. But she is willing to die for her brother who is irreplaceable (*Ant.* 905 ff.). Could there be a certain incestuous tinge

---

[34] For Weil's distinction between a supernatural moral law and a natural or 'social' moral law, which she thinks is already present in Plato, see *SG* 82, 88–9.
[35] Aristotle, *Rhetorics* 1373b, 1375ab.
[36] 'Even a mother's love wears out if all the conditions for its renewal are lacking' (*FLN* 127).
[37] 'An unconditioned love is a madness' (ibid.).

to her love for her brother? Steiner wonders in his book *Antigones*.[38] Perhaps Weil would have agreed with those classicists who believe this passage to be a later addition to the play. But she would have been less willing to admit that Antigone was influenced by her culture, and had mixed motivations.[39]

The moral law is also supernatural in that it requires supernatural motives to obey it. Willpower is not enough. Love in the sense of a folly of love, being 'insensée par amour', is necessary (*IPC* 20).[40] To want to act justly by using only one's own resources, is like believing that by continually jumping up, one will one day be able to fly (*AD* 191). Antigone, in Weil's eyes, is motivated by such a *folie d'amour*, which makes people wrongly think she is mad:[41] 'Car la loi non écrite à laquelle obéissait cette petite fille, bien loin d'avoir quoi que ce fût de commun avec aucun droit ni avec rien de naturel, n'était pas autre chose que l'amour extrême, absurde, qui a poussé le Christ sur la Croix' (*EL* 26).[42] Antigone's famous line that she was born to love and not to hate reinforces Weil's reading. In the end it turns out that Creon lacked sense because his irate pride blinded him (*Ant.* 1260 ff., 1350 ff.). He wants to determine the justice and injustice of people beyond death, such as Polynices whose body he leaves unburied: 'Jamais l'ennemi, même lorsqu'il est mort, n'est un ami', he says in line 522 (*IPC* 19).[43] But ironically, he himself acts unjustly towards the guard, Antigone, Ismene, his son Haemon, and the seer Tiresias, and defeats his own purpose.

Thirdly the moral law is supernatural in its origin for Weil. In a Kantian tone, she writes in her 'Étude pour une déclaration des obligations envers l'être humain' (*Draft for a Statement of Human Obligations*): 'Il est une réalité située hors du monde, c'est-à-dire hors de l'espace et du temps, hors de l'univers mental de l'homme, hors de tout le domaine que les facultés humaines peuvent atteindre. A cette réalité répond au centre du cœur de l'homme cette exigence d'un bien absolu

---

[38] Steiner 1984: 88; Griffith 1999: 33, 50, 63.
[39] Winnington-Ingram 1980: 145.   [40] 'lov[ing] beyond reason' (*IC* 10).
[41] Though Weil does not use the term *folie d'amour* in her interpretation of the *Antigone*, she employs it in her article 'Luttons-nous pour la justice?' which reflects the Creon–Antigone conflict (*EL* 48 ff.). Weil takes over this expression from Plato (*SG* 117).
[42] 'For the unwritten law which this little girl obeyed had nothing whatsoever in common with rights, or with the natural; it was the same love, extreme and absurd, which led Christ to the Cross' (*SE* 20).
[43] 'Never at any time is the enemy, even when dead, a friend' (*IC* 9).

qui y habite toujours et ne trouve jamais aucun objet en ce monde' (*EL* 74).⁴⁴ Though obligations are often linked to finite goods, the absolute character of these obligations cannot be explained in terms of these.⁴⁵ How can something finite such as a country or another human being require the sacrifice of one's life? Perhaps a divine command coming from above adds a categorical character to the obligation. In any case, to deny the divine character of the moral law, and yet maintain its absoluteness is an absurdity, Weil believes, and thus a *morale laïque* (secular morality) cannot be viable (*AD* 191). Hence Antigone's claim that she is obeying the gods is convincing, whether or not it is to be understood in terms of faith.

Finally the moral law is supernatural in its finality. It appeals to what aspires to the good in us, something Weil calls the sacred in every human being, turning one towards the transcendent (*EL* 12–14, 16).⁴⁶ Those who perform truly just actions already participate in eternity to a certain extent. When Christ says that one should store up treasures in heaven: 'Cela signifie qu'il y a des actions qui ont la vertu de transporter de la terre dans le ciel une partie de l'amour qui se trouve dans le cœur d'un homme' (*E* 180–1).⁴⁷ Rather than being the sign of morbidity, Antigone's concern for the dead shows that she is true to her supernatural vocation, but not so Creon; for she knows she will spend more time in the underworld than on earth, and that it is more important to please the gods than men (*Ant.* 74–5).⁴⁸

Though this analysis of the different implicit meanings of the supernatural moral law may seem technical, it reveals the significance the supernatural has in Weil's justification of Antigone. Antigone is not

---

⁴⁴ 'There is a reality outside the world, that is to say, outside space and time, outside man's mental universe, outside any sphere whatsoever that is accessible to human faculties. Corresponding to this reality, at the centre of the human heart, is the longing for an absolute good, a longing which is always there and is never appeased by any object in this world' (*SE* 219).

⁴⁵ 'Jamais dans cet univers il n'y a égalité de dimensions entre une obligation et son objet. L'obligation est un infini, l'objet ne l'est pas' (*E* 137) ('Never in this world can there be any dimensional equality between an obligation and its subject. The obligation is something infinite, the subject of it is not') (*NR* 156).

⁴⁶ Birou 1995: 68–9.

⁴⁷ 'Which means to say that there are certain actions which have the virtue of transporting from earth to heaven part of the love that lies in a man's heart' (*NR* 209).

⁴⁸ However, the supernatural law is not only accessible to the believer. Anybody who seeks the truth and is not blinded by ideology or self-interest can recognize the moral law.

crazy, but motivated by something greater than the three-dimensional reality of the natural world. By obeying the divine commands of the gods, the powerful force of the supernatural breaks in, and shifts the boundaries between the natural and the supernatural. The 'natural' thing for her to do would have been to obey Creon just as her sister did, marry her fiancé Haemon, and let the dead bury the dead. Instead, she dies for her obedience to the divine law.

The supernatural is not simply something added on to the natural, but it radically changes reality: 'Le bien surnaturel n'est pas une sorte de supplément au bien naturel, comme on voudrait, Aristote aidant, nous le persuader pour notre plus grand confort' (*EL* 29).[49] To adopt Creon's narrow rationality and add respect for the gods to it would not be a solution. For the one point of view excludes the other.[50] Creon's *raison d'état* does not allow for the existence of other obligations, which could override it. His idol does not allow for the presence of other gods. As Weil continues: 'Dans tous les problèmes poignants de l'existence humaine, il y a le choix seulement entre le bien surnaturel et le mal' (ibid.).[51] It is not enough, therefore, to choose the natural good, since it does not exclude injustice.

Yet Creon's viewpoint seems reasonable and justified. After all, Polynices committed treason and came to conquer his home-town Thebes together with the enemies from Argos who were going to ravage the temples of the gods (*Ant.* 199 ff.). The gods therefore must desire the punishment of this attempted desecration. In consequence, Creon leaves him outside the city to be eaten by the birds, while his brother Eteocles, who was defending the city, is buried with all honours. Since both brothers are dead, it is for Creon as next of kin to govern the city. Once Creon has issued his edict that whoever attempts to bury Polynices will be stoned, he cannot go back on his own word for the sake of a family member without undermining his newly acquired authority. It seems therefore that for the greater good, Creon should have Antigone executed.

Yet there are, according to Weil, two forms of justice, a natural and a supernatural justice between which she distinguishes in 'Luttons-nous

---

[49] 'Supernatural good is not a sort of supplement to natural good, as we are told, with support from Aristotle, for our greater comfort' (*SE* 23).
[50] For again 'il n'y a pas dans la vie humaine de région qui soit le domaine de la nature' ('there is not any department of human life which is purely natural') (*AD* 167/*WG* 112).
[51] 'In all the crucial problems of human existence the only choice is between supernatural good on the one hand and evil on the other' (*SE* 23).

pour la justice?'(*EL* 46, 48 ff.; *IPC* 136–7). Natural justice reigns between two equal partners who give each other their due. But when that equality subsides, then the stronger uses his power over the weaker. Supernatural justice, on the other hand, respects the weaker person in every way.[52] This compassion cannot be accounted for in natural terms, because of the pull of *pesanteur*. It is the same as love in the sense of *caritas*: 'L'esprit de justice n'est pas autre chose que la fleur suprême et parfaite de la folie d'amour' (*EL* 56).[53] When Antigone risks her life, she acts out of this love which is prescribed by justice: 'Elle périt pour avoir été insensée par amour' (*IPC* 20; *EL* 26).[54] In the Beatitudes Christ does not call his benefactors 'charitable' or 'loving', as Weil points out, but 'just' (*AD* 124–5). Justice demanding love may seem at first contradictory, but is love not the response due to another person?

Creon on the other hand thinks strictly in terms of friends and enemies (*IPC* 19) (*Ant.* 522). He falls prey to the temptation of temporal Messianism by wanting to establish absolute justice concerning the living and the dead: 'Comme chacun se croit suffisamment capable de justice, chacun croit aussi qu'un système où il serait puissant serait assez juste. C'est la tentation que le diable a fait subir au Christ. Les hommes y succombent continuellement' (*E* 134).[55] Weil wrote this about the USSR in 1943, but it could apply just as well to Creon. He thinks he can dictate to the gods who is just and who is not, and thus commits injustices towards Antigone, Polynices, his son, the gods, and ultimately the state. He does not have what Weil calls the 'impartiality of God' who lets the sun shine on the just and on the unjust, but

---

[52] What Weil calls natural justice simply seems to be the law of the stronger, and no justice at all. To call it justice is for the stronger to employ a euphemism to disguise their violence. As Martin Andic puts it in his article 'Supernatural Justice and the Madness of Love': 'Justice is supernatural to the extent that injustice is natural' (Andic 1994: 382).

[53] 'The spirit of justice is nothing other than the supreme and perfect flower of the madness of love' (*SW* 129). If not otherwise indicated, the term 'love' will be used in the sense of *caritas*. Weil herself uses the term *caritas* to express the word *charité* in her unpublished letter to David Bell around 1938/9 (BN Letter to devilboy (Charles Bell), 9/84; SP ii. 194). Regarding the relationship of justice and love in Weil's thought, see Martin Andic's aforementioned article as well as Richard Bell's *Simone Weil: The Way of Justice as Compassion* (1998), especially chs. 4 and 5.

[54] 'She perishes for having loved beyond reason' (*IC* 10). For the coincidence of love and justice see *IPC* 55; *EL* 50; *AD* 40.

[55] 'As each of us considers himself sufficiently capable of practising justice, each of us naturally thinks that a system under which he wielded power would be a reasonably just one. This is the temptation Christ underwent at the hands of the devil. Men are continually succumbing to it' (*NR* 152–3).

wants to separate the wheat from the chaff (*IPC* 18). By impartiality, Weil does not mean that God is indifferent towards his creatures, but rather that his justice is less restricted than our limited rationality. He does not let punishment follow sin immediately except in that injustice carries its own punishment anyway.[56] Paradoxically Antigone has that impartiality though she seems so caught up in her passionate love for her brother that she stubbornly disregards any other reasoning. In spite of the fact that her brother committed treason against the state and intended to commit a sacrilege against the gods of his home town, she does not pass judgement on him, but allows him access to a better afterlife. She is more just than Creon, for she gives her brother what his family owes him, namely a decent burial.

Weil's understanding of the supernatural moral law is based on the objective, metaphysical distinction between good and evil. To deny its existence, she came to see, is disastrous. Therefore one of her primary aims is to convey its objective reality to her readers.[57] It is a fundamental experience of human beings to see this difference, but also to try to avoid it, since it poses a challenge. In her article 'Cette guerre est une guerre de religions' in which she analyses the causes of World War II, Weil points out the different manners of evading this confrontation. One of these is to deny the reality of the difference between good and evil, and to let oneself be governed by one's desires (*EL* 99, 16). Those who live for the sake of experiencing strong sensations, however, fool themselves, as Weil had already written to one of her students in 1934 (which shows that her ontological understanding of right and wrong reaches far back before her mystical experience): 'Il y a des gens qui n'ont vécu que de sensations et pour les sensations; André Gide en est un exemple. Ils sont

---

[56] 'La récompense du bien consiste dans le fait qu'on est bon, la punition du mal dans le fait qu'on est mauvais, et ce sont une récompense et une punition *automatiques*' (*SG* 82) ('The reward for good consists in the fact that one is good and the punishment for evil in the fact that one is evil; and the reward and punishment are *automatic*') (*SG* 82/*SNL* 93). See also Plato, *Gorgias* 469b.

[57] In 1933–4 in her *Cahiers* she wrote: 'La notion de mesure est *partout* perdue [...] Tout s'en trouve corrompu. La vie privée aussi, parce que la tempérance (σωφροσύνη) est impensable. En dehors des règles extérieures (convenances bourgeoises), tout le mouvement moral d'après-guerre (et même d'avant) n'est qu'une *apologie* de l'*intempérance* (surréalisme), donc, en définitive, de la folie' (*OC* vi/1. 99) ('The idea of measure has been lost in *every* sphere [...] Everything is corrupted by it. Including private life, because *temperance* (σωφροσύνη) has become unthinkable. Outside the sphere of external observances (bourgeois formality) the whole moral trend of the post-war years (and even before) has been an *apology* for *intemperance* (surrealism), and therefore, ultimately, for madness') (*FLN* 29).

en réalité les dupes de la vie, et, comme ils le sentent confusément, ils tombent toujours dans une profonde tristesse où il ne leur reste d'autre ressource que de s'étourdir en se mentant misérablement à eux-mêmes' (*CO* 25).[58] Gide with his *acte gratuit* [gratuitous act] along with the Surrealists was responsible for much of the moral degeneration of the inter-war years in Weil's eyes (RL 355–6; *E* 28). The amorality these writers proclaimed had disastrous effects. For Weil believes that human beings need orientation, and when denying them the compass that good and evil provide, they are left at the mercy of their own impulses. Once desire has been satisfied, they fall into a kind of existential despair, an *ennui*. Since 'l'essence même de l'homme est l'effort orienté', he becomes literally mad if the signposts of good and evil are removed (*EL* 99).[59] However, few people have lived this negation completely, and this restraint preserves them from madness (*E* 137–8).

A second way of avoiding the challenge of the moral law, according to Weil, is idolatry. In that case, a social entity, a nation, or an ideology are assigned an absolute value, everything else being sacrificed for their sake. While the first manner of avoiding the moral conflict throws human beings into boredom and despair, this method has the fanaticizing power of a pseudo-religion. Similarly, Creon made the state his idol. He was therefore blind to any moral claims outside those of the *polis* to which everything else must be surrendered.[60] The Nazis adopted this position, Weil claims, which explains their strength, while the French, having chosen the first option, are weak (*EL* 99 ff., 105–6).

At the centre of morality lies a contradiction, Weil admits, namely the fact that an absolute obligation is attached to a finite object. Weil does not suggest a solution to the problem, but accepts the existence of seeming contradictions, the terms of which have to be maintained if one does not want to curtail reality. Those who want to avoid such a contradiction will either fall into a false mysticism by acknowledging only obligations towards God, or will try to introduce an absolute into the world by means of idolatry (*E* 137). Alternatively, one can accept reality as Antigone does, and obey the moral law even when its demands

---

[58] 'There are people who have lived by and for nothing but sensations; André Gide is an example. What they really are is the dupes of life; and as they are confusedly aware of this they always fall into a profound melancholy which they can only assuage by lying miserably to themselves' (*SL* 12).
[59] 'The very essence of man is directed effort' (*SE* 211).
[60] Creon says, for example: 'One must obey the man whom the city sets up in power in small things and in justice and *in its opposite*' (*Ant.* 666–7; my italics).

are attached to such finite things as the burial of a dead brother. However, Weil is aware that the existence of the moral law cannot be demonstrated. For how could an ultimate reality, something *sui generis*, ever be strictly demonstrated? It can only be seen, acknowledged, and analysed in detail, and its denial shown to be contradictory or practically impossible.[61]

In contrast to Weil's interpretation in *Entre Nous*, she now believes that the tragedy 'pourrait être une illustration de la parole: "Il vaut mieux obéir à Dieu qu'aux hommes"' (*IPC* 18).[62] It all comes down to the fundamental choice between obedience to God or obedience to human beings. For Weil, this overrides all the legitimacy that Creon's position might appear to have as well as Antigone's problematic motivations.

This is ultimately a choice everybody must make and should be aware of, for 'il n'y a que la foi, implicite ou explicite, ou bien la trahison' (ibid. 165).[63] Whether one believes in God or not, one has to make a choice for or against him, at least implicitly through one's decisions in relation to justice, truth, love, and the supernatural moral law.[64] Therefore it is not enough to be fighting on the right side. One must also be doing it for the right reasons, as Weil pertinently tells the Free French in 'Luttons-nous pour la justice?'

THE FOLLY OF LOVE VERSUS POLITICAL RATIONALITY

Only true love and compassion can guarantee an authentic form of justice, as Weil points out in 'Luttons-nous'. Furthermore, the *folie d'amour* would be a much more powerful motivation for the Free French than any desire for glory or greatness. But the results, such as

---

[61] In her incomplete essay 'Quelques réflexions autour de la notion de valeur' from probably the beginning of 1941, Weil states that the notion of value is at the centre of human life, and that it cannot be denied without self-contradiction (*Œ* 121 ff.). See also *E* 137-8.
[62] 'might be an illustration of the saying: "We ought to obey God rather than men"' (*IC* 8-9).
[63] 'There is only faith, implicit or explicit, or else betrayal' (ibid. 196).
[64] Similarly T. S. Eliot says in 'Second Thoughts on Humanism' that 'man is man because he can recognize supernatural realities, not because he can invent them. Either everything in man can be traced as a development from below, or something must come from above. There is no avoiding that dilemma: you must either be a naturalist or a supernaturalist' (Eliot 1972: 485).

Christ's death on the cross, are probably not desirable for the French, Weil sarcastically adds: 'Mais nous n'avons pas à craindre ses périls. Elle n'habite pas en nous. Si elle y habitait, cela se sentirait. Nous sommes des gens raisonnables, comme il semble certain qu'il convient de l'être à ceux qui s'occupent des grandes affaires de ce monde' (*EL* 57).[65] Similarly Weil opposes Creon's rationality to Antigone's folly of love in 'La Personne et le sacré'. Creon speaks with 'bon sens', his argument that an enemy can never become a friend is 'parfaitement raisonnable' ('perfectly reasonable'), and he follows his logic to its natural end by telling Antigone: 'Va donc dans l'autre monde, et puisqu'il faut que tu aimes, aime ceux qui demeurent là-bas' (ibid. 25–6) (*Ant.* 524–5).[66] Antigone, on the other hand, seems 'folle' ('mad'), she is motivated by an 'excès d'amour' ('surfeit of love'), and answers Creon's reasonable points with the candour of a 'petite niaise' ('little simpleton') (*EL* 26/*SE* 20). However, Creon's rationality goes beyond the call of reason and ends in injustice and folly.

At first sight Creon's edict concerning Polynices does not seem unusual, given that Plato in his *Laws* prescribes that slayers of kinsmen, robbers of temples, and other kinds of criminals are to be left unburied outside the city.[67] However, Creon could have allowed other kinsmen to bury him far from the city, which was the usual and appropriate solution.[68] Apparently, Creon goes beyond the call of duty and law to punish his nephew. One could expect him to feel torn between his political responsibilities and his family ties. But on the contrary, he is ready to condemn to death not only Antigone—his niece and the fiancée of his son—but also her sister Ismene without trial or proof of the latter's guilt. This is a sign of tyranny, as Bowra points out in his book *Sophoclean Tragedy*, and Creon possesses the typical characteristics of the tyrant which an Athenian audience would have quickly spotted. For Creon does not want to hear any kind of criticism or suggestion contradicting his plan of action, he perceives his subjects as slaves, he

---

[65] 'But we need not fear its perils. It does not dwell in us. If it did, it would be felt. We are reasonable people, as obviously befits those who concern themselves with the great matters of the world' (*SW* 130).

[66] 'Pass, then, to the other world, and if thou must love, love those who dwell there' (*SE* 20).

[67] Plato, *Laws* 9. 873bc, 10. 909c, 12. 960b; Bowra 1944: 70.

[68] Nussbaum 2001: 55; Bowra 1944: 70. Griffith (1999: 29–30), however, doubts that there was a clear-cut consensus among the Greeks about what was to be done with the corpse of an enemy.

executes persons without trial, and he suspects rebellion and corruption everywhere.[69] During his discussion with Haemon, it becomes clear that he thinks the city exists for its ruler and not vice versa:

CREON: Must I rule this land for another and not for myself?
HAEMON: Yes, there is no city that belongs to a single man!
CREON: Is not the city thought to belong to its ruler?
HAEMON: You would be a fine ruler over a deserted city! (*Ant.* 736–9)

Creon collapses the distinction between virtue and the common good, thus turning the state into an absolute, as Martha Nussbaum points out in her book *The Fragility of Goodness*.[70] Weil would say that he is committing idolatry, for she writes in *La Connaissance surnaturelle*: 'On ne peut choisir qu'entre Dieu et l'idolâtrie. Il n'y a pas d'autre possibilité. Car la faculté d'adoration est en nous, et elle est dirigée quelque part dans ce monde ou dans l'autre' (*CS* 88).[71] Creon may well believe he is honouring the gods in punishing dead Polynices who had intended to desecrate their temples, but he does not allow for their presence. When the Chorus suggests in the beginning that the gods may have been responsible for the burial of Polynices, Creon reacts with anger (*Ant.* 280 ff.). As Segal points out in his article '*Antigone*: Death and Love, Hades and Dionysus', it remains ambivalent whether Antigone performs the first burial or whether this is done by the gods.[72] The sandstorm accompanying Antigone at her 'second' attempt to bury Polynices could be a merely natural phenomenon, but its suddenness and strength at such a moment might well appear to the ancient Greeks as a divine sign.[73] But Creon 'defies augury' and even responds to the seer Tiresias' warning with a sacrilegious remark: 'But you shall not hide him in the grave, even if Zeus' eagles should snatch the body and bear the carrion up to their master's throne!' (*Ant.* 1039–41).[74] He thereby blasphemes against the very gods he claims to be honouring, namely the Olympians, while Antigone reveres the deities of the underworld.[75]

---

[69] Bowra 1944: 72–3.   [70] Nussbaum 2001: 55–6.
[71] 'One has only the choice between God and idolatry. There is no other possibility. For the faculty of worship is in us, and it is either directed somewhere into this world, or into the other' (*FLN* 138). Thus also 'tout athée est idolâtre' ('every atheist is an idolater') (*CS* 276/*FLN* 308).
[72] Segal 1990: 170–1.   [73] Steiner 1984: 224–5.
[74] For an analysis of the sacrilege, see Segal 1990: 169.   [75] Knox 1964: 99 ff.

As Simone Fraisse mentions in her article 'Simone Weil et la tragédie grecque', Weil chooses to disregard this distinction.[76] Weil writes: 'Le Dieu qui est présent à cette tragédie n'est pas conçu comme étant dans les cieux, mais sous terre, parmi les morts. Mais cela revient au même. Il s'agit toujours du vrai Dieu, du Dieu qui est dans l'autre monde' (*IPC* 18).[77] Antigone alone is serving the true God whether he be situated in the lower or the upper world, while Creon only claims to be doing so. In reality he is serving his idol, the state. For idols are 'des biens relatifs pensés comme biens hors de toute relation' (*OC* vi/2. 151).[78] Idols made of stone or wood are not really dangerous, for the real crime of idolatry is always committed towards the state or something analogous (*E* 103).[79]

In her sixth *Cahier*, written from the end of 1941 to the beginning of 1942, Weil comments on the passage of St Paul's letter to the Hebrews concerning faith which 'prove[s] the existence of realities that are unseen' (Heb. 11: 1): 'Il n'y a pas de justice sans foi, et la foi est la croyance aux choses invisibles' (*OC* vi/2. 299).[80] Applied to Creon, this would mean that his injustice is due to his lack of faith. He cannot believe that the gods Antigone claims to be obeying—or God, as Weil would put it—really exist to the extent that they would require obedience. The supernatural is not present to him in the same manner as it is to Antigone. From Weil's note, one must infer that justice is supernatural not only in requiring *caritas*, but also in requiring faith, for 'il n'y a pas de justice sans foi' (ibid.). French, Greek, and Hebrew do not distinguish between the legal notion of justice and the moral concept of righteousness as English does. But Weil makes it clear that the first cannot exist without the second. Legal justice depends on moral righteousness, which in its turn hinges on love and faith. The secular is thus rooted in the sacred, and ultimately the secular is either transformed by the sacred or tries to abolish it.

---

[76] Fraisse 1982*a*: 196.

[77] 'The god who presides over this tragedy is not known as being in heaven, but beneath the earth. It comes to the same thing. It is always to the true God, the God who is in the other world, that reference is made' (*IC*: 9). Similarly in his article 'Polis und Hades in der Antigone des Sophokles' Bultmann says that in terms of the conflict between Creon, who does not really respect the gods and Antigone, who does, there is no difference between Zeus and Hades (Bultmann 1967: 314).

[78] 'relative forms of good conceived as being totally unrelated forms of good' (*NB* 145).

[79] On the question of idolatry in Weil see J. P. Little's article 'Le Refus de l'idolâtrie dans l'œuvre de Simone Weil' (1979*a*), José-Maria Pacheco-Gonçalves 'Vrai Dieu, vraie foi, religion vraie selon Simone Weil' (2003: 167 ff.) and my article, 'Simone Weil's Critique of the Zeitgeist' (Cabaud Meaney 2003*b*).

[80] 'There is not justice without faith, and faith is the belief in invisible things.'

Creon's injustice does not only express itself in his outbursts of temper and rash condemnations, but also has epistemological consequences. For to be just means to admit continuously that others are different from what one 'reads' them to be, as Weil explains in her *Cahiers*: 'Justice. Être continuellement prêt à admettre qu'un autre est autre chose que ce qu'on lit quand il est là (ou qu'on pense de lui). Ou plutôt: lire, en lui, aussi (et continuellement) qu'il est certainement autre chose, peut-être tout autre chose, que ce qu'on y lit' (*OC* vi/1. 319).[81] Creon fails to do so at every moment: he believes the guard to be corrupt, Ismene to have helped her sister, Haemon to lack loyalty, and even accuses Tiresias of corruption. He sees in Polynices merely a traitor and not a nephew, and he never tries to understand Antigone. He cannot accept that people are different from what he believes them to be, because he lacks justice. For justice is one of the conditions for an adequate understanding of reality, and its absence leads to error and catastrophe, as the end of the tragedy shows.[82]

When Weil says justice, she clearly means love as well. 'L'amour est le regard de l'âme', she writes in 'Formes de l'amour implicite de Dieu' (*AD* 212).[83] Like the prisoners in Plato's cave allegory who stare at the shadows cast on the wall, human beings tend to look in one direction only. What frees them from their bonds and makes them dare to walk up the steep hill towards wisdom, is love for truth, the good, or beauty (*IPC* 85, 88). Thus 'l'amour voit l'invisible', which is hidden to the world (*AD* 136).[84] Strangely enough it is not so much the Platonic Ideas that Weil has in mind here, but the concrete existence of other people that love makes visible. For morally speaking, most people live in a Ptolemaic world, they perceive themselves as being the centre of the universe, and hardly acknowledge the existence of other people not connected by family bonds or friendship: 'Comme Dieu, étant hors de

---

[81] 'Justice. To be continually ready to admit that another person is something other than what we read when he is there (or when we think about him). Or rather: to read in him also (and continually) that he is certainly something other than what we read—perhaps something altogether different' (*NB* 43).

[82] 'Le don de la lecture est surnaturel, et sans ce don il n'y a pas de justice' (*OC* vi/2. 317) ('The gift of reading is supernatural, and without this gift there is no justice') (*NB* 220).

[83] 'Love is the soul's eye.' 'Il est impossible à l'homme d'exercer pleinement son intelligence *sans la charité*, parce qu'il n'y a pas d'autre source de lumière que Dieu' (*SG* 96) ('Man cannot exert his intelligence to the full *without charity*, because the only source of light is God') (*SNL* 104). Though Weil interprets Plato's thought here, this reflects her own ideas as well.

[84] 'Love sees what is invisible' (*WG* 92).

l'univers, en est en même temps réellement le centre, de même chaque homme a une situation imaginaire au centre du monde. L'illusion de la perspective le situe au centre de l'espace; une illusion pareille fausse en lui le sens du temps; et encore une autre illusion pareille dispose autour de lui toute la hiérarchie des valeurs' (ibid. 147; *IPC* 73–4, 135).[85] What limits the horizon for Weil is not the historicity of human beings, as Gadamer and Jauss would hold, but moral limitations. Thus when she reads history, it is with compassion as a hermeneutic key that she tries to unlock the door to truth. For compassion, she believes, breaks through the veils of grandeur and glory that the conquerors have woven around events. Roman victories seem glorious because they were written by the Romans themselves, but one needs to read between the lines to understand the horrors and crimes perpetrated (*E* 191–2).[86] Only love for the afflicted makes this possible.

Antigone feels compassion for her dead brother, and thus perceives more about him than Creon who looks at the world from an egoistic perspective.[87] Otherwise Creon would 'live and let live': 'Être heureux qu'il y ait des êtres pensants autres que soi; grâce essentielle. Désirer la mort d'un être humain, c'est refuser cette grâce (cf. Créon)', Weil writes in *Cahier* 3 (*OC* vi/1. 335; *IPC* 156).[88] Yet both Antigone and Creon seem locked into their points of view. How could Creon ever understand Antigone, and vice versa? Must it not remain *un dialogue de sourds* ('a deaf men's dialogue')? There is no universal way of perceiving reality, Weil admits, though tyrants would like to impose their world-view on the rest of humanity.[89] One cannot take on the other's perspective: 'Nul effort ne peut amener les uns à lire comme les autres', but 'un

---

[85] 'Just as God, being outside the universe, is at the same time the center, so each man imagines he is situated in the center of the world. The illusion of perspective places him at the center of space; an illusion of the same kind falsifies his idea of time; and yet another kindred illusion arranges a whole hierarchy of values around him' (*WG* 99).

[86] See also Fraisse's article 'Simone Weil contre les Romains' (1980).

[87] Thus, as Weil writes in 'Dieu dans Platon': 'L'usage de l'intelligence a pour condition l'amour surnaturel' ('the condition for using the intelligence is supernatural love') (*SG* 97/*SNL* 105).

[88] 'To be happy that there are thinking beings other than oneself; essential form of grace. To desire the death of a human being is to reject this form of grace (cf. Creon)' (*NB* 57).

[89] 'Forcer quelqu'un à se lire soi-même comme on le lit (esclavage). Forcer les autres à vous lire comme on se lit soi-même (conquête)' (*OC* vi/1. 319) ('To force somebody to read himself as you read him (slavery). To force others to read you as you read yourself (conquest)') (*NB* 43).

effort peut les amener tous à une troisième lecture, la même pour tous' (*OC* vi/1. 315)[90]

One should not try to perceive things exactly the way the other does, but attain a point of view from where everybody can see things in a similar manner. This sounds like a totalitarian position, but is in reality its very opposite, Weil would say. She is critical precisely of the tyrant's attempts to make others see the world as he does (*PG* 135–6; *OC* vi/1. 296). Weil wishes to offer an Archimedian point from which everyone will see things similarly. Archimedes just asked for one point of support to be able to lift the earth: 'Donne-moi un point d'appui, et je soulève le monde' (*OC* vi/3. 272, vi/1. 95, 462 n. 113).[91]

But what could this point be, which transcends the distorting limitations of subjectivity, be they temporal, spatial, or moral? Weil had the experience of such a point in her mystical encounters. She describes it thus in her famous letter to Père Perrin: 'Parfois les premiers mots [du Pater] déjà arrachent ma pensée à mon corps et la transportent en un lieu hors de l'espace d'où il n'y a *ni perspective ni point de vue*. L'espace s'ouvre. L'infinité de l'espace ordinaire de la perception est remplacée par une infinité à la deuxième ou quelquefois troisième puissance. [...] Parfois aussi [...] le Christ est présent en personne' (*AD* 48–9; my italics).[92] When God enters the soul, as she writes in 'L'Amour de Dieu et le malheur': 'L'espace s'ouvre devant nous comme un fruit qui se sépare en deux, car nous voyons l'univers d'un *point situé hors de l'espace*' (*PSO* 129; my italics).[93] Mysticism makes one see things *sub specie aeternitatis*, namely in the light of eternity without the distorting influences of passion or of the *Zeitgeist*. Instead of simply being carried along by events and one's personal interests, seeing things in terms of their eternal value puts them back into perspective: 'Pour échapper aux erreurs de perspective, le seul moyen est de choisir son trésor et de transporter son cœur hors de l'espace, hors du monde, en

---

[90] 'No amount of effort will enable the former to read in the same way as the latter', 'a joint effort can enable them all to arrive at a third reading, the same for all' (*NB* 39).
[91] 'Give me a fulcrum, and I will lift up the world' (ibid. 557).
[92] 'At times the very first words [of the Our Father] tear my thoughts from my body and transport it to a place outside space where there is neither perspective nor point of view. The infinity of the ordinary expanses of perception is replaced by an infinity to the second or sometimes the third degree. [...] Sometimes, also [...] Christ is present with me in person' (*WG* 29).
[93] 'space opens before us as the opening fruit of a plant divides in two, for we are seeing the universe from *a point situated outside space*' (*SNL* 197; my italics).

Dieu' (*IPC* 73).[94] Glory and success are then perceived in terms of their inherent limitations, while other persons become the centre of attention. Contrary to Protagoras' saying, God becomes the measure of all things instead of man, and God commands us to love our neighbour (*SG* 92). The supernatural perspective or 'discernement surnaturel', as Weil calls it a few times, far from shutting one up in an ivory tower, makes one engage in present concerns and care for others (*AD* 16; *OC* vi/2. 378).[95] In obeying the gods, Antigone cares about her brother's decaying body. Creon, on the other hand, sees things only from the limited point of view of the state. His natural perspective makes him hard-hearted to the people around him.

Their points of view are incommensurable. It is not only the difference between master and subject that makes it difficult for the one to see things from the other's perspective, as Weil had emphasized in *Entre Nous*, but that between two worlds. For Creon's condemnation shows that: 'ceux qui ont part seulement à l'amour et non à la haine appartiennent à un *autre monde* et n'ont à attendre de celui-ci que la mort violente' (*IPC* 19; my italics).[96] Antigone's world includes the supernatural while Creon's does not. Therefore he cannot understand her motivations. The supernatural and the natural in the sense of *pesanteur* directly oppose each other. Either the supernatural transforms and redeems sin, or sin tries to eliminate the supernatural. There is no neutral realm where both could happily coexist, for the mediocre part of the soul cannot stand the pure and holy, since they cause its death (*AD* 166–7, 190–1). Rather than dying to self, it will prefer to eliminate the challenge.

---

[94] 'To escape from the errors of a false perspective the only way is to choose one's treasure and to carry one's heart beyond space, and beyond the world, to God' (*IC* 134). 'Justice surnaturelle, opération analogue à celle qui surmonte la perspective. Pas de centre dans le monde, seulement hors du monde. Renoncer par amour pour Dieu au pouvoir illusoire qu'il nous laisse de dire "Je suis"' (*CS* 31/*OC* vi/3. 402) ('Supernatural justice, an operation analogous to the overcoming of perspective. No centre anywhere in the world, only outside the world. Through love of God, to renounce the illusory power he has left to us of saying "I am"') (*FLN* 87). See also *IPC* 137.

[95] The use of the term 'supernatural perspective' should not lead to the impression that I agree with Winch's idea in *Simone Weil: 'The Just Balance'* that the supernatural is for Weil but a way of thinking of earthly things (Winch 1989: 199–200). Winch fails to see that the supernatural is a reality for Weil. Winch's approach remains reductive, despite Allen and Springsted's attempt to defend Winch in their chapter 'Winch on Weil's Supernaturalism' in *Spirit, Nature, and Community* (Allen and Springsted 1994: 82 ff.).

[96] 'those who share only in love and not in hate belong to *another world* and have nothing to expect from this world but a violent death' (*IC*: 9; my italics).

This might explain Creon's hatred towards Antigone which otherwise appears strange.

But how does this fit in with Antigone's harsh temper? In the light of her irascibility, it seems difficult to agree with Weil that Antigone is 'un être parfaitement pur, parfaitement innocent, parfaitement héroïque' (*IPC* 19).[97] However, in her analysis of the Sophoclean *Electra*, Weil claims one of the effects of *malheur* is to become embittered (ibid. 16). This bitterness does not yet reflect in and of itself the person's lack of righteousness. Yet one may wonder whether a *folie d'amour* should not have rendered Antigone loving even towards her enemies, and especially towards her sister who eventually is willing to die with her. However, Antigone's harshness might be explained by her desire to save her sister, by showing to Creon that they did not collaborate. Whatever Antigone's character flaws are, she continues to be motivated by love until the end in spite of her fear of death (ibid. 19–20).

Christ inspires *caritas* and, according to Weil, is the Archimedian point or fulcrum offering the leverage by which one can lift oneself out of one's limited point of view by the means of the cross (ibid. 178–9).[98] This mystical hermeneutics, as I would call it, is not only accessible to the believer or the mystic in the strict sense. Though mysticism is for Weil a loving encounter with God, it includes many stages, implicit love of God being one of them. Love is not only a lens sharpening our sight, it is the very organ of sight: 'L'amour est le regard de l'âme' (*AD* 212).[99] We tend to give people we dislike a less sympathetic ear. It seems that the foundation of a fruitful dialogue demands at least respect, as a *conditio sine qua non*. This truism receives a new slant through Weil: real love, the one that moves mountains and makes one sacrifice one's life for one's friends, belongs to a different dimension of reality, and gives us access to that realm. The supernatural, however, is not simply

---

[97] 'a perfectly pure being, perfectly innocent, perfectly heroic' (ibid. 10).

[98] 'Ainsi la mystique doit fournir la clef de toutes les connaissances et de toutes les valeurs. [...] Le Christ est la clef' (*CS* 43) ('In the same way, mysticism should provide the key for all knowledge and all values. [...] Christ is the key') (*FLN* 98). ' "Donne-moi un point d'appui, et je soulèverai le monde." Ce point d'appui est la Croix. Il ne peut y en avoir d'autre. Il faut qu'il soit à l'intersection du monde et de ce qui n'est pas le monde. La Croix est cette intersection' (*OC* vi/3. 119–20) (' "Give me a fulcrum, and I will lift up the world." This fulcrum is the Cross. There can be none other. It has got to be at the point of intersection between the world and what is not the world. The Cross is this point of intersection') (*NB* 433). For an analysis of the epistemological relevance of suffering, see Ch. 6 on *Prometheus*.

[99] 'Love is the soul's eye.'

something superimposed on reality for Weil. Rather, it *is* reality and permeates the 'natural' world. A purely natural world is the one we have created through our lies. Creon lives in such a world, which he has built around his own self-importance.

Might this gulf between the natural and the supernatural perspective be the reason why one often cannot help feeling sympathy for Creon's position? Perhaps we are similarly affected by his worldly thinking and fail to see things from a supernatural perspective, something Weil suggests in 'La Personne et le sacré': 'Ce n'est pas nous qui pourrions lui donner tort, nous qui, en ce moment, pensons, parlons et agissons exactement comme lui' (*EL* 25).[100] If we readers of Sophocles' play are like Creon, then it will be indeed difficult for us to judge the two opposing characters.[101] We will be biased. But worse than that, Weil accuses us of hypocrisy. If we think that Antigone is obviously in the right, this is probably because we do not experience the conflict as being on our doorstep. Weil implies that in a modern-day conflict between Creon and Antigone, we would probably side with the former. This is a strange thought for someone who was working for the Free French Government, which would more likely than not be viewed as an Antigone-figure in contrast to the Creon-like Vichy-government. Yet it is precisely the officers working for the Free French whom Weil accuses of thinking within the narrow logic of natural justice, as pointed out earlier on. She implicitly parallels Creon to them, or more precisely, she identifies everybody with Creon who does not share Antigone's supernatural perspective, the Free French Government included (ibid. 50). So it is not enough for Weil that we agree with her. She demands that we agree with her for the right reasons. We need to feel the drama of the situation, and not assume hypocritically that we would have done the same as Antigone.[102]

---

[100] 'And we should be the last people to disagree with him; we who at this moment are thinking, talking, and behaving exactly as he did' (*SE* 20).

[101] This would explain the neo-Hegelian trend Brueck (1995: 78 ff.) describes in *The Redemption of Tragedy* which claims that both Antigone and Creon are right and wrong to different degrees, and have adopted limited points of view (of family and state) which should not be mutually exclusive.

[102] Thus, Weil writes in a letter to Jean Wahl in New York 1942, concerning those who condemn the people collaborating with the Vichy government: 'Or, la plupart des gens qui s'érigent en juges ici n'ont jamais eu l'occasion d'éprouver s'ils sont eux-mêmes des héros. J'ai horreur des attitudes faciles, injustes et fausses, surtout quand la pression de l'opinion générale semble les rendre presque obligatoires' (*CSW* 10/1: 3) ('Most of the people here, however, who set themselves up as judges have never had an opportunity

Instead of looking at the world through the distorting glasses of ideology, Weil's goal is a *non-lecture* ('non-reading'), which means restraining oneself from imposing one's perception and idolatrous desires on reality. 'Il s'agit de déraciner les lectures, de les changer, pour parvenir à la non-lecture', she writes in her *Cahiers* probably in February 1942 (*OC* vi/2. 436).[103] Earlier at the turn of the same year, an entry reads 'ne jugez pas, i.e. ne lisez pas',[104] which can be applied *par excellence* to Creon who fails to follow this advice (ibid. 292).[105] To let the text speak for itself, without approaching it through the lens of ideologies and critical theories, would have been, theoretically speaking, Weil's ideal. Whether she practised this herself is a different question.

This *non-lecture* is not easily achieved, however, since it requires death to self. To refrain from imposing a meaning on certain situations may be extremely difficult. There is nothing more tempting, for example, than to make somebody who is experiencing great suffering responsible for it after a while (*AD* 104). The advice Job gets from his well-meaning friends is an example. *Non-lecture*, on the contrary, means accepting the void, which remains if no explanation is provided or imposed, yet focusing with all one's attention on something one does not understand. To wait like the servants for their master in the Gospel, in a position of *attente*, is Weil's ideal in the intellectual as well as the moral realm (ibid. 193; *PSO* 37).[106] Critics are servants of the text and must wait for its meaning to disclose itself at any moment like a thief in the night.[107]

---

to find out if they themselves are heroes. I detest facile, unjust, and false attitudes, and especially when the pressure of public opinion seems to make them almost obligatory') (*SL* 159).

[103] 'It is a question of uprooting our readings of things, of changing them, so as to arrive at non-reading' (*NB* 312).

[104] 'Judge not, i.e. read not' (ibid. 201).

[105] 'Le point de vue est la racine de l'injustice' ('The fixed point of view is the root of injustice'), could also be applied to Creon (*CS* 234/*FLN* 270).

[106] 'Méthode pour comprendre les images, les symboles, etc. Non pas essayer de les interpréter, mais les regarder jusqu'à ce que la lumière jaillisse. [...] D'une manière générale: Méthode d'exercer l'intelligence, qui consiste à regarder' (*OC* vi/2. 458) ('A method is necessary for the understanding of images, symbols, etc. One should not try to interpret them, but contemplate them until their significance flashes upon one. [...] In a general way: a method for exercising the intelligence, which consists of beholding') (*NB* 334).

[107] Weil experienced this herself, when reading the Gospel: 'Il y a des passages de l'Evangile qui me choquaient autrefois et qui sont maintenant pour moi extrêmement lumineux. [...] Si je ne les avais pas lus et relus avec attention et amour, je n'aurais pu parvenir à cette vérité' (*AD* 249) ('There are some passages from the Gospel which shocked me formerly and which are for me now extremely luminous. [...] If I had not

In her essay 'Réflexions sur le bon usage des études scolaires en vue de l'amour de Dieu', she compares the right attitude to assume when faced with a particular intellectual question to 'la situation de l'âme qui, la lampe bien garnie d'huile, attend son époux avec confiance et désir' (*AD* 94–5).[108] Critics, it seems, must be mystics, servants of the text, prudent virgins waiting with their lamps for the logos of the text to disclose itself.

Ideally speaking, Creon should have adopted the supernatural perspective and not have issued his edict in the first place. Once issued, however, the obvious political dictum is that he cannot take back his word without undermining his newly acquired authority. Yet Weil manifestly believes he needs to take it back, if it is proved unjust. Whether Creon risks losing some of his authority or not, he still has to obey God. Perhaps it would not even have affected his political power. People might have respected him all the more. For if Haemon is telling the truth and not lying in order to save his fiancée, then the population is siding more with Antigone anyway (*Ant.* 690–700). In the end, condemning Antigone saves neither Creon's authority nor the *polis*, for his actions are condemned by the gods.[109]

However, one must not underestimate the difficulty of Creon's position. A contradiction appears between his duties towards his family (which he admittedly does not apprehend) and those towards the state. He needs to punish a traitor, yet he also has to bury a kinsman. In a certain sense, Antigone has duties only towards her family, while Creon is in charge of the city.[110] If he had honestly acknowledged this conflict, how could he have resolved it? Mystery and apparent contradiction are part of human life, according to Weil. Human beings are like 'des mouches collées au fond d'une bouteille, attirées par la lumière et incapables d'y aller' (*CS* 258).[111] At the beginning of *L'Enracinement*,

---

read and reread them with attention and love, I could not have reached that truth'). 'S'il y a vraiment désir, si l'objet du désir est vraiment la lumière, le désir de lumière produit la lumière' (*AD* 88). ('If there is a real desire, if the thing desired is really light, the desire for light produces it') (*WG* 93).

[108] 'the position of the soul, which, with its lamp well filled with oil, awaits the Bridegroom's coming with confidence and desire' (*SW* 97).

[109] Griffith 1999: 6 n. 21.

[110] Weil, by the way, saw the seriousness of disobeying the law. For example, she told her young friend Malou, charged with distributing the clandestine paper, *Témoignage chrétien*, that to disobey the law is very serious and should only be done after long reflection (Courtine-Denamy 2000: 158–9; Perrin 1984: 107–8).

[111] 'flies caught inside a bottle, attracted to the light and unable to go towards it' (*FLN* 292).

when analysing the *besoins de l'âme* (needs of the soul), Weil points out that contradictory obligations frustrate the soul's need for order. But whoever simplifies reality so as to avoid the problem 'a conclu en son cœur une alliance avec le crime' (*E* 15).[112] Is this not what Creon is doing? Faced with contradictory obligations, he should have contemplated the problem with *attention* until he could see what must be done: 'Si nous gardons sans cesse présente à l'esprit la pensée d'un ordre humain véritable [. . .] nous serons dans la situation d'un homme qui marche dans la nuit, sans guide, mais en pensant sans cesse à la direction qu'il veut suivre. Pour un tel voyageur, il y a une grande espérance' (ibid. 16).[113] If one lives in an attitude of *attente* towards God's will, one will eventually perceive current obligations. Antigone obeys God, and must therefore have adopted this attitude. Hence her decision to bury her brother is not a sign of one-sided concern for her family. She does not simplify reality like Creon, though she might appear to do so at first sight, but follows a divine command. This, at least, can be concluded from Weil's fragmentary interpretation as well as from her thoughts on morality and conflicting obligations.

Though Creon's decisions seem reasonable at first sight, his most serious mistake is failing to acknowledge the existence of the supernatural which breaks into the play at different moments, signalling him to look beyond his limited point of view. Dionysus is invoked at various times in the tragedy, and one may wonder whether it is not his presence that brings purification to the city in the end.[114] The Chorus asks Dionysus in the first *stasimon* to lead the procession in thanksgiving for the salvation of the city, and in the fifth *stasimon* entreats him to come and heal it (*Ant.* 153–4, 1115 ff.). When Dionysus does come, as we know from Euripides' *Bacchae*, death accompanies him. Might not the demise of Creon's son and wife be understood as retribution instigated by this god? Furthermore, after the guard's announcement of the first attempted burial, the Chorus suggests the gods may have done it (*Ant.* 278–9). As already mentioned, the sandstorm accompanying Antigone at her second attempt to bury Polynices seems numinous. And it is not clear who performed the first burial rites, Antigone or the gods.

---

[112] 'has, in his heart, made a compact with crime' (*NR* 10).
[113] 'If we keep ever-present in our minds the idea of a veritable human order [. . .] we shall be in a similar position to that of a man travelling, without a guide, through the night, but continually thinking of the direction he wishes to follow. Such a traveller's way is lit by a great hope' (ibid. 12). See also *OC* vi/3. 95, 97.
[114] Steiner 1984: 259–61.

Weil refers briefly to the presence of Dionysus in the *Antigone* in her *Cahiers*. She cites or alludes quite a few times to the fifth *stasimon* where Dionysus is asked to appear with his fire: 'Ô feu, chef du chœur des astres qui respirent [...] gardien des voix nocturnes... parais, roi, avec tes thyades qui toute la nuit en extase dansent. Iacchos ordonnateur' (*Ant.* 1146–52) (*OC* vi/3. 226/7, 231, 236; *IPC* 88–9).[115] Though she sees in him a Christ-figure, and admits that he is the 'inspirateur par excellence de toute la tragédie grecque', she does not use his 'epiphanies' as indication of a Christological revelation (*Œ* 669; *IPC* 56–7).[116] The supernatural law is valid without being buttressed by marvels, Weil would have thought, and Creon is punished through the consequences of his own pride rather than through a *deus ex machina*.

FATE AND MALEDICTION

'Those who live by the sword, shall die by the sword.' This summarizes Weil's understanding of fate in Greek tragedy: 'On a très mal compris ce qu'on nomme la fatalité dans la tragédie grecque. Il n'y a pas de fatalité mais cette conception de la malédiction qui, une fois produite par un crime, est transmise par les hommes les uns aux autres, et ne peut être détruite que par la souffrance d'une victime pure, obéissante à Dieu' (*IPC* 20).[117] The question of fate in Greek literature is a difficult one. It is hard to determine from case to case what the responsibility of the persons in question is, the ways in which their character shapes their destiny, what part the gods or simply blind fate have in the sufferings befalling human beings. In her article on the *Iliad*, Weil at least points out this complexity, but with the *Antigone* she focuses on one aspect of fate only (*OC* ii/3. 251–2). Fate, she believes, is nothing else than the consequence of sin, which is essentially self-perpetuating. When one has been hurt by somebody stronger than oneself, the natural reaction is to vent one's pain by hurting someone else. To abstain from acting thus means bearing the pain of the injustice without alleviation.

---

[115] 'O fire, leader of the chorus of stars which breathe [...] guardian of nocturnal voices... manifest thyself, O King, with thy train of Thyiads who all night dance in frenzy, praising Iacchus, the Distributor' (*NB* 525).

[116] 'inspirer *par excellence* of all Greek tragedy'.

[117] 'What is called Fate in Greek tragedy has been very badly misunderstood. There is no such agency apart from this conception of the curse, which, once produced by a crime, is handed down by men from one to another and cannot be destroyed except by the suffering of a pure victim obedient to God' (*IC* 10).

It takes *caritas* or *pureté* to do so. Only a victim who is perfectly pure, an *être pur*, as Weil calls it, is able to stop the *perpetuum mobile* of sin, since 'seule la pureté parfaite ne peut pas être souillée' (*AD* 186).[118] Those who are not wholly pure will reach their natural limits and react with revolt or resentment. It takes perfect love to bear the unbearable: 'Celui qui reçoit et transmet la malédiction ne la laisse pas pénétrer au centre de lui-même. Il ne la sent pas. Celui sur qui elle s'arrête, celui qui l'arrête, celui-là, elle pénètre au centre de lui. Il devient malédiction. Il faut être pur pour devenir malédiction' (*CS* 13/*OC* vi/3. 382).[119] Those who do not stop the ongoing dynamics of sin, but pass it on, are not fully affected by it (*OC* vi/3. 206). Instead of feeling the full brunt of the injustices perpetrated against them, they expel the pain by inflicting it on someone else. The *être pur* on the contrary comes to bear its crushing weight without becoming sinful herself (ibid. 275).[120]

Only God become man, can achieve this, Weil claims. She writes in her *Connaissance* that God himself cannot be affected by our sins, for 'toute offense dirigée directement contre Lui [Dieu le Père] retombe sur l'offenseur sous forme de malédiction' (*CS* 106).[121] Therefore God has to become man to destroy evil by suffering it.

Yet, one may wonder whether Antigone is really such an *être pur* who stops the malediction transmitted from generation to generation, as Weil claims (*IPC* 20; *OC* vi/3. 275–6). The curse resting on her family is well known: her father Oedipus kills his own father and marries his mother. Thus Antigone is born out of an incestuous relationship, as are her sister and her two brothers, who kill each other the day before the play starts.[122] But rather than bringing the malediction to an end, Antigone seems to be perpetuating it. Because of her importunate intervention, she is condemned to death, in consequence of which

---

[118] 'Perfect purity alone cannot be defiled' (*WG* 124).
[119] 'The man who receives and transmits malediction does not let it penetrate to his core. He does not feel it. But it penetrates to the core of the man upon whom it settles, the man who arrests it. He becomes a curse. To become a curse, it is necessary to be pure' (*FLN* 69).
[120] There is only this alternative: 'Quiconque prend l'épée périra par l'épée. Et quiconque ne prend pas l'épée (ou la lâche) périra sur la croix' (*OC* vi/2. 327) ('Everyone that taketh up the sword shall perish by the sword. And everyone that taketh not up the sword (or lets it drop) shall perish on the Cross') (*NB* 229).
[121] 'every offence committed directly against Him falls back upon the offender as a curse' (*FLN* 153).
[122] As early as about 1935 Weil wrote in her *Cahiers* about Antigone: 'sa naissance est impure, mais sa piété est pure' ('her birth is impure, but her piety is pure') (*OC* vi/1. 121/*FLN* 49).

Haemon kills himself as does his mother. Creon is a crushed man, and it is difficult to imagine much happiness for Ismene. However, were it not for Creon's stubbornness in the face of warnings, human and divine, these calamities would not have occurred. Antigone was simply obeying the gods.

Granted that Creon is full of hubris and that he brings about these disasters, is it really Antigone who stops him? Creon has only contempt for Antigone, and is persuaded neither by the Chorus, nor by Haemon, nor by the seer Tiresias. Only after Tiresias' departure, he quickly and anti-climactically changes his mind (*Ant.* 1095 ff.). But the *être pur* is not defined by her capacity to convert the evil-doer anyway (though that may happen as well), but by absorbing evil without passing it on to others. Antigone is a challenge to the path of compromise chosen by Ismene and by the Chorus, and to the idolatry of Creon. Given that Creon is a tyrant, anything could have provoked his hubris to express itself in a destructive way. Antigone, one could claim, just defied him early on, and bore the brunt of his irate pride. In the end, Creon has learnt his lesson. He admits his folly. If it is true that 'l'idolâtrie est une armure; elle empêche la douleur d'entrer dans l'âme', Creon's suit of armour is shattered by the end of the drama (*E* 193).[123] Had Antigone not stood firm, this would perhaps never have occurred.

Yet this does not prevent her from being afraid of death: 'Au moment de l'approche imminente de la mort, la nature en elle défaille et elle se sent abandonnée des hommes et des dieux', Weil writes in her *Intuitions* (*IPC* 19–20).[124] In her famous *kommos*, her death-song, Antigone laments the fact that she is going to death unwedded and unlamented. But rather than diminishing her virtue and courage, this, in Weil's eyes, likens her to Christ. For: '[Le Christ] n'est-il pas allé au supplice dans la joie, mais dans la défaillance de toutes les forces de l'âme, après avoir vainement supplié son Père de l'épargner et avoir vainement demandé à des hommes de le consoler' (ibid. 78).[125] She even wonders in which way she displeased the gods to be punished thus (*Ant.* 921 ff.). This feeling of guilt is natural for someone who feels cast out by gods and men (*Ant.* 923 ff.). The lamb who carries the sin of the people is a

---

[123] 'Idolatry is an armour, prevents pain from entering the soul' (*NR* 224).
[124] 'At the moment when imminent death approaches her[,] her nature betrays her, she feels herself abandoned by men and by the gods' (*IC* 10).
[125] '[Christ] did not go to his martyrdom in joy, but in a swoon of all the powers of the soul, after having vainly implored his Father to spare him and having vainly asked men to console him' (*IC* 138).

'man of sorrows, familiar with suffering' as Isaiah says (Isa. 53: 3). By definition the Passion implies the shameful death of a criminal rather than the heroic sacrifice of one's life for a noble cause (*IPC* 78). Thus Weil sees Antigone as a Christological figure.[126]

SIMONE WEIL AS ANTIGONE

Hence by comparing herself to Antigone, as she liked to do, Weil reveals her desire for a sacrificial, Christlike death.[127] When asking for a post with the Free French, she wrote to Maurice Schumann from New York that she eventually needed a task 'comportant [...] un degré élevé de souffrance et de danger' otherwise she would be paralysed by grief.[128] This, she claims, is not just a question of character, but also part of her vocation (*EL* 200). Like Antigone, one might add, she needs to become a scapegoat, as she writes to him in a letter from London: 'Vous comprenez de cette manière pourquoi la proposition que je vous avais faite—celle du bouc émissaire—est facile pour moi. Elle n'implique rien de plus que ce qui m'était impérieusement imposé de toutes manières' (ibid. 208).[129] She had come to London with the hope of being sent on a no-return mission to France, or at least of pushing through her project of front-line nurses who would give first aid to wounded soldiers. Thus soldiers could be saved, and the presence

---

[126] Weil lists her as a Christ-figure along with Prometheus, Orestes, and Dionysus (*CS* 290–1).

[127] For example in her letters to her parents from 16 Dec. 1942 and 15 June 1943, she refers to herself as Antigone (*EL* 218, 243). Fraisse claims that 'chez ses proches, l'identification semble même être devenue une habitude familière' ('among those close to her the identification seems even to have become a customary habit') (Fraisse 1982*a* 195). Ann Loades suggests in her article 'Simone Weil and Antigone: Innocence and Affliction' that Weil used Antigone as a self-confessional mask (Loades 1993: 278).

[128] 'involving a high degree of hardship and danger' (*SL* 157).

[129] 'In this way you can understand that the proposition I put to you—the proposition of the scapegoat—is an easy one for me. It implies nothing more than was incumbent on me in any case' (ibid. 174). Yet Weil was not a masochist: 'On ne s'inflige jamais le malheur, ni par amour, ni par perversité. Tout au plus peut-on, sous l'une ou l'autre inspiration, faire distraitement et comme à son propre insu deux ou trois pas, qui mènent au point glissant où l'on devient la proie de la pesanteur et d'où l'on tombe sur des pierres qui cassent les reins' (*IPC* 148) ('No one ever inflicts disaster on himself, neither out of love nor perversity. At the most one can, under one or the other inspiration, take distractedly and as if unconsciously two or three steps leading to the slippery point where one becomes a prey to gravity and from which one falls on stones that break one's back') (*IC* 183).

of these nurses would give courage to all at the Front. Furthermore, the heroic love of those nurses would be a powerful symbol opposing the Nazi ideology, as she argues in her 'Projet d'une formation d'infirmières de première ligne' ('Plan for an Organization of Front-Line Nurses'/*SL*) (ibid. 190 ff.). But when her plans did not find approval, she plunged into despair. However, her desire for sacrifice could not be stifled, and she continued with her strict diet, not wanting to eat more than she assumed the French in the occupied zone could procure themselves. This together with her tuberculosis ended her life.

In another letter of 4 August 1943 to her parents she speaks about herself in terms that remind one of Antigone. When seeing *King Lear* in England, she suddenly realized the tragic character of the fools in Shakespeare. They alone tell the truth, yet they are not in a position to be taken seriously. Similarly, one might add, Antigone is treated as a fool. Weil continues: 'Darling M. [Mime, her mother], sens-tu l'affinité, l'analogie essentielle entre ces fous et moi—malgré l'Ecole, l'agrégation et les éloges de mon "intelligence"?' (ibid. 256).[130] One does not call her a fool. On the contrary, one praises her for her intelligence, but this is only a way to avoid the question of whether she is speaking the truth or not. But 'combien j'aimerais mieux leur étiquette!' (ibid.).[131] Her time with the Free French Government was painful to her for these reasons. Her paradoxical spiritual writings were not appreciated in London.

Yet Antigone's attitude turns out to be just. Her folly of love is what the world needs, then and especially when Weil was writing. For as Weil states in 'Luttons-nous pour la justice?': 'Il doit y avoir quelquefois des moments où, du point de vue de la raison terrestre, la folie d'amour seule est raisonnable. Ces moments ne peuvent être que ceux où, comme aujourd'hui, l'humanité est devenue folle à force de manquer d'amour' (ibid. 57).[132] For when there is no love in the world, a different kind of madness arises, namely one of slaughter, war, and genocide. Is this not the madness which strikes Creon because of his hubris? Thus 'la foi est plus réaliste que la politique réaliste',

---

[130] 'Darling M., do you feel the affinity, the essential analogy between these fools and me—in spite of the Ecole and the examination successes and the eulogies of my "intelligence"?' (*SL* 201).
[131] 'How much I would prefer their label!' (ibid.).
[132] 'There must sometimes be moments when, from the point of view of earthly reason, only the madness of love is reasonable. Such moments can only be those when, as today, mankind has become mad from want of love' (*SW* 130).

as Weil states in *L'Enracinement* (*E* 182).[133] Therefore the world needs people like herself, she might say, to remind them of the really important things—the *unum necessarium*—even if tragically one does not listen to them. One may wonder what impact Weil thought her writings could have. She did not write something for the *grand public*, and the number of her readers was rather restricted. Yet, potentially speaking, her writings were going to have a significant influence. Though she writes texts such as 'La Personne et le sacré' and 'Luttons-nous' 'only' for the Free French, the latter were already having some influence on the Resistance and more so in France in the years after the war. Thus by having an impact on them, by disclosing the reality of the supernatural and its rationality, and by suggesting a folly of love as a remedy against the world's evils, she was perhaps hoping to have a wider impact eventually.[134] She obviously did not just want to present some new ideas, but to bring about a change of heart, to make her readers burn with the folly of love, which one day might set the whole country on fire. For example, she writes in 'Cette guerre est une guerre de religions': 'Si une foi surgissait sur ce continent misérable, la victoire serait rapide, sûre et solide. Cela est évident même sur le plan stratégique. [...] Les communications ennemies se font parmi des populations opprimées, et deviendraient impossibles si l'incendie d'une véritable foi se propageait sur tout ce territoire' (*EL* 107).[135]

Similarly Weil wrote her *Intuitions* for a purpose, namely for the lecture-series Perrin organized in the crypt of the Dominican monastery. She bequeathed him the manuscript, before leaving for the United States, so that he might use it in the future. The same holds true for her *Cahiers*, which she gave to Thibon. Though Weil had not thought of publishing them in this format herself, she made her entries with

---

[133] 'Faith is more realist than is realist policy' (*NR* 211).

[134] Immediate success was not something she was expecting anyway, for the good works act like yeast, slowly and unobserved. Their method is obviously different from Hitler's: 'Il [Hitler] joue pour le mal; sa matière est la masse, la pâte. Nous jouons pour le bien, notre matière est le levain. Les procédés doivent différer en conséquence' (*EL* 108) ('He hopes for the triumph of evil; his material is the mass, the dough. We hope for the triumph of good; our material is the yeast. The difference of material calls for different methods') (*SE* 218).

[135] 'If a faith were to arise in this unhappy continent, victory would be rapid, certain, and secure. That is obvious even on the strategic level. Our line of communication is the sea, and can be defended by submarines, whereas the enemy's communications are on land, among the oppressed peoples, and they would be destroyed if all the land were set ablaze by a true faith' (*SE* 218).

the idea of perhaps using them for future articles and books. It is also significant, as Thibon points out, that Weil gave her writings to two Catholics who, she knew, would not deny their faith when making use of her ideas.[136] It is important to keep all of this in mind, for it would be impossible to speak of apologetic purposes in Weil if she did not intend her texts to be read or her ideas to be transmitted in some manner.

CONCLUSION

Though Weil's interpretation is anachronistic, I believe it is a more adequate appropriation than might appear at first sight. One cannot fully reconstitute what the gods meant for the Greeks nor to what extent the audience perceived the presence of the gods in tragedy with 'selective credulity' and 'suspended disbelief'.[137] One may therefore wonder whether Weil's Christological appropriation is not more accessible to modern man than the Greek divinities who are clouded in past and mystery. If the supernatural is central to this tragedy, would not a Christian interpretation do more to bring the text back to life than a historical one that will not be able to avoid anachronisms either? Apologetically speaking, Weil's reading seems successful. She brings the classic back to life, at the same time shedding new light on Christian concepts that are perhaps viewed with contempt because of their familiarity: the moral law, love and justice, sin and fate, and also the supernatural perspective (traditionally called *sub specie aeternitatis*) are presented in a new manner. At the same time, Weil's understanding of the moral law as supernatural, of Antigone's madness consisting of a *folie d'amour,* and fate being the consequence of sin are Weil's special slants among interpretative approaches.[138] One could add that Weil's reading allows for Antigone's fear of death without diminishing her heroism. By comparing Antigone's agony to that of Christ, Weil paradoxically allows her to be fully human and to express her all too human terrors

---

[136] Perrin and Thibon 1967: 17–18. Weil writes to Thibon from Casablanca: 'Elles [les pensées contenues dans les *Cahiers*] vous appartiennent donc, et j'espère qu'après avoir subi en vous une transmutation elles sortiront un jour dans un de vos ouvrages' (*CSW* 4/4: 196) ('They [the thoughts contained in the *Notebooks*] belong to you therefore, and I hope that after having undergone a transmutation in you they will one day appear in one of your works').

[137] Steiner 1984: 221.   [138] Fraisse 1982a: 197

while staying heroically obedient to the gods.[139] One should not forget, however, that Weil's interpretation remains fragmentary. Her compact analysis only reveals its full depth in the light of her other writings. But at the same time her reading of *Antigone* condenses many of her ideas, and thus becomes a powerful means of conveying these concepts in a striking and abbreviated form to her audience.

Weil's interpretation of *Antigone* has not only begun to give us a certain sense of her manner of reading, but could be taken as a paradigm for her whole approach to literature. If critics do not adopt Antigone's supernatural point of view, they will fail to understand great works of art. Thus they might get sucked into Creon's narrow world-view and believe that he has a point, when in reality obstinacy and pride are his driving motivations. Instead, critics should approach the text without preconceived ideas and adopt a mystical hermeneutics, which lets the 'other' break through the boundaries of theory.[140] For Weil herself, literature and mysticism became tightly interlinked. It was when reciting George Herbert's poem 'Love' that the borders between the natural and the supernatural started shifting: 'Je croyais le réciter seulement comme un beau poème, mais à mon insu cette récitation avait la vertu d'une prière' (*AD* 44).[141] Literature turned into prayer; and it was prayer that led to the mystical experience which gave her the appropriate vantage-point to understand texts adequately, namely a place outside space 'd'où il n'y a ni perspective ni point de vue' (ibid. 48).[142] The supernatural is part of reality; therefore acknowledging its presence is an epistemological necessity while disavowing it distorts one's perception.

Weil's understanding of the supernatural is radical in many ways. In its demands, its lack of compromise, and its relationship to the human world, the supernatural does not provide easy answers or consolation. Antigone has to obey the supernatural moral law even though it means her death and does not particularly provide comfort in her agony. It

---

[139] *IPC* 19–20, 78; Brueck 1995: 90–1. Thus Steiner's omission of Weil's interpretation in his book *Antigones*, as well as his dismissal of Ann Loades's claim that Weil had something new to say, does not seem justified (Steiner 1996*a*: 176).

[140] Though Brueck in *The Redemption of Tragedy* presents Weil's approach to literature as being supernaturalist, she does not present her interpretation of *Antigone* as being the paradigm of her ideas on literature, nor does she focus on Weil's ideas on the supernatural perspective (Brueck 1995: 1 ff.).

[141] 'I used to think I was merely reciting it as a beautiful poem, but without my knowing it the recitation had the virtue of a prayer' (*WG* 27).

[142] 'where there is neither perspective nor point of view' (ibid. 29).

does not promise security. Creon, on the other hand, believes he has everything under control. He uses the well-known metaphor of the ship to describe the *polis* (*Ant.* 188–91). But rather than claiming that Antigone needs to be sacrificed to the common good, he claims that there is no justice or piety outside the city-ship, as Nussbaum points out.[143] In contrast, Weil compares the human situation to one of shipwreck. There is no security, only a false sense of security, since all human beings are at the mercy of necessity. Thus, one could add, Creon fools himself with his sense of self-sufficiency which is soon shattered:

Nous sommes comme des naufragés accrochés à des planches sur la mer et ballottés d'une manière entièrement passive par tous les mouvements des flots. Du haut du ciel Dieu lance à chacun une corde. Celui qui saisit la corde et ne la lâche pas malgré la douleur et la peur, reste autant que les autres soumis aux poussées des vagues; seulement ces poussées se combinent avec la tension de la corde pour former un ensemble mécanique différent. (*IPC* 162–3; *CS* 26/*OC* vi/3. 396–7)[144]

The supernatural does not guarantee safety, but its presence changes the world: 'Seul ce qui vient du ciel est susceptible d'imprimer réellement une marque sur la terre' (*EL* 30; *IPC* 163).[145] How Weil tries to make the supernatural more present and transform the world, will unfold in the course of the next chapters.

---

[143] Nussbaum 2001: 58–9.

[144] 'We are like shipwrecked persons clinging to logs upon the sea and tossed in an entirely passive manner by every movement of the waves. From the height of heaven God throws each one a rope. He who seizes the rope and does not let go, despite the pain and the fear, remains as much as the others subject to the buffeting of the waves; only for him these buffets combine with the tension of the cord to form a different mechanical whole' (*IC* 194).

[145] 'It is only what comes from heaven that can make a real impress on the earth' (*SE* 23).

5

Tableau de l'absence de Dieu—A Modern Interpretation of the *Iliad*

> Faire de toute chose un intermédiaire vers Dieu [. . .] Cela ne veut pas dire ajouter Dieu à toute chose [. . .] Chaque chose doit être élaborée pour être changée afin d'être rendue transparente à la lumière.[1]
>
> (*OC* vi/2. 454)

To answer one of the most pertinent questions of her time, namely the reasons for war, Weil turns again to the classics, this time to the *Iliad*.[2] In the face of destruction and battle, Weil looks at their ancient poetic depiction. Though many know the epic, 'une sorte de fatalité nous fait lire sans comprendre' (*OC* ii/3. 50).[3] This may be the time when its true meaning can be understood anew, since the French are about to experience a fate similar to that of the Trojans. In spite of Weil's fear of the suffering that awaits her countrymen, she also sees the possibilities of awakening and conversion that war offers. War reveals certain truths concerning evil that need to be grasped, as she writes in *La Connaissance surnaturelle*: 'Dans la guerre, il faut lire les vérités surnaturelles qui concernent le mal' (*CS* 126).[4] These truths concern the nature of *force*, destiny, the perception of one's enemy, the dynamic of war and its causes. These themes will be examined in detail in this chapter, as well as the reason why Weil calls them supernatural.

---

[1] '[Turning] everything into an intermediary leading toward God [. . .] This does not mean adding God on to everything [. . .] But each thing must be wrought upon to bring about a change so that it may be made transparent to the light' (*NB* 328).
[2] *OC* vi/3. 90.
[3] 'by a sort of [fatality] [. . .], we read it without understanding' (*SE* 155).
[4] 'In war, one should read the supernatural truths concerning evil' (*FLN* 173).

Weil's 1938–9 article 'L'*Iliade* ou le poème de la force' is perhaps the best known of all her writings on ancient classical texts.[5] It is certainly the most complete of her interpretations, and it is among the articles she most reworked.[6] In an earlier text from 1937 'Ne recommençons pas la guerre de Troie', Weil uses the theme of Troy to defend pacifism. Though this piece is not about the epic itself, it is interesting as a contrast to her later explanation of war, and reveals her ideas at the time on the role and responsibility of intellectuals.

In terms of her apologetic intentions, this chapter will look at Weil's use of the epic to prepare her readers for war, *malheur*, and death, so that they may be made aware of the true nature of these realities and put their knowledge to good use. For as she writes in 'L'Amour de Dieu et le malheur': 'D'autre part, à une époque comme la nôtre, où le malheur est suspendu sur tous, le secours apporté aux âmes n'est efficace que s'il va jusqu'à les préparer réellement au malheur' (*AD* 103).[7] Without directly introducing Christianity (except at the end of her article on the *Iliad*), she gives a Christian view of a world lacking redemption, thus underlining its necessity. Without calling for conversion, she prepares the way for it. Instead of letting affliction purposelessly crush human beings, as so often happens, she tries to make use of its potential, which is to awaken them from their dream world, this being the first step on the path towards truth (ML 350–1; *EL* 108). By disclosing these realities, the intellectual—and thus Weil—has a significant role to play in the renewal of civilization.

CHRONOLOGY AND QUOTATIONS

Simone Weil got to know the *Iliad* in depth at Henri IV, for the epic was one of the texts studied with Alain in 1926–7.[8] She read the *Iliad* again when interrupting her teaching for health reasons in January 1938.[9]

---

[5] The classicist MacLeod (1982: 1 n. 1). wrote: 'I know of no better brief account of the *Iliad* than this.' He admits his indebtedness to Weil 'as regards the spirit of the *Iliad* as a whole'.

[6] *OC* ii/3. 308.

[7] 'On the other hand, in a time such as ours, where affliction is hanging over us all, help given to souls is effective only if it goes far enough really to prepare them for affliction' (*WG* 70).

[8] SP i. 79.

[9] Ibid. ii. 216–17. Though Weil mentions the *Odyssey* here and there, and even has it sent to her from Paris when in Marseille, she always seems to have preferred the *Iliad*

In the appendix to vol. ii, pt. 3 of her complete works, there is an excellent article by the editor Simone Fraisse on the genesis of 'L'*Iliade* ou le poème de la force' (*OC* ii/3. 301–3). It is not clear when Weil first had the idea for the piece, probably in 1936 when envisaging a series of articles for *Entre Nous*, after her successful essay on *Antigone* (*CO* 154). On the page where she had written the 'Plaintes d'Électre' for her article on the Sophoclean tragedy, she sketched in the margins the plan for an article on the *Iliad* with the name of the epic featuring as the title. It is divided into six points: 'la guerre' ('war'), 'les horreurs de la guerre' ('the horrors of war'), 'l'âme du guerrier. Achille' ('the soul of the warrior. Achilles'), 'Hector', 'Priam', and 'Philosophie de la vie humaine' ('Philosophy of human life'). As the editor points out, Weil does not use the terms *force* and *chose* (thing), which were going to become key concepts in her later article and which can be found in the class-notes taken by a student from Saint-Quentin in autumn 1937 (*OC* ii/3. 305). Thus this plan must predate her time in Saint-Quentin. Interestingly, Weil intends to concentrate on the nature of war as the two first points indicate, and only then turns her attention to three key figures of the epic, before concluding with a philosophy of human life. Though an equal number of points were supposed to be dedicated to specific figures in the epic and to more general areas, the latter are perhaps significant, given that they frame the projected article.

Probably between 1937 and 1938 Weil translated parts of the *Iliad*, mainly for her friend Posternak who did not know Greek (Œ 648 ff.; *CSW* 10/2: 117 ff.). The number of her translations, striking for their beauty, is astonishing, as is the fact that she did not send most of them.[10] Weil translated mainly the goodbye scene between Hector and Andromache (6. 410–65); the encounter between Achilles and

---

(*OC* vi/1. 208) (for references to the *Odyssey*, see for example *OC* vi/2. 105, 252; *AD* 171; *CS* 128). In contrast, she disliked Virgil's *Aeneid*, for: 'le pieux héros du doux Virgile est représenté plus d'une fois tuant un ennemi désarmé qui implore la vie, et sans prononcer les paroles qui rendent même une scène de ce genre admirable dans l'*Iliade*' (*OC* ii/3. 199) ('the gentle Virgil's pious Aeneas is more than once shown killing a disarmed enemy who begs for life, and without speaking any of those words which, in the *Iliad*, make even a scene of this kind admirable') (*SE* 120). Furthermore, she accuses Virgil of having sold his art to Augustus (*E* 198–9).

[10] The quality and especially the exactness of a translation were very important for Weil (Œ 648 n. 9). In a note at the beginning of her article she points out that each line translates a Greek verse, that the order of words and enjambments were respected as much as possible (*OC* ii/3. 227). Furthermore, in her second letter to Posternak she criticizes the new translation of the *Iliad* published by Budé, because it fails to render the energy present in the language (Œ 656). Because of their exactness and beauty, Weil's

his mother Thetis (18. 79–126); the cries of Briseis over the body of Patroclus (19. 282–302); Lycaon unsuccessfully begging Achilles for his life (21. 35–53, 64–119); Andromache's sorrow over her husband's death (24. 725–45); and Priam's visit to Achilles (24. 477 ff.). Among those scenes she concentrates on certain elements, quoting them frequently: she often mentions the passage on Niobe who had to think about eating even after her children had died (24. 602–13); she also refers a few times to the way Hector's corpse is dragged behind the chariot (22. 401–4); or she points out that Hector is killed 'loin des bains chauds' (22. 442–6).[11] Furthermore she translates certain short sections repeatedly: the loneliness of Bellerophon (6. 200–3); the corpses, which are dearer to the vultures than to their wives (11. 158–62); the passage that identifies a change in battle fortunes as the time of day when a woodcutter prepares his meal after working (11. 84–90). She often augments the translations prepared for her friends with short commentaries.

In her lessons on the *Iliad* at Saint-Quentin she discussed the nature of *force*, even distinguishing between various kinds. The second sentence of the notes taken by a student contains the later title of her article: 'Iliade est le poême qui célèbre la force.'[12] In her *Cahier* I—probably a later entry from 1937—she writes how *force* turns man into a thing, something repeatedly described in the *Iliad*.[13] 'Homère—*Iliade*' features as title to the one and a half pages she dedicates to the theme in this *Cahier*, mentioning some of her favourite quotes, which were going to appear in her article (*OC* vi/1. 83–4).[14]

Perhaps as early as 1938 and certainly by 1939 Weil was working on her article, first entitled 'L'*Iliade* ou la philosophie de la force', and later 'L'*Iliade* ou le poème de la force'. Weil wanted to publish it in the *NRF*, but Jean Paulhan demanded some substantial cuts (*OC* ii/3. 308–9). There were too many quotations, he thought, and when he gave it to some friends to read, they all—with one exception—thought that the *étude* was 'un peu longue et complaisante' (ibid. 309).[15] Weil had used many of the passages she had translated for Posternak. Her

translations seem to have been greatly appreciated by classicists, as Devaux (1982: 92) points out in his short article 'Simone Weil entre la Grèce et l'Inde'.

[11] 'far from the hot baths'.   [12] BN Notes du cours de Saint-Quentin, typed p. 1.
[13] Editorial note *OC* vi/1. 460 nn. 65, 66, ii 3. 307.
[14] *Il*. 11. 161–2; 22. 402–4, 445–6; 6. 456–8; 24. 731–4; 21. 97–8, 114–16; 24. 507–12, 477.
[15] 'a bit long and complacent'.

article, as Fraisse rightly claims, 'est bâti sur ces textes de prédilection' (ibid. 306).[16] Weil refused to accept Paulhan's cuts, and preferred to wait for the article to appear in two parts. This, however, was prevented by the German occupation. Weil then published it in the *Cahiers du Sud* in Marseille where it appeared in two parts in December 1940 and January 1941 under the pseudonym Émile Novis, an anagram of her name.[17]

NE RECOMMENÇONS PAS LA GUERRE DE TROIE

During Weil's life, people were preoccupied with war. How to prevent another war was the natural question to ask after the horrors of World War I. The nationalism and patriotic pride which had fuelled the latter had become unacceptable to many intellectuals in the inter-war period. Pacifism seemed to be the answer to the problem, and Simone Weil embraced it wholeheartedly for many years before reproaching herself bitterly for it (*CS* 317).

Weil greatly admired Jean Giraudoux's play *La Guerre de Troie n'aura pas lieu* when it was performed in Paris in 1935.[18] The title of her article 'Ne recommençons pas la guerre de Troie' (literally 'Let us not restart the War of Troy', though it appeared in English as *The Power of Words*), published in 1937, probably alludes to it. It appeared in two parts on 1 and 15 April in the *Nouveaux Cahiers*, a fortnightly review founded by a group of young industrialists attracted by the personality of Auguste Detœuf who had let Weil work in his factory in 1934.[19]

Weil's pacifist article 'Ne recommençons pas la guerre de Troie' is not about the *Iliad*, but about the question of war. She says the most dangerous conflicts do not seem to have a definite purpose. This is one of the keys to understanding history, and is 'sans doute la clef de notre époque' (*OC* ii/3. 49).[20] When a struggle has a concrete goal,

---

[16] 'is built on these favourite passages'.
[17] In the *Œuvres complètes* Fraisse gives a good overview of the different versions of Weil's article (*OC* ii/3. 304). Even though Weil wrote many versions of the article, it is astonishing with what assurance she composed early on many parts that remained almost unchanged in the final work.
[18] Editorial notes *OC* ii/3. 11.
[19] J. Cabaud 1964: 174. Editorial notes *OC* ii/3. 10.
[20] 'the key to our own period [. . .] [without a] doubt' (*SE* 154).

the parties can find a compromise and can measure the sacrifices they can reasonably make. But in a purposeless war, the sacrifices made become the driving force prolonging the fighting; otherwise one would have to admit that the death of one's comrades had been useless. 'Ce paradoxe', Weil writes, 'est si violent qu'il échappe à l'analyse' (ibid. 50).[21] Most cultivated people read the *Iliad*, 'l'exemple le plus parfait [de ce paradoxe]' but do not understand it (ibid.).[22] The Greeks and Trojans fought for ten years over Helen, whom nobody except Paris really cared about. Everybody, herself included, deplored the fact that she was ever born. There is such lack of proportion between the size of the war and Helen that she is generally thought to be merely a symbol for something else. But a symbol for what, Weil asks? Nobody can tell, for that 'what' simply does not exist. It cannot be the economic interests of the different national economic oligarchies, as often thought, for these are not limited to one nation. In reality, human nature is sufficient to explain war.

Human nature is easily seduced by words that start with capital letters, such as Nation, Capitalism, Communism, Fascism, Democracy, but: 'Si nous saisissons, pour essayer de le serrer, un de ces mots tout gonflés de sang et de larmes nous le trouvons sans contenu' (ibid. 51).[23] Instead of waging war for a woman, for her alleged presence, or for financial reasons, we are fighting for something much less real: we are fighting for words. These words are empty of content, yet have taken on an importance out of all proportion because of the sufferings they have already cost. Yet people are willing to die for these concepts. This is the case, Weil says, partly because they come in pairs: one is willing to sacrifice everything to champion Communism and crush Fascism (and vice versa), even if this means adopting the same methods as one's opponents. These words are empty because one does not make the effort to define their exact meaning. Thus defined, they lose their capital letter and 'il[s] ne peu[vent] plus servir de drapeau ni tenir [leur] place dans le cliquetis des mots d'ordre ennemis' (ibid.).[24] Weil sees the problem of war in intellectual terms, rather than in the religious or moral terms of her later years. She thinks that by clarifying these concepts, much could be gained. Thus the original title of the article had been 'Pour

---

[21] 'This paradox is so extreme as to defy analysis' (*SE* 154).
[22] 'the most perfect example of [this paradox]' (ibid.).
[23] 'If we grasp one of these words, all swollen with blood and tears, and squeeze it, we find it is empty' (ibid. 156).
[24] 'can no longer serve either as a banner or as a hostile slogan' (ibid.).

un peu de clarté' ('For the Sake of a Bit of Clarity').[25] Hence the intellectual has an important part to play in these days of a 'véritable décadence intellectuelle' (ibid.).[26] Superstition has come back in the form of these capital-letter words transforming our political universe, which has become 'exclusivement peuplé de mythes et de monstres' (ibid. 52).[27] Superstition is something of an *Ersatz* for religion, one might add. These are the only ways in which Weil pre-empts her later religious explanation of war. Spiritual renewal was the solution she proposed later on, while for now intellectual rigour is her answer.

Weil's suggestions seem rather optimistic given that she is aware how war has a tendency to perpetuate itself without sufficient reason. It seems impossible to bring the conflict to a halt once it has started. Even if the Trojans had returned Helen, Weil points out, this would have been of no use, for their loss of prestige in the eyes of the Greeks would have made it seem easy to overwhelm them. The only solution, Weil writes in her usual paradoxical way, lies in a miracle. There have been some peaceful periods in history, thus peace is not impossible. More than that: 'La vie humaine est faite de miracles' (*OC* ii/3. 65).[28] Could one believe that a Gothic cathedral could stand, if one did not see the proof of it every day? But Weil's answer is not satisfactory. She leaves us in the dark as to what could bring this miracle about. If human nature is sufficient to explain wars, then what is there within human nature to prevent them? Or must not something external to human nature counteract this tendency to fight? Weil's analysis of *force* was going to give a more satisfying answer to these questions than 'Ne recommençons pas la guerre de Troie'.

L'*ILIADE* OU LE POÈME DE LA FORCE

The Greeks knew about the horrors and the guilt of war: 'L'histoire grecque a commencé par un crime atroce, la destruction de Troie. Loin de se glorifier de ce crime comme font d'ordinaire les nations, ils ont été hantés par ce souvenir comme par un remords. Ils y ont puisé le sentiment de la misère humaine. Nul peuple n'a exprimé comme

---

[25] *OC* ii/3. 283, 311 n. 6.   [26] 'a real intellectual decadence' (*SE* 156).
[27] 'peopled exclusively by myths and monsters' (ibid. 157).
[28] 'Human life is made up of miracles' (ibid. 170).

eux l'amertume de la misère humaine' (*SG* 77).[29] Weil writes this in her essay 'Dieu dans Platon'.[30] Similarly George Steiner in his book *Antigones* speaks about the 'haunted humanism' of the Greeks arising from the 'never-cooling embers of Troy'. They know about the greatness of man who is δεινότερον ['formidable'] — as the Chorus says in the first *stasimon* of the *Antigone* — but behind this greatness lurk madness and disaster (*Ant.* 333).[31] Weil calls this knowledge 'la grandeur propre de la Grèce' (*IPC* 53).[32] In contrast to the Greeks, Weil writes, other nations are unaware of this danger and glory in their victories, France among them (ibid.; *OC* ii/3. 170 ff.). To respect one's enemy, to be saddened by human fate and its subjection to *force*, is the sign of compassion and nobility. It also means understanding the true nature of *force*, which changes sides during war without warning and turns both victim and oppressor alike into a thing, *une chose* (*IPC* 54). The oppressed lose the sense of their humanity and even of being alive. They do not count for other people. Those using *force* become like agents of nature, crushing everybody around them. Both oppressor and oppressed thus deserve our compassion since they become objectified.

Force, she writes provocatively in the first sentence, is the true hero and subject matter of the *Iliad*.[33] In consequence, neither Achilles, nor his wrath, nor the confrontation between Hector and Achilles is at the centre of the epic, which means that Weil implicitly overturns the most widely held interpretations. Therefore Weil does not analyse the nature of Achilles' anger, nor Agamemnon's fault, nor Hector's role as Achilles' counterpart, nor Helen's responsibility in the war.

Force, Weil writes, turns human beings into objects in three ways: through death, imminent death, and slavery. The horror of death strikes us, when we realize that an instant ago there was somebody, while now there is only a corpse. This becomes graphically clear when fair Hector is dragged behind Achilles' chariot (*Il.* 22. 401–4); or when his soul flies off to Hades 'bewailing its fate, leaving manliness and youth' (22. 363); or when the warriors are lying dead on the ground, dearer to

---

[29] 'Greek history began with an atrocious crime: the destruction of Troy. Far from deriving glory for itself from this crime as nations ordinarily do, the Greeks were haunted by the memory of it; that is, by remorse. From this they derived a sense of human misery. No other people has expressed as they have the bitterness of human misery' (*IC* 74–5).
[30] See also *OC* vi/2. 378; *SG* 82; *AD* 245.
[31] Steiner 1984: 263.   [32] 'the innate grandeur of Greece' (*IC* 116).
[33] For a detailed commentary on Weil's article, see Holoka's English edition of the text (S. Weil 2003: 71–105).

the vultures than to their wives (11. 161–2). These scenes are shown in all their *amertume*, which means that one tastes all their bitterness without the comforts of immortality, glory, or patriotism (*OC* ii/3. 228). This becomes all the more painful, when contrasted with the world of family and peace still reigning within the city (22. 442–6). This *amertume*, one would think, is an indirect avowal of the distance between the *Iliad* and Christianity. There is no hope of redemption, of 'changing the face of the earth' or of an afterlife. Yet Weil says: 'L'amertume d'un tel tableau, nous la *savourons* pure, sans qu'aucune fiction réconfortante vienne l'altérer, aucune immortalité consolatrice, aucune fade auréole de gloire ou de patrie' (*OC* ii/3. 228; my italics).[34] The readers are given to drink the bitter cup of seeing war in all its horror without a possibility of escape, thus participating in the cathartic experience of the cross.[35]

Force also turns human beings into stone before they are killed. They lose their reflexes and their capacity to think: 'il n'est plus que matière, encore pensant ne peut plus rien penser' (ibid. 229).[36] Lycaon, a son of Priam, had been captured by Achilles once already, had been sold into slavery, and came back to Troy. On the twelfth day after his return, he encounters Achilles who is now merciless after Patroclus' death. Lycaon begs Achilles for his life, but realizes that it is to no avail (*Il.* 21. 114–16). Similarly Priam is reduced to the point of losing all reflexes. Instead of experiencing horror in front of Achilles when he comes to beg for Hector's body, he kisses the hands of his sons' murderer. Only when reaching a certain level does horror paralyse people, like Lycaon, or deaden them, like Priam.

Whether one agrees with Weil's interpretation of the *Iliad* in terms of *force* or not, her psychological finesse is impressive. Her insights into the effects of *force*, the horrors of slavery, and the dynamics of the relationship between victim and oppressor have the weight of Weil's own experience of a modern form of slavery, namely industrial work in the 1930s. She draws a map of the essential characteristics of war, *force*, and slavery, which remain the same over the ages, thereby hoping to open her readers' eyes to their situation as well as to prepare them for the horrors of war.

---

[34] 'We *taste* the bitterness of such a tableau undiluted, mitigated by no comforting lie, no consoling expectation of immortality, no faded nimbus of glory or patriotism' (*IOPF* 46; my italics).
[35] See also *OC* vi/2. 396.
[36] 'he is no more than matter; still thinking, he can think no more' (*IOPF* 47).

Her interpretation of the encounter of Achilles and Priam is powerful. When Priam asks for Hector's body, this reminds Achilles of his own lonely old father: 'L'autre, songeant à son père, désira le pleurer; | Le prenant par le bras, il poussa *un peu* [ἦκα/ēka] le vieillard' (*OC* ii/3. 230; my italics) (*Il.* 24. 507–8).[37] Achilles pushes Priam away without restraint, because he does not really count for him.[38] He treats him like an object, for he is weaker. Normally the presence of other people changes our behaviour, but when somebody does not count in our eyes, we are not self-conscious and have no self-restraint. Paradoxically, Weil says, it is not out of insensitivity that Achilles pushes Priam away, for to be insensitive means to lack compassion towards somebody who is present. Achilles' behaviour towards the old man is beyond thoughtlessness: it is the expression of complete disregard.

Apart from this instance, however, Achilles is attentive to Priam's safety—something Weil fails to point out. He does not let him sleep in his own tent for fear that his soldiers might see him and report his presence to Agamemnon who would capture him. Nor does he allow Priam to see Hector's corpse immediately. He is afraid Priam might become angry, that in consequence his own anger might flare up and that he might kill Priam. For Weil, indifference and true love seem to intertwine in this scene. Later on she quotes the passage where the two men admire each other, calling it a 'moment [. . .] de grâce' (*OC* ii/3. 247).

Weil takes the passage as a starting point to develop her interesting hermeneutics of oppressor and oppressed. Each reads the world differently. The victim sees nothing but the power of the master while the

---

[37] 'The other, thinking of his father, desired to weep; | Taking him by the arm, he pushed the old man away *a little*' (*IOPF* 48; my italics).

[38] Weil gives different translations of this passage, especially of the word *ēka*. In those joined to her letter to Posternak of May 1937, in her first *Cahier* and in an early version of the article, she writes that Achilles pushes Priam *far* away ('rejeta loin') rather than *un peu* (BN 'Résidues de diverses rédactions du début', MS 49/6 verso; *OC* vi/1. 84). In her lessons of Saint-Quentin, Achilles 'repousse le vieillard et l'envoie rouler à terre' ('pushes the old man away and sends him rolling on the floor') (BN Notes du cours de Saint-Quentin, typed p. 2). Weil obviously twists the text here, for as Michael Ferber points out in his article 'Simone Weil's *Iliad*', *ēka* means 'gentle' (1981: 70–1). According to the Liddell and Scott Greek dictionary, however, *ēka* can also mean 'a bit', though this passage from the *Iliad* is explicitly mentioned under 'gentle'. When Weil renders *ēka* by *loin* she is clearly getting carried away by her interpretation. Yet in the final version of the article as in many of the former versions she translates it by its other possible meaning, 'un peu'. However, 'gentle' seems the correct translation since Achilles helps Priam to get up, accepts his petition and is concerned for his safety.

latter simply does not perceive the former. Yet Weil demands: 'Il faut parvenir à une unité de lecture. Lire dans les apparences quelque chose qu'un autre, situé autrement, ému autrement, peut lire—par le même effort' (*OC* vi/1. 315).[39] Priam and Achilles probably do not achieve this unity of *lecture*, yet they transcend their own pain sufficiently to forgive each other. Priam kisses Achilles' murderous hands, and Achilles gives Priam his son's corpse.

Priam is considered a mere object only for a short period, while slaves are permanently in this condition, as Weil points out. They experience the contradiction of being 'un compromis entre l'homme et le cadavre' (*OC* ii/3. 231).[40] But when the impossible becomes reality, she continues, the soul is torn apart. This happens to Chryseis before she is returned to her father. It is the lot predicted to Andromache and Astyanax, and is already the case for Briseis. Briseis mourns Patroclus since he promised her she would marry Achilles. She was hoping for this marriage in spite of the fact that Achilles had killed her husband and her three brothers. Since slaves are not allowed to express their feelings, the only licit emotion left to show is love for their master: 'Elle dit en pleurant, et les femmes de gémir, | Prenant prétexte de Patrocle, chacune sur ses propres angoisses' (ibid. 232) (*Il.* 19. 301–2).[41] In her first *Cahier* Weil explains the psychological dynamics of slavery in these terms, which could well be applied to Briseis:

À partir d'un certain degré d'oppression, les puissants arrivent nécessairement à se faire *adorer* par leurs esclaves. Car la pensée d'être absolument contraint, jouet d'un autre être, est une pensée insoutenable pour un être humain. Dès lors, si tous les moyens d'échapper à la contrainte lui sont ravis, il ne lui reste plus d'autre alternative que de se persuader que les choses mêmes auxquelles on le contraint, il les accomplit volontairement.   (*OC* vi/1. 114)[42]

This would contradict Oliver Taplin's suggestion in *Homeric Soundings* that a real romantic relationship exists between Achilles and Briseis.

---

[39] 'We must reach a unity in the reading [. . .] To read in outward aspects something which another person, differently situated, differently affected, is able to read—by making the same effort' (*NB* 39).

[40] 'a hybrid of man and corpse' (*IOPF* 48).

[41] 'She spoke weeping, and the women wailed, | taking Patroclus as pretext each for her own anguish' (ibid. 49).

[42] 'By carrying oppression beyond a certain point, the powerful inevitably make their slaves *adore* them. Because the thought of being in absolute subjection as somebody's plaything is a thought no human being can sustain: so if a man is left with no means at all of escaping constraint he has no alternative except to persuade himself that he is doing voluntarily the very things he is forced to do' (*FLN* 41).

Briseis, according to Taplin, is more than simply a concubine, and is even called 'wife' by Achilles in one instance; his relationship with her is the closest he ever gets to marriage.[43] But what is true from Achilles' perspective may not be so for Briseis. Briseis' apparent love would, according to a Weilian analysis, be simply the result of oppression.

Force is ephemeral, but blinds one to this very feature for 'elle enivre' ('it intoxicates') (*OC* ii/3. 233/*IOPF* 51). The *Iliad* makes clear how *force* oscillates between the two sides. There is no set division between victim and oppressor. Everybody in the *Iliad*, according to Weil, must at some point give way to *force*. The great hero Achilles is humiliated and cries in the beginning after Agamemnon has taken Briseis away. Even Agamemnon must humble himself just a few days later and ask Achilles to return to battle, but in vain. Each one in turn must tremble and fear, except for Achilles, though even he runs away from a flooding river.

Destiny, Weil writes, bestows on people a kind of blind justice—a *lex talionis*. The biblical principle that 'those who live by the sword, shall die by the sword', finds its precursor in the *Iliad* in book 18 when Hector says to Polydamas that 'Arès est équitable, et il tue ceux qui tuent' (*OC* ii/3: 235) (*Il.* 18. 309).[44] Nobody can escape this law since the strong are never omnipotent, and the weak not irremediably weak. Without ever using the word, Weil describes the nature of what is in modern terms hubris. The powerful believe nothing can resist them, no other human beings and no justice. This explains the harsh behaviour of many warriors, the way they kill their enemies gratuitously, like Achilles cutting the throats of twelve adolescents on the pyre of Patroclus 'aussi naturellement que nous coupons des fleurs pour une tombe' (*OC* ii/3. 236).[45] But by definition the strong will fall since they overestimate their strength. This geometric law, Weil claims, is what the Greeks called *nemesis*. At the end of the first day of battle described in the epic, the Greeks could have freely obtained Helen and many riches, Weil claims, but they fail to do so since they believe that they will conquer Troy before long anyway.[46] On that same day Hector predicts the fall of his city, yet when he wins the next day, he wants total victory and prevents the Greeks from leaving. After he kills Patroclus and beats

---

[43] Taplin 1992: 212 ff.
[44] 'Ares is just and kills those who kill' (*IOPF* 53). The reference in *OC* ii/3. 235, 319 n. 194, wrongly says book 8, instead of 18.
[45] 'as casually as we cut flowers for a grave' (*IOPF* 53).
[46] This is not quite correct, since Paris refuses during the assembly to return Helen though he is willing to give back the riches (*Il.* 7. 355 ff.).

the Greeks, the Trojans should have retired to the city as Polydamas advises, but Hector has lost all moderation. The next day he is killed. He is not spared the humiliation of running away from Achilles and, once wounded, even asking for a decent burial. But Achilles' victory is short-lived for the readers of the *Iliad* know that he will soon die in turn.

Weil's analysis is obviously meant to be applied to her times.[47] Hitler may be the strongest at the moment. He may conquer the world as the Romans did, but his reign will necessarily come to an end. His power may be great, but it is limited, and he is bound to overrate it, as he eventually did. In her 1940 article 'Réflexions sur les origines de l'Hitlérisme' ('The Great Beast: Some Reflections on the Origins of Hitlerism'/*SE*), Weil draws a parallel between the methods of the Romans and those of Hitler, both characterized by a ruthlessness and cruelty that paralyse their opponents (*OC* ii/3. 181 ff.). But the Roman Empire came to an end, and so will Hitler's. This may be of little consolation to those who suffer under Hitler and who think that the *Reich* might continue for a thousand years. The terror he inspires comes partly from the illusion he creates of omnipotence and of the permanence of his reign. Goliath may be a giant, but David wins since he does not let himself be impressed by size alone. Thus Weil's article on the *Iliad* is of political relevance, even though she does not mention Hitler by name. *Prestige* magnifies power. It is an illusion and can therefore be overcome, something she had already mentioned in 'Ne recommençons pas la guerre de Troie'. Therefore her article on the *Iliad* could not be published in occupied Paris; nor her article on Hitlerism, which appeared only in part in the *Nouveaux Cahiers* on 1 January 1940, the other two parts being rejected by the censors.

Weil's analysis of war is forceful, especially when seen in its historical context, for 'L'*Iliade* ou le poème de la force' was first supposed to appear while the Germans and French were still fighting. War, Weil writes, seems simple before one has entered combat. One leaves for war with a light heart, overestimating one's strength while the enemy is absent. Unless the opponent has a terrifying reputation, one will feel stronger and enter war as if it were a game. In the *Iliad*, the men have already been fighting for so long that they know well the dangers of war. Odysseus tells them:

---

[47] Thus Joseph Summers in his 'Notes on Simone Weil's *Iliad*' thinks of her article 'primarily as a document of its time' (Summers 1981: 87).

> Où sont parties nos vantardises, quand nous nous affirmions si braves,
> Celles qu'à Lemnos vaniteusement vous déclamiez,
> [. . .]
> Qu'à cent ou à deux cents de ces Troyens chacun
> Tiendrait tête au combat; et voilà qu'un seul est trop pour nous!
> (*OC* ii/3. 241) (*Il.* 8. 229-30, 233-4)[48]

Weil's style is at its best here, climactically rising, contrasting the seriousness of war with an abstraction, a children's game, a theatrical pose: 'Le danger est alors une abstraction, les vies qu'on détruit sont comme des jouets brisés par un enfant et aussi indifférentes; l'héroïsme est une pose de théâtre et souillé de vantardise' (*OC* ii/3. 241).[49] This is the psychology of war. Unfortunately, once the horrors of war become reality to the warrior, the soldiers feel they have no future. The *Leitmotiv* of the *Iliad* for Weil, as she says in her lessons at Saint-Quentin, is the line 'Je ne reviendrai pas dans ma patrie.'[50] In order to protect themselves the warriors try to stop thinking about the future or about the purpose of war. Therefore they will not do anything to bring it to a halt, for the only conceivable end they can think of is death and destruction. A moderate compromise seems impossible considering the sacrifices made, Weil says, repeating what she had already written in 'Ne recommençons pas . . .'. When human beings are doomed to die in war and have to suppress their desire to live, they tend to lose all compassion towards others.[51] The healing of one's wounds seems to depend on the death of the enemy who inflicted them. This point could be applied to Achilles even though Weil does not do so explicitly. Achilles is bent on killing Hector and every other Trojan, for the death of his friend

---

[48] 'What happened to our boasts, used to bolster our brave selves, | which you at Lemnos made in your vanity, | [. . .] | That each against one or two hundred of these Trojans | could hold his own in battle; and behold one alone is too much for us!' (*IOPF* 58).

[49] 'Danger is then an abstraction, and the lives one destroys are like playthings broken by a child and just as inconsequential; heroism is histrionic and besmirched by boasting' (ibid.).

[50] BN Notes du cours de Saint-Quentin, typed p. 7. 'I will not return to my fatherland.'

[51] Weil does not seem to think of Achilles' fate as something allotted to him, but rather as an unconscious death-wish due to Patroclus' death: 'Tuer est toujours se tuer. Deux manières de se tuer, *suicide (Achille)* ou détachement' (*OC* vi/1. 316, 306; my italics; *OC* vi/2. 313) (*Il.* 18. 98-100) ('To kill is always to kill oneself. Two ways of killing oneself, suicide (Achilles) or detachment') (*NB* 40).

Tableau de l'absence de Dieu 129

Patroclus has made him merciless.[52] But though he kills Hector, and drags his body round his friend's pyre many times, he finds no peace. The promise of healing that vengeance gives is false.

Thus the *Iliad* is a poem about *force* in all its different aspects.[53] In relation to it, Achilles is no less a victim than Agamemnon. Though Weil does not analyse the nature of Achilles' wrath, it can be explained as his reaction to the dominion exercised over him by Agamemnon.[54] Hector himself, who so admirably defends Troy, cannot escape from this role-play as a victim of *force*. *Force* is par excellence the explanation for war, Helen being merely an excuse. Weil's interpretation may lack the detail that only a close structural analysis could have provided. She gives no direct answers to the most prominent questions which usually spring to mind about the epic. Yet by revealing the main theme of the *Iliad*, Weil gives the key to the whole.

However, her negative view of *force* has been criticized. Rachel Bespaloff, though strongly influenced by Weil, wrote an interesting article 'De l'*Iliade*' in 1943 in which, without mentioning Weil's name, she challenges her views on *force*.[55] She herself admits, in an unpublished letter to Jean Grenier dated 29 October 1941 (who had sent her Weil's article), 'Il y a des pages entières de mes notes qui auront l'air d'être un plagiat.'[56] Yet Bespaloff explains in her article that *force* is not portrayed solely under its negative aspect in the epic, that it is also beautiful:

Ainsi la force apparaît dans l'*Iliade*, à la fois, comme la suprême réalité et la suprême illusion de l'existence. Homère, tout ensemble, divinise en elle la

---

[52] As Taplin points out, Achilles becomes this merciless only once Patroclus is dead, knowing that he himself will die. Formerly he had sold many of Priam's sons for ransom. Now he kills Lycaon whom he calls 'friend', being united by the common bond of mortality (Taplin 1992: 222 ff.).
[53] In *Homer on Life and Death* Griffin (1983: 143) calls the epic 'a poem of death'. But while death is continuously depicted, it is the result of *force*. Thus Weil's concept encompasses Griffin's point, but goes beyond it.
[54] Weil briefly refers to Achilles' wrath in her *Cahiers* in autumn 1941: 'Car la colère d'Achille le pousse à plus de colère. Même au xxive chant il n'est pas guéri, puisque Priam le fuit au milieu de la nuit. La mort seule y mettra fin. Pourtant la connaissance certaine qu'il va mourir introduit une nuance d'apaisement' (*OC* vi/2. 96–7) ('For the wrath of Achilles urges him on to greater wrath. Even by the xxivth canto he hasn't recovered from it, since Priam flees from him in the middle of the night. Death alone will put a stop to it. Still, the certain knowledge that he is going to die has a certain pacifying effect upon him') (*NB* 103).
[55] See note on Bespaloff in Grenier 1997: 51 n. 3.
[56] 'There will be entire pages of my notes that will appear to be plagiarized' (Archives of Jean Grenier at the BN).

surabondance de vie qui éclate dans le dédain de la mort, dans l'extase du sacrifice, et dénonce la fatalité qui la change en inertie: cette poussée aveugle qui la fait aller jusqu'au bout de son développement, jusqu'à l'annulation d'elle-même et des valeurs qu'elle a engendrées.[57]

'Condamner ou absoudre la force', Bespaloff writes later on, 'ce serait condamner ou absoudre la vie même.'[58] But why should *force* equal life? The acts of love and friendship depicted in the epic show that there is more to life than *force*. Weil condemns *force* in its Nietzschean glorification, when it is sheer power and egoism, not life itself.

Steiner criticizes Weil's interpretation in a vein similar to Bespaloff's, for he believes that 'even in the midst of carnage, life is in full tide and beats forward with a wild gaiety'. He thinks that Homer 'proclaims that there is that in men which loves war, which is less afraid of the terrors of combat than of the long boredom of the hearth'.[59] While this statement might have applied to the first years of the Trojan war, it is no longer cogent in the tenth year in which the epic is set. Trojans and Achaeans are both exhausted and yearn for an end to the war. Hector is fearful of his death and of the fall of Troy, while Achilles, bemoaning his destiny, goes back to battle, not with a heart full of love for warfare, but driven by vengeance.

When battle-scenes are depicted and the gruesome deaths of young warriors are described in gory detail, Homer points to the tragic character of their disappearance by evoking the bride, the wife and children, or the old, dependent father left behind. Suddenly the dead youth, portrayed against his family background, gains a human dimension shedding a tragic light on his death. Jasper Griffin highlights this in his book *Homer on Life and Death*, which buttresses Weil's negative interpretation of *force*.[60] Similarly C. W. MacLeod in his commentary on book 24 of the *Iliad* says that its 'central subject is not honour and glory, but suffering and death'.[61] In a letter to David Garnett, the editor of Lawrence

---

[57] Bespaloff 1943: 19. 'Thus, in the *Iliad*, force appears as both the supreme reality and the supreme illusion of life. Force, for Homer, is divine insofar as it represents a superabundance of life that flashes out in the contempt for death and the ecstasy of self-sacrifice; it is detestable insofar as it contains a fatality that transforms it into inertia, a blind drive that is always pushing it on to the very end of its course, on to its own abolition and the obliteration of the very values it engendered' (Bespaloff 1970: 44–5).

[58] Bespaloff 1943: 23; 'To condemn force or to absolve it' 'would be to condemn, or absolve life itself' (Bespaloff 1970: 48).

[59] Steiner and Fagles 1962: 9.   [60] Griffin 1983: 103 ff.

[61] MacLeod 1982: 5. See also what MacLeod writes a bit further on: 'The *Iliad* is concerned with battle and with men whose life is devoted to winning glory in battle;

of Arabia, Weil wrote that what she appreciated in the *Iliad* as in Lawrence's book *The Seven Pillars of Wisdom* was that it described 'war as mirrored in peace-values and peace standards'.[62] Thus peace is the norm and the goal against with the epic is set, rather than a glorification of *force*.

MOMENTS LUMINEUX

Given all the horrors it depicts, the *Iliad* would be a cold and monotonous piece were it not for the 'moments lumineux', as Weil calls them, 'où les hommes ont une âme' (*OC* ii/3. 246).[63] Weil briefly refers to them already in the first entry of her *Cahiers* concerning the *Iliad*: 'Opposée, par éclair, cette paix perdue où on avait égard à l'homme' (*OC* vi/1. 83).[64] In her early draft 'L'*Iliade*, ou la philosophie de la force' she speaks about 'cet autre monde', where 'l'homme reste homme'.[65] These moments when friendship, love, and courage are able to break through are 'brefs et divins' (*OC* ii/3. 246):[66] the tradition of hospitality which Diomedes and Glaucus respect on the battlefield; parental love, love for one's siblings, the conjugal love between Hector and Andromache, friendship between Achilles and Patroclus. These 'moments de grâce', as Weil calls them, are rare, but heighten the sense of loss and tragedy (ibid. 247). In ch. 4 of his book, Griffin refers to the same passages that Weil quotes as well as to others where the contrast between war and peace is highlighted. For example, Weil mentions Hector running away from Achilles around Troy and passing by the washing pools where the women of Troy cleaned their garments in times of peace; the same Hector is described as the 'gardien des épouses chastes et des petits enfants', which is enough 'pour faire apparaître la chasteté souillée par

---

and it represents with wonder their strength and courage. But its deepest purpose is not to glorify them, and still less to glorify war itself. What war represents for Homer is humanity under duress and in the face of death; and so to enjoy or appreciate the *Iliad* is to understand and feel for human suffering. The greatest of all critics of poetry rightly called Homer "the path-finder of tragedy" (*Republic* 598d)' (MacLeod 1982: 8).

[62] BN Letter to David Garnett.   [63] 'when men possess a soul' (*IOPF* 62).
[64] 'And by a flash of contrast, that lost peace when man was still cherished' (*FLN* 14).
[65] BN 'L'*Iliade*, ou la philosophie de la force', p. 1; 'this other world', 'where man remains a man'.
[66] 'fleeting and sublime' (*IOPF* 62).

force et les enfants livrés aux armes' (ibid. 248) (*Il.* 24. 730).[67] Homer's manner of writing, according to Griffin, is 'emotional writing in the dispassionate style'.[68]

For Weil the greatest triumph of love within the *Iliad* is the friendship which arises between two enemies, namely between Achilles and Priam. Not only do they forget their vengeance, but for a moment the distance between benefactor and beggar, between victor and vanquished disappears. They are able to admire each other despite their enmity (*OC* ii/3. 247) (*Il.* 24. 628–33). Though Achilles does not get much gratification from dragging Hector's body round the pyre of Patroclus, it seems almost compulsory, something from which he promises himself some relief.[69] Furthermore, it prolongs the retribution inflicted on Hector and his family. This shows how difficult it must be for Achilles to give Hector's body to Priam. In *La Connaissance surnaturelle* Weil underlines this by pointing to the existential significance of burial through an anachronistic comparison to Christian belief: 'Hector supplie Achille pour son cadavre comme un chevalier du moyen âge implorerait le loisir de se confesser. Achille veut non seulement tuer, mais damner Hector' (*CS* 210).[70] Dead Patroclus' appearance to Achilles further highlights the importance of burial, for he laments that he has not yet been admitted into the company of the dead in Hades since he is still unburied (*Il.* 23. 65 ff.). Thus by handing Hector's body over to Priam, Achilles is giving up his revenge.

These islands of peace and love are not sufficient, however, to stop the ongoing madness of war. None of the characters present in the *Iliad* is an *être pur* like Antigone who can bring sin and hubris to a halt. The epic is without such a redeemer-figure except for Patroclus whom Weil seems to consider briefly in this light.[71] Nobody in the epic has this *générosité*

---

[67] 'protector of chaste wives and small children', '[to] suggest purity defiled by force and children offered up to weapons' (ibid. 64–5). Actually, 'chaste' is not a correct translation of the adjective κεδνός, which really means 'noble' or 'diligent'.

[68] Griffin 1983: 119.

[69] As Redfield writes in *Nature and Culture in the Iliad*: 'The two heroes are locked together in an everlasting dance of hatred—despoiler and victim, predator and prey' (Redfield 1975: 211).

[70] 'Hector begs Achilles to respect his corpse in the way that a medieval knight begged for time to make his last confession. But Achilles wanted not only to kill Hector but to damn him' (*FLN* 248–9).

[71] 'Atè court, la pointe des pieds sur la tête des hommes, de tête en tête—jusqu'à ce qu'un homme l'arrête; alors elle entre en lui. Nul ne l'arrête dans l'*Iliade*' (*CS* 14/*OC* vi/3. 382) ('Atë runs on tiptoe over men's heads—until one man arrests her; then she enters into him. In the *Iliad* no one arrests her') (*FLN* 69). But then: 'Êtres parfaitement

à briser le cœur to respect the life of others—rendered especially difficult when one has had to stifle one's own desire for life—except perhaps Patroclus who ' "sut être doux envers tous" '.[72] Weil considers him to be at the centre of the poem, for he avoids all brutality and cruelty (*OC* ii/3. 244) (*Il.* 27. 671). Yet he kills many Trojans, including Sarpedon, a son of Zeus, and is called the 'bravest among the Achaeans' by Menelaus, and the 'bravest among the Myrmidons' by Achilles, as Villela-Petit points out in her article 'La Force des mots: écho philosophique à "l'étrange mort de Patrocle" '.[73] Villela-Petit suggests that Patroclus probably distinguishes himself from the other warriors by abstaining from insulting his enemies, that he has no hubris. When he finally joins the battle, it is out of pity for the Achaeans who are being massacred by Hector.[74] However, one needs to keep in mind that he dies because he disobeys Achilles who ordered him to return to the ships after having driven back the Trojans. He continues fighting until he comes face to face with Hector who kills him. Patroclus obviously lacks moderation since he gets carried away in the heat of the battle. Weil admits so herself in the second version of her article, but not in the final one: 'Mais Patrocle même, qui vient de périr, c'est la même faute qui l'a tué [i.e. la même folle assurance que Hector]; oublieux des ordres d'Achille, enivré par la victoire, il est allé jusqu'aux remparts, s'est efforcé de les escalader, jusqu'à ce qu'épuisé il ait perdu son armure que lui ôtait pièce par pièce Apollon.'[75]

Homer's Supernatural Perspective

Weil, however, does not give much importance to Patroclus in the final version of her article. It is in an aside that she mentions his virtues. No

---

purs dans l'*Iliade*; Patrocle et Polydamas?' ('Perfectly pure beings in the *Iliad*; Patroclus and Polydamas?') (*CS* 149/*FLN* 194). Weil asks herself not only whether Patroclus is an *être pur*, but also whether Polydamas incarnates such purity since he does not let himself be carried away by the dynamics of war and advises moderation to Hector. See also (*OC* vi/2. 327).

[72] 'heart-rending generosity' (my translation), ' "knew how to be gentle to all" ' (*IOPF* 61).

[73] Villela-Petit 1998: 90. Gaillardot (1982: 186) enumerates some of the warriors he kills.

[74] Taplin 1992: 174 ff.

[75] BN 2ième rédaction de 'L'*Iliade* ou le poème de la force', MS 62/IX 19. 'But Patroclus himself, who has just been killed, had to die due to the same fault [namely the same foolish assurance as Hector's]; forgetting the orders of Achilles, intoxicated by victory, he has gone to the ramparts, tried to scale them, until, exhausted, he loses his armour which Apollon has taken from him piece by piece.'

single figure reveals the supernatural in the *Iliad*. There is no redemption within the epic, as Weil writes in her *Cahier* VIII: 'L'*Iliade*, tableau de l'absence de Dieu' or in her *Cahier* VI earlier on: 'L'*Iliade*; "misère de l'homme sans Dieu"' (*OC* vi/3. 90, vi 2. 327).[76] Though there is no Christ figure, there is, according to Weil, a Christian point of view within the epic. It is the manner in which things are described that shows the supernatural vantage point Homer adopted (*OC* ii/3. 248, 250; *CS* 95, 97; *PSO* 56–7). How else could he have written with the same compassion of both the Trojans and Greeks? Had the *Iliad* been a simple piece of propaganda intended to sing the glory of the Achaeans as the forefathers of the Greeks, it would have treated the two sides differently. This is what Northrop Frye points out in his *Anatomy of Criticism* without, however, referring to the supernatural: 'It is hardly possible to overestimate the importance for Western literature of the *Iliad*'s demonstration that the fall of an enemy, no less than of a friend or leader, is tragic and not comic. With the *Iliad*, once and for all, an objective and disinterested element enters into the poet's vision of human life.'[77] For Weil it is more than that, since to portray affliction with such attention as in the book of *Job* and in the *Iliad*, means loving God (*CS* 297; *OC* vi/2. 360). One's natural reaction is to turn away from unbearable suffering, either by closing one's eyes, by projecting glorifying elements onto it, or by turning cynical. Therefore, 'il ne peut y avoir contemplation de la misère humaine dans sa vérité qu'à la lumière de la grâce' (*OC* vi/3. 90).[78] It is not by what an author says about God that we know where he stands, Weil claims, since he might be a hypocrite. Rather it is the manner in which he talks about the natural world which reveals his real stance. Analogously, 'la foi d'un juge n'apparaît pas dans son attitude à l'église, mais dans

---

[76] 'The *Iliad*: this draws a picture of God's absence' (*NB* 405). 'The *Iliad*; "misery of the man without God"' (*NB* 229). The gods in the epic have no redemptive function. They merely provide in Weil's eyes comic interludes, just as the clowns in Shakespeare do (*PSO* 56; *OC* vi/2. 345). Only when Zeus pulls out his scales and weighs the destiny of people, does he reveal a true aspect of God submitting himself to the necessity of the world (*OC* vi/1. 333; *PSO* 56) (*Il.* 8. 69 ff.).

[77] Frye 1957: 319 (quoted by Ferber 1981: 76).

[78] 'There can be no contemplation of human misery in its very truth otherwise than by the light of grace' (*NB* 405). 'Il n'y a pas de tableau de la misère humaine plus pur, plus amer et plus poignant que l'*Iliade*. La contemplation de la misère humaine dans sa vérité implique une spiritualité très haute' (*SG* 78) ('There is no purer, bitterer, and more poignant picture of human misery than the *Iliad*. The contemplation of human misery in its truth implies a very high spirituality') (*SNL* 90).

son attitude au tribunal' (*CS* 97).⁷⁹ Though a painter does not depict the point from where he paints on the canvas, one can know where he was standing by looking at the picture. Similarly, the manner in which Homer speaks about 'la misère humaine', namely 'aussi lucidement, aussi froidement [. . .] sans perdre la tendresse ni la sérénité', reveals both his vantage point and his love for God (ibid.).⁸⁰ Thus, 'les choses charnelles sont le critérium des choses spirituelles' (ibid. 98).⁸¹ This approach sheds an interesting light on Weil's own method. She does not present Christianity on its own, but discloses her own supernatural point of view indirectly, through her interpretation of the Greek classics, for: 'On témoigne moins bien pour Dieu en parlant de Lui qu'en exprimant, soit en actes, soit en paroles, l'aspect nouveau que prend la création quand l'âme a passé par le Créateur. A vrai dire, même, on témoigne seulement ainsi' (ibid. 95).⁸² This is a revealing statement: it shows that Weil's apologetics must be oblique and indirect. She prefers to speak of the natural world or of art, both of which reveal a new aspect when seen through the eyes of faith, than openly proclaim and defend Christianity itself.

Homer's supernatural point of view, expressing itself in the compassion with which he portrays the warriors from both sides, is what suffuses his poem with *amertume*:⁸³

C'est par là que l'*Iliade* est une chose unique, par cette amertume qui procède de la tendresse, et qui s'étend sur tous les humains, égale comme la clarté du soleil. Jamais le ton ne cesse d'être imprégné d'amertume, jamais non plus il ne s'abaisse à la plainte. La justice et l'amour, qui ne peuvent guère avoir de place dans ce tableau d'extrêmes et d'injustes violences, le baignent de leur lumière sans jamais être sensibles autrement que par l'accent.   (*OC* ii/3. 248)⁸⁴

---

⁷⁹ 'The faith of a judge is not seen in his behaviour at church, but in his behaviour on the bench' (*FLN* 146).
⁸⁰ 'so lucidly and so coolly without losing either tenderness or serenity' (ibid.).
⁸¹ 'earthly things are the criterion of spiritual things' (ibid. 147).
⁸² 'One does not testify so well for God by speaking about Him as by expressing, either in actions or words, the new aspect assumed by the creation after the soul has experienced the Creator. Indeed, the truth is that the latter is the only way' (ibid. 144).
⁸³ Weil has already mentioned *amertume* in her lessons in Saint-Quentin where she says that Homer speaks about war in all of its *amertume* without romanticizing it or reducing it to the touchiness of the gods (typed p. 8).
⁸⁴ 'This is what makes the *Iliad* unique, this bitterness emerging from tenderness and enveloping all men equally, like the bright light of the sun. The tone always is imbued with bitterness but never descends to lamentation. Justice and love, totally out of place in this depiction of extremes and unjust violence, subtly and by nuance, drench all with their light' (*IOPF* 64). See also *OC* vi/2. 363

Amertume is no cynical kind of sadness, nor is it a complaint: 'il ne s'abaisse jamais à la plainte' (ibid.).[85] It suggests drinking the bitter cup of the human condition without seeking escape into the dream-world of wish-fulfilment or by venting one's own suffering on a scapegoat. It means acknowledging the fact that in one way or another all human beings are subject to *force* which is the necessary prerequisite to *caritas*. Thus: 'Il n'est possible d'aimer et d'être juste que si l'on connaît l'empire de la force et si l'on sait ne pas le respecter' (ibid. 251).[86] Could not the depiction of so much affliction lead to despair? Not if it is shown in the light of grace (*OC* vi/3. 90). For to know:

Avec toute l'âme, que tout dans la nature, y compris la nature psychologique, est soumis à une force aussi brutale, aussi impitoyablement dirigée vers le bas que la pesanteur, une telle connaissance colle pour ainsi dire l'âme à la prière comme un prisonnier, quand il le peut, reste collé à la fenêtre de sa cellule, comme une mouche reste collée au fond d'une bouteille par son élan vers la lumière. (*IPC* 53)[87]

Only those who are unprepared and for whom suffering has only a natural dimension are in danger of falling into despondency (*AD* 103).

Significantly, Weil writes about the meaning of suffering in the light of God's love and the *Iliad* in her last letter to Perrin from Casablanca on 26 May 1942. Though recognizing God's presence does not diminish suffering itself: 'On sait d'une manière certaine que l'amour de Dieu pour nous est la substance même de cette amertume et de cette mutilation. Je voudrais, par gratitude, être capable d'en laisser le témoignage. Le poète de l'*Iliade* a suffisamment aimé Dieu pour avoir cette capacité' (ibid. 70).[88] And she continues: 'Car c'est là la signification implicite du poème et l'unique source de sa beauté. Mais on ne l'a guère compris' (ibid.).[89] To mention the epic in such a letter where she speaks about

---

[85] 'never descends to lamentation' (*IOPF* 64).

[86] 'It is impossible to love and to be just unless one understands the realm of force and knows enough not to respect it' (ibid. 67).

[87] 'Not abstractly but with the whole soul, that all in nature, including psychological nature, is under the dominance of a force as brutal, as pitilessly directed downward as gravity, such a knowledge glues, so to speak, the soul to prayer like a prisoner who, when he is able, remains glued to the window of his cell, or like a fly stays stuck to the bottom of a bottle by the force of its urge toward the light' (*IC* 116).

[88] 'But we know quite certainly that God's love for us is the very substance of this bitterness and this mutilation. I should like out of gratitude to be capable of bearing witness to this. The poet of the *Iliad* loved God enough to have this capacity' (*WG* 44).

[89] 'This indeed is the implicit signification of the poem and the one source of its beauty' (ibid.). For how could the depiction of death and misery be beautiful in art

the nature and meaning of suffering, as she herself is leaving for an uncertain future, shows again the importance the *Iliad* had for Weil.

LESSONS TO BE LEARNT: HOMER AND WEIL AS EDUCATORS OF THEIR TIME

War has a lesson to teach. One needs to grasp the universal power of *force* without being seduced by it. If applied to France's situation at the time, Weil's article makes the readers come to the conclusion that the French should be aware of *force* and prepare themselves for its rule. They should not look down on those who are in a worse situation, for they might soon share their plight. It is not right either to blacken the Germans for they too are dying in this war, leaving their wives, children, and parents to mourn them.[90] Nor should one envy the powerful, for they too are affected by *force*, and may soon be subjected to its regime, led astray by their hubris. Weil's article gives an admirable lesson to her contemporaries, if only they are willing to listen and to understand the *Iliad* better; then they will recognize in the epic 'le plus pur des miroirs' (*OC* ii/3. 227).[91] Instead of using a modern example to understand an ancient text, Weil employs the reverse technique. One might think it would be easier to comprehend something distant in time by something analogous which is closer to the present. Yet at certain moments one is too close to a situation to perceive it *sine ira et studio*. Thus Weil's use of an ancient text places her readers at an emotive distance from their

---

otherwise? 'Dans la peinture vraie du malheur, ce qui suscite la beauté, c'est la lumière de la justice dans l'attention de celui qui a tracé le tableau, attention rendue contagieuse par la beauté. Seul un juste parfait pouvait écrire l'*Iliade*' (*CS* 307) ('In the true portrayal of affliction, what creates beauty is the light of justice in the attention of the man who portrays it; this attention becomes contagious through beauty. Only a just man made perfect could have written the *Iliad*') (*FLN* 336). See also *EL* 37.

[90] Furthermore, we are not any better than they are, Weil writes in 'Cette guerre est une guerre de religions': 'Pourtant nous ne devons pas méconnaître que l'Allemagne est pour nous tous, gens du xxe siècle, un miroir. Ce que nous apercevons là de tellement hideux, ce sont nos propres traits, seulement grossis' (*EL* 102) ('Nevertheless, we ought not to hide from ourselves, we people of the twentieth century, that Germany is a mirror for all of us. What looks to us so hideous is our own features, but magnified') (*SE* 214). Summers (1981: 87) writes admiringly about Weil: 'That anyone of left sympathies could see anything pitiable in the triumphant German armies of Hitler was remarkable enough; that a Frenchwoman and a Jew who passionately identified with the defeated and the oppressed could do so struck me as miraculous.'

[91] 'the most beautiful and flawless of mirrors' (*IOPF* 45).

own times, thus making an objective evaluation easier. At the same time the *Iliad* is brought closer to the readers in revealing to them those very truths about war, death, and love, which they are experiencing. Weil wants her French contemporaries to adopt the same compassionate and objective attitude to their own situation as Homer showed towards the Greeks and Trojans. Only then will they be able to learn from their own plight and assess it rightly. War can paradoxically teach true *caritas*: to be just, one has to know the empire of *force* without being seduced by it. Weil herself assumes that the older parts of the *Iliad* were written some time after the sack of Troy, which would have given its author(s) the necessary objective distance from the event. The Achaeans themselves were conquered eighty years after the conquest of Troy according to Thucydides, and some songs of the *Iliad* may derive from the vanquished Achaeans of those days. This would have placed them in a situation where they could judge war from the point of view of the loser as well as that of the winner, which would explain the objective perspective within the poem (ibid. 250).

Towards the end of her article Weil starts mentioning Christianity. The spirit of justice and compassion which permeates the epic in its depiction of human suffering is ultimately Christian for her. Or rather, the Gospel came to express the Greek spirit fully, which the *Iliad* manifested first (ibid. 251). Yet, one might object, there are many elements of the epic which are hardly Christian in tone. Though warriors may be humiliated, such as Achilles by Agamemnon or Hector who begs for a proper burial, they are far from being humble. Hector dies because he refuses to lose face before the Trojans, as he would by escaping from Achilles into the city. If Dodds is correct, then the Homeric culture is a shame culture and not a guilt culture.[92] Appearance and success are more important than the 'quiet' values of solidarity. In contrast, humility remains specifically a Christian virtue: 'La vertu chrétienne a pour centre, pour essence, pour saveur spécifique l'humilité, le mouvement librement consenti vers le bas. C'est par là que les saints ressemblent au Christ' (*E* 124).[93] Quite opposite is κλέος/*kléos*, the glory the epic heroes strive to achieve. The self-worth of a warrior depends on the glory he obtains that

---

[92] Dodds 1966: ch. 2. However, Dodds's view has been criticized by Rutherford, for example, who points out that the two are no longer seen to be mutually exclusive (Rutherford 1996: 42; Lloyd-Jones 1983: 15, 24 ff.).

[93] 'The essential fact about the Christian virtues, what lends them a special savour of their own, is humility—the freely accepted movement towards the bottom. It is through this that the saints resemble Christ' (*NR* 140).

will outlive him. He is to a certain extent determined by his reputation within society, in contrast to the Christian—ideally speaking at least. While Weil was very critical of Corneille's concept of *gloire*, which she thought contradicted Christianity, she does not seem to have been aware that *kléos* and humility cancel each other out (*E* 124; *PSO* 54; *CS* 193; *OC* ii/3. 31, 213, 293). However, Weil does not claim that the warriors themselves are saints or Christian in spirit, but that Homer portrayed them from a Christian perspective. That the characters think highly of glory does not mean that Homer does so. For as we have seen, Homer depicts the misery of the epic heroes without embellishment and their death without the trimmings of military glory.

In her article 'La Force des mots' Villela-Petit proposes an interpretation which takes into account both Weil's reading of the *Iliad* and the concept of *kléos*. There are two manners of speaking about the dead in Greek culture according to Gregory Nagy's book *The Best of the Achaeans*: one is to bemoan their lot and feel great sorrow over their death as Achilles does over Patroclus (πένθος/*pénthos* and ἄχος/*ákhos* refer to this pain), the other is to sing their glory, namely their κλέος ἄφθιτον/*kléos áphthiton*.[94] The family members and friends express their sorrow in γόοι/*góoi*, but the professional singers intone the funeral songs called θρῆνοι/*thrēnoi*.[95] Whilst the *góoi* are depicted in the *Iliad*, the *thrēnoi* are simply mentioned. Villela-Petit suggests that this may be because the *Iliad* itself is supposed to be a *thrēnos* on the destruction of holy Troy and its heroes, while at the same time conferring on Achilles his *kléos*. This tension between *force*, the misery of human beings, and the lamentation of their lot, and on the other hand the glory of their heroic actions, would thus be at the very centre of the epic poem. Hence, Villela-Petit suggests, the *Iliad* could have contributed to a dramatic change of values in a warrior society by depicting its negative aspects. It might be considered the true educator of Greece.[96]

Could the same be said of Weil's article? She is trying to educate her times, to portray war and power for the benefit of a world racked by both, and thus help reset people's scale of values. Her article bemoans the fate not only of ancient Troy, but indirectly of a France in danger of destruction. Compassion is the attitude she suggests should be adopted towards one's country, as she writes in *L'Enracinement*, rather than the desire for *gloire* (*E* 147 ff.). Compassion explains Homer's supernatural perspective from which he can perceive the truths about war, *force*, and

[94] Nagy 1979: 94 ff.   [95] Ibid. 112–13.   [96] Villela-Petit 1998: 97–9.

human destiny. It is the perspective that makes these truths supernatural even though they do not directly relate to the supernatural realm, for they could not be understood adequately from any other point of view (*CS* 126; *AD* 103).

In 'Ne recommençons pas...' Weil advocated pacifism by showing the purposelessness and absurdity of war. She claimed that human nature is enough to explain war, and she still believes this in 1939–40. But now it is human nature at the mercy of *force* which accounts for war, while a few years later in 'Cette guerre...' it was going to be human nature trying to avoid the religious question. The miracle needed to arrest the course of war remains undefined in 'Ne recommençons pas...'. In her article on the *Iliad* Weil hints at the *être pur* who would be necessary to bring the frenzy to a halt, while in the *Connaissance* she states that there is no such person in the epic (*CS* 14/*OC* vi/3. 382). Patroclus foreshadows such a figure, but becomes himself a victim of *démesure* (immoderation).[97] In 'Cette guerre...' Weil suggests that only an acceptance of God will prevent ideologies from exercising their reign of terror and bring the war to a halt.[98] Faith is the answer to World War II, since its cause is the denial of God (*EL* 107). God must be put again at the centre of civilization to prevent such man-eating ideologies as Nazism or Communism having their way.[99]

---

[97] In Weil's unfinished tragedy *Venise Sauvée*, set in the seventeenth century, there is such an *être pur*, namely Jaffier, who stops the otherwise unrestrained reign of *force*. After planning to conquer and destroy Venice, he is moved by compassion and saves the city. Contrary to agreements made, the city officials execute his companions, and he is rejected as traitor both by them and by the Venetians. Significantly Weil started writing the piece in 1940, and it embodies many of her ideas on *force*, redemptive love, and the importance of roots. It is an indirect appeal to her contemporaries to let themselves be motivated by compassion rather than nationalistic patriotism. In the original version of the thesis, I give a detailed analysis of *Venise Sauvée*. I am the first to draw a parallel between the tragedy and Weil's interpretation of the *Iliad* as a poem about *force* (M. Cabaud 2001*a*: 172–80).

[98] In *Writing as Resistance: Four Women Confronting the Holocaust*, Rachel Feldhay Brenner (1997) draws a parallel between Weil, Edith Stein, Anne Frank, and Etty Hillesum who responded to the horrors of war and of the Holocaust with their own moral self-improvement. Yet Brenner wrongly believes that it is the remnant of Enlightenment optimism that motivated these women—at least in Weil's case who was fully aware of the abyss of evil into which human beings can fall due to the pull of *pesanteur*.

[99] Weil thought that the Cathars, like the Greeks, were very perceptive about the nature of *force* and condemned it. She wrote two articles, 'L'Agonie d'une civilisation vue à travers un poème épique' ('A Medieval Epic Poem'/*SE*) and 'En quoi consiste l'inspiration occitanienne?' ('The Romanesque Renaissance'/*SE*), for a special issue of the *Cahiers du Sud* which was to appear in Feb. 1943 when she had already left

CONCLUSION

Trying to inspire a country is difficult, for it stands in contradiction to the widespread practice of propaganda in Weil's time. In an article written for the *Cahiers du Sud*, published in December 1942, Weil concludes by saying that: 'Nous sommes comme revenus à l'époque de Protagoras et des sophistes, l'époque où l'art de persuader, dont les slogans, la publicité, la propagande par réunions publiques, journal, cinéma, radio, constituent l'équivalent moderne, tenait lieu de pensée' (*S* 207–8).[100] Propaganda has been studied extensively, as Weil states in *L'Enracinement*, and has replaced real inspiration. For in contrast to the latter, propaganda: 'ferme, elle condamne tous les orifices [de l'âme] par où une inspiration pourrait passer; elle gonfle l'âme tout entière avec du fanatisme' (*E* 161).[101] In contrast, inspiration, one could add, opens the soul to the transcendent and to real values, such as truth, goodness, and justice, which is what Weil is trying to do, and wherein she sees the true task of the intellectual and apologist.

Force has been the theme of this chapter. The greatness of the Greeks is due to their understanding of the nature of *force*, a cognizance the French should acquire as well: 'La connaissance de la force comme chose absolument souveraine dans la nature tout entière, y compris toute la partie naturelle de l'âme humaine avec toutes les pensées et tous les sentiments qu'elle contient, et en même temps comme chose absolument méprisable, c'est la grandeur propre de la Grèce' (*IPC* 53).[102] At the moment the French are still in bondage, and are therefore

---

France. Though Weil wrongly identifies Catharism with Occitan civilization and projects her own Christian Platonism into it, the point is that Weil looked for inspiration in Catharism for her own times. Like the Cathars, she believes that modern civilization needs to put God in its centre. For a more detailed analysis of Weil's interpretation of the Cathars, see M. Cabaud 2001*a*: 180–2.

[100] 'It is as though we had returned to the age of Protagoras and the Sophists, the age when the art of persuasion—whose modern equivalent is advertising slogans, publicity, propaganda meetings, the press, the cinema, and radio—took the place of thought and controlled the fate of cities and accomplished coups d'état' (*SNL* 64).

[101] 'it closes, seals up all the openings [of the soul] through which an inspiration might pass; it fills the whole spirit with fanaticism' (*NR* 186).

[102] 'The recognition of might as an absolutely sovereign thing in all of nature, including the natural part of the human soul, with all the thoughts and all the feelings the soul contains, and at the same time as an absolutely detestable thing; this is the innate grandeur of Greece' (*IC* 116).

not able to understand objectively the cause of their suffering: 'Mais un poème comme l'*Iliade*, nous n'en sommes pas capables; la grâce d'écrire un tel poème nous a été enlevée parce que depuis trop de siècles nous avons oublié d'être justes. Nous ne savons plus connaître et décrire la force, parce que au plus profond de nous-mêmes, et sans vouloir le reconnaître, nous sommes à genoux devant elle' (*OC* ii/3. 299).[103] For works like the *Iliad* to be written at this point, a spiritual renewal would be necessary and had yet to occur. Weil wanted contribute to its advent.

---

[103] 'But we are incapable of a poem like the *Iliad*; the grace of writing such a poem has been taken away from us, for we have forgotten to be just for too many centuries. We are no longer able to know and describe might, for in our very depths and without wanting to acknowledge it, we are kneeling in front of it.'

6

Prometheus Bound — An Apologetics of the Cross

> Jamais, dans toute l'histoire actuellement connue, il n'y a eu d'époque où les âmes aient été tellement en péril qu'aujourd'hui à travers tout le globe terrestre. Il faut de nouveau élever le serpent d'airain pour que quiconque jette les yeux sur lui soit sauvé.[1]
>
> (*AD* 53)
>
> Heureux ceux pour qui le malheur entré dans la chair est le malheur du monde lui-même à leur époque. Ceux-là ont la possibilité et la fonction de connaître dans sa vérité, de contempler dans sa réalité le malheur du monde. C'est là la fonction rédemptrice elle-même.[2]
>
> (*PSO* 76)

How a good and omnipotent God can allow evil and suffering is a question which has haunted humanity at all times. But during World War II it was a particularly pertinent problem. It led some to atheism and others—such as Weil—to develop a theodicy which usually belongs to every apologetic endeavour. The *malheur* of her contemporaries obsessed Weil. She was tempted 'de pleurer des larmes

---

Some of the ideas in this and the following chapter have already appeared in 'Mystique et herméneutique: Simone Weil et sa lecture christologique d'*Electre* et du *Prométhée enchaîné*' in the *Cahiers Simone Weil* who allowed me to reproduce them here (Cabaud 2000). The *St Austin Review* kindly allowed me to reproduce sections from my article 'The Vocation of the Cross: Simone Weil's Theodicy' (Cabaud Meaney 2003*a*).

[1] 'In all the history now known there has never been a period in which souls have been in such peril as they are today in every part of the globe. The bronze serpent must be lifted up again so that whoever raises his eyes to it may be saved' (*WG* 32).

[2] 'Fortunate are those in whom the affliction which enters their flesh is the same one that afflicts the world itself in their time. They have the opportunity and the function of knowing the truth of the world's affliction and contemplating its reality. And that is the redemptive function itself' (*SL* 137).

de sang', when thinking of those who are unable bear their suffering (*PSO* 130).³ In a letter to Maurice Schumann from New York, she wrote: 'Le malheur répandu sur la surface du globe terrestre m'obsède et m'accable au point d'annuler mes facultés' (*EL* 199).⁴ Thus the question of theodicy was particularly close to Weil's heart, and she addressed it especially in her essay 'L'Amour de Dieu et le malheur', as well as in many of her other writings in a more fragmentary form. Though she does not explicitly mention the question of theodicy in her interpretation of Aeschylus' *Prometheus Bound*, it seems to me that in her reading of the ancient tragedy she is indirectly presenting her readers with an 'answer' to this problem. For by describing Prometheus' suffering as an illustration of Christ's Passion, she is providing the reader with what alone can give meaning to affliction: 'La seule source de clarté assez lumineuse pour éclairer le malheur est la Croix du Christ' (*PSO* 124).⁵

Prima facie, of all the Greek texts that Weil discusses in any detail, Aeschylus' *Prometheus Bound* lends itself the most to a Christological reading. Prometheus seems to be the most Christlike figure in Greek mythology: he loved human beings to the extent that he saved them from extinction by bringing them fire against the explicit orders of Zeus, and was consequently nailed to a high rock in the Caucasus. Thus the nature of his suffering (crucifixion) and its cause (his love for humanity) are similar to Christ's. On the other hand, Prometheus suffers because he disobeyed Zeus, in contrast to Christ who obeyed his Father unto death. Prometheus rails against Zeus, whilst Zeus heaps greater sufferings upon him. Weil's reading of this drama contradicts the text perhaps the most among her interpretations. Weil claims that 'tout est liberté dans ce drame fait de chaînes et de clous' though the protagonist is immobilized throughout the drama (*IPC* 104).⁶ What she means is that Prometheus accepted this suffering freely. He knew what was awaiting him, yet decided to ensure the survival of the human race by his gift of fire. In Weil's eyes, he experiences an abandonment similar to that of Christ on the cross. In reality his disagreement with Zeus is merely apparent. Neither he nor Zeus really hate each

---

³ 'weep tears of blood' (*SNL* 198).
⁴ 'The suffering all over the world obsesses and overwhelms me to the point of annihilating my faculties' (*SL* 156).
⁵ 'The Cross of Christ is the only source of light that is bright enough to illumine affliction' (*SNL* 194).
⁶ 'All is freedom in this drama built of chains and of nails' (*IC* 69).

other. Freely the one accepts suffering, and freely the other bestows it—a surprising idea, given Prometheus' angry words when talking about Zeus.

For Weil to claim that Prometheus and Zeus love each other, she must think that the suffering Zeus inflicts on the Titan does not contradict his love for him, just as human suffering does not contradict God's love for us. This leads to the question of theodicy to which Weil gives various answers that need to be taken into account to understand her interpretation. Not only does suffering leave her faith in God's goodness and omnipotence unscathed, but she believes that it can even become the sign of his loving presence. Prometheus may not be aware of this at the moment of his greatest distress, just as many human beings have the impression that God has abandoned them in their affliction. But they need to learn to read God's/Zeus' hidden presence behind the veil of pain.[7]

Thus I will analyse Weil's Christological interpretation of Prometheus' suffering as a Passion, and show how this ultimately is the answer Weil gives to the question of theodicy. In order to do so, I will assemble Weil's different approaches to theodicy. Despite her unorthodox reading of the drama, I will try to situate it among the various interpretations of the play. This drama is central, in Weil's eyes, for an understanding of Greek culture, and thus for the re-Christianization of Europe by means of the classics. As will be shown, it can also be seen as a paradigm of Weil's understanding of art and artistic creation.

CHRONOLOGY AND QUOTATIONS

Though Weil quotes a few lines from Aeschylus' tragedy on the inside front cover of her *Cahier* I, her interest in the play only arose later in her life (*OC* vi/1. 69) (*Prom.* 88–92). She does not mention it in connection with her projected articles for *Entre Nous*. In the early pages of her first *Cahier* she briefly refers to a *Propos* on *Prometheus* written by

---

[7] Once again, Weil identifies Greek gods with the Christian God. For example, she writes in her short text 'Zeus et Prométhée': 'Zeus [dans les tragédies d'Eschyle] semblait y être regardé comme étant le Dieu suprême—c'est-à-dire le seul Dieu' ('Zeus [in Aeschylus' tragedies] seems to be regarded therein as the supreme God, that is to say, the only God') (*SG* 44/*IC* 57). Zeus and God will therefore be used interchangeably in this chapter.

Alain, probably that of 5 April 1924 (ibid. 86–7).[8] Her interest in the Prometheus theme seems to have been awakened only in 1937. Was it her contact with Christianity that gave the impetus or simply her first personal experience of antiquity during her first trip to Italy in 1937?[9] In any case, she wrote her poem 'Prométhée' after this trip to Italy, during which in the chapel of Santa Maria degli Angeli she had knelt down for the first time in her life.[10] Weil had written only three poems before then, namely the 'Vers lus au goûter de la Saint-Charlemagne' ('Verses read for afternoon tea on Saint-Charlemagne'), for the occasion at Henri IV in January 1926; then 'A une jeune fille riche' ('To a rich young girl') which she also composed during her years of study; and finally 'Éclair' ('Lightning') in 1929, after which she did not write any poetry for eight years. 'Prométhée' opened a new creative phase in her life, for it was followed by another five poems and her tragedy *Venise sauvée*.

Weil sent her 'Prométhée' to Paul Valéry, who wrote back mentioning a series of criticisms as well as some positive points (*P* 9–10). 'Prométhée' starts off by describing the savage state to which human beings would have been reduced without the help of Prometheus. Then it enumerates the gifts he gave to humanity, starting with fire, the wheel, the lever, religious rites and temples, languages, writing, and numbers. The last stanza ends with a description of Prometheus' sufferings counterbalancing the depiction in the first verse of the miseries which would have awaited humanity without his help. Weil's poem is not religious, nor is her interpretation of Prometheus. The last line of the second stanza, speaking of the gift of fire, says: 'Qu'il vous aima, pour faire un don si beau', without taking on a redemptive connotation.[11] In v. 4 she mentions that Prometheus is the author of religious rites and the temple, but this is not emphasized. In the last stanza the Titan 'pend crucifié' and '[l]a douleur froide entre comme une lame' which reminds

---

[8] *OC* vi/1. 461, n. 86. While Alain interprets the Aeschylean figures allegorically, Weil's comments seem disconnected from Alain's interpretation, for she meditates on the power of a tyrant who can damn an innocent person by making him lose his mind, his innocence, and ultimately his soul (ibid. 86–7).

[9] In the spring of 1938 she writes in her fifth letter to Posternak to whom she had sent her poem 'Prométhée' that '[l]'Italie [. . .] a ressuscité en moi la vocation pour la poésie, refoulée depuis l'adolescence' ('Italy [. . .] reawakened the impulse to write poetry which I had repressed [. . .] since adolescence') (*CSW* 10/2: 129/*SL* 93) (SP ii. 164).

[10] SP ii. 164.

[11] 'How he must have loved you, to make you such a beautiful gift.'

one of the centurion's lance piercing Christ's side.[12] Yet these lines are only echoes of Christianity, for the poem does not present Prometheus as a prefiguration of Christ, as Weil's later interpretation will.

Though 1937 shows Weil's budding interest in the Prometheus theme, the Aeschylean drama had not yet captivated her attention sufficiently for her to translate passages for Posternak as she did from the *Iliad*. But by the time she left Marseille in 1942, *Prometheus Bound* was part of her canon, for she translated sections for both Bousquet and Thibon:[13] therein she gives the framework of the play, starting with Prometheus' monologue, then his first speeches in dialogue with the Chorus, and ends with his final words which he cries out before being buried under the rocks. Prometheus' first speech, his monologue in lines 88–108, are among Weil's favourite, since she quotes them often in her *Cahiers* (*OC* vi/1. 263, 370, 372, vi/2. 154–5). In *La Source grecque* and in her *Intuitions* she compares this passage to the end of the book of Job, where suffering allows for a greater revelation of the world's beauty (*SG* 45–6; *IPC* 37).[14] To Thibon she simply sent the last lines of the play, 1080–1 and 1089 ff., both in French and in Greek. On a few pages of her *Cahier* 3, Weil translates sections of the play at greater length, for example: Hephaistos expressing his reluctance to obey Zeus' order to nail Prometheus to the rocks (*Prom.* 18–28, 31–4); or Prometheus speaking to the daughters of Ocean or bemoaning his fate (*OC* vi/1. 369–70) (*Prom.* 136–43, 152–8).[15] She ends her *Cahier* with five quotations from *Prometheus*, whilst she gives only two from *Antigone*, one from *Electra*, and one from the *Iliad* (*OC* vi/1. 379). It is in her long section on *Prometheus* in her *Intuitions pré-chrétiennes*, however, that Weil translated the most extensively from the tragedy (*IPC* 94 ff.).[16]

Among her interpretations of Greek tragedies, Weil devoted the most space to the *Prometheus*. There are about thirteen consecutive pages in the *Intuitions*, and many references to it throughout her other works. There is also a fragment called 'Zeus et Prométhée', published in *La Source grecque*. These references have not been considered all together

---

[12] 'hangs crucified', 'the cold pain enters like a blade'.
[13] For Bousquet she translated ll. 88–108, 112–13, 119–26, 141–3, 152–8, and the last lines of the tragedy, namely 1080–93 (*Œ* 664–6; *CSW* 19/2: 147–9).
[14] Weil's comparison of Job to Christ is criticized by Sourisse in his article 'Job, figure du Christ?' (2003).
[15] Weil also translates ll. 239–40, 514, 546–50.
[16] ll. 89–112, 118–26, 141–4, 152–9, 190–5, 208–10, 218–20, 233–43, 248, 250–2, 267–72, 306–8, 386–8, 393, 437–40, 442–51, 469–75, 505–10, 542–4, 612–17, 755–7, 760–2, 764, 768–70, 1080–93.

before, nor has any study been made of Weil's reading of the drama.[17] Together with *Agamemnon* she thought *Prometheus* was the best among Aeschylus' tragedies, and it is of *Prometheus* that she gives the most detailed interpretation (*OC* vi/2. 389).[18]

PROMETHEUS CHRISTUS

The similarities between Christ and Prometheus are so obvious that one might think that many interpreters must have drawn the parallel before. According to Raymond Trousson in *Le Thème de Prométhée dans la littérature européenne*, many nineteenth- and twentieth-century scholars thought that the Church Fathers had done so. But as Trousson points out, they failed to see that only Tertullian seems to have made the comparison.[19] In fact, only one passage in Tertullian's *Adversus Marcionem* would allow for this interpretation, namely when he speaks of the 'crucibus Caucasorum' ('the crosses of the Caucasus'), and the 'verus Prometheus deus omnipotens blasphemiis lancinatur' ('the true Prometheus, the almighty God, lacerated by blasphemies').[20] However, in his *Apologetics* Tertullian points to Christ as being the real Prometheus in contrast to the mythical one, which was invented merely to depreciate in advance the Christian truths: 'De[us] unic[us] [...] qui universa condiderit, qui hominem de humo struxerit; hic enim est verus Prometheus' ('there is but one God who made the universe and formed man from the earth. He is the true Prometheus, who has regulated the world with a fixed order and fixed endings for the ages').[21] Weil obviously knew the first quotation since she refers to it in her *Connaissance*, but there is no indication that she knew about the second quotation as well (*CS* 55).[22]

Both Prometheus and Christ are crucified, one on a mountain, the other on the cross. The tragedy significantly ends with the word

---

[17] Except in M. Cabaud 2000.
[18] She mentions Prometheus first in her list of 'images du Christ' (*CS* 290).
[19] Trousson 1976: i. 73 ff.   [20] Ibid. i. 73; Tertullian 1972: 1. 1. 5 (my trans.).
[21] Trousson 1976: i. 77; Tertullian 1889: ch. 18 p. 61/1950: 54.
[22] Trousson (1976: i. 65 n. 24) mentions Ronsard, Schlegel, Quinet, and Paul de Saint-Victor who made more detailed, but facile comparisons between the two figures: for example the eagle's beak ripping Prometheus' breast stands for the lance's point piercing Christ's side, or the Oceanides are the holy women at the foot of the cross.

πάσχω, which, according to Weil, shows that Prometheus undergoes a Passion (*IPC* 99). Prometheus cannot change his fate. Though he knows who the son is whom Zeus will father and who will then overturn his reign, Prometheus does not give his secret away. To do so would only make his release less likely, even if he could thereby avoid the greater punishment that Zeus threatens him with and carries out by the end of the tragedy. Similarly, Christ is submitted to his fate, but in contrast to Prometheus, in obedience to his Father's will.[23]

Like Christ, and like Isaiah's 'righteous one'—'maltraité, injurié, il n'ouvrait pas la bouche'[24]—Prometheus is silent when he is nailed to the Caucasus by an unwilling Hephaistos (Isa. 53: 7). He makes himself heard only when Hephaistos, Power, and Force have left the scene, in 'une explosion de douleur', indicating the physical nature of his suffering (*IPC* 94).[25] Earlier on, in an analysis of the perfectly just man in Plato's *Republic*, Weil gives a more detailed account of the Passion, at the end of which she refers to Prometheus:

> C'est l'absence de prestige, et non pas la souffrance, qui est l'essence même de la Passion. Les mots d'Isaïe 'homme de douleurs, expert en maladies', n'ont leur vrai sens que pour un peuple où la maladie était méprisée. Mais la maladie aurait été trop peu. Il fallait une souffrance de caractère pénal, car l'homme n'est vraiment dépouillé de toute participation au prestige social que quand la justice pénale l'a retranché de la société.   (ibid. 78)[26]

Christ was punished like a common criminal, as is Prometheus for stealing fire and disobeying Zeus. Christ is spat upon and ridiculed, while Prometheus is insulted by Power and by Hermes who comes at the end to try to obtain his secret. It is humiliating to be punished publicly and sneered at: 'Mais dans l'air ballotté misérablement, | mes ennemis font leur joie de ma souffrance' (ibid. 95) (*Prom.* 158–9).[27] Others who

---

[23] For the Christological character of Prometheus, see e.g. *E* 251; *PSO* 60; *OC* vi/2. 361; *AD* 238.
[24] 'ill-treated and afflicted, he never opened his mouth'.
[25] 'an explosion of pain' (*IC* 88).
[26] 'It is the absence of prestige, and not the physical suffering, which is the very essence of the Passion. The words of Isaiah: "a man of sorrows and acquainted with grief" have their true meaning only for a people among whom illness is despised. But the physical suffering would have been too little. A suffering of penal character was required, for man is not truly stripped of all participation in social prestige until penal justice has cut him off from society' (ibid. 137).
[27] 'But here, wretchedly battered by the wind, | my enemies exult over my suffering' (ibid. 62).

die for the sake of an idea, or for religious or political reasons, are often admired, since there is a certain prestige attached to that kind of death. But Christ 'a été ridiculisé comme ces fous qui se prennent pour des rois, puis a péri comme un criminel de droit commun' (*IPC* 78; *AD* 108).[28] He did not die with heroic elation, but after having asked his Father in vain to spare him and men to console him. Similarly Prometheus is 'haï des dieux, abandonné des hommes'.[29] He feels ashamed because of the 'humiliation du malheur' and would prefer to be hidden from the sight of all (*IPC* 102) (*Prom.* 152 ff.). However, Prometheus is not as abandoned as Weil claims. Not only do the daughters of Ocean keep him company, but Ocean himself visits him, as does Io. As Oliver Taplin points out in *The Stagecraft of Aeschylus*, the Chorus sings that the whole earth 'Asians, Colchians, Scythians, and Arabians, the sea, Hades, and the rivers [...] all lament in sympathy for Prometheus' (*Prom.* 407 ff.).[30] However, according to Weil, Prometheus receives the visit of Ocean and Io, not because Aeschylus wants to show that the Titan is not so lonely after all, but because a drama requires a certain amount of interaction on the stage. Prometheus is abandoned in a deserted place and experiences solitude, and this is what the play intends to convey (*IPC* 102).

Prometheus suffers out of love for mortals, which is why he cannot console himself with thoughts of glory. He pitied them, but was not pitied himself—just like Antigone, as Weil points out. The thought that Love is unloved made St Francis of Assisi weep, and Weil believes that the Greeks were haunted by the same thought (ibid. 99).[31] It is true that Prometheus does not glory at the thought of his revolt against Zeus. This contradicts later appropriations which see him as the symbol of human revolt against God, authority, religion, etc. Weil's interpretation would thus be closer to the original than some of the readings of the *Sturm und Drang* or of the Romantics.[32]

However, Weil fails to see that Prometheus does not fulfil the ideal of perfect love. The Titan has a temperament similar to that of Zeus,

---

[28] 'He was ridiculed like those madmen who take themselves for kings; then he perished like a common criminal' (*IC* 138).
[29] 'hated by the gods, abandoned by men' (ibid. 67).
[30] Taplin 1977: 264.
[31] Weil also draws a parallel between the figure of Love in Diotima's myth in the *Symposium* and Prometheus. Love is the child of *Penia* (Poverty) and of *Poros* (Plenty), and inherits from both parents attributes which are similar to Prometheus' characteristics (*IPC* 65 ff., 99–100; *CS* 152). Both are mediators bringing redemption to humanity as Christ does.
[32] Trousson 1976: i. 234 ff., ii. 299–300.

for 'both are "harsh", "bold", "unbending", "full of rage and pride"', as Mark Griffith points out in his introduction of the tragedy.[33] As the drama develops, Prometheus' anger towards Zeus grows increasingly violent. Furthermore, Prometheus is himself a traitor to his race, for he sided with Zeus in an earlier conflict, and this is what brings about the decline and fall of the Titans. So when Zeus turns against Prometheus, this is not so very different from what Prometheus himself did.

From the human perspective one tends to see Prometheus positively, namely as the saviour of the human race. Yet how beneficial is Prometheus' gift ultimately? According to the myth as related in Plato's *Protagoras*, the fire the Titan gave to human beings was not sufficient for their survival.[34] It took *Dike*, justice, which Zeus bestowed on them, to make life in community possible; but this version of the myth is, of course, later than Aeschylus' adaptation.[35] In the Aeschylean tragedy Prometheus does not give human beings fire only, but also the knowledge of numbers, of technology, and generally 'l'intelligence de l'ordre du monde', as Weil calls it (*IPC* 102).[36] Concerning the doom of death, Prometheus grants them 'd'aveugles espérances' (ibid. 96) (*Prom.* 252).[37] Rather than allowing them to understand their desperate situation, the Titan infuses into their hearts vain hopes. But Weil takes this to mean that he gives them supernatural hope, namely the belief in immortality which is to be upheld in the face of death (*IPC* 102). The hope is 'blind' because it has to survive the dark night of the soul, as St John of the Cross calls it. But on a supernatural level it is not blind, for it perceives otherwise invisible realities. Thus the fire that Prometheus brings to human beings symbolizes for Weil the Holy Spirit:

La vertu propre de la foudre consiste à produire le consentement aux commandements de Dieu. Donc la foudre est l'Amour, autrement dit le Saint-Esprit. C'est le feu que le Christ est venu jeter sur terre. Cela éclaire la signification de l'acte de Prométhée dérobant la foudre à Zeus pour donner le feu aux hommes. (*SG* 161–2)[38]

---

[33] Griffith 1983: 10; see also Scully 1975: 15.
[34] Griffith 1983: 4; Plato, *Protagoras* 320c–323a.
[35] Aeschylus also does not refer to the punishment human beings incur because of Prometheus, as related in the Hesiodic poems (Griffith 1983: 1) (*Theogony* 521–616).
[36] 'knowledge of the order of the world' (*IC* 67).   [37] 'blind hopes' (ibid. 62).
[38] 'The special virtue of the lightning is that it induces consent to God's commands. Therefore the lightning is Love, in other words the Holy Spirit. It is the fire which Christ came to throw upon earth. This clarifies the meaning of Prometheus' theft of Zeus' lightning in order to give men fire, a gift which prevented Zeus from annihilating them, therefore a redemptive gift' (*SNL* 138). See also *OC* vi/2. 455; *CS* 312.

Weil writes this in a short note on the *Hymn to Zeus* by Cleanthes. The Holy Spirit in the guise of fire bestows wisdom or supernatural reason which makes one understand the mysteries of faith. But to attain this wisdom one must embrace the cross: 'Saint Jean de la Croix savait qu'il y a une raison surnaturelle, lui qui écrivait qu'on pénètre seulement par la Croix dans les secrets de la Sagesse de Dieu' (*CS* 56).[39] Reason transformed by love, tested by the fire of suffering, can thus acquire a supernatural perspective. If the cross is the path to wisdom, then Prometheus' own suffering must be a lesson to human beings. In this light Ocean's rather trite-sounding words, 'ton malheur est un enseignement' take on a new meaning for Weil, namely of how suffering teaches wisdom (*IPC* 97, 104) (*Prom.* 393).[40] In consequence, Prometheus' suffering would itself be his greatest present to humanity, and illogically the gift of fire would actually depend on it, rather than vice versa.[41]

Weil also sees a connection between Ocean's comment and the line from the *Agamemnon*: 'par la souffrance la connaissance' (*IPC* 104) (*Ag.* 177).[42] The question is, however, who is gaining knowledge through suffering? Instead of becoming wiser, Prometheus becomes more harsh and irate. The cruel punishment he inflicts on the Titan and the message he sends through Hermes indicate that Zeus does not show any signs of increasing wisdom either. Anyway, as Weil points out, Prometheus *is* the wisdom of Zeus which ensured him his victory over the Titans, but which he also loses once he punishes him (*IPC* 103).[43] Is it perhaps the audience that is supposed to be learning through Prometheus' suffering? If this is the case, then the tragedy would be an initiation into the meaning of suffering in the light of the divine. But what exactly do the spectators learn? The later section in this chapter on Weil's theodicy will perhaps offer an answer.

---

[39] 'St. John of the Cross knew that there is a supernatural reason, for he wrote it is only by the Cross that one penetrates the secrets of the Wisdom of God' (*NB* 110).

[40] 'Thy calamity [...] is a lesson' (*IC* 63).

[41] 'C'est en crucifiant Prométhée que Zeus a ouvert aux hommes la route de la sagesse' (*SG* 45). ('It is in crucifying Prometheus that Zeus has opened the way of wisdom to men') (*IC* 58).

[42] 'By suffering comes understanding' (*IC* 69).

Weil ascribes great depth to this phrase, while Lloyd-Jones in his article 'Zeus in Aeschylus' calls it proverbial (*IPC* 103) (Lloyd-Jones 1956: 62).

[43] However, Weil's identification of Prometheus with Zeus annuls the conflict within the tragedy, as Fraisse points out, apart from being contradictory (Fraisse 1982a: 205–6).

Prometheus Bound 153

DIFFERENT INTERPRETATIVE APPROACHES

The manner in which Zeus is presented in *Prometheus* is quite different from his positive depiction in *Agamemnon*. This has led some critics to believe that *Prometheus Bound* is not by Aeschylus, or at least only partially so.[44] In many ways the drama is unusual. For example the protagonist is on stage from beginning to end—which was normally not the case in Greek drama. However, the question of the play's authenticity is not significant here. Of more avail is the debate about the development of the plot. The sequel to *Prometheus Bound* was probably *Prometheus Unbound*.[45] Hence the question arises how the conflict between Zeus and the Titan was resolved, and here different answers have been given.[46]

The so-called evolutionary theory claims that Zeus develops in the course of the trilogy, that he goes from being a harsh tyrant to being a kind and wise ruler. L. Séchan, G. Thomson, and E. R. Dodds, for example, defend this position.[47] Yet nowhere else in Greek mythology does a god change so radically, as Lloyd-Jones points out in the aforementioned article. The Furies in the *Eumenides* do not alter, but simply make a deal with the Athenians, as will Zeus in *Prometheus Unbound*. Furthermore, Zeus does not have to change in order to come to an agreement with Prometheus. Had he done so, Prometheus would not have needed to sell his knowledge in return for his freedom.[48] However, there are some indications of a transformation in Zeus. From the fragments extant of *Prometheus Unbound*, it becomes clear that Zeus releases the Titans, and Winnington-Ingram suggests that even Cronus might have been freed and sent to the island of the blessed.[49] Furthermore, the reconciliation of Zeus and Prometheus is announced in lines 194–5. Both will come together by their own free will (σπεύδων σπεύδοντι/*speúdon*

---

[44] See e.g. Schmid in *Untersuchungen zum Gefesselten Prometheus* or Taplin whose analysis of the structural originality of the play in ch. 5 of *The Stagecraft of Aeschylus* leads him to this conclusion (Schmid 1929: 281 ff.; Conacher 1980: 124; Taplin 1977: 240 ff.).

[45] See Lloyd-Jones's (1983: 97 ff.) discussion of the sequence within the trilogy (if there was a trilogy), as well as Dodds' suggestions (1985: 37 ff.).

[46] In *Aeschylus' Prometheus Bound: A Literary Commentary*, D. J. Conacher gives an excellent survey of the different approaches adopted by various scholars (Conacher 1980: 120 ff.).

[47] Lloyd-Jones 1956: 56; 1983: 95; Conacher 1980: 121 ff.

[48] Lloyd-Jones 1956: 57, 66–7; 1983: 97.   [49] Winnington-Ingram 1983: 185.

speúdonti) as Weil points out (*IPC* 105; *OC* vi/3. 225). Prometheus uses the word ἀρθμόν/*arthmón* to speak about their future reconciliation: in Weil's eyes, this is wordplay on ἀριθμόν/*arithmón*, 'number', and suggests the Pythagorean notion of harmony. This would indicate that the newly established bond between the two would be strong and harmonious (*IPC* 100–1) (*Prom.* 94).[50] According to Conacher, however, the words ἀρθμόν and φιλότητα/*philótēta*, which are used to describe the future agreement between Zeus and Prometheus, have a political ring to them. The nature of Prometheus' liberation, as announced in the tragedy, seems to be a compromise. He may even need to find a substitute for himself, namely the centaur Chiron who, wounded by the poisoned arrow of Heracles, is willing to give up his immortality in order to put an end to his pain.[51] Furthermore in a fragment from *Prometheus Unbound* the Titan says to Heracles after being rescued by him: 'This dearest child of the Father *I hate*!' which is another sign that their reconciliation is of a political nature.[52]

Thus Conacher's reading is political, as is Lloyd-Jones's. It is not so much Zeus as the political circumstances that change within the trilogy and reveal a different side of Zeus' character.[53] For Lloyd-Jones, Zeus' justice is the same in all Aeschylus' plays. His justice consists in his rule of others, and is not necessarily a guideline he is himself obliged to follow.[54]

In contrast to the evolutionary theory, some scholars such as Wilamowitz and Solmsen think that the *Prometheia* (the trilogy around the Prometheus-theme) simply portrays the evolution of humanity's concept of God. It is not Zeus who changes, but the Greeks' understanding of Zeus.[55] In Weil's terms one could say that it is all a question of *lecture*. It is our reading of Zeus' or God's actions that determines our concept of why he lets Prometheus or human beings suffer. He may seem to have ordered Power and Might to punish the Titan, but perhaps

---

[50] Similarly Weil sees in the use of the word ἐρρύθμισμαι/*errúthmismai*, a hidden reference to rhythm, which indirectly points to the concept of number and harmony, and would thus be another Pythagorean reference (*IPC* 100–1).

[51] Conacher 1980: 135. Weil is aware of this aspect of the myth, as her entry in the *Connaissance* shows: Chiron 's'est, dit-on, substitué à Prométhée dans le Tartare' ('it is said [...] took the place of Prometheus in Tartarus') (*CS* 184/*FLN* 225–6). And in her earlier *Cahiers* from Marseille she writes: 'Héraclès delivre Prométhée' ('It is Heracles who releases Prometheus') (*OC* vi/3. 253/*NB* 543).

[52] My italics. This fragment is from Plutarch's *Life of Pompey the Great* (Scully 1975: 108, frag. 14).

[53] Conacher 1980: 133 ff.

[54] Lloyd-Jones 1956: 57 ff., 60, 65–6; 1983: 95 ff., 102.

[55] Conacher 1980: 122; Wilamowitz 1914: 150; Solmsen 1995: 147–8.

he merely lets necessity take its course, as Weil suggests: 'A ce moment Dieu apparaît comme soumis à la nécessité; non seulement Dieu comme victime, mais Dieu comme bourreau; non seulement le Dieu qui a pris la forme d'un esclave, mais aussi le Dieu qui a gardé la forme du maître' (*IPC* 105).[56] Though Weil talks here about Hephaistos who unwillingly chains Prometheus to the rock, what she says can be applied to Zeus as well. For Weil speaks about both gods in terms of God, perhaps revealing different aspects of him. If Zeus and Prometheus are only apparently separated, like Christ on the cross from his Father, then both have subjected themselves in different ways to necessity. Prometheus/Christ has to obey Zeus/his Father, and Zeus/God agrees to let the Titan/his Son suffer.

The points raised in this chapter have already shown how difficult it is to reconcile Weil's Christological reading with the actual Greek text. For Zeus is 'severe', 'harsh', 'he in rancour hath set his soul inflexibly and keepeth in subjection the race sprung from Uranus', and Prometheus considers himself to be his enemy (*Prom.* 77, 189, 163–6, 119). In contrast, Christ's cry is one of distress, not of accusation and hatred.

Yet if Wilamowitz and Solmsen are right, then Weil's reading is not that far off the mark, regardless of her anachronisms and Christological projections. If the trilogy portrays in fact the evolution of the Greeks' concept of Zeus rather than describing his own development (if there is a development), then Prometheus' perception of him as well as that of the other characters may well be wrong. For Wilamowitz's theory to be true, the characters' and spectators' perception of Zeus would have had to undergo a complete reversal in the *Prometheus Unbound*, which is what Weil is expecting (*IPC* 103, 105). Prometheus would have learnt through suffering to perceive Zeus' 'true' nature. Similarly Weil advocates in her theodicy that human beings need to learn to read God's loving presence behind the experience of affliction.

THE RIGHTEOUSNESS OF PROMETHEUS

Both Prometheus and Zeus are ambiguous characters. Although Prometheus is perceived positively from a human perspective since he saves the human race, his behaviour towards the Titans is problematic. He

---

[56] 'At this moment God appears as submitting to necessity; not only God as victim but God as executioner; not only the God who has taken the form of a slave but also the God who has kept the form of the master' (*IC* 70).

sides with Zeus in a conflict between the parties, and in consequence the Titans lose and are sent to Tartarus. However, he had offered his services first to the Titans who refused (*OC* vi/3. 234). Thus he may legitimately turn to Zeus who is more willing to let himself be guided by wisdom, rather than by the mere power exercised by the Titans.[57] According to Weil, Prometheus is righteous, and he embodies the 'truly just man' of Plato's *Republic* mentioned earlier on (*IPC* 79; *CS* 18/*OC* vi/3. 387). Paradoxically suffering has an important epistemological significance to play, according to Plato, in determining who is truly just and who is not. Without suffering, people may seem to be acting justly when in reality they are motivated by the very prestige which the appearance of justice bestows on them. Only when they have nothing to win, can one be sure that they are authentically just. Weil translates the relevant passages from the *Republic* in her *Intuitions*: 'Il faut qu'il [l'homme juste] soit rendu nu de toutes choses excepté la justice... que ne commettant rien d'injuste, il ait la plus grande réputation d'injustice, afin que ce soit une pierre de touche pour sa justice, si la mauvaise réputation et ses conséquences ne la font pas fondre, si au contraire il reste inébranlable, paraissant injuste toute sa vie, mais réellement juste' (IPC: 79).[58] Prometheus and Christ had to suffer and to appear like criminals for their justice to be ultimately revealed. The Passion has become an epistemological necessity, an indispensable criterion in order to discern the truly just man. However, Prometheus' suffering, as Weil admits, is more of a redemptive nature than of epistemological significance (ibid. 85). Yet there is a link between the two. Because of original sin, appearance and reality do not coincide. Those who appear to be just, are not necessarily so.

Prometheus seems to be loving human beings too much. He speaks himself of his 'too great love for mankind' (ibid. 95) (*Prom.* 122). Conversely, one might think that the Hippolytus of Euripides loves the gods (or at least Artemis) too much at the expense of other human

---

[57] Furthermore the Titans ate Dionysus Zagreus, the son of Zeus and Persephone, for which they were struck by lightning. Thus Prometheus would have been justified in turning to Zeus rather than to them, as Weil writes in her *Cahiers* (*OC* vi/3. 168, 174–5).

[58] Plato, *Republic* 2. 360e–362c. 'Let him [the just man] be shown naked of all things except justice... that while committing no injustice he may have the greatest reputation for injustice in order that this may be a touchstone for his justice, to prove whether this evil reputation, and the consequences thereof, make him waver, or whether on the contrary he continues steadfast, seeming all his life to be unjust but being truly just' (*IC* 138).

Prometheus Bound 157

beings, as Weil suggests in her *Connaissance*. But this is only a question of perspective:

La notion des couches planes verticalement superposées dans la vie de l'âme, et dont la plus haute est au-dessus de la conscience et du psychologique, il n'y a rien de plus important. Ce qui est vrai dans la plus haute est faux au-dessous, et réciproquement. Ainsi c'est dans le secret de la plus haute que l'amour de Dieu et l'amour du prochain ne font qu'un. Au-dessous, dans la conscience, l'amour authentique de Dieu apparaît comme une trahison à l'égard des hommes (Hippolyte) et l'amour authentique de l'homme comme une trahison à l'égard de Dieu (Prométhée): Le Christ unit les deux. (*CS* 132–3)[59]

As became clear in Ch. 4, Weil is very critical of any attempt to exclude the supernatural, since by its elimination morality becomes an absurdity and certain actions become unintelligible. In consequence, Antigone giving up her life to bury her brother, people dying for their faith, or renouncing everything to enter a monastery, cause scandal. But from a supernatural perspective their behaviour makes sense and may even be required. A reductive approach, on the other hand, would probably perceive their behaviour as masochism or as fear of life. But what Weil rightly says about Christ, namely that he combines the love of God with the love of human beings, is difficult to apply to the Titan for his hatred does not look like a disguised form of love.

As with Antigone, Weil sees in Prometheus an *être pur*, assuming suffering without passing it on (*CS* 13–14/*OC* vi/3. 382). Not only does he suffer for the sake of human beings, but he is also concerned about the fate of those trying to help him; he dissuades Ocean from pleading in vain with Zeus for fear that he might be punished as well (*Prom.* 346 ff.). Eventually his situation becomes worse, when Zeus sends an eagle every day to eat his liver, which grows back overnight. This leads Weil to draw a eucharistic parallel between Christ and the Titan: 'La chair vive est entamée et dévorée. (Prométhée, comme le Christ, est mangé)' (*CS* 178).[60]

---

[59] 'The idea of vertically superimposed levels in the life of the soul, the highest of them being above consciousness and the psychological—there is nothing more important. What is true on the highest level is false lower down, and reciprocally. Thus it is in the secrecy of the highest level that the love of God and the love of one's neighbour are one love. Below, in consciousness, the authentic love of God appears as treachery towards men (Hippolytus) and the authentic love of man as treachery towards God (Prometheus). Christ unites the two' (*FLN* 179).
[60] 'The living flesh is attacked and is being devoured. (Prometheus, like Christ, is eaten)' (ibid. 220).

Furthermore, he is an *être pur* since Weil surprisingly believes that he did not really disobey Zeus: 'Prométhée n'a pas désobéi à Zeus, quoiqu'il ait souffert un châtiment' (*OC* vi/3. 112).[61] If he is punished, Weil wonders whether it is for his disobedience—'ce ne serait donc pas pour le punir [que Zeus le fait souffrir]?'—or so that he may receive wisdom (ibid. 98).[62] Thus in reality, 'il n'y a pas eu de vol de la part de Prométhée',[63] for Zeus agreed to this initiative; otherwise would Zeus not have taken back the fire from human beings? 'Mais Prométhée n'en savait rien'—and feels punished and abandoned by Zeus, just as anybody who experiences affliction will feel abandoned by God (ibid. 112):[64] 'Le malheur rend Dieu absent pendant un temps, plus absent qu'un mort, plus absent que la lumière dans un cachot complètement ténébreux' (*AD* 102).[65] Weil is now leading us into the realm of pure speculation. To understand her reading of the drama, however, her theodicy needs to be investigated in order to comprehend her justification of Zeus fully. How far removed it may be from the actual play is a different question.

THE RIGHTEOUSNESS OF ZEUS—WEIL'S THEODICY

Weil was aware of the questions the drama of human suffering poses about God's goodness, power, and even his very existence.[66] It was not only a theoretical question for her, but one she had experienced herself during her year of industrial work and during her headaches, which brought her to the brink of suicide (*AD* 41–2; *PSO* 80). She wrote the following to Schumann: 'J'éprouve un déchirement qui s'aggrave sans

---

[61] 'Prometheus did not disobey Zeus, although he was made to suffer punishment' (*NB* 426).
[62] '[Zeus therefore makes him suffer] *not* [in order] [. . .] to punish him?' (ibid. 413).
[63] 'there was no theft on the part of Prometheus' (ibid. 426).
[64] 'but Prometheus knew nothing about it' (ibid.).
[65] 'Affliction causes God to be absent for a time, more absent than a dead man, more absent than light in the utter darkness of a cell' (*SNL* 172).
[66] Weil does not offer a systematic answer to the problem of evil and suffering. Her reflections on theodicy are scattered throughout her work and sometimes seem inconsistent. The problems involved are complex, and go beyond the scope of this book. For a more detailed analysis of specific incongruencies, see Gabellieri's excellent and detailed article 'La Nuit du don' (1996), Birou's 'Introduction à la problématique du mal chez Simone Weil' (1996), and Sourisse's 'Sur une aporie concernant le problème du mal chez Simone Weil' (1996).

cesse, à la fois dans l'intelligence et au centre du cœur, par l'incapacité où je suis de penser ensemble dans la vérité le malheur des hommes, la perfection de Dieu et le lien entre les deux' (*EL* 213).[67] But in her essay on the question, 'L'Amour de Dieu et le malheur', she describes how *malheur* may ultimately become an occasion for greater union with God though it first seems to separate us from him.[68]

Affliction or *malheur* remains the great enigma of human life. It is not astonishing that the innocent are killed, tortured, enslaved, and chased from their country, Weil surprisingly says, for there will always be criminals ready to commit atrocities. But what is astonishing is that God gives *malheur* the power to take hold of the soul, and crush it 'comme un ver à moitié écrasé' (*PSO* 87–8).[69] One could add that those who have the strength and vitality to live up to the challenge of torture and enslavement, may grow through the experience, but not those who are simply crushed by it. Thus John Hick's idea of 'soul-making' (of moral growth through suffering)—even if seen from an eschatological perspective—is not satisfactory for those who are overwhelmed by suffering.[70] For what sense and purpose can there be to such misery?

To demand justice, to ask God 'why', and even to accuse him like Job, saying that 'il se rit du malheur des innocents', is not blasphemous, but 'un cri authentique arraché à la douleur'.[71] Job is the paradigmatic example of all those who suffer, and 'une pure merveille de vérité et d'authenticité' (ibid. 89).[72] Anything diverging from this model must in some way be lying, according to Weil. For the experience of God's absence belongs to the trial of *malheur*, as does the sense of its purposelessness (*AD* 102; *OC* vi/3. 183).

Job accuses God while his friends offer well-meaning but unhelpful advice. Their standard answer that suffering is the punishment for past sins is not accepted by God. Job's attitude is preferable, for at least he

---

[67] 'I feel an ever increasing sense of devastation, both in my intellect and in the centre of my heart, at my inability to think with truth at the same time about the affliction of men, the perfection of God, and the link between the two' (*SL* 178).
[68] Weil wrote this essay for Père Perrin and gave it to him just before leaving Marseille. It was then published in *Attente de Dieu*. Afterwards a slightly different version with a new part added on to it, which must have been written in Casablanca, was found in Weil's papers. Both the first and the second version were published in *Pensées sans ordre concernant l'amour de Dieu*, and can be found in English in *SNL*.
[69] 'like a half-crushed worm' (*SNL* 172).   [70] Hick 1977: 253 ff. and ch. 15.
[71] 'he laughs at the affliction of the innocent', 'a genuine cry of anguish' (*SNL* 172).
[72] 'a pure marvel of truth and authenticity' (ibid.).

is honest, he cries out to God in his agony, and asks him why he lets him suffer so much (*PSO* 88–9). Though God does not give him a satisfactory answer on one level, he shows him that things look different from a divine perspective. God is bigger than the universe, so how can Job expect to understand these mysteries?

Weil's approach is not systematic, but an experiential one. She starts with the experience of pain on the one hand, and her faith in God's love on the other, and strives to reconcile the two. Though God seems to be absent in affliction, this never leads her to consider the possibility of his non-existence. 'L'Amour de Dieu et le malheur' deals exclusively with the enigma of affliction, but in the *Intuitions*, in the *Connaissance* and in some of her other *Cahiers*, the question of theodicy appears frequently as well.

God's Responsibility

The stumbling-block for Christianity is the question of God's responsibility in the occurrence of moral and of natural evil. If God is the all-good and omnipotent creator of the universe, why did he not create a cosmos where no natural catastrophes would happen and where human beings would be good to each other? St Augustine, for example, responded to these questions by pointing out that moral evil is the result of free will. In creating free persons, God automatically allowed for the possibility of evil, for they are able to choose between good and evil.[73] Even the angels who are ontologically superior to human beings had this choice with the same result. This does not disprove God's omnipotence, but shows that in creating persons, he has to allow for their free choice otherwise they would neither be free nor persons. For God to create persons without freedom would not prove his power, but would be absurd, apart from being impossible.[74] Natural evil, on the other hand, is the consequence of original sin, according to Catholic doctrine. Though God created a good universe, human beings overturned its goodness by choosing evil. The consequences of the Fall thus influenced all creation, and this explains the occurrence of natural catastrophes, sickness, death, and sin.[75]

---

[73] Hick 1977: 59 ff.   [74] Plantinga 1990: 89 ff.
[75] In *Does God Suffer?* Thomas Weinandy gives a good overview from the Catholic perspective of the different kinds of sufferings, their causes, and various manners of responding to them (Weinandy 2000: 262 ff.). See also the *Catechism of the Catholic Church*, §§ 309, 311, 385, 403.

Weil addresses the problem of divine responsibility by saying that the act of creation was a loving abdication by God. God decided not to be everything, and restricted himself by creating the universe. Though God is indirectly the cause of everything, he is directly responsible only for spiritual goodness, not for evil. His omnipotence is 'une abdication volontaire en faveur de la nécessité' (*CS* 262).[76] Similarly Weil holds that Zeus has given over his power to necessity which—in the shape of Power and Force—inflicts suffering on Prometheus (*IPC* 105).

Thus it is a false alternative to say that if God permits evil, either he cannot be good or omnipotent, or he does not exist. Perhaps he does not command everywhere he could, Weil suggests in 'Formes de l'amour implicite de Dieu' (*AD* 131). This abdication is not the cruel indifference of a deistic God, leaving creation to its own devices, but is motivated by love: 'L'Amour consent à tout et ne commande qu'à ceux qui y consentent. L'Amour est abdication. Dieu est abdication. [...] L'Amour consent à être haï. Dieu permet au mal d'exister. Nous devons en faire autant pour le mal que nous n'avons pas la possibilité de détruire' (*CS* 267–8).[77] So in reality, the apparent absence of God 'est le plus merveilleux témoignage de parfait amour' (*OC* vi/3. 88).[78] For God needs to restrict himself, to allow our freedom to exert itself. Weil looks at moral evil from God's perspective, so to speak. Rather than saying: 'How can God allow us to suffer, and let others inflict suffering on us?' Weil shows what it means for God to leave human beings their freedom: they can choose to hate him, who is Love itself, and choose to do evil to each other: 'Celui qui souffre injustement doit avoir pitié d'abord de Dieu contraint de permettre l'injustice. De même pour les souffrances d'autrui' (*EL* 165).[79]

Not only does God let evildoers exist, but he maintains them and everything in existence, as Weil writes at the beginning of 'Réflexions sans ordre sur l'amour de Dieu': 'Notre être même, à chaque instant, a

---

[76] 'an abdication in favour of necessity' (*FLN* 296).

[77] 'Love consents to all things and commands only those who are willing to obey. Love is abdication. God is abdication. [...] Love consents to be an object of hatred. God allows evil to exist. We ought to do the same for any evil that we have no means of destroying' (ibid. 300).

[78] 'is the most marvellous testimony of perfect love' (*NB* 403).

Thus Weil does not believe in Providence in the usual sense of the word (Vetö 1971: 22) (*IPC* 31; *OC* vi/2. 193, 374, 477; *CS* 83).

[79] 'The one who suffers unjustly must first have pity on God who is constrained to allow injustice. The same holds for the sufferings of others.'

pour étoffe, pour substance, l'amour que Dieu nous porte.'[80] So when God creates or when he maintains his creation in existence, he dies to himself. The Passion is therefore the continuation and the fulfilment of his creative act (*PSO* 35).[81] It is part of God's loving omnipotence to abdicate his power, even to the extent that he cannot help those suffering, except through other human beings (*CS* 281). So rather than holding God responsible for evil, one needs to see that he is its first victim, in terms of the Passion and in terms of all offences directed against him, directly or indirectly. In Weil's eyes, there was a separation within God between his power and his love when he created the universe. He had to abdicate from some of his power to permit the existence of other persons who could decide for or against him.

Aeschylus' tragedy reflects this theological point, according to Weil, since there too, Zeus (power) and Prometheus (wisdom and love) are separated (*OC* vi/3. 249, 251, 252, 275, 436, vi/2. 545–6). Zeus punishing Prometheus would be suffering himself from this punishment. This, however, is only true in so far as he has separated himself from the one who can save him from a future revolution by his foreknowledge.

It is easier for Weil to come to terms with her own suffering than with that of others: 'Parvenir à aimer Dieu à travers la misère d'autrui est bien plus difficile encore que de l'aimer à travers sa propre souffrance. Quand on l'aime à travers sa propre souffrance, cette souffrance en est transfigurée, devient selon le degré de pureté de l'amour soit expiatrice, soit rédemptrice. Mais l'amour ne peut transfigurer la misère des autres' (*OC* vi/2. 360).[82] Thus Weil can empathize with Ivan Karamazov's statement in Dostoevsky's *The Brothers Karamazov*, that he cannot accept the existence of a God who lets children suffer (*OC* vi/3. 119). However, she cannot approve of Karamazov's attitude, for if he were really upset about the suffering of the innocent, he would have tried to improve their situation. Had he done so despite his revolt against God, he would have been loving God implicitly. However, by failing to help,

---

[80] 'The love that God bears us is, at any moment, the material and substance of our very being' (*SNL* 153).
[81] There are interesting similarities on this question between Weil and Jürgen Moltmann (who also thought that divine suffering must already have started with the act of creation) which would be worthwhile investigating (Fiddes 1988: 6–7).
[82] 'To manage to love God through and beyond the misery of others is very much more difficult than to love him through and beyond one's own suffering. When one loves him through and beyond one's own suffering, this suffering is thereby transfigured; becomes, depending upon the degree of purity of that love, either expiatory or redemptive. But love is unable to transfigure the misery of others' (*NB* 255).

he adopts the same attitude he accuses God of, namely of neglecting the suffering children and overlooking their existence (*OC* vi/2. 398). On a natural level, there is no justification for the suffering of the innocent, there cannot be any reason to accept it. Only an intelligence illuminated by supernatural love can accept the answer, namely that God wants it, even though he may only allow it to happen (*OC* vi/3. 119). Why God may allow it, will become clearer in the following sections.

The Epistemological Significance of Suffering

The epistemological significance Weil attributes to suffering has already been mentioned earlier in this chapter. It is wrong to think, however, that affliction automatically teaches wisdom. On the contrary, Weil says in 'L'Amour de Dieu', for: 'La pensée placée par la contrainte des circonstances en face du malheur fuit dans le mensonge avec la promptitude de l'animal menacé de mort et devant qui s'ouvre un refuge' (*PSO* 114).[83] Christ, however, stayed true to reality even during his Passion. He saw suffering as it is, and neither became cynical nor escaped into a dream world. Thus Christ overcame the world by the mere fact that he is Truth and that he remained Truth during his agony.[84] One cannot look at affliction closely unless one is willing to die to oneself for the sake of truth. This, according to Weil, is what Plato meant by 'philosopher, c'est apprendre à mourir' (ibid.).[85] Thus to be willing to know *malheur* is miraculous, more miraculous than walking on water, and requires supernatural grace (ibid. 116).

Prometheus suffers in order to obtain wisdom. Zeus, Weil writes, established this law in Aeschylus' *Agamemnon*: 'Τῷ πάθει μάθος. Par la souffrance la connaissance' (*OC* vi/3. 112; *Ag.* 177).[86] Thus Zeus 'a donc dû crucifier Prométhée pour une raison tout autre [...] que le châtiment d'un vol'.[87] Etymologically, Weil believes that Prometheus'

---

[83] 'When thought finds itself, through the force of circumstance, brought face to face with affliction it takes immediate refuge in lies, like a hunted animal dashing for cover' (*SNL* 188).

[84] In *Le Bouc émissaire* René Girard similarly claims that Christ was the only victim who did not take on his persecutors' perspective and thereby broke through their web of lies once and for all (Girard 1982: 147 ff.). See also Girard's *Je vois Satan tomber comme l'éclair* (1999).

[85] 'to philosophize is to learn to die' (*SNL* 188).

[86] 'Knowledge through suffering' (*NB* 426).

[87] 'must, therefore, have crucified Prometheus for a totally different reason [...] [than] the punishment for a theft' (ibid.).

name might derive from μανθάνω (to learn) or from μάθος (knowledge), thus confirming her idea (*OC* vi/3. 112, 98–9/*NB* 426). What is that wisdom? She speaks about 'les secrets de la sagesse divine' or 'les profondeurs de la sagesse de Dieu' in the sense of St John of the Cross (*PSO* 58; *OC* vi/3. 125).[88] The secret at the heart of divine wisdom must be that God is love, the only truth which is really worthwhile witnessing to, according to Weil (*CS* 201).

In her *Connaissance* Weil compares the human soul to scales. But the scales are wrong. Only when God fully takes possession of the soul do they indicate the correct weight. This happens through a nail fastening the scales in their midpoint: 'La balance est agitée en tous sens. Un clou en fixe le centre. Désormais elle marque juste. Le clou ne marque aucun chiffre, mais par le clou l'aiguille marque juste' (ibid. 103).[89] This nail is the cross through which human beings participate in the suffering of Christ. But why is suffering necessary to share in Christ's universally true, supernatural perspective, thereby reaching the Archimedian point?

Perhaps because the cross goes through the very heart of the universe: 'l'univers entier dans la totalité de l'espace et du temps a été créé comme la Croix du Christ' (*IPC* 167).[90] In consequence, to understand the cosmos and to attain wisdom, one needs to know the cross and experience it. Christ as the Logos holds the universe together. He is the key to all knowledge (ibid. 164). Therefore those who participate in his cross, Weil continues, have to realize that this is a privilege giving access to wisdom: 'Ceux qui ont le privilège immense de participer par tout leur être à la Croix du Christ traversent la porte, passent du côté où se trouvent les secrets même de Dieu' (ibid.).[91] 'La porte' is, for Weil, this world that shuts off the supernatural: 'Ce monde est la porte fermée. C'est une barrière, et en même temps c'est le passage' (*OC* vi/3. 191).[92] To go through the door means crossing the border, entering the supernatural where God's secrets can be found. In her poem *La*

---

[88] 'the secrets of divine wisdom', 'the depth of God's wisdom'.

[89] 'The scales tip every way. But there is a nail that fixes the centre. Therefore the register is true. The nail does not indicate any figure, but because of the nail the pointer marks accurately' (*FLN* 151).

[90] 'the whole universe, in the totality of space and of time, has been created as the Cross of Christ' (*IC* 198).

[91] 'Those who have the immense privilege of participating with their whole being in the Cross of Christ, go through that door, they pass to the side where the secrets of God Himself are to be found' (ibid. 195–6).

[92] 'This world is the closed door. It is a barrier, and at the same time it is the passage-way' (*NB* 492).

Porte, written in 1941, Weil describes what it means to be standing in front of the closed door and not to be admitted. In the first verse the authorial voice, speaking in the plural, asks to be let in: 'Ouvrez-nous donc la porte'—behind which meadows, flowers, and cooling water are expected to be found.[93] The voice is demanding and threatening: 'S'il le faut nous romprons cette porte avec nos coups.'[94] But it remains 'close, inébranlable' ('closed, immovable'). Despair sets in, when suddenly the door opens: 'La porte en s'ouvrant laissa passer tant de silence.'[95] No meadows and no flowers appear. Only the immensity of space and light, which fills the heart and washes the eyes 'presque aveugles sous la poussière'; at which point the poem ends (*PSO* 11–12).[96]

The earlier expectation of pleasure is not fulfilled, for there are no flowers, no streams, and no meadows. But something much greater is offered that satisfies the heart—'combla le cœur'—namely the immensity of space suffused with emptiness and light. The door lets in an overpowering silence, which banishes flowers and meadows. In her *Cahiers* Weil calls the Logos 'le silence de Dieu' (*OC* vi/2. 373).[97] Weil describes this silence in her mystical experience as 'un silence qui n'est pas une absence de son, qui est l'objet d'une sensation positive, plus positive que celle d'un son' (*AD* 48–9).[98] This silence is the presence of Christ.

So when Weil speaks in her *Intuitions* about 'les secrets mêmes de Dieu' which one discovers when going through the door, it is God himself whom one finds (*IPC* 164).[99] What one discovers is that he is a hidden God. Seeing this rectifies one's vision, and delivers one from the value-blindness induced by worldly considerations: 'Et lava les yeux presque aveugles sous la poussière' (*PSO* 12).[100] The cross thus brings about an epiphany, a revelation of God himself, but paradoxically as a hidden God.

When human beings keep asking for the reason and purpose of their suffering, they will one day hear: 'Le silence même comme quelque chose d'infiniment plus plein de signification qu'aucune réponse, comme la parole même de Dieu. Elle [l'âme] sait alors que l'absence de Dieu

---

[93] 'Do open us the door.'
[94] 'If we must, we will break open the door with our blows.'
[95] 'Upon opening the door let so much silence through.'
[96] 'almost blind beneath the dust'.   [97] 'the silence of God' (*NB* 266).
[98] 'a silence which is not an absence of sound but which is the object of a positive sensation, more positive than that of sound' (*WG* 29).
[99] 'the secrets of God Himself' (*IC* 196).
[100] 'And washed the eyes almost blind beneath the dust'.

ici-bas est la même chose que la présence secrète ici-bas du Dieu qui est aux cieux' (*IPC* 168).[101] Thus Weil turns around the very argument often used against the existence and goodness of God. His silence is not a sign of his non-existence nor of his disinterest in human suffering. In itself it is already an answer, but one that takes patience and humility to understand. The answer is love, expressing itself in silence, which alone can make suffering meaningful though it does not elucidate God's reasons for allowing it. Only those who truly love will perceive that divine silence as an answer, and not simply as a void: 'C'est ce silence éternel que Vigny a reproché amèrement à Dieu; mais il n'avait pas le droit de dire quelle est la réponse du juste à ce silence, car il n'était pas un juste. Le juste aime' (*PSO* 129).[102] It is not the fact that Vigny asked how God can allow suffering that is problematic, but his attitude. For Job and everyone undergoing affliction will ask the same question. It depends whether the 'why' has become a simple accusation or is still waiting for an answer. God's participation in human history is discreet. Christ's advent in the world was humble, not that of a temporal king. His response to suffering was therefore humble as well: he did not abolish it, but participated in it and gave it new meaning, as the next section will show (*CS* 104).[103]

Imitatio Christi

Yet, Weil was profoundly troubled by the *malheur* of those who did not believe in God (*PSO* 130). What about the case of slaves in antiquity who did not know about Christ's Passion and could therefore find no meaning in suffering (*AD* 188; *CS* 132)? As a matter of justice, Weil believes that Christ's Passion must therefore have been accessible in some way to everybody since the beginning of time.

For it ultimately takes Christ to understand affliction, as already mentioned at the beginning of this chapter: 'La seule source de clarté assez lumineuse pour éclairer le malheur est la Croix du Christ', Weil

---

[101] 'the very silence as something infinitely more full of significance than any response, like God himself speaking. It knows then that God's absence here below is the same thing as the secret presence upon earth of the God who is in heaven' (*IC* 199). See also *OC* vi/3. 355–6.

[102] 'This is the eternal silence for which Vigny bitterly reproached God; but Vigny had no right to say how the just man should reply to the silence, for he was not one of the just. The just man loves' (*SNL* 197).

[103] Thus Vigny's or Karamazov's revolt against God is due to their fallacious idea of him as a sovereign (*OC* vi/2. 393).

writes in her second version of 'L'Amour de Dieu et le malheur' (*PSO* 124).[104] The promise of future happiness or the attempt to understand the providential reasons for one's suffering cannot really counterbalance the horrors of affliction. Paradoxically only the cross can make one accept real *malheur*. Love makes one want to have a share in the sufferings of the persons one loves (ibid. 125). For those who love Christ, suffering becomes a gift, for it was central to his life, and is part of God's creative act: 'Dans cet état, l'âme est déchirée, clouée aux deux pôles de la création, la matière inerte et Dieu. Ce déchirement est la reproduction dans une âme finie de l'acte créateur de Dieu' (*CS* 298).[105] This rupture even affects the Trinity, for the abandonment experienced by Christ was extreme: 'Cette distance infinie entre Dieu et Dieu, déchirement suprême, douleur dont aucune autre n'approche, merveille de l'amour, c'est la crucifixion. Rien ne peut être plus loin de Dieu que ce qui a été fait malédiction' (*PSO* 92).[106] Thus Weil comes to the conclusion that the cross is the fulfilment of the human vocation, since it allows for a response and a participation in God's love: 'La crucifixion est l'achèvement, l'accomplissement d'une destinée humaine. Comment un être dont l'essence est d'aimer Dieu et qui se trouve dans l'espace et le temps aurait-il une autre vocation que la croix?' (*OC* vi/2. 375).[107] Without suffering, human beings could not answer God's love to the same extent, as Weil explains in her *Intuitions*: 'Il n'est pas surprenant que ce monde soit par excellence le lieu du malheur, car sans le malheur perpétuellement suspendu nulle folie de la part de l'homme ne pourrait faire écho à celle de Dieu' contained in his creative act (*IPC* 148).[108] Human beings should freely accept the suffering they

---

[104] 'The Cross of Christ is the only source of light that is bright enough to illumine affliction' (*SNL* 194).
[105] 'In this state the soul is lacerated, nailed to the two poles of creation: inert matter and God. This laceration is a copy, within a finite soul, of God's creative act' (*FLN* 328). See Charot's article 'Le Mal: Brisure originelle entre l'amour et la puissance dans l'acte créateur' for a good explanation of *décréation* as experienced by God in his creation and Passion, and by human beings (1995).
[106] 'This infinite distance between God and God, this supreme tearing apart, this incomparable agony, this marvel of love, is the crucifixion. Nothing can be further from God than that which has been made accursed' (*SNL* 174–5).
[107] 'The crucifixion is the conclusion, the accomplishment of a human destiny. How could a being whose essence it is to love God and who finds himself situated in space and time have any other vocation than the cross?' (*NB* 268).
[108] 'It is not surprising that this world should be the place of affliction above all other, for without perpetually suspended disaster no folly on man's part could echo that of God' (*IC* 182–3).

cannot avoid, and imitate God's *décréation*. This ambiguous term may sound like nihilistic self-annihilation, but is in reality the self-abdication of love, as Gabellieri claims in his article 'La Nuit du don'.[109] However, Christianity is not morbid. *Malheur* is something that is by definition inflicted upon the victim, not something sought out, or it would not really be *malheur* (*PSO* 108, 122; *IPC* 148; *OC* vi/2. 363).

In her article 'Horrendous Evils and the Goodness of God' the philosopher Marilyn McCord Adams similarly points out that horrible suffering can find an answer only in Christ. Only God's goodness can engulf it. For to know that globally, good balances out evil on earth and defeats it, and that their suffering does not weigh in the ultimate picture of things, cannot console suffering individuals.[110] Alone God's goodness and love can outweigh the horrors of extreme suffering. Thus Weil writes in 'L'Amour de Dieu': 'Le vrai malheur, une seule chose permet d'y consentir, c'est la contemplation de la Croix du Christ. Il n'y a rien d'autre. Cela suffit' (*PSO* 125).[111]

Lecture and Union

The lack of visible purpose makes it particularly hard for human beings to bear pain. But if they trust God throughout this experience, Weil claims that they will discover his love behind it: 'On n'a pas le courage de regarder la face du malheur; autrement, au bout de quelque temps, on verrait que c'est le visage de l'amour' (*PSO* 123).[112] Everything will be seen as a sign of God's love: 'Tout événement qui s'accomplit est une

---

[109] Gabellieri 1996: 25–6, 42–4, 54. See also ch. 8 of Gabellieri's *Être et don* (2003*b*).
[110] McCord Adams 1990: 213 ff., 218 ff. In 'Suffering as Theodicy' Robert Arp claims that McCord Adams offers an answer that Weil's theodicy does not contain for it applies only to 'spiritually mature' people who can unite themselves through their suffering to God. McCord Adams holds that even those who cannot do so, such as babies or the severely mentally handicapped, are implicitly united to Christ, such that they will also be able to say in the light of the beatific vision that these sufferings are now engulfed by God's love (Arp 2000: 428–30). But could one not trace such an implicit participation in Christ's suffering also in Weil, for example when she writes: 'Les hommes frappés de malheur sont au pied de la Croix' ('Men struck down by affliction are at the foot of the Cross') (*PSO*: 92–3/*SNL* 175)?
[111] 'There is only one thing that enables us to accept real affliction, and that is the contemplation of Christ's Cross. There is nothing else. That one thing suffices (*SNL* 195).
[112] 'We dare not look affliction in the face; otherwise we should see after a little time that it is the face of love' (ibid. 193). See also *IPC* 153.

syllabe prononcée par la voix de l'Amour lui-même' (*IPC* 40).[113] Weil compares it to the situation where one has not seen a good friend for a long time: everything that friend tells one becomes precious, even if one has a terrible headache and every word he says hurts. Similarly God speaks to us through every event, even if it is through the effects of pure necessity, which should in consequence be accepted lovingly (ibid. *OC* vi/2. 373, vi 3. 73; *PSO* 101):

Dieu établit avec ses amis un langage conventionnel. Chaque événement de la vie est un mot de ce langage. [...] Le sens commun à tous ces mots, c'est: je t'aime.

[...] Dieu est comme une femme importune collée à son amant et lui disant tout bas dans l'oreille, pendant des heures, sans arrêter: 'Je t'aime—je t'aime—je t'aime—je t'aime...'

Ceux qui sont des commençants dans l'apprentissage de ce langage croient que certains de ces mots seulement veulent dire 'je t'aime'.

Ceux qui connaissent le langage savent qu'il ne s'y trouve qu'une signification. (*CS* 76–7; *OC* vi/2. 447)[114]

Those who continue loving God while they are being crushed by suffering are nailed to the very centre of the universe: 'Celui dont l'âme reste orientée vers Dieu pendant qu'elle est percée d'un clou se trouve cloué sur le centre même de l'univers. C'est le vrai centre, qui n'est pas au milieu, qui est *hors de l'espace et du temps*, qui est Dieu' (*PSO* 104; my italics).[115] Weil uses the same language as for her mystical encounter to describe the transcending of space and time, the reaching of a point which goes beyond all subjectivity, and which is the real centre of the universe. This centre, strangely enough, 'n'est pas au milieu' for this would imply that it is located within space.[116] Though it is the centre of all things, it is not situated in this world, for it is the 'super'-natural.

---

[113] 'Every event that takes place is a syllable pronounced by the voice of Love himself' (*IC* 104).
[114] 'God establishes a conventional language with his friends. Every event in life is a word of this language. [...] The meaning common to all these words is: I love you. [...] God is like an importunate woman who clings to her lover, whispering in his ear for hours without stopping: "I love you—I love you—I love you—I love you..." Those who are beginning to learn this language think that only some of its words mean "I love you". Those who know the language know that it has only one meaning' (*FLN* 128).
[115] 'The man whose soul remains oriented towards God while a nail is driven through it finds himself nailed to the very centre of the universe; the true centre, which is not in the middle, which is *not in space and time*, which is God' (*SNL* 183; my italics).
[116] 'not in the middle' (ibid.).

Ultimately it is God, it is the Logos that holds all things together. Though suffering has the tendency to enclose human beings within themselves, there also lies at its heart the means whereby one can leave one's subjective point of view and accede to the supernatural level. From this one can see that while 'nous sommes les esclaves de la nécessité [. . .] nous sommes aussi les fils de son Maître' (ibid. 111; *IPC* 153).[117] To attempt to resolve the problem of theodicy without this perspective of love is doomed to failure. One has to go 'du côté de Dieu' in order to see God's love behind the opaqueness of suffering (*IPC* 153; *PSO* 37).[118] If all reality were transparent to God's presence, we would simply enjoy the sensation this causes rather than love God. If all reality were opaque, Weil continues, then we could not know about God's existence. The latter is the case only sometimes: 'Quand nous ne [. . .] voyons pas [Dieu], quand la réalité de Dieu n'est rendue sensible à aucune partie de notre âme, alors, pour aimer Dieu, il faut vraiment se transporter hors de soi. C'est cela aimer Dieu' (*PSO* 37).[119] To love God truly, human beings in a way need to suffer. When God allows us to suffer, it is 'le témoignage le plus précieux de sa tendresse' (ibid. 123).[120] No wonder, one might want to exclaim, that St Paul called the cross 'an obstacle to the Jews and foolishness to the Gentiles' (1 Cor. 1: 23).

Beauty and Suffering

Paradoxically suffering opens one's eyes not only to the love of God, but also to the beauty of the world. The end of the book of Job and the first verses pronounced by Prometheus point to this mysterious link, according to Weil, since in both cases the beauty of the universe is revealed (*IPC* 37) (*Prom.* 88–92).[121] Necessity is just one aspect of

---

[117] 'We are the slaves of necessity, but we are also the sons of her Master' (ibid. 186).
[118] 'to God's side' (*IC* 187).
[119] 'It is when we do not see God, it is when his reality is not sensibly perceptible to any part of our soul, that we have to become really detached from the self in order to love him. This is what it is to love God' (*SNL* 154).
[120] 'the most precious evidence of his tenderness' (ibid. 193). Thus Marilyn McCord Adams ends her article 'Redemptive Suffering: A Christian Approach to the Problem of Evil' in the following way: 'For Christians as for others in this life, the fact of evil is a mystery. The answer is a more wonderful mystery—God himself' (McCord Adams 1986: 267).
[121] Weil does not mention of which verses in Job she is thinking. Perhaps it is when Yahweh speaks about the mysteries of the universe and describes his creation in detail (Job 38 ff.).

beauty, Weil claims, the other being the good. When an apprentice hurts himself, the saying goes that 'c'est le métier qui lui rentre dans le corps' (*IPC* 36).[122] Similarly, Weil thinks that through suffering beauty itself enters one's body.

But more than that, the crucifixion itself creates a music, the underlying harmony of the universe:

> Ce déchirement [entre Christ et le Père] par-dessus lequel l'amour suprême met le lien de la suprême union résonne perpétuellement à travers l'univers, au fond du silence, comme deux notes séparées et fondues, comme une harmonie pure et déchirante. C'est cela la parole de Dieu. La création toute entière n'en est que la vibration. Quand la musique humaine dans sa plus grande pureté nous perce l'âme, c'est cela que nous entendons à travers elle.   (*PSO* 92)[123]

The cross is at the root of all great music, and, one could add, of all great art. Masterpieces reflect something of this tragic separation between Father and Son, as well as their loving union beyond it. This means that the cross is at the centre of artistic creation whether the artist is aware of it or not.

Probably in 1938 or 1939 Weil wrote a letter to Charles Bell whom she had met at the abbey of Solesmes.[124] Since Bell wanted to become a writer, Weil speaks to him about literature and artistic creation: 'It was not till Christ had known the physical agony of crucifixion, the shame of blows and mockery, that he uttered his immortal cry, a question which shall remain unanswered through all times on this earth "My God, why hast thou forsaken me?" When poetry struggles toward the expressing of pain and misery, it can be great poetry only if that cry sounds through every word' (*SL* 103).[125] Aeschylus must have heard this tragic harmony to an unusual degree to be able to portray this separation within the Trinity in such detail. Perhaps one could draw out Weil's thought even further and see Prometheus as a figure not only of Christ, but of the artist during the creative act. For the cross is not only part of the depiction of suffering, but essential to the creative act itself: 'L'art est attente. L'inspiration est attente. Il portera des fruits dans l'attente.

---

[122] 'it is the craft entering into the body' (*IC* 101).
[123] 'This tearing apart, over which supreme love places the bond of supreme union, echoes perpetually across the universe in the depth of the silence, like two notes, separate yet blending into one, like a pure and heart-rending harmony. This is the Word of God. The whole creation is nothing but its vibration. When human music in its greatest purity pierces our soul, this is what we hear through it' (*SNL* 175). See also *IPC* 168–9; *AD* 106.
[124] SP ii. 192.   [125] Weil wrote this letter in English.

L'humilité participe à l'attente de Dieu. L'âme parfaite attend le bien avec autant de silence, d'immobilité et d'humilité que Dieu lui-même. Le Christ cloué sur la croix est la parfaite image du Père' (*CS* 91).[126]

Like Christ on the cross, the artist needs to wait for inspiration in perfect obedience, humility, and love, otherwise he will produce a minor work which will simply be the result of his personality and talent, instead of being due to a transcendent inspiration (*IPC* 22; *E* 241).[127] The artist has the choice between an inspiration which is 'au-dessus' ('above') or 'au-dessous des cieux' ('below the sky') (*CS* 276). To seek one's inspiration in the transcendent, as Weil writes in the *Connaissance*, is nothing else than being obedient and '[de] chercher d'abord le royaume et la justice du Père céleste, et recevoir ce qui est donné' (ibid. 277).[128] Depending on his inspiration the artist will be either religious or an idolater, independently of what he depicts. Hence he may profess religious beliefs, yet create idolatrous art, if his inspiration comes from a source 'au-dessous des cieux'. Weil's words are strong: in order to create great art the artist must in a way share in Christ's cross, be nailed to the centre of the universe to receive inspiration from above. She describes the experience in her *Cahiers*:

La faculté d'intuition [...] se développe par la contemplation face à face de l'inintelligible—mais de l'inintelligible qui est au-dessus de la signification, non pas de celui qui est au-dessous. Elle constitue le génie. Elle a besoin d'une vocation [...] en ce sens que la contemplation qui en constitue l'exercice est *si pénible, si déchirante, constitue un tel arrachement*, qu'aucun mobile, aucun motif humain ne serait suffisant pour s'y résoudre. (*OC* vi/3. 162–3; my italics)[129]

Artists are not the only ones who have access to this transcendent realm of inspiration, Weil points out, saints do so too. However, the

---

[126] 'Art is waiting. Inspiration is waiting. He shall bear fruit in patience. Humility partakes in God's patience. The perfected soul waits for the good in silence, immobility and humility like God's own. Christ nailed on the cross is the perfect image of the Father' (*FLN* 141).

[127] See also Broc-Lapeyre 1987: 363.

[128] '[to] seek first the kingdom and the justice of the heavenly Father, and then receive whatever is given' (*FLN* 308).

[129] 'The intuitive faculty [...] is developed by contemplation face to face with the unintelligible—but with the unintelligible that lies above significance, not that which lies below it. It is this faculty which constitutes genius. It is in need of a vocation [...] in the sense that the contemplation in which its exercise consists is *so painful, so harrowing, constitutes such a spiritual disruption*, that no incentive, no human motive of any kind would suffice to bring one to make up one's mind to it' (*NB* 465; my italics).

former do not need to be as moral as the latter to gain that access (*OC* vi/2. 365–6). Though sanctity and genius are close and sometimes inseparable for Weil, it is not morality that is the most central feature of either, especially not in the case of the genius (*E* 199–202). Obedience to God or to the transcendent inspiration, the humility, which should ensue, and the renunciation to self, are key—at least during the creative act.[130] Both saint and artist must ultimately be with Christ on the cross. The critic as well, it follows, for to judge a work of art adequately he has to hear the harmony of the cross vibrating through the cosmos. The critic should therefore not only be in a certain sense a mystic, as concluded in Ch. 4, but must also be crucified.[131]

PROMETHEUS AND APOLOGETICS

What may seem to have been a divergence from the main line of argument, has in fact been essential for a better understanding of Weil's interpretation of the *Prometheus*. Without presenting various aspects of Weil's theodicy, it would have been more difficult to comprehend why both Prometheus and Zeus are justified in her eyes and are really united by bonds of love. Apologetically speaking the Prometheus myth is essential for Weil. For her, the cross is at the centre of the universe, and thus the tragedy expresses a fundamental truth about the structure of the cosmos and about the nature of humanity. Weil writes again in 'L'Amour de Dieu et le malheur': 'La notion de la nécessité comme matière commune de l'art, de la science et de toute espèce de travail est la porte par où le christianisme peut entrer dans la vie profane et la pénétrer de part en part. Car la Croix, c'est la nécessité elle-même mise en contact avec le plus bas et le plus haut de nous-mêmes' (*PSO* 126).[132] Thus: 'Il n'y a, il ne peut y avoir, dans quelque domaine que

---

[130] See *AD* 135; *CS* 276–7, 305–6.
[131] I have not presented Weil's theodicy exhaustively: for example, Weil's unorthodox idea that God himself only reaches his perfection on the cross when the virtual union of his divinity and humanity is rendered fully actual (*CS* 136–7); or that the Trinity only finds its perfection there (*IPC* 132); furthermore that Christ learnt obedience and humility to such a degree on the cross as would have been unobtainable in another way (*CS* 43, 314). Weil also believes that Christ's incarnation did not happen for the sake of human beings, but that the latter were created for the sake of God who wanted to give many brothers to the crucified Christ. Thus human beings have to share in Christ's suffering (*IPC* 132, 167; *CS* 325).
[132] 'The idea of necessity as the material common to art, science, and every kind of labour is the door by which Christianity can enter profane life and permeate the whole

ce soit, aucune activité humaine qui n'ait pour suprême et secrète vérité la Croix du Christ' (ibid.).[133] Necessity, for Weil, is the structure that holds the universe together, and that needs to be taken into account in all human activities. The cross is the embodiment of necessity, and must therefore be at the core of all human action, especially in art.

At the end of her interpretation of *Prometheus* in her *Intuitions*, Weil claims that apart from the New Testament and the liturgy of the Holy Week, one cannot find anywhere else such poignant words 'pour exprimer l'amour que Dieu nous porte et la souffrance liée à cet amour' (*IPC* 106).[134] By presenting the tragedy Weil can paradigmatically compress what she writes in 'L'Amour de Dieu et le malheur'. By showing how Prometheus and Christ suffer for their love of humanity, Weil can convey the significance of the cross for humanity and for an understanding of our suffering. If the cross really is 'the only source of light that is bright enough to illumine affliction', then her presentation of Prometheus' suffering as a Passion already contains a theodicy (*PSO* 124/*SNL* 194).

Furthermore, she can show that the Passion is at the source of Greek culture, which is so appreciated by unbelievers: 'N'est-ce pas une chose extrêmement forte à pouvoir dire à tous les incrédules que celle-ci: Sans la hantise de la Passion, cette civilisation grecque dans laquelle vous puisez toutes vos pensées sans exception ne se serait jamais produite' (*IPC* 106).[135] She obviously thinks this is a particularly convincing argument.

She does not seem aware, however, that this reasoning might be turned against her. By showing the Christian character of Greek tragedy, is she not afraid of really arguing for the mythical character of the Gospels? The Church Fathers were concerned about this, and consequently adopted a critical attitude towards ancient mythology. Yet Weil dismisses this concern: 'Comme parmi les ressemblances entre l'histoire de Prométhée et celle du Christ il n'y en a aucune qui soit d'ordre anecdotique, elles ne peuvent en aucun cas servir d'argument contre le caractère historique des

---

of it. For the Cross is necessity itself brought into contact with the lowest and the highest part of us' (*SNL* 195).

[133] 'There is not, there cannot be, any human activity in whatever sphere, of which Christ's Cross is not the supreme and secret truth' (ibid. 195–6).

[134] 'to express the love God bears us and the suffering linked to this love' (*IC* 71).

[135] 'Is it not an extremely powerful thing to be able to say this to all the unbelievers: without the haunting of the Passion, this Greek civilization, from which you draw all your thoughts without exception, would never have existed' (ibid.).

Prometheus Bound 175

Évangiles' (ibid.).¹³⁶ On the contrary, such an event as the crucifixion of God 'ne peut ne pas être réfractée dans l'éternité', for how could a historical event of such magnitude happening to a divine person not have some impact on eternity?¹³⁷ Thus 'Pascal parle de "Jésus en agonie jusqu'à la fin du monde". Saint Jean, avec l'autorité souveraine des textes révélés, dit qu'il a été égorgé dès la fondation du monde' (ibid.).¹³⁸ But this is due to an 'anecdote historique', a real historical event. No such event can be traced back to the Prometheus-myth, is Weil's claim. Instead Christ's Passion, which is inscribed into the cosmos and vibrates through the universe, inspired the Prometheus-myth. Thus Christ's Passion is not undermined by the Passion of another figure. It is historically unique, Weil seems to be saying, even though it is reflected in other stories. Instead of undermining Christianity, Weil thinks these similarities actually confirm it. If it is metaphysically unthinkable that Christ's Passion would not affect the whole of creation from all eternity, how could this not be in some way captured in art? On the contrary, if no such pre-Christian intuitions were present, one might well doubt the cosmological significance and the historical reality of such an event.¹³⁹

CONCLUSION

To show the presence of the Passion and the cross within ancient cultures was a powerful apologetic tool in Weil's eyes: to indicate the eternal character of Christ's crucifixion discloses the meaning of suffering, and sheds light on ancient Greek culture as well as showing that the cross

---

[136] 'Among the resemblances between the story of Prometheus and that of the Christ there is none that could be of an anecdotal order. They can in no case serve as arguments against the historical character of the Gospels' (ibid. 70–1). Canciani believes that Weil was not really influenced by modern historical criticism of Scripture (Canciani 2000: 12–13).

[137] 'cannot [but] be refracted into eternity' (*IC* 70).

[138] 'Pascal speaks of "Jesus in agony until the end of the world." St. John, with the sovereign authority of revealed texts, says that He has been slain since the foundation of the world' (ibid.).

[139] The writer and convert C. S. Lewis first saw Christianity as one among many myths. Later he came to understand it as a myth come true, as the only myth which became reality (Hooper 1996: 582–5). Weil, on the other hand, sees it in terms of metaphor: 'Il faut retrouver la notion de la métaphore réelle. Autrement l'histoire du Christ, par exemple, perd soit sa réalité, soit sa signification' (*CS* 163) ('We must rediscover the idea of the metaphor which is real. Otherwise the story of Christ, for example, loses either its reality or else its meaning') (*FLN* 207).

stands at the heart of pure civilizations. For though she admits that 'il y a toutes sortes d'arguments contre une telle conception de l'histoire', she believes that 'dès qu'on y est entré elle apparaît d'une vérité tellement criante qu'on ne peut plus l'abandonner' (*IPC* 106).[140] Rather than addressing individual objections, Weil seems to think that the most persuasive approach is simply to unfold and explain her interpretation.

However, Weil's reading of the Aeschylean tragedy remains contradictory: it is difficult to reconcile her interpretation with the actual text. For example she says that it would be reductive to believe that Prometheus does not love God/Zeus just because he loves human beings to such a degree (*CS* 132–3). However, one does not doubt Prometheus' love for Zeus primarily because he suffers for the sake of human beings, but because he insults the Olympian god throughout the tragedy.

Though Weil did not choose the Prometheus-figure to embody the artist, her idea that art is intrinsically linked to the cross leads one to make the association. Art rooted in the cross is a particularly striking concept at a time when some wondered whether all art would not come to an end in the light of the terrible sufferings of World War II, especially of the Holocaust. The sufferings of occupied France, Weil thought, were perhaps going to lead to a renewal of art as she writes in her 'Lettre aux *Cahiers du Sud* sur les responsabilités de la littérature': 'Si les souffrances actuelles amènent jamais un redressement [dans le domaine de l'art], il ne s'accomplira pas par l'effet des slogans, mais dans le silence et la solitude morale, à travers les peines, les misères, les terreurs, dans le plus intime de chaque esprit' (RL 357).[141] She speaks from her own experience, since suffering ultimately proved fruitful for her spiritual development and her writings.

Weil's understanding of Prometheus is in line with her general approach to suffering. It is that of a mystic who has experienced God's love, who wants to participate in the suffering of the Trinity and who can thus say that 'l'Amour infiniment tendre [...] m'a fait le don du malheur' (*AD* 82).[142] The human heart is meant to be broken in some

---

[140] 'There are all sorts of arguments against such a conception of history', 'as soon as one enters into this one, it appears to be of such a crying truth that one can never abandon it' (*IC* 71).

[141] 'If our present suffering ever leads to a revival, this will not be brought about through slogans but in silence and moral loneliness, through pain, misery, and terror, in the profoundest depths of each man's spirit' (*SNL* 169).

[142] 'infinitely tender Love [...] made me the gift of affliction' (*WG* 52). Weil's famous 'exemple de prière' also needs to be read in this light. She asks God for the worst

way. Weil hopes to inspire her readers to let God break it rather than anything else: 'L'amour est une chose divine. S'il entre dans un cœur humain, il le brise. Le cœur humain a été créé pour être ainsi brisé. C'est le plus triste des gaspillages, quand il est brisé par autre chose. Mais il préfère être brisé par n'importe quoi plutôt que par l'amour divin. Car l'amour divin ne brise que les cœurs qui consentent à l'être. Ce consentement est difficile' (CS 294).[143]

sufferings, to become 'un paralysé, aveugle, sourd, idiot et gâteux' ('a paralytic—blind, deaf, witless and utterly decrepit') (CS 204–5/FLN 243–4). Similarly Weil's famous line from her fourth letter to Perrin where she writes that 'toutes les fois que je pense à la crucifixion du Christ, je commets le péché d'envie' ('every time I think of the crucifixion of Christ I commit the sin of envy') needs to be understood from this perspective (AD 62/WG 38). See Charot's article 'Simone Weil: la Croix et le péché d'envie' (1991).

[143] 'Love is a divine thing. If it enters a human heart it breaks it. The human heart was created in order to be broken in this way. It is the saddest waste if it is broken by anything else. But it prefers to be broken by anything rather than by the divine love. Because the divine love breaks only those hearts which consent to be broken; and this consent is difficult to give' (FLN 324).

7

Electra—Waiting on God

Dieu traverse l'univers et vient jusqu'à nous. Par-dessus l'infinité de l'espace et du temps, l'amour infiniment plus infini de Dieu vient nous saisir. Il vient à son heure. Nous avons le pouvoir de consentir à l'accueillir ou de refuser. Si nous restons sourds il revient et revient encore comme un mendiant, mais aussi, comme un mendiant, un jour ne revient plus. Si nous consentons, Dieu met en nous une petite graine et s'en va. A partir de ce moment, Dieu n'a plus rien à faire ni nous non plus sinon attendre. Nous devons seulement ne pas regretter le consentement que nous avons accordé, le oui nuptial.[1]

(*AD* 117–18)

> O très aimée lumière.
> Très aimée, j'en suis témoin.
> O voix, tu es là?
> Plus jamais ailleurs n'interroges.
> Je t'ai dans mes bras?
> Ainsi désormais, tiens-moi toujours.[2]
>
> (*IPC* 16; *El.* 1224–6)

The recognition-scene between Electra and her brother Orestes from the Sophoclean *Electra* is one of Weil's favourite passages in Greek tragedy,

---

[1] 'God crosses the universe and comes to us. Over the infinity of space and time the infinitely more infinite love of God comes to possess us. He comes at his own time. We have the power to consent to receive him or to refuse. If we remain deaf he comes back again and again like a beggar, but also, like a beggar, one day he stops coming. If we consent, God places a little seed in us and he goes away again. From that moment God has no more to do; neither have we, except to wait. We have only not to regret the consent we gave, the nuptial Yes' (*SNL* 181).
[2] 'Electra: O beloved light! | Orestes: Beloved, I am its witness. | Electra: O voice—are you there? | Orestes: No longer question elsewhere. | Electra: I have you in my arms? | Orestes: Thus henceforth forever hold me' (*IC* 7).

since it symbolizes in her eyes a mystical encounter: 'La reconnaissance d'Oreste et d'Électre dans Sophocle ressemble au dialogue de Dieu et de l'âme dans un état mystique succédant à une période de "nuit obscure"' (*PSO* 58).[3] The tragedy is thus of great apologetic significance, since Weil believes that mysticism is an essential element of every authentic religion.[4] To revive Christianity, which in its turn will lead to a renewal of Western civilization, means to bring mysticism back to the fore. The mystical experience is for Weil the loving encounter between God and the soul to whom he reveals himself. It brings about a radical and painful transformation in the person. This, Weil admits, makes it difficult to imagine that a whole civilization would be willing to undergo such a change. Though it may fail to achieve the latter, at least 'la vie entière de tout un peuple peut être *imprégnée* par une religion qui soit tout entière orientée vers la mystique' (*EL* 103; my italics).[5] Hence, she attempts to prepare her contemporaries for a mystical experience, or at least to give them a sense of the hidden presence of God who can manifest himself at any moment. After her mystical encounter, the question of the existence of God was no longer an irresolvable intellectual problem, but had found its answer (*AD* 45). Thus, to the incredulity and materialism of her contemporaries, she responds with the description of divine encounters, of the madness of God's love, and of the stages of a mystical experience. However, as already mentioned in the preceding chapters, she writes only to Perrin and Bousquet about her own mystical experience. There is no direct reference to it in the *Intuitions* though this work was meant to assemble texts on the love of God from all cultures and times. Yet hers would have been a prime example of the authentic mystical experience of a non-baptized person as well as of the reality of the implicit love of God. The context in which Weil speaks about mystical encounters and maps out its different stages is the Sophoclean *Electra*, the myth of Persephone, the already mentioned 'Duc de Norvège', and her own 'conte mystique' (mystical tale), as Gabriël Maes calls it, namely her famous *Prologue* (*IPC* 9 ff., 13 ff., 15 ff.; *CS* 9–10/*OC* vi/3. 369–70, 445–7).[6] Hence her interpretations and the *Prologue* need to be analysed

---

[3] 'The recognition of Orestes and Electra in Sophocles resembles the dialogue between God and the soul during a mystical state following upon the period of a "dark night".'
[4] Kahn 1985: 378.
[5] 'the whole life of a people may be *permeated* by a religion entirely oriented towards mysticism' (*SE* 215; my italics).
[6] Maes 2000: 219.

in detail for they reveal Weil's ideas on (and experience of) mysticism in the condensed and visual form intended for her readers.[7]

In her interpretation of the Sophoclean *Electra*, Weil bypasses the usual problems the tragedy poses to critics. In contrast to the versions of Aeschylus and of Euripides who each wrote a tragedy on the same theme, the problem of matricide does not seem to be addressed in the Sophoclean drama. Orestes comes back from his exile and avenges the murder of his father Agamemnon who, on his return from Troy, had been killed by his wife Clytemnestra and her lover Aegisthus. In consequence, in Aeschylus' *Choephoroe* Orestes is persecuted for his matricide by the Furies, until Apollo, who gave him the order to kill Clytemnestra in the first place, appeases the Furies together with Athena. Euripides in his *Electra* emphasizes the cruelty of such a divine command which runs counter to the laws of kinship. In Sophocles' play, however, the Furies do not appear, nor do Electra or Orestes show any pangs of conscience. Whether Sophocles really overlooks this problem or whether he addresses it in a different manner is a question which has received various answers. Weil is aware of the problem but she focuses on another aspect of the play.

CHRONOLOGY AND QUOTATIONS

Weil's interest in the *Electra* goes back to her pre-mystical days. She wrote the aforementioned lines (*El.* 1224–6) from the recognition scene between Electra and her brother in big letters in Greek on the front cover of her first *Cahier*. She translates them in her article for *Entre Nous* in 1936 in a manner which is less prone to a mystical interpretation than her later rendition (*OC* ii/2. 347). In the same *Cahier* she refers to the tragedy several times. She even briefly addresses the question of the Furies by saying that instead of their appearance at the end of the tragedy, Orestes is holding Electra in his arms (*OC* vi/1. 120). Orestes brings Electra peace and salvation, rather than the continuation of her woes in the shape of the Furies. Weil already uses the religious term *salut* ('salvation') early on to describe Orestes' arrival, in her short summary of the play in the same *Cahier* (ibid. 101/*FLN* 32). However, this does not

---

[7] Similarly in 'L'Aspect mystique de la pensée de Simone Weil', Kahn concentrates on these texts rather than on Weil's explicit thoughts on mysticism, since the former reveal her spontaneous approach to the question (Kahn 1985: 377–8).

yet foreshadow her later religious understanding of the text, but simply indicates how strongly she interprets the relief Electra experiences when her brother comes to save her from her sufferings. The play is clearly of great importance to Weil, since she writes a few pages later: 'Électre: c'est la victoire de la pureté sur l'impureté... Toujours cette lecture me consolera' (ibid. 121).[8]

Electra was the second Greek tragedy Weil wrote about for *Entre Nous*. The article, however, was not published since Weil had offended Bernard (the technical director of the factory who was also in charge of the journal) by showing her joy about the general strikes during the *Front Populaire* government. As in her article on *Antigone*, Weil tries to make the tragedy accessible to the workers by pointing out the parallels between their condition and Electra: 'Cette histoire d'Électre est bien faite pour toucher tous ceux qui, au cours de leur vie, ont eu l'occasion de savoir ce que c'est que d'être malheureux' (*OC* ii/2. 339–40).[9] Electra is struck down by wretchedness and humiliation. This, Weil points out, is nothing new and happens every day. Electra is alone in her woe, for even the Chorus feels sorry for her 'comme on plaint d'ordinaire les malheureux, c'est-à-dire avec beaucoup d'incompréhension et une bonne dose d'indifférence' (ibid. 341–2).[10] When her brother comes back and makes himself known to her, 'elle se laisse aller tout de suite à la douceur des confidences, si apaisante au cœur des malheureux' (ibid. 347).[11] In the end Electra is liberated and the oppression is over. On this note the article ends: 'L'oppression est enfin brisée. Électre est libre' (ibid. 348).[12] For Weil the main theme of the tragedy is clearly Electra's misery and her ensuing liberation.

Weil does not even mention the moral dilemma of matricide which the two children have to face. Theirs is clearly the right action, for it leads from darkness and submission to light and joy: 'Tout se termine dans la joie la plus pure' (ibid. 339).[13] Chrysothemis, Electra's sister, chooses the easy path of compromise. She flatters Aegisthus who has

---

[8] 'Electra: the triumph of purity over impurity... I shall always be consoled by reading this' (*FLN* 50).
[9] 'This story of Electra is well adapted to touch all those who have had the occasion to experience during their lives what it means to be unhappy.'
[10] 'as one normally feels sorry for the afflicted, that is to say with much incomprehension and a good dose of indifference'.
[11] 'she immediately surrenders to the sweetness of confiding in him, which is so soothing to the heart of the afflicted'.
[12] 'The oppression is broken. At last Electra is free.'
[13] 'Everything ends in the purest joy.'

reigned with Clytemnestra since the death of Agamemnon, and she submits herself to the new rulers (ibid. 342–3). Weil does not quite do justice to Chrysothemis for it is nowhere mentioned that she flatters Aegisthus, though she keeps quiet in contrast to Electra. She intends to obey her mother at first and to offer a sacrifice in the latter's name on the tomb of Agamemnon, which is a sacrilege. But Electra convinces her not to do so.[14]

Weil gives a significant number of quotations in the article as well as in her *Cahiers*. In her article she quotes from the early speeches in which Electra bemoans her fate, then a few lines from her first dialogue with Chrysothemis, before citing passages of her sorrow over Orestes' death. At the end Weil translates her favourite lines from the recognition scene.[15] She quotes the latter frequently, for example in her *Intuitions*, in a letter to Posternak, and in a fragment called 'Plaintes d'Électre' ('The Laments of Electra'/*IC*) of 1942 (*IPC* 15–16; *Œ* 660; *SG* 53–4; *El.* 1218–29).[16] In the 'Plaintes', Weil translates almost the same sections as in her article, except that the recognition scene is quoted at greater length.[17] It is interesting to note that Weil never gives any quotation from the discussion between Electra and her mother, nor from the scene of the actual murder. Clytemnestra has no 'case' in Weil's eyes, she is in no way justified for her murder of Agamemnon by the fact that he killed their daughter Iphigenia. Therefore Weil does not mention passages where we might feel some sympathy for Clytemnestra: for example when the queen is torn, on hearing the news of the death of her son, between her sorrow as a mother and her relief at the death of

---

[14] In his article '*Electra* by Sophocles: The Dialectical Design', Thomas Woodard (1964: 185) claims that Chrysothemis is in a certain sense more active than her sister, since she disobeys her mother by throwing away her mother's sacrifice and offering libations on Agamemnon's tomb to beg for his revenge. However, Woodard fails to see that Electra cannot engage in a more active opposition at this point, since her mother would never think of entrusting her with such a task. Furthermore Electra bears the consequences of her words while Chrysothemis does not need to account for her action. Electra's oppressors fear her, for they are about to imprison her. She abstains from action since she counts on her brother to take revenge. But once she learns he is dead, she intends to kill her father's murderers herself.

[15] These are the lines Weil translates in her article: *El.* 118–20, 164–72, 185–92, 263–5, 307–9, 359–64, 387, 391, 394–5, 795, 796, 808, 812–15, 817–19, 1126–30, 1149–51, 1158–9, 1164–5, 1170, 1171–2, 1179–81, 1195–6, 1199–200, 1217–26.

[16] She also sends these lines to Bousquet and to Thibon (*Œ* 668) (BN textes destinés à Gustave Thibon).

[17] In her *Cahiers*, Weil also translates some of these lines (*OC* vi/2. 191–2; *El.* 1126–30, 1136–45, 1149–51, 1165–70). Sometimes she just gives the Greek quotations (*OC* vi/1. 276; *El.* 1132–37, 1143–5, 1149–51, 1165–72).

her potential murderer; or, for example, when she is being murdered and begs for mercy.[18]

Though Weil gives some quotations from the Aeschylean *Oresteia*, she never makes any reference to Euripides' *Electra*.[19] She may have disapproved of Euripides' critical attitude towards the gods.[20] Concerning Aeschylus' *Choephoroe*, Weil briefly discusses the nature of Orestes' act, as well as the nature of the Furies, but this will be investigated later (*OC* vi/1. 302, 120).

Weil devotes only about two pages to the Sophoclean *Electra* in her *Intuitions*. There are about nine pages of the aforementioned 'Plaintes d'Électre' in *La Source grecque*, most of which are translations from the tragedy but for two pages of comments. Once again, Weil's observations are scattered through her *Cahiers* and her other writings, and will be brought together in this chapter.

THE MORAL DILEMMA

The Sophoclean *Electra* has given rise to much disagreement among classicists. J. H. Kells in the introduction to his commentary distinguishes between three different approaches among scholars to the question of the matricide, namely the 'justificatory', the 'amoral', and the 'ironic' theory.[21] T. B. L. Webster defends the 'justificatory' theory, claiming that the matricide is ultimately approved of. Others such as R. C. Jebb and J. D. Denniston espouse the 'amoral' theory, maintaining that Sophocles is simply not interested in the ethical or legal aspect of the question.[22] The 'ironic' theory, on the other hand, as held by J. T. Sheppard, claims that Sophocles is very subtle in his criticism of

---

[18] Furthermore Weil does not refer to the second scene between Chrysothemis and Electra (*El.* 871 ff.).
[19] Though, according to the editors, there might be a passing reference in her *Cahiers* (*OC* vi/3. 402 n. 107).
[20] For example, she writes: 'C'est seulement dans Euripide que les histoires d'adultères racontées au sujet des dieux servent d'excuse à la luxure des hommes; or Euripide était un sceptique. Dans Eschyle et Sophocle, les dieux n'inspirent que le bien' (*PSO* 57) ('It is only in Euripides that the stories about the adulteries of the gods serve as an excuse for the lust of men; this is because Euripides was a sceptic. In Aeschylus and Sophocles, the gods only inspire goodness').
[21] Kells 1973: 2 ff.
[22] It is also called the 'Homeric' view, since its defenders claim that the tragedy is simply the expansion on the remarks found in the *Odyssey* which indicate neither guilt nor remorse (Ringer 1998: 129).

the matricide. Though it seems to be approved by the gods, in reality the oracle, which Orestes questions before performing the deed, only answers his question of *how* and not *whether* to execute it in the first place.

Neither Orestes nor Electra seem to have any doubt about the righteousness of their action or any anxiety concerning it. Electra even encourages Orestes to strike twice when she hears her mother screaming inside the palace (*El.* 1415). Contrary to the *Oresteia* and to the Euripidean *Electra*, the Furies do not appear in Sophocles' play. This fact is emphasized by the sequence of the murders: Clytemnestra dies first, and Aegisthus is killed only afterwards, contrary to the other two versions. Since it is Clytemnestra's death that should awaken the Furies, Sophocles seems to be making a point by reversing the order of their deaths: if there is a time lapse after the queen's death, yet no Furies appear, then they were probably not meant to come, and the matricide was therefore justified.[23]

On the other hand, Winnington-Ingram in his book *Sophocles* suggests that the Furies are present, and that they are embodied by Electra and Orestes themselves. Sophocles mentions the Erinyes four times in the play (*El.* 112, 276, 491, 1080).[24] Orestes and Electra avenge the murder of Agamemnon by killing his assassins, but only after inspiring them with fear, as the Furies would do. If Sophocles had meant to make the public forget the traditional ending, why did he make references to the Erinyes up to the very end of the play? For some reason, he did not want to look to the future with its peaceful resolution as Aeschylus does, but concentrated on the past and on its result for the present. For Winnington-Ingram there is no right mode of conduct given the tragic circumstances, and Electra is both the 'victim and agent of the Furies'.[25]

Yet one might point out with Weil that 'Oreste, au lieu des furies, c'est: "ἔχω σε χερσίν; ὡς τὰ λοίπ' ἔχοις ἀεί" [Je t'ai dans mes bras?—Ainsi désormais tiens-moi toujours]' (*OC* vi 1. 120; *El.* 1226).[26] The note of deliverance is stronger than the possibility of future Furies and pangs of conscience. Bowra claims that Sophocles shows the religious, moral, and legal reasons for the matricide.[27] Nobody other than Orestes can perform the deed since he is the only male descendant left. Because

---

[23] Bowra 1944: 258.   [24] See also l. 1388 (Winnington-Ingram 1980: 218).
[25] Ibid. 233, 226, 228, 239, 246. See also Ringer 1998: 203, 210, 212.
[26] 'Orestes, instead of the furies it is: [. . .] [Do I hold you in my arms?—May you hold me for ever]' (*FLN* 49).
[27] Bowra 1944: 229.

the authority and power are in the hands of the murderers themselves, only he is able to reinstate justice. If the murder of a husband were to remain unpunished, then a great rule would be violated: it would be 'the end of reverence and of the piety of all mortals!' Apollo needs to 'show mortals with what wages the gods reward impiety', and it is a necessary preventive measure against further crime (*El.* 249–50, 1382–3, 1505–7). It is Electra and Orestes who make these claims, but Bowra's and Weil's interpretation is strengthened by the fact that Clytemnestra is shown in such a negative way, and that the play ends with the approving comment of the Chorus. Weil, by the way, does not even seem to interpret the Furies in the Aeschylean version of the *Electra* as the sign of Orestes' guilt and of the wrongness of the matricide, for she writes: 'L'être pur qui arrête la malédiction des Pélopides est Oreste dans Eschyle (l'*Électre* de Sophocle ne se place pas dans cette perspective)' (*IPC* 20).[28] Aeschylus' Orestes is an *être pur* who stops the history of sin and crime in his family. The Furies persecuting him thus symbolize the suffering he has taken on himself, and the subjective feeling of guilt which is not due to a real crime.

The 'justificatory' theory seems to have been so obviously right in Weil's eyes, that she does not even go to any lengths to defend it. If it were not for the aforementioned passage in her *Cahiers* where she refers to the Furies, one might have wondered whether she was even aware of the moral dilemma (*OC* vi/1. 120). The matricide is not evil and Clytemnestra cannot be justified, as Weil's early interpretation of the figure already seems to indicate. In her article for *Entre Nous*, she claims that Clytemnestra is incapable of waiting for ten years for her husband, and therefore takes a lover (*OC* ii/2. 340). Nowhere does she mention that Clytemnestra might have killed her husband to avenge Iphigenia in spite of the fact that Clytemnestra defends herself with this argument (*El.* 530 ff.). Weil adopts Electra's point of view, which is to see Clytemnestra's crime as motivated by her adultery rather than by her motherly feelings (*El.* 558 ff.).[29] Thus the tragedy's conclusion is truly a liberation rather than the beginning of new family woes (*CSW* 8/4: 319–20).[30]

---

[28] 'The guiltless person who stops the curse of the Pelopids is Orestes in Aeschylus (the *Electra* of Sophocles is not in that perspective)' (*IC* 10).
[29] Similarly Bowra (1944: 238) believes that her adulterous love is the only reason for her crime.
[30] As Weil's unsent letter to Jean Giraudoux on his *Électre* in 1937 shows, she is not in principle set against the idea of Furies or against Clytemnestra; for she compliments

Orestes' Act

While Orestes is reluctant to kill his mother in Euripides' tragedy, and while he dreads it in the *Choephoroe*, he does not seem to have any problems with it in Sophocles' drama (*Choe*. 899, Euripides' *El*. 966 ff.). This could either be the sign of great hardness of heart or of the moral certainty that righteousness gives.[31] It might have been unjust to let Clytemnestra live. Interestingly Weil contrasts Orestes to Hamlet. The Shakespearean hero cannot make up his mind to avenge his father, while Orestes goes straight to action. Weil writes in her *Cahier* 3:

Si, contemplant la chose qui paraît bonne et contemplant non moins fixement le risque infini, l'action se fait—l'action n'est-elle pas bonne?
Hamlet ne sait pas contempler ainsi.
'. . . *is sicklied o'er*', ce n'est pas la vraie pensée.
Au contraire, Oreste, dans Sophocle.   (*OC* vi/1. 334)[32]

Ironically Weil does not accuse Hamlet—who does nothing but think about what he should do—of lacking readiness to act, but of the incapacity to contemplate. Instead of going neurotically back and forth like Hamlet, one needs to determine the right manner of action by gazing attentively and patiently at the question until it becomes clear what one needs to do. Then one must obey, rather than act according to one's own wishes. As Weil writes in her essay 'Réflexions sans ordre sur l'amour de Dieu': 'Mais il ne faut pas agir, ni d'ailleurs s'abstenir d'agir, par volonté propre. Il faut faire seulement en premier lieu ce à quoi on est contraint par une obligation stricte, puis ce qu'on pense honnêtement nous être commandé par Dieu' (*PSO* 38).[33] Orestes

---

him on his idea of letting the Eumenides first appear as children who then grow up in the course of the play. It is merely in the context of Sophocles' tragedy that she denies their presence and does not allow for any mitigating instances for Clytemnestra (*CSW* 8/4: 319–20). For more details concerning this letter to Giraudoux, see M. Cabaud 2001*a*: 234–5.

[31] In his commentary Kells questions whether Orestes or the oracle call the murder righteous, ἐνδίκου/*endíkou*. Only in the latter case would it be a sign of its righteousness (Kells 1973: 82; *El*. 35–7). One might also want to question Orestes' integrity, since he justifies his lies in the beginning by the idea that the end justifies the means (*El*. 61).

[32] 'If, contemplating the thing which seems good and contemplating no less fixedly the infinite risk, the action is carried out—is not the action a good one? Hamlet does not know how to contemplate in this way. ". . . is sicklied o'er", that is not true thought. On the other hand, Orestes, in Sophocles' (*NB* 56).

[33] 'But one must not act, or, indeed, abstain from acting, by one's own will. In the first place, we must perform only those acts to which we are constrained by a strict obligation, and then those which we honestly believe to have been enjoined upon us by

believes that Apollo ordered him to kill the murderers of his father, and he obeys his command.

But one may wonder whether vengeance is not motivating the two children of Agamemnon, at least in part. Electra bloodthirstily asks Orestes to strike Clytemnestra twice (*El.* 1416). In her *Connaissance*, Weil distinguishes between the punishment inflicted on the criminal for his own good in order to heal him of his guilt, and the punishment exercised for the sake of the victim. In the latter case: 'La satisfaction n'a pas pour but la guérison du criminel, mais de l'offensé, qui ne peut oublier l'offense ou y penser sans trouble qu'après avoir vu souffrir le coupable. Cela répond au besoin de transférer la souffrance' (*CS* 105).[34] Might this not apply to Electra? Not in the eyes of Weil, since she seems to think that Electra acts more out of a desire for justice than out of vengeance. Orestes, not having suffered as much as Electra nor having the same harsh temper, has less reason to take revenge for his own sake rather than out of a sense of justice. Weil considers, for example, that the Aeschylean Orestes embodies to a certain extent impersonal justice: 'Il est mauvais et je le punis. En réalité: je le vois mauvais et il est puni. Oreste—Ce n'est pas moi, c'est ton acte passé qui te tue. Si en même temps, tout en frappant, il ne juge pas cet acte passé, il est pur' (*OC* vi/2. 291).[35] If she believes this of the Aeschylean Orestes, how much more of the Sophoclean figure who is less obviously condemned within the play—if at all. Similarly, Weil refers implicitly to two lines from Aeschylus' tragedy in a different *Cahier*, namely when Orestes says: 'The fate meted out to my father condemns thee to death' and 'It is thou, not I, who wilt kill thyself' (*OC* vi/1. 302 nn. 68, 69/*NB* 29 nn. 1, 2) (*Choe.* 927, 923). In that same passage she calls a *belle action* the one 'qui sort d'une situation, qui l'exprime'.[36] Thus the matricide committed by

---

God' (*SNL* 154–5). One should always do what one believes to be God's will: 'Car nous pouvons nous tromper sur la volonté de Dieu—mais nous pouvons regarder comme certain que Dieu veut que nous exécutions tout ce que nous croyons conforme à sa volonté' (*CS* 102) ('Because we may be mistaken about God's will—but we can regard it as certain that God wishes us to do everything that we believe is in conformity with his will') (*FLN* 150).

[34] 'The purpose of reparation is not to cure the criminal but the injured party, who cannot forget the offence or think of it without distress until he has seen the criminal suffer. This corresponds with the need to pass suffering on' (*FLN* 153).

[35] 'He is bad and I punish him. In reality: I see him as bad and he is punished. Orestes—I do not kill thee; thine own past act killeth thee. If at the same time, while in the act of killing, he does not judge this past act, he remains pure' (*NB* 201).

[36] 'which springs from a situation, which expresses it' (ibid. 29).

Orestes is more the impersonal consequence of Clytemnestra's crime, the just response to her murderous deed, than an act of vengeance.[37]

Electra

Electra, on the other hand, is a more problematic character. She is passionate, full of hatred for her mother, and immoderate in her grief. She admits herself that she is not good: 'Dans ces conditions je ne puis être ni raisonnable, amies, | ni bonne. Ceux à qui on fait trop de mal | ne peuvent pas s'empêcher de devenir mauvais' (*SG* 47) (*El.* 307–9).[38] When she points out to her mother that by justifying herself with the *lex talionis* Clytemnestra is condemning herself, the same could be said of her (*El.* 580–1). If Electra does not admit any good reasons for killing one's husband (for example, because he sacrificed Iphigenia), how could there be any good reasons for killing one's mother? However, Electra's point is precisely that her mother's motivations were unjust. She slew Agamemnon because she wanted to continue her adulterous relationship and govern Mycenae with her lover. Iphigenia is just an excuse for the murder.[39] Thus she cannot really justify herself with the *lex talionis*.

Early, in her article for *Entre Nous*, Weil tried to understand Electra in terms of her terrible situation. She is treated like a slave by those who killed her father, sees her father's murderer married to her mother, and is suffering from hunger and cold. It is no wonder that 'son caractère s'aigrit' and that 'elle n'a plus d'équilibre', something Weil emphasizes in her *Intuitions* as well (*OC* ii/2. 341; *IPC* 16).[40] It is part of *malheur* to feel evil even when one is innocent: one cannot distinguish between one's suffering and one's sin. On the other hand, the criminal paradoxically does not feel evil, as Weil writes in 'L'Amour de Dieu et le malheur': 'Le malheur durcit et désespère parce qu'il imprime jusqu'au fond de l'âme, comme avec un fer rouge, ce mépris, ce dégoût et même cette répulsion de soi-même, cette sensation de culpabilité et de souillure, que le crime devrait logiquement produire et ne produit pas. Le mal

---

[37] An example of 'action non-agissante' Weil liked to reflect upon is that of Arjuna in the *Bhagavadgītā* who has to kill his family in war, since it is his *dharma*, his duty and a necessity (Vetö 1971: 134–5).
[38] 'Under such conditions, dear friends, I cannot be either good | Or reasonable. Those to whom evil is done | cannot save themselves from becoming evil' (*IC* 11–12).
[39] However, Weil does not approve of Iphigenia's sacrifice (*OC* vi/3. 275–6).
[40] 'her character becomes embittered', 'she loses her balance'.

habite dans l'âme du criminel sans y être senti. Il est senti dans l'âme de l'innocent malheureux' (*AD* 103).[41] This explains Electra's sense of guilt. For really, Electra has acted rightly by speaking out against her father's murderers. Were she to remain silent like Chrysothemis, she would seem to be condoning their action, and would lose her integrity. She loses her temper in the process, but this does not diminish her righteousness.[42] However, Charles Segal in *Tragedy and Civilisation* believes that Electra's personality has been destroyed by her hatred. She is enclosed in the obsessive repetition of certain acts which lock her into the vicious circle of hatred. Electra's stubbornness is another sign that the natural order of things has been inverted in the tragedy. But, one may ask, how could Electra have behaved without losing her integrity? Given the unrepented murder in her family, it is difficult to live in peace. As Segal himself admits, the preceding crimes in the family have set the tone: Clytemnestra has become the man in the house and prevents her daughter from getting married and having children. Electra is the only voice daring to speak out the truth, yet she is about to be locked up, perhaps even killed (*El.* 378 ff.).[43] Her behaviour may seem irrational for it means choosing death over life. But as already discussed in the Antigone chapter, in some situations one has to risk death to do the right thing. The Gospel says so, and Weil affirms this idea in 'Réflexions sans ordre sur l'amour de Dieu': 'il faut choisir entre la vérité et la mort ou le mensonge et la vie' (*PSO* 43).[44] Electra would have to lie in order to live in comfort. Weil is clearly thinking of her in this passage, since she mentions her a few lines further on. Chrysothemis, on the other hand, has chosen to survive, as Weil already writes in *Entre Nous*, but lives with a lie: 'La vie est tellement plus commode quand on sait se plier aux pires injustices, et oublier que ce sont des injustices!' (*OC* ii/2. 343).[45]

The Chorus thinks that Electra grieves too much and fails to accept human mortality, especially her father's (*El.* 137 ff., 153 ff.). What may

---

[41] 'Affliction hardens and discourages because, like a red-hot iron, it stamps the soul to its very depths with the contempt, the disgust, and even the self-hatred and sense of guilt and defilement which crime logically should produce but actually does not. Evil dwells in the heart of the criminal without being felt there. It is felt in the heart of man who is afflicted and innocent' (*SNL* 173). See also *OC* vi/3. 349–50.

[42] Bowra 1944: 242.

[43] For an analysis of the internal chaos in Mycenae, see Segal 1981: 250, 252 ff., 262 ff., and Ringer 1998: 128.

[44] '[one] must either choose truth and death or falsehood and life' (*SNL* 158).

[45] 'Life is so much easier when one knows how to submit to the worst injustices and forget that they are injustices!'

seem obsessive, is in reality essential to great affliction, as Weil writes in her *Cahiers*: 'L'obsession est l'unique souffrance humaine [. . .] une douleur non obsédante n'en est pas une' (*OC* vi/1. 142).[46] The pain over her father's murder is so intense, because she is permanently reminded of it by the presence of his murderers. It is understandable therefore that it has become an *idée fixe*. More positively, it also keeps her sense of justice alive and guarantees her integrity.

Electra seems unreasonable and even crazy, but she is not medically insane according to Weil's world-view, for: 'Le critère des choses qui viennent de Dieu, c'est qu'elles présentent tous les caractères de la folie, excepté la perte de l'aptitude à discerner la vérité et à aimer la justice' (*CS* 323).[47] Because she has not adopted the perspective of the rulers, she has become an outsider and looks like a fool. But in reality she is the only one reacting rightly in being horrified by a truly horrible situation. If the world is out of joint, it will not be set right by pretending that everything is all right. Though Segal's analysis of the various elements of disorder and inversion is to the point, he is wrong in believing that Electra has been perverted as well. For she is the only one standing up for truth and justice in the tangle of sin in which her family is enmeshed.[48]

What looks like bloodthirsty revenge at first sight, is in reality a desire for justice. Yet justice without *caritas* is no real justice, as shown in Ch. 4. Does Electra's desire for justice not eventually lead her to be unjust and cruel? Electra's love for Agamemnon is supernatural, Weil claims in her *Connaissance*. For to continue to love the dead, when life in all its fullness tempts one to forget them, implies detachment.[49]

---

[46] 'Obsession is the only human suffering [. . .] a pain that is not obsessive is not a real one.'

[47] 'The criterion for those things which come from God is that they show all the characteristics of madness except for the loss of capacity to discern truth and love justice' (*FLN* 351).

[48] Weil writes about Sophocles' characters in general: 'La raison surnage dans le malheur [dans Sophocle] (dans Eschyle, il y a toujours une atmosphère de folie). [. . .] *Aucun* de ses personnages n'a le moindre grain de folie, encore que *tous* soient dans des situations à rendre fou' (*OC* vi/1. 120–1) ('Reason floats above the tide of affliction (whereas in Aeschylus there is always an atmosphere of madness). [. . .] In *none* of his characters is there the tiniest seed of madness, although *all* of them are in situations to drive one mad') (*FLN* 49).

[49] 'Il n'est pas vrai que l'amour humain soit plus fort que la mort. La mort est beaucoup plus forte. Il est soumis à la mort. Aimer ce qui est vivant est facile. Il est difficile d'aimer ce qui est mort. [. . .] Mais un tel amour, s'il est amour et non pas rêve, est surnaturel. [. . .] l'amour d'Électre est l'amour surnaturel' (*CS* 292) ('It is not true that human love is stronger than death. Death is much stronger. Love is subdued to death. It is easy to love what is alive. It is difficult to love what is dead. [. . .] But

Electra could easily have followed in Chrysothemis' footsteps. Instead she chooses suffering, neglect, and ill-treatment by continuing to accuse the murderers. Even upon hearing that Orestes is dead, she only despairs briefly before planning to kill Agamemnon's slayers herself (*OC* vi/2. 138, 579 n. 427). Weil interprets this as a sign of supernatural hope, which is part of her mystical interpretation of the tragedy.

The Mystical Encounter

Weil's mystical reading of the *Electra* hinges on the recognition scene between Electra and Orestes. In her pre-mystical period she already had a predilection for this scene. The scene is significant, as Bowra points out, since it gives Orestes the occasion to become aware of his sister's ill-treatment and the hideousness of his mother's crime. Thus his duty to kill his father's murderers becomes less abstract. Electra, on the other hand, goes from 'hate to love, from despair to hope, from solitude to intimate companionship'.[50] Similarly in *Entre Nous*, Weil indicates how in this scene Electra's suffering becomes Orestes', and how they go from wretchedness to 'un même élan de joie pure' (*OC* ii/2. 347).[51]

Later, in her *Intuitions* Weil interprets the scene in terms of a mystical encounter. Mysticism for Weil means a personal and loving encounter between the soul and God who reveals himself.[52] It is not the search for special feelings or ecstasy, which, for example, drugs can provide, and which Weil calls a 'fausse mystique' ('false mysticism') (*AD* 165/*WG* 111).[53] All mystical experiences follow a certain pattern, and the different stages in various accounts can be differentiated.[54] Weil

---

such a love, if it really is love and not day-dreaming, is supernatural. [. . .] Electra's is supernatural') (*FLN* 323).

[50] Bowra 1944: 250.   [51] 'the same élan of pure joy'.

[52] Marie-Madeleine Davy's *Encyclopédie des mystiques* gives a good introduction to mysticism, especially her 'Préface', which is strongly influenced by Weil to whom she dedicates a section in the second volume (1977). She published *The Mysticism of Simone Weil* as early as 1951. Another good introduction to mysticism is David Knowles's *What is Mysticism?* (1966). See also Kahn's aforementioned article on Weil's understanding of mysticism (Kahn 1985: 378).

[53] Thus as Birou points out in his article 'Simone Weil, mystique dans sa vie et dans son œuvre', Weil's understanding of mysticism is utterly opposed to Bataille's, which focuses on the individual's imagination and feelings, and ends up with a mysticism without God (Birou 1988: i. 45, 47).

[54] 'Les récits de voyage, les cartes, sont ainsi un moyen de discrimination. Tels sont les récits d'expériences mystiques, si on en fait cet usage' (*OC* vi/2. 487) ('Travel reports, maps, are thus a means of discrimination. So are the accounts of mystical experiences,

believes that Electra has an authentic mystical experience, after going through great suffering and aridity of the soul:

> C'est quand l'âme épuisée a cessé d'attendre Dieu, quand le malheur extérieur ou la sécheresse intérieure lui fait croire que Dieu n'est pas une réalité, si néanmoins elle continue à l'aimer, si elle a horreur des biens d'ici-bas qui prétendent le remplacer, c'est alors que Dieu après quelque temps vient jusqu'à elle, se montre, lui parle, la touche. C'est ce que saint Jean de la Croix nomme nuit obscure. (*IPC* 17)[55]

There is a double recognition, according to Weil, namely by the soul and by God. God recognizes the soul by its tears (ibid.; *PSO* 58). Only those servants who are ready, those who have their wedding garments on, whose lamps are filled with oil will be acknowledged by God and be rewarded for their good service. Electra's tears represent this wedding gown, for they are the sign of her faithfulness to justice over whose absence she cries, and thereby of her implicit love for God. Though she cannot hope any more for justice to prevail, she still possesses supernatural hope for 'elle ne songe pas un instant à pactiser', as Weil writes in 'Plaintes d'Électre':[56] 'La croyance en apparence certaine que ce qu'elle aime n'existe absolument pas ne diminue aucunement son amour, mais au contraire l'augmente. C'est cette espèce de folie dans la fidélité qui contraint Oreste à se révéler' (*SG* 55; *IPC* 17).[57]

When Orestes, whom Electra has not recognized yet, wants the urn with 'his' ashes back from her before revealing his identity, this symbolizes for Weil the absolute detachment God demands from the soul. Yet Electra remains in the perfect attitude of *attente*, which the Greek term ἐν ὑπομονῇ/*en hupomone* expresses. As Weil writes in 'Formes de l'amour implicite de Dieu' about the nature of *attente*:

> [C'est] l'immobilité attentive et fidèle qui dure indéfiniment et que ne peut ébranler aucun choc. L'esclave qui écoute près de la porte pour ouvrir dès que

too, if this use is made of them') (*NB* 362) 'Il y a une mécanique spirituelle, aux lois aussi rigoureuses que l'autre, mais autre' (*CS* 253) ('There is a spiritual mechanics with laws as rigorous as our mechanics, only different') (*FLN* 287).

[55] 'Just when the soul is spent and has ceased to wait for God, when the external affliction or the interior aridity forces it to believe that God is not a reality, if then nevertheless the soul still loves, and holds in horror those worldly riches which would take His place, then it is that God comes to the soul, reveals Himself, speaks to it, touches it. This is what St. John of the Cross names the dark night of the soul' (*IC* 8).

[56] 'she never for an instant dreams of compromising'.

[57] 'Belief in the apparently certain evidence that he whom she loves is absolutely non-existent never diminishes her love, but on the contrary increases it. This is the sort of fidelity raised to the point of madness which compels Orestes to reveal himself' (*IC* 17).

le maître frappe en est la meilleure image. Il faut qu'il soit prêt à mourir de faim et d'épuisement plutôt que de changer d'attitude. Il faut que ses camarades puissent l'appeler, lui parler, le frapper sans qu'il tourne même la tête. Même si on lui dit que le maître est mort, même s'il le croit, il ne bougera pas. (*AD* 193; *PSO* 144–5)[58]

The Chorus and Chrysothemis tell Electra that she is unreasonable 'sans qu'[elle] tourne même la tête' (*AD* 193).[59] For 'elle aime mieux l'absence d'Oreste que la présence de quoi que ce soit d'autre' (ibid. 212).[60]

To see Electra's attitude in terms of (implicit) supernatural hope is less radical than to interpret the whole recognition scene in terms of a mystical encounter. The latter is already an allegorical reading. How does Weil justify such an interpretation? First of all she thinks that the theme of recognition is frequent in folktales, which she reads in a similarly mystical way, as for example in her interpretation of the 'Duke of Norway'. It is also present in St John's Gospel, when Mary Magdalene recognizes the resurrected Lord whom she first takes to be the gardener (*IPC* 16; John 20: 15 ff.). Since the motif of mystical recognition is often reflected in literature, why should it not also be present in Sophocles' tragedy? Weil is implying. The words in the recognition scene have a double meaning. There is 'un sens mystique tout à fait manifeste', more prominent than the literal meaning, which is only the 'sens *extérieur*' (*SG* 49; my italics).[61] One looks at something, and suddenly recognizes another reality beneath: 'Reconnaître, ce n'est pas apprendre un état civil. Électre après avoir vu le sceau, regardant Oreste, voit manifestement, immédiatement que c'est lui dont elle se souvenait [...] Reconnaissance, c'est *lecture*' (*OC* vi/3. 67).[62] Weil wants her readers to have the same experience of recognition, to see for themselves the mystical significance of the tragedy.

---

[58] 'It is the waiting or attentive and faithful immobility that lasts indefinitely and cannot be shaken. The slave, who waits near the door so as to open it immediately when the master knocks, is the best image of it. He must be ready to die of hunger and exhaustion rather than change his attitude. It must be possible for his companions to call him, talk to him, hit him, without his even turning his head. Even if he is told that the master is dead, and even if he believes it, he will not move' (*WG* 128).
[59] 'without [her] [...] even turning [her] [...] head' (ibid.).
[60] 'she prefers the absence of Orestes to the presence of anything else'.
[61] 'a perfectly manifest mystical sense', 'external sense' (*IC* 13).
[62] 'Recognition does not mean apprehending a certain particular civil status. Electra, having seen the stamp, and beholding Orestes, sees clearly, immediately that it is he whom she remembered [...] Recognition means *reading*' (*NB* 389–90). 'LA SCÈNE DE LA RECONNAISSANCE DANS ÉLECTRE EST LE MEILLEUR EXEMPLE DE LECTURE' (*OC* vi/2. 256). ('The recognition scene in Electra is the best example of reading') (*NB* 183).

Electra assures herself of Orestes' presence through the three senses of sight, hearing, and touch. Orestes' lines in that passage 'n'ont de sens que de la part de Dieu':[63] 'Bien-aimée, j'en suis témoin', 'Plus jamais ailleurs n'interroge', 'Ainsi désormais aie-moi toujours' (*SG* 54–5; *El.* 1224–6).[64] Weil does not explain the mystical meaning of these lines. Probably Orestes as Christ-figure can testify ('j'en suis témoin') that he is truly the light of the world (John 8: 12). Furthermore once the soul has found God, its deepest thirst has been quenched ('plus jamais ailleurs n'interroge'): 'inquietum est cor nostrum, donec requiescat in te' ('our heart is restless, until it finds its rest in thee'), as St Augustine puts it.[65] Finally line 1226 takes on a particular meaning, if pronounced by God who tells the soul that it may possess him forever. Weil translates these lines slightly differently than in her article for *Entre Nous* so that they can better reflect the spiritual meaning she attributes to them. In the article she writes for example 'garde-moi ainsi toujours', instead of the later, more radical 'aie-moi toujours'; or she translates later on 'plus jamais ailleurs n'interroge' instead of the earlier 'ne tends plus l'oreille ailleurs' (*SG* 54; *OC* ii/2. 347). It is difficult to see, however, why these lines would make sense only in the mouth of God. The literal meaning seems much more obvious. Weil also picks passages such as 'un vivant n'a pas de tombeau', which she interprets to refer to the resurrected Christ (*IPC* 15) (*El.* 1219).[66] When Electra cries out that 'un stratagème l'a fait mourir, à présent un stratagème l'a sauvé', Weil sees behind it a reference to divine intervention (*IPC* 17–18, 69, 72) (*El.* 1228–9).[67] For the word μηχανή/*mechanē*, she thinks, should not be translated by 'stratagème', but by 'moyen' ('means'), and corresponds to the Latin idea of the *deus ex machina*.[68] Thus Orestes is more than just a human hero, he is a divine saviour, come to liberate Electra and reinstitute justice.

For Weil the mystical sense of this scene is obvious: 'Si on lit ces vers sans songer à l'histoire d'Électre et d'Oreste, la résonance mystique est évidente' (*IPC* 16).[69] In a letter to Perrin's assistant she writes that

---

[63] 'are without meaning, unless spoken by God' (*IC* 16).
[64] 'Well-Beloved; I am witness to it', 'Henceforth never doubt', 'Thus hold me forever' (ibid.). The 'bien-aimée' refers to the 'bien-aimée lumière' of the preceding line.
[65] St Augustine, *Confessions* 1. 1. 1.
[66] 'The living have no tomb' (*IC* 6). See also *OC* vi/3. 298.
[67] 'A stratagem caused his death, now a stratagem has saved him' (*IC* 8).
[68] Similarly Ringer believes that the machinations which bring Orestes back to life are meant to remind the audience of the *deus ex machina* (Ringer 1998: 193).
[69] 'If one reads these lines without thinking of the story of Electra and Orestes, the mystical overtones are evident' (*IC* 7).

the identification of Orestes with Christ, as well as of Electra with the human soul, 'est presque aussi sûre pour moi que si j'avais moi-même écrit ces vers' (*AD* 64).[70] Weil speaks with the authority of her own experience, when she writes in 'Formes de l'amour implicite de Dieu': 'Celui à qui est arrivé l'aventure d'Electre, celui qui a vu, entendu et touché, avec l'âme elle-même, celui-là reconnaît en Dieu la réalité de ces amours indirects qui étaient comme des reflets' (ibid. 212–13).[71]

Her allegorical reading shocks modern sensibilities, especially because of her assured tone. But there is an inbuilt indeterminacy or openness to different meanings within myth of which the multiple interpretations of myths over the ages are the empirical proof. Because of the indeterminate potential of myth, its possible readings are to a certain extent wilful. These readings explain the text and reveal other possible meanings, but also bend it into a new shape. Weil's interpretation does not contradict the text on its literal level though her Christian allegorical reading is unusual for her times. The problem does not lie with its allegorical character, but with Weil's claim that it is authorially intended and that it is *the* inscribed and only meaning of the text, apart from the literal one (*SG* 55; *AD* 64). This aside, how successful is Weil's allegorical reading?

It is difficult to determine the criteria of a good allegory. Perhaps its explanatory function is the main criterion, the way it sheds light, if not (or not only) on the literal meaning of the text, but on the realities the allegory points to. For allegory, according to Deborah Madsen in *Rereading Allegory*, is not only 'speaking other', but also 'speaking of the Other', meaning that it leads to a higher reality.[72] If the recognition scene between Orestes and Electra can be interpreted as an allegory of a mystical experience, what does this tell us about the latter? First of all that God comes to the soul and not vice versa—one of Weil's pet themes. The soul has to wait for him, be it explicitly or through implicit forms of love. But it is God who has to cover the infinite distance between them, for as Weil writes in 'L'Amour de Dieu et le malheur': 'Quand même nous marcherions tout au long des siècles, nous ne ferions pas autre chose que tourner autour de la terre. Même en avion, nous ne pourrions pas faire autre chose. Nous sommes hors d'état

---

[70] 'is almost as certain for me as if I had written these verses myself' (*WG* 39–40).

[71] 'He who has had the same adventure as Electra, he whose soul has seen, heard, and touched for itself, he will recognize God as the reality inspiring all indirect loves, the reality of which they are as it were the reflections' (ibid. 141).

[72] Madsen 1994: 29.

d'avancer verticalement. Nous ne pouvons pas faire un pas vers les cieux. Dieu traverse l'univers et vient jusqu'à nous' (*AD* 117).[73] He chooses the occasion and time, for 'il vient à son heure' (ibid.).[74] But Weil's interpretation of the tale of the Duke of Norway in her *Intuitions* tells us more about God than her allegorical reading of the *Electra* (*IPC* 13 ff.). In the former Weil emphasizes the point that God comes to the soul as a beggar, waiting to be let in. The Duke of Norway, who stands for the soul, assumes the shape of an animal during the day, while retaining his human appearance during the night. A princess/God marries him, and destroys his outward animal skin, which he divests during the night. This represents God's attempt to bring to light our humanity, hidden beneath our sinful animal nature. Yet the duke/soul flees, forgets the princess/God, and gets engaged to another woman, who symbolizes the flesh. The mediocre part of the soul flees the presence of purity since it means its death, and seeks the pleasures of this world instead (*AD* 166).[75] The princess searches for her lost husband, and on her way encounters an old woman who gives her three magic nuts. She comes to the palace where the forgetful duke is to be married. She gets hired as a kitchen maid, which means that God approaches the soul in the guise of a beggar. She breaks one of the nuts, out of which comes a beautiful dress. She offers it to the fiancée of the duke in exchange for spending the night with him, which signifies that God gains access to the soul by seducing the flesh through beauty. But the fiancée gives the duke a sleeping potion, so that he does not wake up when his wife sings to him. Only on the third night—after gaining access to the duke by the same means on this and the previous night—just before break of dawn, does the duke wake up, recognize his true wife, and send his fiancée away.

---

[73] 'Even if we were to walk for endless centuries we should do no more than go round and round the world. Even in an aeroplane we could not do anything else. We are incapable of progressing vertically. We cannot take one step towards the heavens. God crosses the universe and comes to us' (*SNL* 181).

[74] 'He comes at his own time' (ibid.).

[75] 'L'âme ne veut s'unir à la vérité que dans la nuit, dans l'inconscience. Voyant paraître une lueur de vérité, l'âme fuit et se tourne vers la chair. La vérité doit la chercher et séduire la chair pour obtenir accès jusqu'à l'âme. Mais l'âme dort. Si elle s'éveille un instant, alors elle se tourne vers l'union légitime' (*OC* vi/3. 46). ('It is only in the night, in a state of unconsciousness that the soul wants to be united to truth. As soon as it sees a glimmer of truth appear, the soul flees and turns itself toward the flesh. Truth has got to seek it out and seduce the flesh in order to gain access to the soul. But the soul is asleep. If it wakes up for an instant, it then turns itself toward the legitimate form of union') (*NB* 370).

In her reading of the *Electra* Weil focuses on the nature of *attente* and on the dark night of the soul, rather than on the means God employs to conquer it. To present the notion of *attente* is apologetically very significant, since it is so central to salvation: 'Désirer Dieu et renoncer à tout le reste, c'est cela seul qui sauve. L'attitude qui opère le salut ne ressemble à aucune activité. [. . .] C'est l'attente' (*AD* 193; *PSO* 41–2).[76] Many feel discouraged in the spiritual life, since they think that everything depends on their own effort. One tends to believe that Christianity is just a question of morality, an ethical programme, which one has to follow. Instead, as David Knowles points out in *What is Mysticism?*, it is a participation in the divine life of God.[77] Therefore *attente* is key, for it will eventually lead one to see God's presence behind every event, as explained in the last chapter. Weil points out that the usual experience of God is one of absence.[78] God speaks to us through the events of our life, and we must learn to perceive him therein. Therefore everything can become the means of uniting oneself to God. A continual contact is possible, be it in the ecstasy of a mystical experience or a dark night of the soul. Weil writes twice in her *Connaissance*: 'Tout le problème de la mystique et des questions connexes est celui du degré de valeur des sensations de présence' (*CS* 150, 153).[79] During a mystical experience God's presence is felt so strongly as to seem more real than anything else. In the dark night, his presence is experienced as absence; for the grace he infuses blinds the unpurified soul. Weil's interpretation of the *Electra* is therefore apologetically important, since it conveys some of the central elements of Christianity, showing what the basis for a relationship with God is.

When Weil describes Electra's mystical experience in the *Intuitions*, she writes about it in terms of God '[qui] se montre, lui parle, la touche' (*IPC* 17).[80] In 'Plaintes d'Électre', she says that Electra 's'émerveille successivement de la présence du bien-aimé aux trois sens, vue, ouïe et toucher' (*SG* 55).[81] This is astonishing given that when Christ came

---

[76] 'To long for God and to renounce all the rest, that is alone what saves. The attitude that brings salvation is unlike any activity. [. . .] This means to wait.'
[77] Knowles 1966: 15 ff.
[78] Therefore Kahn calls Weil's mysticism not one of effusion, but of 'retrait' (Kahn 1985: 385). See also Broc-Lapeyre 1999: 272.
[79] 'The whole problem of mysticism and kindred questions is that of the degree of value of sensations of presence' (*FLN* 195).
[80] 'reveals Himself, speaks to it, touches it' (*IC* 8).
[81] 'marvels at the presence of her beloved with three senses successively: sight, hearing and touch' (ibid. 16).

to Weil 'ni les sens ni l'imagination n'ont eu aucune part' (*AD* 45).[82] Yet Weil speaks about the mystical encounter in the physical terms of a real contact: 'je l'ai touchée' (ibid. 69), 'le Christ [...] m'a prise' (ibid. 45), 'contact réel, de personne à personne' (ibid.), 'soudaine emprise du Christ sur moi' (ibid.), 'Dieu [...] vient saisir l'âme et la lève' (ibid. 91), 'l'amour infiniment plus infini de Dieu vient nous saisir' (ibid. 117).[83] Though the senses are not involved in the mystical encounter, Weil uses especially the sense of touch to emphasize the reality of the experience, for the mystic needs to use ordinary language to express realities which are beyond its scope. A mystical experience is like sense-perception in its realness, though the reality perceived is greater and more certain than the one the senses could ever yield. As Weil writes to Bousquet: 'j'ai senti [...] une présence plus personnelle, plus certaine, plus réelle que celle d'un être humain' (*PSO* 81).[84]

In her interpretation of the myth of Persephone or Core, Weil focuses on the apologetic role of beauty as well as on the different stages of the mystical experience. Core/the soul is attracted by beauty, which works as a trap in Hades'/God's favour. Before God lets her go back to her mother Demeter/the natural world, he gives her a pomegranate seed to eat (*IPC* 9–13; *OC* vi/3. 58–9). This operates like the mustard seed Christ speaks about which, though the smallest seed, grows until the birds of heaven can live in it (Luke 13: 18–19). It symbolizes the 'yes' the soul has said to God almost without realizing it. Later, the soul has to give a more explicit affirmation. There are two stages of the mystical encounter: one where God takes the soul almost by force, the other where the soul needs to give its consent (*IPC* 12). Once the soul belongs to God, it has to experience a dark night: 'elle doit à son tour, mais à tâtons, traverser l'infinie épaisseur du temps et de l'espace pour aller à ce qu'elle aime. Cela, c'est la Croix' (*OC* vi/3. 115).[85] In the end God will reveal himself (*AD* 153).

---

[82] 'neither my senses nor my imagination had any part' (*WG* 27). In her letter to Bousquet she writes that Christ's presence during the mystical encounter is 'inaccessible et aux sens et à l'imagination' ('inaccessible both to sense and to imagination') (*PSO* 81/*SL* 140).

[83] 'I have touched it [God's mercy]' (*WG* 43), 'Christ himself [...] took possession of me' (ibid. 27), 'a real contact, person to person' (ibid.), 'this sudden possession of me by Christ' (ibid.), 'God [...] comes down and possesses the soul' (ibid. 61), 'the infinitely more infinite love of God comes to possess us' (ibid. 79).

[84] 'I felt [...] a presence more personal, more certain, and more real than that of a human being' (*SL* 140).

[85] 'it has, in its turn, groping as best it may, to cross the infinite thickness of time and space to go to what it loves. *That* is what constitutes the Cross' (*NB* 429).

Weil's allegorical reading intends to reveal the supernatural, but does Weil's outdated allegorical interpretation of Greek tragedy not bewilder modern readers rather than draw them to the realities the mystical experience discloses? Allegory has been used for apologetic purposes throughout the ages. The ancient Greeks employed it to explain shocking passages about the gods in myth. Therefore the gods were interpreted in terms of natural forces or moral symbols, or the whole myth was read as the embodiment of some philosophical idea—something the Stoics liked to do.[86] While Weil's arbitrariness is reminiscent of classical allegory, her Christological approach reminds one of the typological reading of Scripture mentioned in Ch. 2.[87] Though Christianity is Weil's starting point for interpreting Greek myth, and though she emphasizes, like St Augustine, the importance of love for a correct perception of things, her understanding of Christianity is heterodox to start with.[88]

The Prologue

Weil herself wrote 'a brief allegory of a mystical encounter', as Dargan calls it, or a 'conte mystique' ('mystical tale') according to Maes, entitled *Prologue*.[89] This text describes a mystical experience. In his close-reading of the *Prologue* in his article 'Lecture(s) de Prologue', Maes criticizes those who too quickly see Weil's own mystical experience described

---

[86] Madsen 1994: 34.

[87] Weil was respectful, at least in theory, of the literal sense of myth and folklore: 'Il vaut mieux risquer de les prendre trop littéralement que trop peu' (*OC* vi/2. 458) ('It is preferable to run the risk of taking them too literally than insufficiently so') (*NB* 334).

[88] 'Je médite tous les problèmes relatifs à l'étude comparée des religions [. . .] à la signification mystérieuse des textes et des traditions du christianisme; tout cela sans aucun souci d'un accord ou d'un désaccord possible avec l'enseignement dogmatique de l'Église' (*PSO* 150) ('I meditate on all the problems relative to the comparative study of religions [. . .] to the mysterious meaning of the texts and traditions of Christianity; all of this without any regard for any agreement or disagreement with the dogmatic teaching of the Church'). For Augustine's hermeneutics, see e.g. Rollinson 1981: 42 ff.

[89] Dargan 1999: 52; Maes 2000: 196 ff. There are three versions of the text, as pointed out by the editors of the *Œuvres Complètes* and by Maes (*OC* vi/3. 445). The oldest version, a draft containing the most corrections, was found on a loose page in the first *Cahier* written in the US (K12). Weil wrote another version at the end of her eleventh *Cahier* (K11) which she left with Thibon and which starts with the words 'Commencement du livre (le livre qui contiendrait ces pensées et beaucoup d'autres)' ('Beginning of the book (the book which should contain these thoughts and many others)') (*FLN* 63). The third version entitled *Prologue* is contained at the end of the twelfth *Cahier*, probably reconstituted with the help of the draft and therefore slightly different from the second version.

therein, or who try to situate the event described in time and space.[90] Weil never calls Christ by name, but only says 'il'. The 'je' to whom 'il' speaks is never specified, and is masculine as the 'je n'ai pas été *baptisé*' indicates and which buttresses the idea that Weil is not referring to herself (*OC* vi/3. 369; my italics).[91] The text starts with 'il' coming into the room of the subject: 'Il entra dans ma chambre et dit: "Misérable qui ne comprends rien, qui ne sais rien. Viens avec moi et je t'enseignerai des choses dont tu ne te doutes pas." Je le suivis' (ibid.).[92] He then takes the subject to a modern, ugly church, where he tells it to kneel down.[93] When 'je' says that it has not been baptized, he tells it to kneel 'devant ce lieu avec amour, comme devant le lieu où existe la vérité', which 'je' then does.[94] They go to an attic room from which the whole city can be seen where 'il' speaks and sometimes somebody comes in and joins the conversation. Sometimes he shares some bread with 'je' which he takes out of the cupboard: 'Ce pain avait vraiment le goût du pain. Je n'ai jamais plus retrouvé ce goût.'[95] They also drink wine 'qui avait le goût du soleil et de la terre où était bâtie la cité'.[96] Sometimes they lie down on the floor to sleep. One day he tells 'je' to leave. Though 'je' begs him on its knees, he throws 'je' out onto the staircase, and it leaves the house, wanders through the streets, and cannot remember where the house was. Nor does 'je' try to find it again, believing it was called by mistake in the first place. The text ends in the following way: 'Je sais bien qu'il ne m'aime pas. Comment pourrait-il m'aimer ? Et pourtant au fond de moi quelque chose, un point de moi-même, ne peut pas s'empêcher de penser en tremblant de peur que peut-être, malgré tout, il m'aime' (ibid. 370).[97] Though Maes criticizes any attempt to see in this text a description of Weil's own mystical experience, he does admit

---

[90] He criticizes those who read the text with an intuitive approach, but analyses it himself with his own presuppositions, namely that no analogies may be drawn, no similarities seen.
[91] 'I have not been baptized' (*FLN* 65).
[92] 'He came into my room and said: "You poor wretch, who understand nothing and know nothing—come with me and I will teach you things you have no idea of." I followed him' (ibid.).
[93] I will refer to 'je' as 'it' in order to distinguish the subject better from 'il'.
[94] 'before this place, with love, as before the place where truth exists' (*FLN* 65).
[95] 'That bread truly had the taste of bread. I have never found that taste again' (ibid.).
[96] 'which tasted of the sun and of the soil on which that city was built' (ibid.).
[97] 'I well know that he doesn't love me. How could he love me? And yet there is something deep in me, some point of myself, which cannot prevent itself from thinking, with fear and trembling, that perhaps, in spite of everything, he does love me' (ibid. 66).

that it is of a mystical nature. Thus the subject is the soul, and it seems obvious to me that 'il' stands for Christ. For 'il' speaks with authority, makes the subject kneel, promises a teaching, shares bread and wine (the eucharistic connotation is evident), and sends the subject away, as experienced during a dark night of the soul. Yet Weil does not mention Christ by name. What could the reason for this be? Maes explains the lack of references in the following way: 'C'est pour donner plus de force et une plus grande portée à son message qu'elle l'a dépouillé de tout ce qui ne regardait qu'elle et ne relevait que des conditions individuelles, religieuses.'[98] One might indeed think that the presence of Christ is not just the fortuitous element of an individual mystical experience. Weil's mystical encounters were Christological, and she believes that the mysticism of all cultures and religions is the same (*LR* 53).[99] On the other hand, why would she want to state the obvious? To give the text such bareness gives it greater power. The readers are first intrigued as to who this 'il' is who can come into a room and give orders with such authority, before soon realizing his identity.[100] Though Maes is right in pointing out the text's starkness, which gives it greater universal import, Weil has her own mystical experience to start from.[101] Though she may not want to describe her own mystical encounter specifically, it must in some form be contained therein, though stripped of all details. After all, the subject is somebody who has not been baptized, like Weil, yet Christ comes to 'je' and asks it to kneel and adore. The suddenness with which he walks into the room may indicate the unexpectedness of Weil's own

---

[98] Maes 2000: 218–19. 'It is in order to give her message greater power and a greater impact, that she stripped it of everything that concerned her alone and pertained only to individual, religious circumstances.'

[99] 'En fait, les mystiques de presque toutes les traditions religieuses se rejoignent presque jusqu'à l'identité. Ils constituent la vérité de chacune' (*LR* 53) ('In practice, mystics belonging to nearly all the religious traditions coincide to the extent that they can hardly be distinguished. They represent the truth of each of these traditions') (*LTP* 47). 'La vérité mystique est une comme la vérité arithmétique ou géométrique' (*CS* 204) ('Mystical truth is one, like arithmetical or geometrical truth') (*FLN* 243).

[100] Similarly Weil simply knew that it was Christ who had taken her, as Kahn points out (*PSO* 81; Kahn 1978*b*: 36–7, 40).

[101] There are some details contained in the text that I cannot go into: there is a river flowing through the city; the season is no longer winter, nor yet spring; 'je' says that its place is not in that attic, but in 'un cachot de prison, dans un de ces salons bourgeois pleins de bibelots et de peluche rouge, dans une salle d'attente de gare' ('a prison cell, in one of these bourgeois salons full of knick-knacks and of red plush, in the waiting room of a train station'). This made Weil's mother suggest that her daughter was thinking of specific locations in Paris and in Rouen, where she visited her brother André who had been jailed in spring 1940 for refusing conscription (*OC* vi/3. 447).

mystical encounter.[102] Christ feeds the subject and promises to teach it, but: 'il ne m'enseigna rien'.[103] Rather, 'nous causions de toutes sortes de choses, à bâtons rompus, comme font de vieux amis'.[104] Then comes the description of the experience of abandonment so familiar to Weil. This enigmatic and powerful text has been widely accepted as being a key text for Weil's thought.[105] In the version given to Thibon, she wrote at the top of the page: 'Commencement du livre (le livre qui contiendrait ces pensées et beaucoup d'autres)' (*OC* vi/3. 369).[106] It is supposed to stand at the beginning of her work, in particular of her *Cahiers*, which need to be read in its light.[107] Thus a mystical experience is meant to explain, and is in some way at the centre of, her whole *œuvre*.[108] Through this text, as Maes rightly points out, Weil opens mysticism in some form or other to everybody, for it is within the reach of everybody who seeks God with perseverance: 'le désir seul oblige Dieu à descendre. Il ne vient qu'à ceux qui lui demandent de venir; et ceux qui demandent souvent, longtemps, ardemment. Il ne peut pas s'empêcher de descendre vers eux' (*AD* 91–2).[109]

By heading her *œuvre* with a mystical text, Weil confronts her readers with the reality of God as experienced in a mystical encounter. She puts them on the spot, challenges them with a reality beyond their experience of the world. They can either accept it or not, continue to read or not. As Dargan says about the *Prologue*: 'There is no room for argument. One assents or one does not. One climbs to her point of elevation or,

---

[102] Micheline Mazeau writes in 'Commentaire du *Prologue* de Simone Weil': 'Le visiteur mystérieux ne frappe pas, on ne lui dit pas d'entrer. Il surgit, il s'impose et il s'impose au cœur de la maison à l'endroit le plus intime, dans la chambre' (Mazeau 1978: 15) ('The mysterious visitor does not knock, is not told to come in. He appears suddenly, asserts himself and thrusts himself into the heart of the house, at the most intimate place, in the room').

[103] 'he taught me nothing' (*FLN* 65).

[104] 'We talked in a rambling way about all sorts of things, as old friends do' (ibid.).

[105] Maes 2000: 191.

[106] 'Beginning of the book (the book which should contain these thoughts and many others)' (*FLN* 63).

[107] At the end of the text is written in brackets: 'Suit une masse non ordonnée de fragments' ('Follows a mass of non-ordered fragments') (*OC* vi/3. 370).

[108] Perrin confirms this: 'Car Simone voulait faire comprendre qu'à l'origine de tous ces écrits il n'y avait pas seulement son travail, son érudition, mais une présence mystérieuse qui a tout éclairé, tout inspiré' (Canciani 2000: 134) ('For Simone wanted to make it clear that at the origin of all her writings there was not only her work, her erudition, but a mysterious presence which illuminated everything, inspired everything').

[109] 'desire alone draws God down. He only comes to those who ask him to come; and he cannot refuse to come to those who implore him long, often, and ardently' (*WG* 61).

remaining below, one accepts her teachings; it is impossible to stay on one's own terms.'[110] Similarly Christ calls the soul to high places, to the challenges of an ascent, to an arid night during which it has to cross the distance that God traversed first.

Yet this ascent yields a much better view, since one can see from the *mansarde* 'toute la ville, quelques échafaudages de bois, le fleuve où l'on déchargeait des bateaux'.[111] In the chapter on *Antigone* I have shown the relevance of the mystical or supernatural approach for an adequate perception of reality. This is confirmed by Weil's more explicit thoughts on mysticism:

Postulat: ce qui est inférieur dépend de ce qui est supérieur.
Il n'y a qu'une source unique de lumière. La pénombre, ce ne sont pas des rayons venant d'une autre source, mi-obscure, c'est la même lumière dégradée. Ainsi *la mystique doit fournir la clef de toutes les connaissances et de toutes les valeurs.* [. . .]
Le Christ est la clef.   (*CS* 43; my italics)[112]

Whether we realize it or not, our perception depends on the Logos. If we are united to the Logos, explicitly or implicitly, we can look on things from a higher plane, and have a more comprehensive and adequate perspective. God is the source of light, and at least the implicit condition of cognition: 'Dieu est la source de la lumière; cela veut dire que toutes les espèces d'attention sont seulement des formes dégradées de l'attention religieuse' (*OC* vi/3. 215).[113]

However, the mystical experience is a secret event. Modesty forbids that one talk about it: 'La pudeur dans l'amour charnel n'est qu'une figure de la vraie pudeur, celle qui recouvre le contact avec "le Père qui est dans le secret", et qui a pour raison d'être qu'il habite seulement dans le secret' (ibid. 361).[114] The mystical encounter happens silently in the secret of the soul (*PSO* 129). Others can only know about it by the

---

[110] Dargan 1999: 51.
[111] 'the whole town, some wooden scaffoldings, and the river where boats were unloading' (*FLN* 65).
[112] 'Postulate: what is inferior depends on what is superior. There is only one unique source of light. Dim light does not consist of rays coming from another source, which is dim; it is the same light, degraded. In the same way, *mysticism should provide the key for all knowledge and all values.* [. . .] Christ is the key' (ibid. 98; my italics).
[113] 'God is the source of light; this means to say that all the different kinds of attention are only debased forms of religious attention' (*NB* 515).
[114] 'The modesty shown in carnal love is simply an image of the true modesty, that which shrouds the contact with the "Father which is in secret", and whose *raison d'être* lies in the fact that He dwells only in secret' (ibid. 631).

persons' behaviour, not by the way they talk about God: 'Quand dans la manière d'agir à l'égard des choses et des hommes, ou simplement dans la manière de les regarder, il apparaît des vertus surnaturelles, on sait que l'âme n'est plus vierge, qu'elle a couché avec Dieu' (CS 97).[115] Weil is not afraid of using the language of sexuality to express the love between God and the soul, for: 'Reprocher à des mystiques d'aimer Dieu avec la faculté d'amour sexuel, c'est comme si on reprochait à un peintre de faire des tableaux avec des couleurs qui sont composées de substances matérielles. Nous n'avons pas autre chose avec quoi aimer' (OC vi/3. 170; AD 163).[116] Weil has different ways of speaking about the mystical encounter. André Devaux calls Weil's mysticism a 'mystique de *traversée*' ('mysticism of crossing').[117] God crosses the infinite distance between himself and us: 'par-dessus l'infinité de l'espace et du temps, l'amour infiniment plus infini de Dieu vient nous saisir' (AD 117).[118] The soul then has to pass through the same distance to rejoin God, but without leaving the body, which is tied to time and space (PSO 105). The soul enters a new dimension—walks through 'la porte' where 'l'espace s'ouvre' ('space opens')—which is filled by the silence of God (AD 48–9).[119]

CONCLUSION

One might have thought that Weil's highly personal and exceptional mystical experiences would make her rank such encounters as being off the beaten spiritual track, and that they would therefore not feature in her apologetic endeavours. On the contrary, mysticism is for her at the core of religion and is therefore of central apologetic significance. For those who believe—as she did in the past—that the question of the

---

[115] 'When a man's way of behaving towards things and men, or simply his way of regarding them, reveals supernatural virtues, one knows that his soul is no longer virgin, it has slept with God' (FLN 145–6).

[116] 'To reproach mystics with loving God by means of the faculty of sexual love is as though one were to reproach a painter with making pictures by means of colours composed of material substances. We haven't anything else with which to love' (NB 472).

[117] Devaux 1985: 74.

[118] 'Over the infinity of space and time the infinitely more infinite love of God comes to possess us' (SNL 181).

[119] To express this reality, Weil likes to compare it to a chick piercing its eggshell, and entering another world (PSO 74).

existence of God cannot be resolved, it overturns intellectual difficulties and prejudices (*PSO* 43 ff.). It questions the prejudices of materialists by confronting them with a reality more real than matter. At a time when people became fanatical partisans of Marxism or Nazism, Weil saw in the fire of divine love the only powerful antidote to these ideologies. The folly of love that animates Antigone, the fire that Prometheus brings to the earth, is what Weil wants to convey to her times. There is a smouldering ember of Christian love left, but it must be newly rekindled: 'Nous restons perdus si de ces charbons et des étincelles qui crépitent sur le continent il ne sort pas une flamme capable d'allumer l'Europe' (*EL* 107).[120] Weil's allegorical interpretation of the *Electra* is unusual for her times. Yet her original reading offers her the opportunity to speak about God's reality and love in the context of a mystical experience which, though not her own, possesses all the power and intensity of a personal encounter.

Like Electra, Weil's contemporaries were experiencing grave injustices. Like Electra, the French could do little against their oppressors. The temptation was great to keep quiet like Chrysothemis and compromise with the enemy. But the greatest danger, in Weil's eyes, was the attraction and dynamics of mass movements. Nobody likes to be an outsider, jeered at, and perhaps even killed. By joining mass movements, one becomes part of the *gros animal* ('great beast'), an expression Weil borrowed from Plato (*SG* 89 ff.).[121] The *gros animal*, which stands for 'le social', can get pulled in any direction, independently of truth and justice. Opinion, not truth, is its guiding principle. Demagogues can manipulate it by means of propaganda. To resist its attraction, one must set one's heart on God, lay up one's treasure in the other world, and seek truth and justice (*OC* vi/3. 164). For God is the only power capable of undermining the opium of ideologies (*OL* 229; *E* 83).

There is a specific date for each individual, when he or she is confronted with the choice between God and evil. Weil writes about this to Bousquet, hoping to prepare him for this choice by telling him about her own mystical encounter. She tries to do the same for her readers, namely to prepare them for this existential choice with which they will be confronted by showing them the mystical dimension of the Electra myth: 'Pour chaque être humain, il y a une date, inconnue

---

[120] 'We are still lost unless those embers and the flickering sparks on the Continent can be fanned into a flame to kindle the whole of Europe' (*SE* 217).
[121] Plato, *Republic* 6. 493a–d.

de tous et de lui-même avant tout, mais tout à fait déterminée, au-delà de laquelle l'âme ne peut plus garder cette virginité. Si avant cet instant précis, éternellement marqué, elle n'a pas consenti à être prise par le bien, elle sera aussitôt après prise malgré elle par le mal' (*PSO* 77).[122] For there is no middle way, only the radical choice between the supernatural/God/the good, and evil: 'Désirer Dieu et renoncer à tout le reste, c'est cela seul qui sauve' (*AD* 193).[123]

---

[122] 'For every human being there is a point in time, a limit, unknown to anyone and above all to himself, but absolutely fixed, beyond which the soul cannot keep this virginity. If, before this precise moment, fixed from all eternity, it has not consented to be possessed by the good, it will immediately afterwards be possessed in spite of itself by the bad' (*SL* 138).

[123] 'To long for God and to renounce all the rest, that alone can save us' (*WG* 128).

8

Conclusion: Simone Weil—An Apologist of the Supernatural

L'unique intermédiaire par lequel le bien puisse descendre de [cette réalité située hors du monde] [...] au milieu des hommes, ce sont ceux qui parmi les hommes ont leur attention et leur amour tournés vers elle.[1]

(*EL* 74–5)

Comme le Christ, nous avons tous été envoyés en ce monde pour témoigner pour la vérité; et quoi que nous fassions, nous témoignerons.[2]

(*CS* 225)

We have seen that Weil is not only a strong reader, but that she is also in some sense an apologetic writer. Her concerns were apologetic, especially in the last years of her life. She was aware of the urgency of conversion given the dangers of her times, and felt the obligation to prepare the ground for a (re-)Christianization of society. She tried to show Christianity's universality by revealing the presence of Christian intuitions in ancient societies. Furthermore, through her interpretations of classical Greek texts she attempted to convey certain Christian ideas, as my analysis has made clear. The question now remains as to how convincing her approach is, and how successful she is as an apologist.[3]

---

[1] 'Those minds whose attention and love are turned towards that reality [outside the world] are the sole intermediary through which good can descend from there and come among men' (*SE* 219).
[2] 'All of us have been put into this world, like Christ, in order to witness to the truth; and whatever we may do, we shall be bearing witness to it' (*FLN* 262).
[3] The *Cahiers Simone Weil* have recently published some issues on the reception history of Weil's works in different countries without, however, focusing on the apologetic dimension of her work (*CSW* 28/1–3).

Weil, as we have seen, sometimes twists the texts to make them fit her Christological interpretation. At first glance this discredits her approach. Historical accuracy was not her goal, as we know, and Jacques Cabaud summarizes this well in *Simone Weil à New York et à Londres*: 'Au lieu de se livrer à une critique approfondie des sources, elle préférait se fier à cette faculté divinatoire qu'était son extraordinaire pouvoir d'invention. Un jour, sur une question d'histoire ancienne, André [son frère] lui déclara: "Cela ne repose sur rien." Simone répliqua: "Cela repose sur ceci que c'est beau. Si c'est beau, cela doit être vrai."'[4] Even if we differentiate between those elements of Weil's interpretations which distort the original text and those which do not, the question remains whether the presence of pre-Christian intuitions is demonstrable. Even if we see similarities between ancient cultures and Christianity, how can we know that we are not projecting a Christian spirit onto them? Or how can we be sure that Christianity did not take some elements from those cultures to integrate them into its own theology and spirituality? Faith is often required, so it seems, in order to perceive pre-Christian elements in ancient cultures on the one hand, and on the other hand not to reduce Christianity to a mere myth that borrowed elements from ancient mythology; for it takes faith to believe in the revelation that stands at the origin of Christianity.[5] Since Christianity proclaims its truth with such absoluteness and universality, it makes sense to look at all things from its standpoint once one has accepted it, especially since 'il n'y a pas le point de vue chrétien et les autres, mais la vérité et l'erreur. Non pas: ce qui n'est pas chrétien est faux, mais: tout ce qui est vrai est chrétien' (*CS* 24/*OC* vi/3. 395).[6] Thus the early Christians read the Scriptures in the light of the New Testament, which they saw as their fulfilment. Therefore Weil interprets ancient cultures from the perspective of Christianity in the belief that they express its spirit, as perhaps the Catholic Church

---

[4] J. Cabaud 1967: 29. 'Instead of submitting her sources to a thorough critique, she preferred to trust that divining faculty of hers, her boundless inventiveness. One day, André [her brother] told her regarding a question of ancient history: "This has no foundation." Simone answered: "It is founded on the fact that it is beautiful. If it is beautiful, it must be true."'

[5] I do not mean to say, however, that faith is something irrational or that it is simply a question of like or dislike. Nor do I mean to imply that faith is the necessary condition for seeing in Christianity something more and radically other than the preceding religions and myths.

[6] 'There is not a Christian point of view and other points of view; there is truth and error. It is not that anything which isn't Christian is false, but everything which is true is Christian' (*FLN* 80).

never has. One may wonder, however, what the point is of an apologetic argument that presupposes what it wants to bring about—faith. As pointed out in Ch. 2, Weil believes that ancient Greece—one of the roots of European culture—was Christian. Europe failed to see this, and was therefore never really Christianized through the Catholic Church. To achieve this now, Europe needs to be made aware of its Christian roots predating Christ's incarnation. Weil does not want to convince us of the truth and universality of Christianity directly, but rather tries to show that the Greek classics cannot be understood except in the light of Christ. Though she herself uses Christianity as her starting point for reading the classics, she wants to lead her readers via the classics towards Christianity. It is not her primary intention to demonstrate the existence of pre-Christian intuitions. Rather, by unfolding the truth and depth of the texts through her Christological approach, she aims to show by default that they cannot be fully understood except from that perspective, thereby indicating the presence of pre-Christian intuitions. She writes at the end of her *Intuitions*: 'La pensée humaine et l'univers constituent ainsi les livres révélés par excellence, si l'attention éclairée par l'amour et la foi sait les déchiffrer. Leur lecture constitue une preuve, et même l'unique preuve certaine. Après avoir lu l'*Iliade* en grec, nul ne songerait à se demander si le professeur qui lui a appris l'alphabet grec ne l'a pas trompé' (*IPC* 171).[7] Thus, once one has perceived the Christological inspiration at the source of the Greek classics, one can no longer doubt their Christocentric nature; it would be irrational to do so.

As we have seen, it was after her first mystical experience that Weil started to look at antiquity from this Christological perspective. It was also through literature—though not ancient literature—that this divine encounter took place. She was reciting Herbert's poem 'Love', when Christ came down and took her:

> Love bade me welcome; yet my soul drew back
> Guilty of dust and sin.
> But quick-eyed Love, observing me grow slack
> From my first entrance in,
> Drew nearer to me, sweetly questioning,
> If I lacked anything.

---

[7] 'Human thought and the universe constitute the books of revelation *par excellence*, if the attention, lighted by love and faith, knows to decipher them. The reading of them is a proof, and indeed the only certain proof. After having read the *Iliad* in Greek, no one would dream of wondering whether the professor who taught him the Greek alphabet had deceived him' (*IC* 201).

Without realizing it, she was saying this poem like a prayer. Conversely, one can also recite a prayer like a beautiful poem, as Weil had done with the Salve Regina before (*AD* 47). But great literature, especially tragedy, can reveal spiritual realities, as Weil writes in her *Cahiers*: 'Grandes œuvres littéraires: des voiles devant la vérité, mais transparents. *Électre. Antigone*' (*OC* vi/2. 273).[8] Truth is revealed, yet hidden in literature. The veils covering it are transparent. The presence of truth within literature is like the parables in the Gospel, which are told in such a way 'that they may be heard and not understood'. Christ then explained them to his apostles. Similarly, Weil tries to reveal to her readers the meaning of ancient Greek texts. She explains to them the significance of the supernatural perspective, the absoluteness of the moral choice, and the nature of idolatry in her reading of the *Antigone*. In her analysis of the *Iliad*, she discloses the nature of war and of power within an unredeemed world. The *Prometheus*, while supplying a theodicy, brings home the nature of Christ's Passion, its import for the Trinity, and the meaning of suffering. Finally, the *Electra* allows Weil to unveil the reality of God, to stress the possibility of a mystical encounter, and to pinpoint the centrality of such attitudes as *attente*, *attention*, and desire for salvation.

Yet the classics, which are used as an apologetic trap, also keep Weil out of the Catholic Church, which, in her eyes, fails to fulfil its call to universality. She wants to remain with everything that is true and good, even if it is outside the Church, and with all those people who are thus marginalized: 'L'amour de ces choses qui sont hors du christianisme visible me tient hors de l'Eglise' (*AD* 76).[9] Weil, as we have seen, if she does propose Christianity, does not always define it in an orthodox way. Among Catholics, her apologetic significance has therefore been judged diversely. Charles Moeller, in *Littérature du XXe siècle et Christianisme*, warns of the danger that her heterodox ideas present to believing Catholics.[10] Others, such as François Mauriac, admired her although she was heterodox and lived 'sur les confins de l'Eglise', because, as he claims, 'la lumière qui [la] [. . .] traverse [. . .] peut-être parce qu'elle ne s'exprime pas dans les formules traditionnelles

---

[8] 'Great literary works: veils drawn in front of the truth, but transparen[t] veils. *Electra. Antigone*' (*NB* 195).
[9] 'The love of those things that are outside visible Christianity keeps me outside the Church' (*WG* 48).
[10] Moeller 1953: 230, 255.

m'illumine d'autant mieux'.[11] Similarly, Weil had some impact on Pope John XXIII who read *La Connaissance surnaturelle* and on Pope Paul VI who counted her together with Pascal and Bernanos as one of the three greatest influences on his intellectual development.[12] Perrin addresses the concerns of Catholics by saying that 'elle n'est pas une solution, mais une question; pas une réponse, mais un appel; pas une conclusion, mais une exigence'.[13] Weil challenges her readers, thereby provoking different responses. As Nevin writes in the preface to his book *Simone Weil: Portrait of a Self-Exiled Jew*: 'What she does do is excite people one way or another. To judge from the hundreds of essays and reviews on Weil and her works, it would seem impossible for anyone to be left indifferent toward her.'[14] She speaks with the tone and authority of a prophet who is jeered at by some and listened to by others. The prophet, as Marchetti says, does not primarily predict the future, but reveals what others do not want to see because of their moral blindness and indifference.[15] Yet Perrin thinks that she may precisely have something to say to the young for 'avec l'évolution des mentalités, je serais porté à croire que cette authenticité spirituelle correspond mieux aux jeunes d'aujourd'hui. Beaucoup d'entre eux n'ont pas peur de cette relation à l'Au-delà, à ce qui dépasse la raison.'[16]

But what is it that makes Weil so appealing, even though she speaks in an apodictic tone, which leads people such as Dargan to say that she leaves her readers no room? What is it that makes her readers want to read the *Intuitions*, even though they are soon aware of its historical shortcomings? There are many answers to these questions. Something new emerges from Weil's imaginative approach to great literature. As we have seen, she uncovers new depths of meaning in the well-known classics and sheds new light on the eternal questions of moral choice, theodicy, the nature of idolatry, the reasons for war, and so on. There is still a factor that is hard to prove, but makes Weil attractive to many:

---

[11] Croc 1995: 166–7; Mauriac 1962: 100. 'on the borders of the Church', 'the light which passes through her illuminates me all the more, perhaps because she does not express herself in traditional ways'.
[12] McLellan 1990: 268.
[13] Perrin and Thibon 1967: 31. 'She is not a solution, but a question; not an answer, but a call; not a conclusion, but a demand.'
[14] Nevin 1991: p. xi.   [15] Marchetti 2000: 131.
[16] Canciani 2000: p. viii. See also J.-M Emmanuelle's testimony 'Simone Weil et mon baptême' (1964). 'With the evolution of mentalities, I would be drawn to believe that this spiritual authenticity corresponds better to the young today. Many among them are not afraid of this relationship with the Beyond, of what goes past reason.'

she has a sense of the supernatural and succeeds in conveying its reality. Weil, I would claim, is an apologist of the supernatural. As Philippe de Saint-Robert puts it in *La Vision tragique de Simone Weil*, she is 'sans doute le seul écrivain de ce siècle qui ait été infatigablement de plain-pied avec le surnaturel'.[17] And Thibon assures us that 'jamais le mot *surnaturel* ne m'est apparu plus gonflé de réalités qu'à son contact'.[18]

Yet Weil claimed: 'L'objet de ma recherche n'est pas le surnaturel mais ce monde. Le surnaturel est la lumière. On ne doit pas oser en faire un objet, ou bien on l'abaisse' (*OC* vi/2. 245).[19] Though the supernatural may not be Weil's object of research, she mentions it so frequently that her last notebooks were published under the title of *La Connaissance surnaturelle*. Furthermore, she views everything from a supernatural perspective, just as she believes is the case in great works of art. For she thought that 'le surnaturel est présent partout en secret', and she attempted to disclose its reality to her contemporaries (*AD* 167).[20] However, this is difficult since it can only be apprehended through personal contact. This, she admits, may seem contradictory, for how could that which is supra-natural, and transcendent, and which goes beyond mere human faculties become an object of experience (*OC* vi/2. 343)? As seen in Ch. 3, words endowed with some kind of sacramental effectiveness can bring about this result. But ultimately only faith can give us a direct contact with the supernatural: 'par définition on ne peut pas percevoir le surnaturel là où on ne dirige pas le regard de la foi, mais seulement les reflets du surnaturel dans la nature' (ibid. 469).[21] Though she cannot instil that faith in her readers, she can at least point to the reflections of the supernatural as present in the heroic courage of Antigone, in the objective perspective of the *Iliad* on friends and foes alike, in the redemptive Passion of Prometheus, and in the mystical hope of Electra. If, in consequence, one accepts the gift of faith when offered and rids oneself of one's idolatrous ideologies, one will gain access to a

---

[17] Saint-Robert 2000: 8. 'without a doubt the only writer of this century that tirelessly has been at home with the supernatural'.

[18] Perrin 1964: 44. 'Never did the word supernatural seem more filled with realities than at her contact.'

[19] 'The object of my search is not the supernatural, but this world. The supernatural is the light. We must not presume to make an object of it, or else we degrade it' (*NB* 173).

[20] 'The supernatural is secretly present throughout' (*WG* 112).

[21] 'since by definition one cannot discern the supernatural except where one has first turned the eyes of faith, but only the reflections of the supernatural in nature' (*NB* 344–5).

supernatural perspective opening new vistas and giving one a grasp of the whole otherwise unattainable: 'D'un endroit élevé, on voit un vaste espace; des lieux que celui qui est dans la plaine voit successivement, celui qui est sur un sommet les voit d'un regard, en même temps' (*OC* vi/1. 353).[22]

Furthermore, if the reasons for the current loss of the sense of the supernatural can be pinned down, the remedy may still be found: 'La perte du passé équivaut à la perte du surnaturel. Quoique ni l'une ni l'autre perte ne soit encore consommée en Europe, l'une et l'autre sont assez avancées pour que nous puissions constater expérimentalement cette correspondance' (*EHP* 375).[23] That is why Weil wants to recall the inspiration of times gone by and place the supernatural at the centre of society. This shows once again that her reasons for her revival of the Greek classics are of an apologetic nature. Did she not claim that 'le très grand art est surnaturel' (*OC* vi/2. 200; *AD* 160)?[24] Masterpieces are bridges leading to a reality that is 'située hors du monde, c'est-à-dire hors de l'espace et du temps, hors de l'univers mental de l'homme, hors de tout le domaine que les facultés humaines peuvent atteindre' (*EL* 74).[25] This reality, which sounds so abstract, is in effect far more than a mere Platonic Idea, since it is a person, and this person is a Love no less substantial than God himself, whom Weil describes as 'l'Amour qui depuis l'origine nous a dans ses bras' (*PSO* 75).[26]

But perhaps the greatest witnesses to this truth are the saints who make this reality visible to others and who embody the supernatural in a unique manner: 'L'unique fait surnaturel ici-bas, c'est la sainteté elle-même et ce qui en approche' (*E* 226).[27] Sanctity, according to this passage, is the only mode in which the supernatural is present in this world—though there are other ways to access it (*OC* vi/3. 310). Thus saints must, by definition, be the principle vehicles of Europe's

---

[22] 'From an elevated spot one commands a vast expanse; places which he who is in the plain can only see successively, he who is on the heights can take in at a glance, at the same time' (ibid. 71).
[23] 'The loss of the past is equivalent to the loss of the supernatural. Even though neither one nor the other loss is yet complete in Europe, both are sufficiently advanced for us to be able to affirm this correspondence through direct experience' (*SWC* 116).
[24] 'All very great art is supernatural' (*NB* 155).
[25] 'outside the world, that is to say, outside space and time, outside man's mental universe, outside any sphere whatsoever that is accessible to human faculties' (*SE* 219).
[26] 'Love who holds us in his arms from the beginning' (*SL* 137).
[27] 'The unique supernatural fact in this world is holiness itself and what lies near to it' (*NR* 264).

re-Christianization: 'Le monde a besoin de saints qui aient du génie comme une ville où il y a la peste a besoin de médecins' (*AD* 82).[28] And she adds: 'Là où il y a besoin, il y a obligation'[29]—an obligation she herself tried to fulfil for sanctity is 'si j'ose dire, le minimum pour un chrétien' (*EL* 209).[30] But she believes this sanctity must take on a new form: 'Aujourd'hui ce n'est rien encore que d'être un saint, il faut la sainteté que le moment present exige, une sainteté nouvelle, elle aussi sans précédent' (*AD* 81).[31] The modern saint, for example, would belong to an order consisting of laypeople whose clothes do not distinguish them from others. This new sanctity would uncover layers of truth to which people have become blind: 'C'est la mise à nu d'une large portion de vérité et de beauté jusque-là dissimulées par une couche épaisse de poussière' (ibid.).[32] Through the saints the supernatural, that is to say God, becomes visible through a mirror not so darkly, to alter St Paul slightly. They lift the veil and become the doorway that gives access to God, washing the eyes 'presque aveugles sous la poussière' ('almost blinded by dust'), as Weil described it in her poem 'La Porte' (*PSO* 12).

The saints are transformed by the Love incarnate to which they witness, becoming thereby eucharistic offerings for others: 'La sainteté est une transmutation comme l'eucharistie' (*CS* 41).[33] Weil herself wanted to become such a eucharistic oblation through her life and through her writings (ibid. 205). She would have wanted her readers to respond to her own texts, as the sinner does to Love in George Herbert's poem who offers him, it seems, his own flesh to eat: ' "You must sit down," says Love, "and taste my meat," So I did sit and eat.' Of her own reading habits she said: 'je ne lis pas, je mange' (*AD* 45).[34] What she wrote was not for mere perusal, but was meant to be assimilated, and, as it were, to be eaten and digested. In turn, her texts would transform the reader. For she believed that she was leaving behind 'un

---

[28] 'The world needs saints who have genius, just as a plague-stricken town needs doctors' (*WG* 51).
[29] 'Where there is a need there is also an obligation' (ibid.).
[30] 'if I dare say so, the minimum for a Christian' (*SL* 175).
[31] 'Today it is not nearly enough merely to be a saint, but we must have the saintliness demanded by the present moment, a new saintliness, itself also without precedent' (*WG* 51). See Lucchetti Bingemer 2005 on sanctity in Weil's thought.
[32] 'It is the disclosure of a large portion of truth and beauty hitherto concealed under a thick layer of dust' (ibid.).
[33] 'Sanctity is a transmutation like the Eucharist' (*FLN* 96).
[34] 'I do not read, I *eat*' (*WG* 27).

dépôt d'or pur' (*EL* 250).³⁵ Ultimately there was only one truth she was trying to convey: 'Il n'y a qu'une vérité qui vaille la peine d'être l'objet d'un témoignage. C'est que Dieu est Amour' (*CS* 201).³⁶ For 'Dieu seul vaut qu'on s'intéresse à lui, et absolument rien d'autre.'³⁷ What happens to all those interesting things, which do not speak of God? 'Faut-il conclure que ce sont des prestiges du démon? Non, non, non. Il faut conclure qu'elles parlent de Dieu.'³⁸ This is what Weil is trying to show, for 'il est urgent aujourd'hui de le montrer' (ibid. 74).³⁹

³⁵ 'a deposit of pure gold' (*SL* 196).
³⁶ 'There is only one truth that is worth the trouble of witnessing to. It is that God is Love' (*FLN* 240).
³⁷ 'God alone is worthy of interest, and absolutely nothing else' (ibid. 126).
³⁸ 'Must we conclude that they are the devil's shows? No, no, no. We must conclude that they do speak about God' (ibid.).
³⁹ 'Today it is urgently necessary to demonstrate this' (ibid.).

Appendix: References to Ancient Greek Texts in the Works of Simone Weil

I do not repeat references appearing in earlier editions of Weil's works that are also contained in the *Œuvres complètes*, but will simply refer to the latter. Thus I will only refer to 'L'*Iliade* ou le poème de la force' in the *Œuvres complètes*, and not to its earlier publication in *La Source grecque*. However, I will refer to other texts in the *Source*, since they are not yet available in the complete edition. Furthermore, I will refer to the first part of 'L'Amour de Dieu et le malheur' as it is printed in *Attente de Dieu*, and to the second part as it is found in *Pensées sans ordre*.

ANTIGONE

CO 154–6; *CS* 17, 222, 291, 306; *EL* 25–6, 218, 243; *IPC* 18–20, 99; *OC* ii/2. 333 ff., ii/3. 61, 211, vi/1. 68, 101–2, 335, vi/2. 273, 389, vi/3. 87, 219, 226–7, 231, 236, 275, 276, 316, 386.

References to specific lines:
Dialogue between Ismene and Antigone: 63–4, 67, 79, 555, 559 (*OC* ii/2. 335–6); 99 (*IPC* 20).
Hymn to the sun: 100–9 (*OC* ii/2. 335; vi/1. 260–1).
Concerning the unwritten laws: 453–4, 504–7 (*OC* ii/2. 335); 450–2 (*EL* 25).
Dialogue between Creon and Antigone: 512–23 (*IPC* 18–19); 450–7 (*EL* 25); 518–24 (*EL* 25–6; *OC* ii/1. 336); 521 (*EL* 25; *OC* vi/1. 380).
To love, not to hate: 523 (*EL* 26; *IPC* 19; *OC* ii/2. 336, vi/1. 68, 219, 379, vi/3. 87; *Œ* 655; *S* 120).
Creon's cynical remark to Antigone to go down to the dead: 524–5 (*IPC* 19; *OC* vi/3. 227, 316).
The discussion between Haemon and his father: 736–9 (*OC* ii/2. 336).

Appendix 217

The Eros hymn: 781–800 (*OC* ii/1. 337, vi/1. 123, 196, 224, 261–2, 368–9; *Œ* 664; *CSW* 5/2: 155, 25/2: 120); 781, 790 (*OC* i. 278).

Antigone's death song: 806–10 (*OC* ii/2. 337); 806–16 (*OC* vi/1. 261); 876–82 (*OC* vi/1. 268); 916–28 (*OC* ii/2. 337–8).

At least Antigone will be dear to her father and mother in Hades for what she has done: 897–9 (*OC* vi/3. 87).

Antigone suffers impiety for having acted piously: 942–3 (*IPC* 99).

The Chorus' hymn to Dionysus: 1146–52 (*IPC* 88–9; *OC* vi/3. 226–7, 231, 236).

The last lines of the tragedy: 1350–3 (*OC* ii/2. 338).

THE *ILIAD* AND HOMER

AD 46, 70, 112, 239, 242, 244–5; *CO* 154; *CS* 14, 95–7, 99, 149, 197, 209, 210, 239, 244, 291–2, 297, 307, 323; *E* 124, 191, 199, 252; *EHP* 66, 372; *EL* 16, 31, 37, 231; *IPC* 54, 107, 171; *LP* 168, 238; *LR* 15; ML 351 *OC* i. 95, 101; ii/2. 70, 273, 274, 356; iii/3. 50 ff., 64, 199, 213, 222, 227 ff., 284; vi/1. 74, 83–4, 86, 79, 105, 118–19, 171, 222 n. 15, 236, 306, 316, 317, 319, 333, 353; vi/2. 88, 96–7, 296, 313, 319, 327, 355, 359, 360, 363, 396, 419, 462; vi/3. 90, 138, 144, 207, 255, 256, 284, 295; *Œ* 177, 648 ff., 656; *PSO* 51, 56–7; *SG* 78; *S* 137, 221, 272; *CSW* 10/2: 130; 15/1: 22.

References to specific lines:

Scene between Andromache and Hector (*Il.* 6): 410–13; 447–55; 456–8; 464–5 (*OC* ii/3. 247, 231, 237–8); 429–30 (*OC* vi/1. 74); 447–9 (*OC* vi/1: 68); 456–8 (*OC* ii/2. 274; ii/3. 231; vi/1. 83); 458 (*OC* ii/2. 70, 171, 356; vi/2. 87 n. 207); 441–65 (BN textes non-envoyés à Posternak).

Encounter between Achilles and his mother Thetis (*Il.* 18): 79–126 (*Œ* 648–9); 98–100, 114–16 (*OC* ii/3. 243); 94–5 (*OC* ii/3. 246); 98–100 (*OC* vi/1. 68); 112–13 (*OC* vi/1. 68, 283, 379, 317 n. 123).

The cries of Briseis over the body of Patroclus (*Il.* 19): 291–302 (*OC* ii/3. 232); 293 (*OC* ii/3. 246); 282–302 (BN textes non-envoyés à Posternak).

Lycaon begging for his life: (*Il.* 21): 35–53, 64–119 (*Œ* 649–50); 64–6, 71–2, 74–85, 97–8, 106–13, 114–19 (*OC* ii/3. 229, 244); 45–8 (*OC* ii/3. 248); 74 (*IPC* 107); 97–8 (*OC* vi/1. 84); 114–16 (*OC* vi/1. 84).

Appendix

Combat between Agamemnon and Hector (*Il.* 11): 159–62 (*OC* ii/3. 227).

Combat between Achilles and Hector; Hector's flight (*Il.* 22): 99–100, 104–7, 111–13, 122–5, 136–7, 159–61, 338 (*OC* ii/3. 239–40).

Andromache's sorrow over her husband's death (*Il.* 24): 730 (*OC* ii/3. 248); 731–4 (*OC* ii/3. 231; vi/1. 83); 725–8, 743–5 (*OC* ii/3. 247); 725–45 (BN textes non-envoyés à Posternak).

Priam's visit to Achilles (*Il.* 24): 477–516 (BN textes non-envoyés à Posternak); 477–9 (*OC* ii/3. 230); 477 (*OC* vi/1. 84); 480–4 (*OC* ii/3. 230); 506 (*OC* vi/2. 296); 507–12 (*OC* ii/3. 230; vi/1. 84); 510 (*OC* vi/2. 355); 525–33 (*OC* vi/2. 377, 393 n. 438 (l. 533)); 540–2 (*OC* ii/3. 240); 571 (*OC* ii/3. 231); 628–33 (*OC* ii/3. 247); 602–17 (BN textes non-envoyés à Posternak).

Agamemnon refuses to give Chryseis back to her father (*Il.* 1): 29–31 (*OC* ii/3. 231).

Achilles cries after Briseis has been taken away from him (*Il.* 1): 348–50 (*OC* ii/3. 234).

Agamemnon humiliates Achilles (*Il.* 1): 185–7 (*OC* ii/3. 234). (*Il.* 2): 176–8 (*OC* ii/3. 243).

Odysseus encourages the men (*Il.* 2): 198–202 (*OC* ii/3. 234).

The loneliness of Bellerophon (*Il.* 6): 200–3 (BN textes non-envoyés à Posternak).

Thersites (*Il.* 2): 266–70 (*OC* ii/3. 234).

Diomedes and Glaucus (*Il.* 6): 224, 246 (*OC* ii/3. 246).

Hector challenges the Achaeans (*Il.* 7): 92–3, 215–17 (*OC* ii/3. 235).

Zeus and his scales of gold (*Il* 8): 69–72 (*OC* ii/3. 235; vi 2. 88 n. 212).

Agamemnon to the Achaeans (*Il.* 8): 229–34 (*OC* ii/3. 241).

'Arès est équitable' (*Il.* 8): 309 (*OC* ii/3. 235; BN cours de Saint-Quentin, p. 5).

Hector wants to keep the Achaeans from leaving (*Il.* 8): 509–11, 513, 515–16 (*OC* ii/3. 238).

Achilles to Odysseus (*Il.* 9): 401–2, 406, 408 (*OC* ii/3. 240).

Attack of Agamemnon (*Il.* 11): 155–9 (*OC* ii/3. 245).

The Trojans are fleeing (*Il.* 11): 172–3, 177–8 (*OC* ii/3. 238).

The corpses are more dear to the vultures (*Il.* 11): 158–62 (BN textes non-envoyés à Posternak); 161–2 (*OC* vi/1. 83).

The tree-cutters (*Il.* 11): 84–90 (*OC* ii/3. 249; BN: textes non-envoyés à Posternak); 87–9 (*OC* vi/1. 70).

Agamemnon kills Iphidamas (*Il.* 11): 241–2 (*OC* ii/3. 248).

Ajax (*Il.* 11): 544–6 (*OC* ii/3. 235).

(*Il.* 14): 85–7 (*OC* ii/3. 241); 88–9 (*OC* ii/3. 243).
Attack on Hector (*Il.* 15): 630–2, 636–8 (*OC* ii/3. 245).
Death of Erymas (*Il.* 16): 348–50 (*OC* ii/3. 249).
About Patroclus (*Il.* 17): 671 (*OC* ii/3. 244).
Hector does not heed Polydamas' counsel (*Il.* 18): 293–6, 310 (*OC* ii/3. 239).
Achilles to his horse Xanthos (*Il.* 19): 421–3 (*OC* ii/3. 243).
Hector flees (*Il.* 22): 153–7 (*OC* ii/3. 249).
Hector's death (*Il.* 22): 362–3 (*OC* ii/3. 228).
Hector's body dragged behind the chariot (*Il.* 22): 401–4 (*OC* ii/3. 228; BN textes non-envoyés à Posternak); 402–4 (*OC* vi/1. 83).
Hector killed 'loin des bains chauds' which Andromache is preparing for him (*Il.* 22): 442–6 (*OC* ii/3. 228; BN textes non-envoyés à Posternak); 445–6 (*OC* vi/1. 83).
Achilles cries over Patroclus (*Il.* 24): 3–5 (*OC* ii/3. 247).
'Les deux tonneaux de Zeus' (*Il.* 24): 525–33 (*OC* vi/2. 377); 527–8 (*OC* ii/3. 233); 531–3 (*OC* ii/3. 233); 531–42 (BN textes non-envoyés à Posternak); 527–34 (*SG* 78).
Niobe (*Il.* 24): 602–13 (*OC* ii/3. 233; Œ 663); 602 (*OC* vi/3. 256); 613 (*OC* vi/3. 110).
(*Il.* 11): 89 (*OC* vi/2. 63 n. 30).
Diomedes asks for a continuation of war (*Il.* 7): 400–2 (*OC* ii/3. 237).
Reference to Ethiopia (*Il.* 1): 423–4; (*Il.* 23): 205–7 (*OC* vi/3. 295).
Other killing scenes (*Il.* 27): 51 (*OC* ii/3. 248).

PROMETHEUS

AD 170, 230, 236, 238; *CS* 14, 15, 17, 18, 19, 55, 56, 57, 133, 135, 152, 168, 178, 184, 187, 210, 218, 219, 247, 290, 298, 312, 316; *E* 251; *EL* 48, 107; *IPC* 12, 18, 20, 34, 37, 41, 49, 51, 55–6, 62, 67, 69–70, 79, 85, 93–106, 110; *LR* 23, 24, 29, 32, 95; *OC* vi/1. 86; vi/2. 212, 299, 305, 320, 322, 335, 361, 385, 389, 445, 455, 481, 487, 545–6; vi/3. 40, 49, 57, 58, 98–9, 112, 125, 126, 138, 157, 168, 186, 219–23, 224–6, 227, 231, 233, 234, 235, 239, 249, 251, 252, 253, 275, 279, 284, 285, 292, 294, 295, 304, 339, 342, 382, 384, 386, 387, 388, 426, 436; *PSO* 58, 60; *SG* 43–6, 110, 111, 127, 134, 135, 139, 142, 162; *S* 234; *CSW* 10/1: 4; 19/2: 140.

References to specific lines:
Prometheus is tied to the rock by Power, Force, and Hephaestus: 11 (*OC* vi/3. 219); 14 (*IPC* 105); 18–28 (*OC* vi/1. 369); 19 (*IPC* 105);

220 *Appendix*

21–2 (*OC* vi/3. 99); 22–3 (*IPC* 69); 28–30 (*OC* vi/3. 339); 31–4 (*OC* vi/1. 369).

Prometheus' first speech: 88–108 (*OC* vi/1. 263, 370, 372; vi/2. 154–5; *Œ* 664–5); 88–92 (*IPC* 37; *OC* vi/2. 69); 88–97 (*Œ* 688); 89–112 (*IPC* 94–5); 94–5 (*OC* vi/1. 379); 103–4 (*IPC* 67; *OC* vi/3. 219); 106–10 (*IPC* 67); 108 (*IPC* 70); 110–11 (*OC* vi/3. 219); 112–13 (*Œ* 665); 112 (*IPC* 69); 118–26 (*IPC* 95); 119–26 (*Œ* 665); 123 (*OC* vi/3. 219).

Prometheus talks to the daughters of Ocean: 136–43 (*OC* vi/1. 369); 141–3 (*IPC* 95; *Œ*: 665); 143 (*OC* vi/3. 225); 152–8 (*OC* vi/1. 369; *Œ*: 666); 152–9 (*IPC* 95); 158 (*IPC* 69, 101); 188–92 (*OC* vi/3. 225); 194 (*IPC* 56, 100); 195 (*IPC* 100, 105); 190–5 (*IPC* 95–6); 208–10 (*IPC* 96); 218 (*OC* vi/3. 219); 220 (*IPC* 55); 218–20 (*IPC* 96); 231–41 (*OC* vi/3. 220); 233–43 (*IPC* 96); 239–40 (*OC* vi/1. 370); 243 (*IPC* 100–1); 248–50 (*OC* vi/3. 220); 248 (*IPC* 96); 250–2 (*IPC* 96); 252 (*OC* vi/3. 220); 254 (*OC* vi/3. 220); 265–70 (*OC* vi/3. 220–1); 267–72 (*IPC* 96–7); 268 (*IPC* 55, 100, 105; *OC* vi/3. 239); 271 (*IPC* 101).

Prometheus and Ocean: 304 (*OC* vi/3. 221); 306–8 (*IPC* 97); 347–8 (*OC* vi/3. 221); 350 (*OC* vi/3. 221); 386–8 (*IPC* 97); 387 (*EL* 48); 391 (*OC* vi/3. 221); 393 (*IPC* 97, 104).

Prometheus talks to the daughters of Ocean: 437–40 (*IPC* 97); 439–40 (*OC* vi/3. 221; *IPC* 101); 442–51 (*IPC* 97); 447–50 (*OC* vi/3. 222); 459 (*IPC* 100); 469–75 (*IPC* 97); 469–71 (*OC* vi/3. 222); 506 (*IPC* 62); 505–10 (*IPC* 98); 508–10 (*OC* vi/3. 222); 514 (*OC* vi/1. 370); 542–4 (*IPC* 98); 542–3 (*OC* vi/3. 498); 545–6 (*OC* vi/3. 222); 546–50 (*OC* vi/1. 370).

Prometheus and Io: 612–17 (*IPC* 98); 755–7 (*IPC* 98); 760–2 (*IPC* 98); 761–2 (*OC* vi/3. 226); 764 (*IPC* 98); 768–70 (*IPC* 98).

Prometheus and Hermes: 944 (*OC* vi/3. 222); 946 (*OC* vi/3. 219); 980–1 (*OC* vi/1. 379); 989–91 (*OC* vi/3. 222); 1078 (*OC* vi/1. 379).

Prometheus' final lines: 1080–1 (*OC* vi/1. 369, 379; BN, sent to Thibon); 1080–93 (*IPC* 99; *Œ* 666); 1089–93 (*OC* vi/1. 369, 370, 371; BN, sent to Thibon); 1091–3 (*OC* vi/1. 379); 1091 (*OC* vi/3. 99).

ELECTRA

AD 64, 212; *CS* 36, 188, 262, 291; *E* 67; *IPC* 15–18, 20, 69; *OC* ii/2. 274, 339 ff.; vi/1. 101 102, 120, 121, 222, 334; vi/2. 137–8, 256;

vi/3. 67, 86–7, 222, 275, 277, 298–9, 406; *PSO* 43, 58; *SG* 47–55; *CSW* 8/4: 319, 321.
References to specific lines:
From Electra's first speech: 118–20 (*OC* ii/2. 342; *SG* 47).
Electra's complaints: 151–2 (*OC* vi/2. 256); 164–72 (*OC* ii/2. 342; *SG* 47); 171 (*OC* vi/1. 235); 185–92 (*OC* ii/2. 342; *SG* 47); 263–5 (*OC* ii/2. 342; *SG* 47); 307–9 (*OC* ii/2. 342; *SG* 47).
Electra and Chrysothemis: 359–64 (*OC* ii/2. 343; *SG* 48); 387 (*OC* ii/2. 343; *SG* 48); 391 (*OC* ii/2. 343; *SG* 48); 392–6 (*SG* 48); 394–5 (*OC* ii/2. 343).
Electra and Clytemnestra: 795–6 (*OC* ii/2. 344).
The effects of the news of Orestes' death on Electra: 808 (*OC* ii/2. 344; *SG* 48); 812–15 (*OC* ii/2. 344; *SG* 48); 817–19 (*OC* ii/2. 344; *SG* 48).
Electra holds the urn: 1126–73 (*SG* 49–50); 1126–30 (*OC* ii/2. 345; vi/2. 191); 1132–7 (*OC* vi/1. 276); 1136–45 (*OC* vi/2. 191); 1142 (*OC* vi/2. 347); 1143–5 (*OC* vi/1. 276, 400; vi/2. 138, 248); 1149–51 (*OC* ii/2. 346; vi/1. 276; vi/2. 192); 1158–9 (*OC* ii/2. 346); 1164–5 (*OC* ii/2. 346); 1165–72 (*OC* vi/1. 276; vi/2. 192); 1170 (*OC* ii/2. 346; vi/1. 400); 1171–2 (*OC* ii/2. 346).
Electra and Orestes—the recognition scene: 1173–229 (*SG* 50–4); 1179–81 (*OC* ii/2. 346); 1195–6 (*OC* ii/2. 347); 1199–200 (*OC* ii/2. 347); 1217–19 (*OC* ii/2. 347); 1218–29 (*IPC* 15–16; *Œ* 660; *SG* 53–4); 1220–3 (*OC* ii/2. 347); 1224–6 (*OC* ii/2. 347; vi/1. 67, 101, 120, 283, 379; vi/3. 87, 277); 1228–9 (*IPC* 17).

OTHER TRAGEDIES BY AESCHYLUS, SOPHOCLES AND EURIPIDES

References to Aeschylus' Plays:
Agamemnon: *IPC* 20–1, 103; *E* 191; *OC* ii/3. 211; vi/1. 67, 119, 219, 257, 259–60, 262, 275–6, 289, 367–8, 379; vi/2. 60, 64–5, 152–4, 389; vi/3. 67–9, 112, 114, 119, 120, 121, 125, 163, 181, 183, 231, 249, 269, 275, 276, 299; *Œ* 663–4, 667; *PSO* 58; *SG* 43 ff.; *BN* 'textes adressés au P. Perrin'.
Choephoroe: *OC* vi/1. 119, 258, 302; vi/2. 291 n. 41.
Eumenides: *OC* vi/1. 258–9; vi/3. 227.
Persians: *OC* vi/3. 348 n. 73.
Seven against Thebes: *IPC* 20 (an indirect reference); *OC* vi/1. 256, 335.

Suppliants: *IPC* 31, 54, 106–8; *OC* vi/1. 262, 288; vi/2. 59, 146, 283, 414; vi/3. 40, 223–5, 356, 386, 427; *PSO* 50.
Fragment 44 Nauck *The Danaids*: *OC* vi/1. 123, 252, 260.

References to Sophocles' Plays:
Ajax OC ii/1: 260–1; ii/2. 274; vi/1. 69, 120–1; *OL* 11.
Oedipus Rex: *OC* ii/2. 274; vi/1. 101, perhaps also 120–1; *OC* vi/2. 347.
Oedipus Coloneus: *OC* vi/1. 101.
Philoctetes: *E* 67; *OC* ii/2. 274, 557; vi/1. 67, 96, 101, 102–4, 120, 261, 283, 379; vi/2. 138; vi/3. 253.
Trachinae: *OC* vi/1. 101.

References to Euripides' Plays:
Alcestis: *LP* 273–4.
Bacchae: *OC* vi/2. 343–5, 347.
Hecuba: *OC* vi/2. 323.
Helen: simple allusion in *OC* ii/3. 55, 311 n. 10.
Hippolytus: *CS* 168; *IPC* 34, 60, 89; *OC* ii/2. 274; vi/2. 320, 322, 328, 384, 385, 389, 404, 445, 455; vi/3. 40, 57, 63, 87, 114, 235, 275, 279, 287; *PSO* 58; *SG* 79, 82.
Ion: *OC* vi/3. 304.
Medea: *OC* vi/1. 69.
Oreste: *OC* vi/3. 402.

Bibliography

ADKINS, A. W. H. (1960). *Merit and Responsibility: A Study in Greek Values* (Oxford: Clarendon).
AESCHYLUS (1996). *Prometheus Bound*, trans. Herbert Weir Smyth, Loeb 145 (1922; repr. Cambridge, Mass.: Harvard University Press).
ALAIN (1956–70). *Propos*, La Pléiade, 2 vols. ([Paris]: Gallimard).
ALLEN, D. (1984*a*). 'Simone Weil on Suffering and Reading', *Communio*, 11: 297–304.
—— (1984*b*). 'The Witness of Nature to God's Goodness and Existence', *Faith and Philosophy*, 1/1: 27–43.
—— (1985). 'George Herbert and Simone Weil', *Religion and Literature*, 17/2: 17–34.
—— (1990). 'Natural Evil and the Love of God', in McCord Adams and Adams (1990: 189–208).
—— (1993). 'The Concept of Reading and the "Book of Nature"', in Bell (1993*a*: 93–115).
—— (1994). 'Manifestations of the Supernatural according to Simone Weil', *CSW* 17/3: 290–307.
—— and SPRINGSTED, E. O. (1994). *Spirit, Nature, and Community: Issues in the Thought of Simone Weil* (Albany: State University of New York Press).
ALLEN, D. C. (1970). *Mysteriously Meant: The Rediscovery of Pagan Symbolism and Allegorical Interpretation in the Renaissance* (Baltimore: Johns Hopkins University Press).
ANDIC, M. (1992). 'Fairy Tales', *CSW* 15/1: 61–91.
—— (1993). 'Discernment and the Imagination', in Bell (1993*a*: 116–49).
—— (1994). 'Supernatural Justice and the Madness of Love', *CSW* 17/4: 373–405.
—— (1996). 'Simone Weil and Shakespeare's Fools', in Dunaway and Springsted (1996: 197–215).
ARP, R. (2000). 'Suffering as Theodicy', *CSW* 23/4: 413–33.
BELL, R. H. (1993*a*) (ed.). *Simone Weil's Philosophy of Culture: Readings toward a Divine Humanity* (Cambridge: Cambridge University Press).
—— (1993*b*). 'Reading Simone Weil on Rights, Justice, and Love', in Bell (1993*a*: 214–34).
—— (1998). *Simone Weil: The Way of Justice as Compassion* (Lanham, Md.: Rowman & Littlefield).
BERNADETTE, S. (1983). 'Foi et connaissance de Dieu dans l'argument ontologique de Simone Weil (I. partie)', *CSW* 6/4: 346–55.
—— (1984). 'Foi et connaissance de Dieu dans l'argument ontologique de Simone Weil (II. partie)', *CSW* 7/1: 68–79.

BESPALOFF, R. (1943) *De l' Iliade* (New York: Brentano's).
—— (1970). *On the Iliad*, trans. Mary McCarthy (Princeton: Princeton University Press).
BIROU, A. (1983). 'Simone Weil et le catharisme', *CSW* 6/4: 340–5.
—— (1985). 'L'Articulation entre le surnaturel et le social chez Simone Weil', *CSW* 8/1: 50–66.
—— (1988). 'Simone Weil, mystique dans sa vie et dans son œuvre', I-III, *CSW* 11/1: 45–56; *CSW* 11/2: 145–54; *CSW* 11/3: 215–26.
—— (1991). '*Venise sauvée* de Simone Weil et la tragédie grecque' suivi de: 'La Conjuration de Venise a-t-elle existé?', *CSW* 14/2: 119–34.
—— (1992). 'Le Christ, médiateur et rédempteur selon Simone Weil', *CSW* 15/4: 333–51.
—— (1995). 'Enracinement, obligation, surnaturel et *metaxu*', *CSW* 18/1: 59–78.
—— (1996). 'Introduction à la problématique du mal chez Simone Weil', *CSW* 19/2: 155–75.
BLONDEL, M. (1956). '*Les Premiers écrits de Maurice Blondel: Lettre sur les exigences de la pensée contemporaine en matière d'apologétique' avec 'Histoire et Dogme*' (Paris: PUF).
—— (1995). *Œuvres complètes*, 2 vols. (Paris: Presses universitaires de Paris).
BLUM, L. A., and SEIDLER, V. J. (1989). *A Truer Liberty: Simone Weil and Marxism* (New York: Routledge).
BLUM-DAVID, M.-L. (1979). 'Témoignages sur Simone Weil', *CSW* 2/4: 181–2.
—— and RABI, W. (1981). 'Entretien sur Simone Weil, la résistance et la question juive', *CSW* 4/2: 76–84.
BOITIER, D. (1991). 'L'Impossible enracinement de Simone Weil: Simone Weil entre "judaïsme" et "catholicisme"', *CSW* 14/4: 329–40.
—— (1994*a*). 'Le Beau, "présence réelle de Dieu dans la matière"', *CSW* 17/1: 35–54.
—— (1994*b*). 'L'Impossible conversion', *CSW* 17/4: 363–72.
BONNARDOT, J. (1979). 'Rencontre de Simone Weil et de Marie Noël', *CSW* 2/3: 139–60.
BOULANGER, A. (1925). *Orphée: rapports de l'orphisme et du christianisme* (Paris: Rieder).
BOWRA, C. M. (1930). *Tradition and Design in the Iliad* (Oxford: Clarendon).
—— (1944). *Sophoclean Tragedy* (Oxford: Clarendon).
BRENNER, R. FELDHAY (1997). *Writing as Resistance: Four Women Confronting the Holocaust: Edith Stein, Simone Weil, Anne Frank, Etty Hillesum* (University Park: Pennsylvania University Press).
BROC-LAPEYRE, M. (1978*a*). 'Simone Weil et l'histoire', in Kahn (1978*a*: 167–91).
—— (1978*b*). 'Les Hébreux', in Kahn (1978*a*: 123–34).

—— (1980). 'Simone Weil et son refus de Nietzsche', *CSW* 3/1: 19–32.
—— (1985). 'Simone Weil et Platon: amour et beauté', *CSW* 8/2: 128–38.
—— (1987). 'Le Souci du mot juste', *CSW* 10/4: 358–67.
—— (1989). 'Simone Weil et Bergson', *CSW* 12/1: 18–28.
—— (1999). 'Simone Weil ou la mystique nihiliste', *CSW* 22/3: 263–75.
—— (2002). 'Une toute autre idée de Dieu', *CSW* 25/4: 305–17.
BRUECK, K. T. (1985). 'Simone Weil et Dostoïevsky: une lecture de *Crime et Châtiment* à la lumière du dualisme weilien', *CSW* 8/3: 273–80.
—— (1989). 'The Mysticism of Simone Weil and François Mauriac's *Viper's Tangle*: Affliction, Gravity, and Grace', *Mystics Quarterly*, 15/4: 166–76.
—— (1995). *The Redemption of Tragedy: The Literary Vision of Simone Weil* (Albany: State University of New York Press).
—— (1996). 'The Tragic Poetics of Simone Weil', in Dunaway and Springsted (1996: 109–21).
BRUNEL, P. (1971). *Le Mythe d'Électre* (Paris: Colin).
BUCHER, J. (1978). 'L'Humilité de Simone Weil et l'orgueil de Frédéric Nietzsche', *CSW* 1/1: 22–9.
BULTMANN, R. (1967). 'Polis und Hades in der Antigone des Sophokles', in Hans Diller (ed.), *Sophokles* (Darmstadt: Wissenschaftliche Buchgesellschaft), 311–24.
BUSH, W. (1985). 'Simone Weil et Georges Bernanos: amour de Dieu et souffrance de l'homme', *CSW* 8/3: 281–92.
CABAUD, J. (1957). *L'Expérience vécue de Simone Weil* (Paris: Plon).
—— (1964). *Simone Weil: A Fellowship in Love* (New York: Channel).
—— (1967). *Simone Weil à New York et à Londres* ([Paris]: Plon).
—— (1985). 'Albert Camus et Simone Weil', *CSW* 8/3: 293–303.
—— (1993). 'Simone Weil à Londres', *CSW* 16/4: 275–311.
CABAUD, M. (2000). 'Mystique et herméneutique: Simone Weil et sa lecture christologique d'*Electre* et du *Prométhée enchaîné*', *CSW* 23/1: 51–77.
—— (2001*a*). 'Literature and Apologetics: Simone Weil's Christological Interpretations of Ancient Greek Texts', D.Phil. thesis (Oxford).
—— (2001*b*). 'Why Antigone Was Right After All: Simone Weil's Mystical Hermeneutics', in Emily Butterworth and Kathryn Robson (eds.), *Shifting Borders: Theory and Identity in French Literature* (Oxford: Peter Lang), 123–38.
CABAUD MEANEY, M. (2003*a*). 'The Vocation of the Cross: Simone Weil's Theodicy', *Saint Austin Review*, 8–11.
—— (2003*b*). 'Simone Weil's Critique of the Zeitgeist', *Faith and Reason*, 28: 319–42.
Cahiers Simone Weil (Paris).   1/3 'Lettre de Simone Weil à Déodat Roché' (1978), 3–5.
—— 2/4 'Lettre à Alain' (1979), 177–8.
—— 3/2 'Un échange de lettres entre Simone Weil et Jacques Maritain' (1980), 68–74.

Cahiers Simone Weil (Paris). 3/3 'Deux lettres sur le travail et les machines' (1980), 162–6.
—— 4/2 'Simone Weil, Gustave Thibon: correspondance' (1981), 65–74.
—— 4/3 'Simone Weil, Gustave Thibon: correspondance, suite' (1981), 129–38.
—— 4/4 'Simone Weil, Gustave Thibon: correspondance, suite' (1981), 193–200.
—— 6/4 'Un épisode de la guerre d'Espagne vu par Simone Weil' (1983), 293–6.
—— 7/3 'Lettres à Antonio' (1984), 201–17.
—— 7/4 'Une lettre inédite de Simone Weil à Emmanuel Mounier' (1984), 313–19.
—— 8/3 'Essai sur la notion de lecture' (1985), 215–20.
—— 8/4 'Lettre à Jean Giraudoux à propos d'Electre' (1985), 319–21.
—— 9/2 'Remarques sur un article de Louis Aragon' (1986), 121–2.
—— 9/3 'Une chronique philosophique à Marseille en 1941' (1986), 229–35.
—— 10/1 'Lettre à Jean Wahl' (1987), 1–5.
—— 10/2 'Lettres à Jean Posternak' (1987), 101–36.
—— 11/1 'Deux lettres à René et Véra Daumal' (1988), 1–4.
—— 14/3 'Quatres lettres à Huguette Baur' (1991), 195–205.
—— 15/1 'Lettres à Boris Souvarine' (1992), 1–22.
—— 15/2 'Lettres à Boris Souvarine' (1992), 117–29.
—— 17/1 'Deux lettres à Huguette Baur' (1994), 1–6.
—— 18/2 'Lettre au *Cri du Peuple*' (1995), 105–8.
—— 19/2 'Deux lettres inédites à Joë Bousquet' (1996), 137–54.
—— 21/1–2 'Lettre à Robert Guihéneuf' (1998), 1–20.
—— 22/1 'Textes inédits de New York' (1999), 3–58.
—— 25/2 ['Lettres à Déodat Roché'] (2002), 139–46.
CAHILL, P. J. (1967). 'Apologetics', in Catholic University of Washington (ed.), *New Catholic Encyclopedia* (New York: McGraw-Hill), 669–74.
CANCIANI, D. (1996). *Simone Weil: il coraggio di pensare: impegno e riflessione politica tra le due guerre* (Roma: Lavoro).
—— (2000). *L'Intelligence et l'amour: réflexion religieuse et expérience mystique chez Simone Weil*, trans. Domenico Canciani, F. Chiappone, and S. Mazurelle (Paris: Beauchesne).
Catechism of the Catholic Church (London: Geoffrey Chapman, 1994).
CHADWICK, H. (1966). *Early Christian Thought and the Classical Tradition: Studies in Justin, Clement, and Origen* (Oxford: Clarendon).
CHAROT, G. (1991). 'Simone Weil: la croix et le péché d'envie', *CSW* 14/2: 97–106.
—— (1995). 'Le Mal: brisure originelle entre l'amour et la puissance dans l'acte créateur', *CSW* 18/3: 257–83.
CHENAVIER, R. (1991). 'Simone Weil, "la haine juive, de soi"?', *CSW* 14/4: 291–328.

CHESTERTON, G. K. (1993). *The Everlasting Man* (1925; 2nd repr. San Francisco: Ignatius).
CHISHOLM, R. M. (1990). 'The Defeat of Good and Evil', in McCord Adams and Adams (1990: 53–68).
CLEMENT (1867, 1869). *The Writings of Clement of Alexandria*, trans. William Wilson, Ante-Nicene Christian Library 12, 2 vols. (Edinburgh: T&T Clark).
—— (1981). *Les Stromates: Stromate V*, ed. Alain Le Boulluec, trans. Pierre Voulet, Sources Chrétiennes 278, 2 vols. (Paris: Cerf), ii.
—— (1991). *Stromateis 1–3*, trans. John Ferguson, The Fathers of the Church 85 (Washington: Catholic University of America Press).
—— (1999). *Les Stromates: Stromate VI*, ed. and trans. Patrick Descourtieux, Sources Chrétiennes 446 (Paris: Cerf).
COCKBURN, D. (1992). 'The Supernatural', *Religious Studies* 28: 285–301.
COLIN, M.-E. (1984). 'Simone Weil et l'Egypte', *CSW* 7/1: 56–67.
COMTE-SPONVILLE, A. (1991). 'Le Dieu et l'idole (Alain et Simone Weil face à Spinoza)', *CSW* 14/3: 213–33.
CONACHER, D. J. (1980). *Aeschylus' Prometheus Bound: A Literary Commentary* (Toronto: Toronto University Press).
COURTINE-DENAMY, S. (2000). *Three Women in Dark Times: Edith Stein, Hannah Arendt, Simone Weil; or, Amor Fati, Amor Mundi*, trans. G. M. Goshgarian (Ithaca: Cornell University Press).
—— (2001). 'Hannah Arendt, Simone Weil: Athènes, Rome, Jérusalem', in Michel Narcy and Étienne Tassin (eds.). *Les Catégories de l'universel: Simone Weil et Hannah Arendt* (Paris: L'Harmattan), 137–63.
CROC, P. (1995). 'François Mauriac et Simone Weil', *CSW* 18/2: 155–67.
CUGNO, A. (1988). 'Jean de la Croix et Simone Weil', *CSW* 11/4: 299–319.
CULLEN, H. E. (1999). 'Simone Weil on Greece's Desire for the Ultimate Bridge to God: The Passion', *Faith and Philosophy*, 16/3: 352–67.
DALY, G. (1980). *Transcendence and Immanence: A Study in Catholic Modernism and Integralism* (Oxford: Clarendon).
DANIÉLOU, J. (1964). 'Hellénisme, judaïsme, christianisme', in Perrin (1964: 19–39).
DARGAN, J. (1987). 'Les Conditions de la création poétique', *CSW* 10/4: 383–94.
—— (1996). 'Trésor éparpillé: The Treasure of Scattered Texts in Works by René Char and Simone Weil', in Dunaway and Springsted (1996: 69–82).
—— (1997). 'Weil and Tsvetaeva on Poetics', *CSW* 20/3: 206–13.
—— (1999). *Simone Weil: Thinking Poetically* (Albany: State University of New York Press).
DARVY, C. (1991). 'Simone Weil et le théâtre', *CSW* 14/2: 135–41.
DAVY, M.-M. (1951). *The Mysticism of Simone Weil*, trans. Cynthia Rowland (London: Rockliff).
—— ([1956]). *Simone Weil* (Paris: Éditions Universitaires).

DAVY, M.-M. (1966). *Simone Weil: sa vie, son œuvre avec un exposé de sa philosophie* (Paris: PUF).
—— (1977). *Encyclopédie des mystiques*, 4 vols. (Paris: Seghers).
DESGRÂCES, A. (1991). 'Simone Weil, la structure de l'expérience spirituelle', *CSW* 14/4: 341–62.
DEVAUX, A. A. (1982). 'Simone Weil entre la Grèce et l'Inde', *CSW* 5/2: 92–4.
—— (1985). 'Passion de la vérité et expérience mystique chez Simone Weil', *CSW* 8/1: 67–84.
—— (1988). 'Simone Weil, l'esprit de vérité et l'écriture', *Revue des deux mondes* (February): 122–31.
—— (1990). 'Simone Weil et Blaise Pascal', in Little and Ughetto (1990: 75–99).
—— (1993*a*). 'Du bon usage de la mort selon Simone Weil', *CSW* 16/4: 259–73.
—— (1993*b*). 'On the Right Use of Contradiction according to Simone Weil', in Bell (1993*a*: 150–7).
—— (1995). 'Présence de Descartes dans la vie et dans l'œuvre de Simone Weil', *CSW* 18/1: 1–24.
—— (1999). 'De Marseille à Ashford, le singulier compagnonnage de Simone Weil et Simone Deitz', *CSW* 22/3: 315–20.
Dictionnaire de Théologie Catholique (Paris: Vacant-Mangenot, 1923).
DODDS, E. R. (1966). *The Greeks and the Irrational* (2nd edn., Berkeley: California University Press).
—— (1985). *The Ancient Concept of Progress and other Essays on Greek Literature and Belief* (1973, repr. Oxford: Clarendon).
DOERING, E. J., and SPRINGSTED, E. O. (2004) (eds.). *The Christian Platonism of Simone Weil* (Notre Dame, Ind.: Notre Dame University Press).
DORIVAL, G. (1998). 'L'Apologétique chrétienne et la culture grecque', *Les Apologistes chrétiens et la culture grecque*, ed. Bernard Pouderon and Joseph Doré, Théologie historique 105 (Paris: Beauchesne), 423–65.
DROGE, A. J. (1989). *Homer or Moses: Early Christian Interpretations of the History of Culture*, Hermeneutische Untersuchungen zur Theologie 26 (Tübingen: Mohr).
DROZ, C. (1994). 'Simone Weil et l'imagination', *CSW* 17/2: 125–44.
—— (1999). 'Mystique et exigence de raison chez Simone Weil', *CSW* 22/3: 277–97.
DRU, A. (1995). 'Introduction', in Maurice Blondel, *'The Letter on Apologetics' and 'History and Dogma'*, trans. Illtyd Trethowan (Edinburgh: T&T Clark), 13–116.
DUCHEMIN, J. (1974). *Prométhée: histoire du mythe, de ses origines orientales à ses incarnations modernes* (Paris: Les Belles Lettres).
DULLES, A. (1971). *A History of Apologetics* (London: Hutchinson).
DUNAWAY, J. M. (1984). *Simone Weil* (Boston: Twayne).

—— (1985). 'Estrangement and the Need for Roots: Prophetic Visions of the Human Condition in Albert Camus and Simone Weil', *Religion and Literature*, 17/2: 35–42.
—— (1996). 'Simone Weil on Morality and Literature', in Dunaway and Springsted (1996: 99–107).
—— and SPRINGSTED, E. O. (1996) (eds.). *The Beauty that Saves: Essays on Aesthetics and Language in Simone Weil* (Macon, Ga.: Mercer University Press).
DUSO-BAUDUIN, G. (2000). 'Les Notions de "métaphysique" chez Gabriel Marcel et de "surnaturel" chez Simone Weil', *CSW* 23/3: 249–81.
EASTERLING, P. E. (1997). 'A Show for Dionysus', in P. E. Easterling (ed.), *The Cambridge Companion to Greek Tragedy* (Cambridge: Cambridge University Press), 36–53.
EDELMAN, J. T. (1998). 'Suffering and the Will of God', *Faith and Philosophy*, 10: 380–8.
EDWARDS, M. (1999). *Apologetics in the Roman Empire: Pagans, Jews and Christians* (Oxford: Oxford University Press).
EDWARDS, M. W. (1987). *Homer: Poet of the Iliad* (Baltimore: Johns Hopkins University Press).
EDWARDS, T. R. (1971). 'Epic and the Modern Reader: A Note on Simone Weil', in *Imagination and Power: A Study of Poetry on Public Themes* (London: Chatto & Windus), 10–16.
ELIOT, T. S. (1972). 'Second Thoughts on Humanism', in *Selected Essays* (3rd enlarged edn., London: Faber), 481–91.
EMMANUELLE, J.-M. (1964). 'Simone Weil et mon baptême', in Perrin (1964: 153–71).
EPTING, K. (1978). 'Le Beau', in Kahn (1978*a*: 245–56).
ESCHYLE (1931–5). Ed. Paul Mazon, 2 vols. (Paris: Les Belles Lettres).
EUSEBIUS (1989). *The History of the Church*, ed. Andrew Louth, trans. G. A. Williamson (2nd edn., London: Penguin).
EVANS, C. A. (1996). 'The Power of Parabolic Reversal: The Example in Simone Weil's Notebooks', *CSW* 19/3: 313–24.
FERBER, M. K. (1981). 'Simone Weil's *Iliad*', in George Abbott White (ed.), *Simone Weil: Interpretations of a Life* (Amherst: Massachusetts University Press), 63–85.
FESTUGIÈRE, A. J. (1932). *L'Idéal religieux des grecs et l'évangile* (Paris: Gabalda).
—— (1936). *Contemplation et vie contemplative selon Platon* (Paris: Vrin).
—— (1942). 'L'Héritage moral de l'Antiquité', *Renaître*, 11: 18–36.
—— (1969). *De l'essence de la tragédie grecque* (Paris: Aubier-Montaigne).
FIDDES, P. S. (1988). *The Creative Suffering of God* (Oxford: Clarendon).
FINCH, H.-L. (1983). 'L'Universalisme de Simone Weil', *CSW* 6/3: 275–83.
FIORI, G. (1987). *Simone Weil: une femme absolue* (Paris: Félin).

FIORI, G. (1989). *Simone Weil: An Intellectual Biography* (Athens: Georgia University Press).
FLEURÉ, E. (1978). 'Albert Camus devant Simone Weil', *CSW* 1/2: 10–17.
FORNI ROSA, G. (2000). 'Ontologie et christologie chez Simone Weil', *CSW* 23/3: 333–48.
FRAISSE, S. (1974). *Le Mythe d'Antigone* (Paris: Colin).
—— (1978). 'Simone Weil et le monde antique', in Kahn (1978*a*: 193–201).
—— (1980). 'Simone Weil contre les Romains', *CSW* 3/1: 5–18.
—— (1982*a*). 'Simone Weil et la tragédie grecque', *CSW* 5/3: 192–207.
—— (1982*b*). 'La Représentation de Simone Weil dans *Le Bleu du ciel* de Georges Bataille', *CSW* 5/2: 81–91.
—— (1989). 'Simone Weil et Péguy', *CSW* 12/1: 1–17.
FRÉMONT, A. (1987). 'Analyse et commentaire d'un conte selon l'esprit de Simone Weil', *CSW* 10/2: 171–80.
—— (1988). 'Correspondance entre le poème *La Porte* de Simone Weil et le récit *La Grotte* d'Ali Ahmed Jan (Nager, Pakistan)', *CSW* 11/2: 136–44.
FREUND, R. A. (1987). 'La Tradition mystique juive et Simone Weil', *CSW* 10/3: 289–95.
—— (1991). 'Simone Weil: le chaînon manquant dans la pensée et l'identité juives modernes', *CSW* 14/4: 363–72.
FRYE, N. (1957). *Anatomy of Criticism: Four Essays* (Princeton: Princeton University Press).
GABELLIERI, E. (1994). 'Une Convergence inattendue: Maurice Blondel et Simone Weil', *Bulletin de l'Institut Catholique de Lyon*, 107: 33–51.
—— (1996). 'La Nuit du don: origine et décréation du mal chez Simone Weil', *CSW* 19/1: 19–65.
—— (1998). 'Blondel, S. Weil et le panchristisme: vers une *métaxologie*', in Marie-Jeanne Coutagne (ed.), *Maurice Blondel et la quête du sens* (Paris: Beauchesne), 53–65.
—— (2003*a*). 'Simone Weil entre le paganisme et la Bible: un dialogue herméneutique avec Ricœur, Lévinas, Schelling et Pascal', *CSW* 26/1: 27–49.
—— (2003*b*). *Être et don: Simone Weil et la philosophie*, Bibliothèque philosophique de Louvain 57 (Louvain: Peeters).
GAILLARDOT, J. (1982). 'L'*Iliade* poème de la force?', *CSW* 5/3: 184–91.
GANDILLAC, M. DE (1941). *La Philosophie de Nicolas de Cues* ([Paris]: Aubier/Montaigne).
GAUTHIER, P. (1980). 'Simone Weil et la Grèce antique', *Commentaire*, 3/10: 243–50.
GEISLER, N. L. (1999). *Baker Encyclopedia of Christian Apologetics* (Grand Rapids: Baker Books).
GENCE, A. (1994). 'Dieu n'est pas abstrait, en témoigne la beauté', *CSW* 17/1: 23–33.

GILLI, C.-A. (2000). 'Simone Weil—Paul Claudel: une confrontation impossible, une confrontation sur l'impossible', *CSW* 23/4: 369–90.
GINIEWSKI, P. (1978). *Simone Weil ou la haine de soi* (Paris: Berg International).
GIRARD, R. (1982). *Le Bouc émissaire* (Paris: Grasset).
—— (1999). *Je vois Satan tomber comme l'éclair* (Paris: Grasset).
GOLDHILL, S. (1997). 'Modern Critical Approaches to Greek Tragedy', in P. E. Easterling (ed.), *The Cambridge Companion to Greek Tragedy* (Cambridge: Cambridge University Press), 324–47.
GOLDSCHLÄGER, A. (1982). *Simone Weil et Spinoza: essai d'interprétation* (Sherbrooke: Naaman).
GRENIER, J. (1997). *Sous l'occupation*, ed. Claire Paulhan (Paris: Claire Paulhan).
GRIFFIN, J. (1983). *Homer on Life and Death* (Oxford: Clarendon).
—— (1986). 'Homeric Words and Speakers', *Journal of Hellenic Studies*, 106: 36–57.
GRIFFITH, M. (1983) (ed.). *Aeschylus: Prometheus Bound* (Cambridge: Cambridge University Press).
—— (1999). *Sophocles: Antigone* (Cambridge: Cambridge University Press).
GUTBROD, G. (1994). 'Théorie et pratique de la poésie chez Simone Weil', *CSW* 17/2: 145–58.
HADOT, P. (1981). *Exercices spirituels et philosophie antique* (Paris: Études Augustiniennes).
—— (1995). *Qu'est-ce que la philosophie antique?* ([Paris]: Gallimard).
HAMBLET, W. C. (1999). 'Suffering in the Cosmos: The Redemption of Evil in Levinas and Weil', *Philosophical Writings*, 10: 69–79.
D'HAUTEFEUILLE, F. (1970). *Le Tourment de Simone Weil* ([Paris]: Desclée de Brouwer).
HEIDSIECK, F. (1978). 'Simone Weil et la beauté du monde', *CSW* 1/2: 2–9.
—— (1982). 'Platon, maître et témoin de la connaissance surnaturelle', *CSW* 5/4: 241–9.
—— (2001). 'L'Eschatologie paradoxale de Simone Weil', *CSW* 24/2: 121–9.
HERLING-GRUDZINSKI, G. (1990). 'Venise sauvée', *CSW* 13/1: 1–13.
HICK, J. (1977). *Evil and the God of Love* (2nd edn., London: Macmillan).
HOMER (1999). *The Iliad*, trans. A. T. Murray, rev. William F. Wyatt, Loeb 170, 171, 2 vols. (1924; 2nd edn., Cambridge, Mass.: Harvard University Press).
HOOPER, W. (1996). *C. S. Lewis: A Companion and Guide* (London: Harper Collins).
HOURDIN, G. (1989). *Simone Weil* (Paris: La Découverte).
HOWATSON, M. C. (1989). *The Oxford Companion to Classical Literature* (2nd edn., Oxford: Oxford University Press).
KAHN, G. (1965). 'L'Idée d'une beauté diabolique chez Simone Weil', in Max Milner (ed.), *Entretiens sur l'homme et le diable* (Paris–La Haye: Mouton), 115–22.

KAHN, G. (1978a) (ed.). *Simone Weil: philosophe, historienne et mystique: communications* (Paris: Aubier).
—— (1978b). 'Simone Weil et le christianisme', in Kahn (1978a: 33–53).
—— (1978c). 'La Vérité des religions', in Kahn (1978a: 67–73).
—— (1982). 'Simone Weil et le stoïcisme grec', *CSW* 5/4: 270–84.
—— (1985). 'L'Aspect mystique de la pensée de Simone Weil', *CSW* 8/4: 377–85.
—— (1987). 'Le Style narratif', *CSW* 10/4: 379–82.
—— (1989). 'Simone Weil et Paul Valéry', *CSW* 12/3: 210–11.
—— (1991). 'Simone Weil et Alain', *CSW* 14/3: 206–12.
—— (1993). 'Les Critères d'appréciation de Simone Weil', *CSW* 16/1: 31–6.
KELLS, J. H. (1973) (ed.). *Sophocles: Electra* (London: Cambridge University Press).
KIRKWOOD, G. M. (1994). *A Study of Sophoclean Drama* (2nd edn., Ithaca: Cornell University Press).
KLEIN, J. (1987). 'Théorie et pratique de la poésie chez Simone Weil d'après ses *Cahiers* et son poème *A une jeune fille riche*', *CSW* 10/4: 368–78.
KNOWLES, D. (1966). *What is Mysticism?* (London: Sheed & Ward).
KNOX, B. M. W. (1964). *The Heroic Temper: Studies in Sophoclean Tragedy* (Berkeley: California University Press).
KRAUSE, G., and MÜLLER, G. (1978). 'Apologetik', in Siefgried M. Schwertner (ed.), *Theologische Realenzyklopädie* (Berlin: de Gruyter), 371–429.
KRAUSE, W. (1958). *Die Stellung der frühchristlichen Autoren zur heidnischen Literatur* (Vienna: Herder).
KÜHN, R.(1982). 'L'Inspiration religieuse et philosophique en Grèce vue à partir des mystères d'Eleusis (éléments d'une philosophie religieuse chez Simone Weil)', *CSW* 5/3: 161–83.
—— (1989). *Deuten als Entwerden: eine Synthese des Werkes Simone Weils in hermeneutisch-religionsphilosophischer Sicht* (Freiburg im Breisgau: Herder).
LANFRANCHI, G. (1983). 'Pureté valéryenne et "mystique" pure: méditation présentée à partir d'un moment de "mystique" pure chez Simone Weil ', *CSW* 6/3: 215–42.
LATOURELLE, R. (1994) (ed.). *Dictionary of Fundamental Theology* (Slough: St Paul).
LEMARCHAND, F. (1983). 'Quelques précisions sur les rencontres de Simone Weil à Solesmes en 1938', *CSW* 6/2: 167–77.
LITTLE, J. P. (1970a). 'Society as Mediator in Simone Weil's *Venise sauvée*', *Modern Language Review*, 65: 298–305.
—— (1970b). 'The Symbolism of the Cross in the Writings of Simone Weil', *Religious Studies*, 6: 175–83.
—— (1973). *Simone Weil: A Bibliography* (London: Grant & Cutler).
—— (1978). 'Signification de la mythologie et des contes chez Simone Weil', in Kahn 1978a: 105–18.

—— (1979a). 'Le Refus de l'idolâtrie dans l'œuvre de Simone Weil', *CSW* 2/4: 197–213.
—— (1979b). *Simone Weil: A Bibliography: Supplement No.1* (London: Grant & Cutler).
—— (1985). 'Simone Weil et la culture populaire', *CSW* 8/4: 322–31.
—— (1988a). *Simone Weil: Waiting on Truth* (Oxford: Berg).
—— (1988b). 'Contribution à une étude de l'usage du paradoxe chez Simone Weil', *CSW* 11/2: 105–14.
—— (1990). 'Simone Weil, ou la pensée analogique', in Little and Ughetto (1990: 51–60).
—— (1991). 'Simone Weil, Albert Camus et la tragédie moderne', *CSW* 14/2: 107–17.
—— (1993a). 'Simone Weil's Concept of Decreation', in Bell (1993a: 25–51).
—— (1993b). 'La Création artistique chez Simone Weil', *CSW* 16/1: 17–30.
—— (1996). 'Simone Weil and the Limits of Language', in Dunaway and Springsted (1996: 39–54).
—— and Ughetto, A. (1990) (eds.). *Simone Weil: la soif de l'absolu, Sud* 87/88 (Marseille: Sud).
LLOYD-JONES, H. (1956). 'Zeus in Aeschylus', *Journal of Hellenic Studies*, 76: 55–67.
—— (1982). *Blood for the Ghosts: Classical Influences in the Nineteenth and Twentieth Centuries* (London: Duckworth).
—— (1983). *The Justice of Zeus* (2nd edn., Berkeley: University of California Press).
LOADES, A. (1985). 'Eucharistic Sacrifice: Simone Weil's Use of a Liturgical Metaphor', *Religion and Literature*, 17/2: 43–54.
—— (1993). 'Simone Weil and Antigone: Innocence and Affliction', in Bell (1993a: 277–94).
LUCCHETTI BINGEMER, M. C. (2005). 'Simone Weil et Albert Camus: Sainteté sans Dieu et mystique sans église', *CSW* 28/4: 365–86.
LUSSY, F. de (1988). 'Marche de l'écriture, progression de la pensée', *CSW* 11/2: 115–26.
—— (1990). 'Folklore et spiritualité', in Little and Ughetto (1990: 37–49).
—— (1994). 'Paul Valéry et Simone Weil: deux natures mystiques, deux natures antithétiques', *CSW* 17/4: 407–29.
MCCOOL, G. A. (1994). *The Neo-Thomists*, Marquette Studies in Philosophy 3 (Milwaukee: Marquette University Press).
MCCORD ADAMS, M. (1986). 'Redemptive Suffering: A Christian Approach to the Problem of Evil', in Robert Audi and William J. Wainwright (eds.), *Rationality, Religious Belief, and Moral Commitment: New Essays in the Philosophy of Religion* (Ithaca: Cornell University Press), 248–67.
—— (1990). 'Horrendous Evils and the Goodness of God', in McCord Adams and Adams (1990: 209–21).

McCord Adams, M. and Adams, R. Merrihew (1990) (eds.). *The Problem of Evil* (Oxford: Oxford University Press).

McLellan, D. (1990). *Utopian Pessimist: The Life and Thought of Simone Weil* (New York: Poseidon).

MacLeod, C.W. (1982) (ed.). *'Iliad' Book XXIV* (Cambridge: Cambridge University Press).

Macquarrie, J. (1988). *20th Century Religious Thought* (4th edn., London: SCM).

Madsen, D. L. (1994). *Rereading Allegory: A Narrative Approach to Genre* (New York: St Martin's).

Maes, G. (2000). 'Lecture(s) de *Prologue*', *CSW* 23/2: 191–221.

Malan, I. R. (1979). 'Simone Weil et la responsabilité des écrivains', *CSW* 2/3: 161–8.

Malone, G. K. (1967). 'Apologetics, Practical', in Catholic University of Washington (ed.), *New Catholic Encyclopedia* (New York: McGraw-Hill), 674–7.

Mambrino, J. (1997). 'Simone Weil et George Herbert', *CSW* 20/3: 161–72.

Mansau, A. (1983). 'Simone Weil et la civilisation d'Oc', *CSW* 6/2: 96–104.

—— (1988). 'L'Écriture théâtrale de *Venise sauvée*', *CSW* 11/2: 127–35.

Marchetti, A. (1983). *Simone Weil: la critica disvelante* (Bologna: Clueb).

—— (1987). 'L'espace giottesque: lecture d'après l'esthétique de Simone Weil', *CSW* 10/2: 153–69.

—— (1989). 'Poétique et inspiration chez Simone Weil et Joë Bousquet', *CSW* 12/3: 212–25.

—— (1990). 'Les Pensées et les mots', in Little and Ughetto (1990: 61–73).

—— (1994). 'Poésie et mise en œuvre de la vérité', *CSW* 17/2: 159–75.

—— (1997). 'Poésie et prophétie chez Simone Weil et chez Joë Bousquet', *CSW* 20/3: 177–93.

—— (2000). 'Conscience du mal(heur) et charité de l'écriture', *CSW* 23/2: 129–44.

Martin, R. P. (1989). *The Language of Heroes: Speech and Performance in the Iliad* (Ithaca: Cornell University Press).

Mauriac, F. (1962). *Ce que je crois* (Paris: Grasset).

Mazeau, M. (1978). 'Commentaire du *Prologue* de Simone Weil', *CSW* 1/1: 15–21.

Moeller, C. (1953). 'Simone Weil', in *Littérature du XXe siècle et christianisme*, 5 vols. (Tournai: Casterman), i. 220–55.

Molard, J. (1998). 'Simone Weil et Émile Guillaumin: une rencontre insolite', *CSW* 21/3: 207–19.

Mueller, M. (1978). 'Knowledge and Delusion in the *Iliad*', in John Wright (ed.), *Essays on the Iliad: Selected Modern Criticism* (Bloomington: Indiana University Press), 105–23.

MÜLLER, W. (2000). 'Une relecture théologique de l'expérience mystique chez Simone Weil', *CSW* 23/1: 36–50.
—— (2002). 'La Théorie des quatre sens et la lecture biblique de Simone Weil', *CSW* 25/4: 297–304.
MUSURILLO, H. (1967). *The Light and the Darkness: Studies in the Dramatic Poetry of Sophocles* (Leiden: Brill).
NAGY, G. (1979). *The Best of the Achaeans: Concepts of the Hero in Archaic Greek Poetry* (Baltimore: Johns Hopkins University Press).
NARCY, M. (1967). *Simone Weil: malheur et beauté du monde* (Paris: Centurion).
—— (1982). 'Le Platon de Simone Weil', *CSW* 5/4: 250–67.
—— (1984). 'Simone Weil, mystique ou politique?', *CSW* 7/2: 105–19.
—— (1985). 'Ce qu'il y a de platonicien chez Simone Weil', *CSW* 8/4: 365–76.
—— (1995): 'A propos du *Timée* de Simone Weil: Descartes relayé par Platon?', *CSW* 18/1: 25–34.
—— (1998): 'Simone Weil et Lawrence d'Arabie', *CSW* 21/4: 329–45.
NEVIN, T. R. (1991). *Simone Weil: Portrait of a Self-Exiled Jew* (Chapel Hill: University of Carolina Press).
The New Jerusalem Bible (1990). (London: Darton, Longman & Todd).
NICOLA, G. P. DI (1995). 'Le Mal et la nécessité: réflexions sur Venise sauvée', *CSW* 18/2: 123–42.
NUSSBAUM, M. (1990). *Love's Knowledge: Essays on Philosophy and Literature* (Oxford: Oxford University Press).
—— (2001). *The Fragility of Goodness: Luck and Ethics in Greek Tragedy and Philosophy* (rev. edn., Cambridge: Cambridge University Press).
OLLIVIER, S. (1995). 'Le Problème du mal chez Simone Weil et Dostoevski', *CSW* 18/4: 367–87.
OXENHANDLER, N. (1995). *Looking for Heroes in Postwar France: Albert Camus, Max Jacob, Simone Weil* (Hanover: University Press of New England).
PACHECO-GONÇALVES, J.-M. (2003). 'Vrai Dieu, vraie foi, religion vraie selon Simone Weil: quelques annotations', *CSW* 26/2: 161–79.
PARAIN-VIAL, J. (1990). 'L'Influence de Platon sur la théorie de la justice dans l'œuvre de Simone Weil', *CSW* 13/3: 253–63.
PASCAL (1954). *Œuvres complètes*, ed. Jacques Chevalier, La Pléiade ([Paris]: Gallimard).
PASSOT, C. (1994). 'Des beaux-arts à la beauté (d'Alain à Simone Weil)', *CSW* 17/3: 256–69.
PEDUZZI, A. C. (1985). 'Simone Weil et Héraclite', *CSW* 8/1: 13–24.
PÉPIN, J. (1961). *Les Deux Approches du Christianisme* (Paris: Éditions de Minuit).
PERRIN, J.-M. (1964) (ed.). *Réponses aux questions de Simone Weil* (Paris: Aubier).
—— (1983). 'Simone Weil au Portugal', *CSW* 6/2: 135–6.

PERRIN, J.-M. (1984). *Mon dialogue avec Simone Weil* (Paris: Nouvelle Cité).
—— (2003). *Simone Weil as We Knew Her*, trans. Emma Crauford (1953; repr. London: Routledge).
—— and THIBON, G. (1967). *Simone Weil telle que nous l'avons connue* ([Paris]: Fayard).
PÉTREMENT, S. (1973). *La Vie de Simone Weil*, 2 vols. ([Paris]: Fayard).
—— (1988). *Simone Weil: A Life*, trans. Raymond Rosenthal (repr. New York: Schocken).
PIRRUCELLO, A. (1994). 'Overcoming Self: Simone Weil on Beauty', in Ann W. Astell (ed.), *Divine Representation: Postmodernism and Spirituality* (New York: Paulist Press), 34–46.
—— (1996). 'Simone Weil's Violent Grace', *CSW* 19/4: 397–411.
PLAGNOL, J. (1997). 'Poésie et musique des sphères chez Simone Weil et Rainer Maria Rilke', *CSW* 20/3: 194–205.
PLANTINGA, A. (1990). 'God, Evil, and the Metaphysics of Freedom', in McCord Adams and Adams (1990: 83–109).
PRÉMONT, L. (1964). *Le Mythe de Prométhée dans la littérature française contemporaine* (Quebec: Presses de l'université Laval).
PUENTE, F. R. (1996). 'Simone Weil, Friedrich Nietzsche et la Grèce', *CSW* 19/1: 67–96.
PURCELL, D. (1996). 'Iris Murdoch's *The Green Knight* and Simone Weil', *CSW* 19/2: 225–38.
RABI, W. (1971). 'Simone Weil (1909–1943) ou l'itinéraire d'une âme: les derniers jours—le baptême *in extremis*', *Les Nouveaux Cahiers*, 26: 51–62.
—— (1978). 'La Conception weilienne de la création: rencontre avec la Kabbale juive', in Kahn (1978*a*: 141–54).
RAHNER, H. (1945). *Griechische Mythen in christlicher Deutung* (Zürich: Rhein-Verlag).
RAPER, D. (1978). 'Les Modèles de religion et la notion de vérité', in Kahn (1978*a*: 59–66).
REDFIELD, J. M. (1975). *Nature and Culture in the 'Iliad': The Tragedy of Hector* (Chicago: Chicago University Press).
REINHARDT, K. (1933). *Sophocles* (Frankfurt am Main: Klostermann).
—— (1979). *Sophocles*, trans. Hazel Harvey and David Harvey (Oxford: Blackwell).
RHEES, R. (2000). *Discussions of Simone Weil*, ed. D. Z. Philips (Albany: State University of New York Press).
RIAUD, J. (1983). 'Simone Weil et les Cathares', *CSW* 6/2: 105–12.
RICHARDSON, N. (1993). *The Iliad: A Commentary*, vi. *Books 21–24* (Cambridge: Cambridge University Press).
RINGER, M. (1998). *Electra and the Empty Urn: Metatheater and Role Playing in Sophocles* (Chapel Hill: University of North Carolina Press).

ROLLINSON, P. (1981). *Classical Theories of Allegory and Christian Culture* (Pittsburgh: Dusquesne University Press).
RUTHERFORD, R. B. (1996). *Homer, Greece & Rome*, New Surveys in the Classics 26 (Oxford: Oxford University Press).
ST JUSTIN MARTYR (1997). *The First and Second Apologies*, ed. and trans. Leslie Barnard, Ancient Christian Writers 56 (New York: Paulist Press).
SAINT-ROBERT, P. DE (2000). *La Vision tragique de Simone Weil* (Paris: de Guibert).
SAVINEL, P. (1960). 'Simone Weil et l'hellénisme', *Bulletin de l'Association Guillaume Budé* 4/1: 122–44.
SCHLETTE, H. R. (1996). 'The Language of the Marketplace and the Language of the Nuptial Chamber: The Theological Significance of a Distinction in the Philosophy of Language', in Dunaway and Springsted (1996: 31–7).
—— (2001). 'Histoire des religions et "théologie" des religions chez Simone Weil', *CSW* 24/2: 73–88.
SCHMID, W. (1929). *Untersuchungen zum gefesselten Prometheus*, Tübinger Beiträge zur Altertumswissenschaft 9 (Stuttgart: Kohlhammer).
SCHMIDT, L. W. (1992). 'Simone Weil on Religion: a Voegelinian Critique', *CSW* 15/3: 263–73.
SCHUMANN, M. (1974). *La Mort née de leur propre vie: Péguy, Simone Weil, Gandhi*, ([Paris]: Fayard).
—— (1993). 'Henri Bergson et Simone Weil', *Revue des deux mondes* (November): 194–203.
SCHWEYER, M. (2001). 'La "fable du progrès" et la "superstition de la chronologie"', *CSW* 24/1: 35–49.
SCULLY, J. (1975) (ed.). *Aeschylus: Prometheus*, trans. James Scully and C. J. Herington (London: Oxford University Press).
SEELHÖFER, D. (2001). 'Reinhold Schneider et Simone Weil', *CSW* 24/3: 217–31.
SEGAL, C. (1981). *Tragedy and Civilisation: An Interpretation of Sophocles* (Cambridge, Mass.: Harvard University Press).
—— (1990). '*Antigone*: Death and Love, Hades and Dionysus', in Harold Bloom (ed.), *Sophocles*, Modern Critical Views (New York: Chelsea House), 161–206.
SEIFERT, J. (1996). *Gott als Gottesbeweis: Eine Phänomenologische Neubegründung des ontologischen Arguments* (Heidelberg: Winter).
SEZNEC, J. (1940). *La Survivance des dieux antiques: essai sur le rôle de la tradition mythologique dans l'humanisme et dans l'art de la Renaissance* (London: Warburg Institute).
—— (1953). *The Survival of the Pagan Gods: The Mythological Tradition and its Place in Renaissance Humanism and Art*, trans. Barbara F. Sessions (New York: Pantheon).

SHEPPARD, J. T. (1927). '*Electra*: A Defence of Sophocles', *The Classical Review*, 41: 2–9.
SHERRY, P. (1993). 'Simone Weil on Beauty', in Bell (1993*a*: 260–76).
SHIBATA, M. (1993). 'La Beauté du monde comme la voix qui nous appelle', *CSW* 16/1: 1–16.
—— (1995). 'Le Mal et la beauté chez Simone Weil', *CSW* 18/2: 109–22.
SIMONSUURI, K. (1985). 'Simone Weil's Interpretation of Homer', *French Studies*, 34/2: 160–75.
SMYTH, H. W. (1924). *Aeschylean Tragedy* (Berkeley: University of California Press).
SOLMSEN, F. (1995). *Hesiod and Aeschylus* (2nd edn., Ithaca: Cornell University Press).
SOPHOCLES (1864). Ed. and trans. G. Dindorf ([Paris]: Firmin Didot).
—— (1922–34). Ed. Paul Masqueray (Paris: Les Belles Lettres).
—— (1997). *Ajax, Electra, Oedipus Tyrannus*, ed. and trans. Hugh Lloyd-Jones, Loeb 20 (1994; repr. with corrections Cambridge, Mass.: Harvard University Press).
—— (1998). *Antigone*, ed. and trans. Hugh Lloyd-Jones, Loeb 21 (1994; repr. with corrections, Cambridge, Mass.: Harvard University Press).
SOURISSE, M. (1985). 'Simone Weil et la tradition cartésienne', *CSW* 8/1: 25–41.
—— (1996). 'Sur une aporie concernant le problème du mal chez Simone Weil', *CSW* 19/2: 177–98.
—— (2000). 'Simone Weil et maître Eckhart', *CSW* 23/1: 1–35.
—— (2003). 'Job, figure du Christ?', *CSW* 26/2: 119–48.
SPRINGSTED, E. O. (1981). 'Théorie weilienne et théorie platonicienne de la nécessité', *CSW* 4/3: 149–67.
—— (1982). 'Métaphysique de la transcendance et théorie des *metaxu* chez Simone Weil', *CSW* 5/4: 285–306.
—— (1983). *Christus Mediator: Platonic Mediation in the Thought of Simone Weil* (Chico, Calif.: Scholars Press).
—— (1986). 'Droits et obligations', *CSW* 9/4: 394–404.
—— (1994). 'The Baptism of Simone Weil', in Allen and Springsted (1994: 3–18).
—— (1996). 'Contradiction, Mystery and the Use of Words in Simone Weil', in Dunaway and Springsted (1996: 13–29).
SPROUL, R. C. (1984). *Classical Apologetics: A Rational Defense of the Christian Faith and a Critique of Presuppositional Apologetics* (Grand Rapids: Zondevan).
STEINER, G. (1984). *Antigones: The Antigone Myth in Western Literature, Art and Thought* (Oxford: Oxford University Press).
—— (1989). *Real Presences* (Chicago: Chicago University Press).
—— (1996*a*). 'Sainte Simone—Simone Weil', in *No Passion Spent: Essays 1978–1996* (London: Faber), 171–9.

—— (1996b) (ed.). *Homer in English* (London: Penguin).
—— and FAGLES, R. (1962) (eds.). *Homer: A Collection of Critical Essays* (Englewood Cliffs: Prentice-Hall).
STOKES, T. (1996). *Audience, Intention, and Rhetoric in Pascal and Simone Weil* (New York: Peter Lang).
STUMP, E. (1996). 'Aquinas on the Suffering of Job', in Daniel Howard-Snyder (ed.), *The Evidential Argument from Evil* (Bloomington: Indiana University Press), 49–68.
SUMMERS, J. H. (1981). 'Notes on Simone Weil's *Iliad*', in George Abbott White (ed.), *Simone Weil: Interpretations of a Life* (Amherst: University of Massachusetts Press) 87–93.
SUTHERLAND, S. R. (1984). *Faith and Ambiguity* (London: SCM).
SWINBURNE, R. (1991). *The Existence of God* (rev. edn., Oxford: Clarendon).
—— (1996). 'Some Major Strands of Theodicy', in McCord Adams and Adams (1990: 30–48).
TAPLIN, O. (1977). *The Stagecraft of Aeschylus: The Dramatic Use of Exits and Entrances in Greek Tragedy* (Oxford: Clarendon).
—— (1992). *Homeric Soundings: The Shaping of the Iliad* (Oxford: Clarendon).
—— (1999). 'Greek with Consequence', *Classical Association Presidential Address* (Sherborne: Remous).
TERTULLIAN (1889). *Apologeticus adversus gentes pro christianis*, ed. T. H. Bindley (Oxford: Clarendon).
—— (1950). *Apologetical Works and Minucius Felix Octavius*, trans. R. Arbesmann, E. J. Daly, and E. Quain (Washington DC: Catholic University of America Press).
—— (1972). *Adversus Marcionem*, ed. and trans. E. Evans (Oxford: Clarendon).
TILLIETTE, X. (1990). *Le Christ de la philosophie: prolégomènes à une christologie philosophique* (Paris: Cerf).
TRABUCCO, G. (1995). 'Su *Venezia salva* di Simone Weil', *CSW* 18/2: 143–54.
TROUSSON, R. (1976). *Le Thème de Prométhée dans la littérature européenne* (2nd edn., Geneva: Droz).
UGHETTO, A. (1990). 'La Méditation de la justice chez Simone Weil', in Little and Ughetto (1990: 117–26).
VERNANT, J. P. (1988). *Myth and Tragedy in Ancient Greece* (New York: Zone Books).
VETÖ, M. (1964). 'Le Piège de Dieu', *La Table Ronde*, 197: 71–88.
—— (1971). *La Métaphysique religieuse de Simone Weil* (Paris: Vrin).
—— (1985). 'Thèmes kantiens dans la pensée de Simone Weil', *CSW* 8/1: 42–9.
—— (1994). *The Religious Metaphysics of Simone Weil*, trans. Joan Dargan (Albany: State University of New York Press).
VILLELA-PETIT, M. (1995). 'Résister au mal chez Simone Weil et Etty Hillesum', *CSW* 18/4: 343–56.

VILLELA-PETIT, M. (1998). 'La Force des mots: écho philosophique à "l'étrange mort de Patrocle"', *Diogène* 181: 89–99.
—— (2002). 'Une lecture élective et analogique de la Bible', *CSW* 25/4: 281–95.
—— (2003). 'Simone Weil, Martin Heidegger et la Grèce', *CSW* 26/2: 181–218.
WEIL, A. (1990). 'Propos sur Simone Weil (entretien avec Malcolm Muggeridge)', in Little and Ughetto (1990: 9–23).
WEIL, S. (2003). *Simone Weil's The Iliad or The Poem of Force*, ed. and trans. James P. Holoka (New York: Peter Lang).
WEINANDY, T. G. (2000). *Does God Suffer?* (Edinburgh: T&T Clark).
WERGE, T. (1996). 'Sacramental Tension: Divine Transcendence and Finite Images in Simone Weil's Literary Imagination', in Dunaway and Springsted (1996: 85–97).
WILAMOWITZ-MOELLENDORFF, U. VON (1914). *Aischylos Interpretationen* (Berlin: Weidmann).
WINCH, P. (1989). *Simone Weil: 'The Just Balance'* (Cambridge: Cambridge University Press).
WINNINGTON-INGRAM, R. P. (1980). *Sophocles: An Interpretation* (Cambridge: Cambridge University Press).
—— (1983). *Studies in Aeschylus* (Cambridge: Cambridge University Press).
WITTGENSTEIN, L. (1980). *Culture and Value*, ed. G. H. von Wright, trans. Peter Winch (Oxford: Blackwell).
WOODARD, T. M. (1964). '*Electra* by Sophocles: The Dialectical Design', *Harvard Studies in Classical Philology*, 68: 163–205.
ZAMBON, F. (1996). 'La Douleur et le mal dans la doctrine cathare et chez Simone Weil', *CSW* 19/1: 1–17.

Index

Aeschylus
  Oresteia 183, 184
  Agamemnon 15, 24, 79
  Choephoroe 180, 183, 185, 186, 187
  Eumenides 153
  Prometheus Bound 1, 15, 79, 80, 143–177
  Suppliants 24
aesthetes 61
aesthetics, *see* beauty
Alain (Emile Chartier) 4, 9, 14, 16, 17, 27, 116, 146
allegory 22, 193, 195–6
amertume 123, 135–6
Anouilh, Jean 26
Anselm of Canterbury 66
Apollo 21, 34
Archimedes 99, 101
Aristotle 86, 89
art 62, 171–4, 176
artistic creation 19, 171–3
atheism 2, 41, 52, 143
attente 31, 33, 49–50, 103, 105, 171–2, 192–3, 197
attention 105
Aubigné, Agrippa d' 25
Augustine of Hippo, Saint 40, 160, 194, 199

Ballard, Jean 6
Balzac, Honoré de 26, 27
baptism 31–2, 37, 39, 59, 72, 200, 201
Baudelaire, Charles 15, 26
beauty 12, 170–3, 196, 198
  and apologetics 60–5, 68
  and suffering 170–3
Bell, Charles 5, 171
Bergson, Henri 40, 57
Bernanos, Georges 11
Bernard, Victor 81–2, 84, 181
Bespaloff, Rachel 129–30
Bhagavadgītā 6, 15, 188

Bible
  New Testament 16, 18, 36, 49, 103, 138, 174–5, 189, 193
  Old Testament 20, 44–9
Blondel, Maurice 54–7
Bousquet, Joë 6, 58–9, 78, 79, 147, 179, 198, 205
Boyer, Johan 27–8
Brooke, Rupert 26
Buck, Pearl 26
Bultmann, Rudolf 18

Camus, Albert 8, 11
caritas 39, 61, 90, 96, 100, 101, 107, 136, 138
Cathars 140–1
Catholic Church 30–2, 34, 41–2, 53–4, 59, 208–10
Ceppède, Jean de La 26
Cervantes, Miguel de 25
Chesterton, G. K. 35
Christ 2, 5, 16, 18, 19, 34, 36, 40, 43, 49, 90, 101, 144, 148–50, 155–7, 163–4, 166, 175, 200–1, 203
Christianity 2, 4, 16, 30, 34–5, 39, 47–8, 55, 116, 123, 135, 138–9, 179, 197, 199, 208–9
Church Fathers 16, 44–9, 148, 174
civilization 2, 34, 48, 116, 140, 174, 176, 179
Claudel, Paul 26
Cleanthes 152
Clement of Alexandria 24, 45, 46–7
communism 4, 9, 120, 140, 205
conversion/*retournement* 23, 27, 33, 38–40, 60, 115, 116
  obstacles 33–5
Core, *see* Persephone
Corneille, Pierre 14, 26, 79, 139
Couturier, Marie-Alain Père 10
creation 161–2, 167
cross 19, 45, 52, 101, 123, 152, 164, 166–8, 171–4, 175–6
culture 12, 20–1, 27, 33, 56

Dante, Alighieri 15, 26
Daumal, René 6
death 108, 109, 122, 128, 130
décreation 167–8
Deitz, Simone 31
déracinement (uprooting) 33, 38
Descartes, René 4, 25
destiny, *see* fate
Detœuf, Auguste 119
Dionysus 2, 21, 24, 34, 105–6
Diotima 4
Donne, John 26
Dostoevsky, Fyodor 11, 26, 162
Duke of Norway (tale) 63, 179, 193, 196
Durkheim, Émile 18

education 70
Entre Nous 15, 24, 27, 79, 80, 81, 180, 181, 185, 194
Erinyes, *see* Furies
être pur 107–8, 132, 140, 157–8, 185
Eucharist 37, 73, 157, 201, 214
euhemerism 22, 45
Euripides 183
 Bacchae 24, 105
 Electra 180, 183, 184, 186
 Heracles 24
 Hippolytus 24, 156–7
 Medea 15
evil, *see* sin

faith 38, 40, 52, 56, 60, 93, 96, 110–11, 140, 208–9, 212
 implicit 35, 57
fascism, *see* Nazism
fate 76, 106–9, 126
Festugière, André-Jean Père 16–17
folly 85, 94, 108, 110, 190
 folly of love 83, 86–7, 90, 93–4, 101, 110–11
force 117, 118, 122–3, 126, 129–31, 136, 137–8, 139–40, 141
France/the French 6, 92, 115, 122, 137–8, 139, 141–2, 176, 205
Francis of Assisi, Saint 26, 48, 150
Frazer, Sir James George 18–19
Free French Government 6, 7, 9, 77–8, 93–4, 102, 109, 110, 111
Freud, Sigmund 14, 78
Furies 153, 180, 183, 184–5

Gadamer, Hans-Georg 98
genius 69, 172–3
Germany 4, 137
Gide, André 26, 91–2
Giraudoux, Jean 119
God 2, 16–17, 20, 24, 40–1, 49–50, 59–62, 80, 91, 93, 96, 100, 107, 134–5, 140, 145, 155, 158–73, 192, 195–8, 203–4
gods 45, 80, 89, 90, 95, 96, 105, 108, 112, 183
Goethe, Johann Wolfgang von 15, 26
good, the 67, 77–8
grace
 see also supernatural 52, 56, 86, 163, 197
Greece 1, 12, 16, 20–1, 30, 36, 45, 48, 121–2, 139, 150, 174
Greek tragedy 14, 15, 16, 22, 23, 25, 28
Grenier, Jean 129
Grévin, Jean 26
Grimm, Gebrüder 27
Guillaumin, Émile 27

Ham 47–8
Hamp, Pierre 27
Heidegger 12
Heracles 154
Herbert, George 2, 5, 26, 113, 209, 214
Hitler, Adolf 6, 127
history 98, 119, 176
Holy Spirit 151–2
Homer 79, 134–5
 Iliad 2, 14, 15–16, 79, 106, 115–42
 Odyssey 15
Horace 15
hubris 108, 110, 126, 133, 137
Hugo, Victor 26

ideology 39, 77–8, 92, 140, 205
idolatry 39, 49, 77, 92, 95–6, 108, 172
 idol 44, 53, 89, 96
impartiality of God 90–1
inspiration 56, 69, 141, 172

Jauss, Hans Robert 98
Job 103, 134, 147, 159–60, 166, 170
Jodelle, Estienne 26

John of the Cross, Saint 48, 151–2, 164, 192
John XXIII, Pope 211
Judaism/Jewish people 29, 31, 38, 44, 48–9
justice 87, 96–7, 190
 natural 77–8, 86, 89–90
 supernatural 78, 90–1, 96
Justin Martyr, Saint 24, 35, 45, 47, 48
Juvenal 15

kléos 138–9

La Boétie, Étienne de 25
Lamartine, Alphonse de 25
language 74–5
law 85–93
 natural law 77, 85–6
 positive law 86
 supernatural moral or divine law 77, 85–9, 91–3
Lawrence of Arabia, T. E. 130–1
Le Senne, René 3
lecture 97, 99, 124–5, 154, 193
 non-lecture 103
Lewis, C. S. 175
literature 11, 16, 19, 25, 27, 28, 68–70, 78, 210
 approach to literature 27–8, 103–4, 113, 173
 Greek 82
Logos 18, 45–7, 164, 165, 170, 203
love 64, 84, 97–8, 101, 131–2, 150, 161, 164, 205
 implicit love 35, 101, 179, 192
 love of God 8, 24, 48, 69, 136, 166, 168–70, 174, 176–7
 love of neighbour, see *caritas*
 see also folly of love
Lucretius 15

malheur 15–6, 59–60, 69, 101, 116, 134, 136, 143–5, 158–73, 188–90
Mallarmé, Stéphane 15, 25
Marcus Aurelius 15
Marie-Noël 11
Maritain, Jacques 10
Marlowe, Christopher 26
Marxism, *see* communism
Mauriac, François 11, 26, 210
Melchisedek 20, 48

Michelangelo 26
Minotaur 62
miracle 42–3, 53, 121
Molière (Jean Baptiste Poquelin) 25
Montaigne, Michel de 25
Montesquieu, Charles de Secondat, baron de 25
moral law, *see* law
morality 26–7, 69, 88, 91–2, 157, 173, 197
Moses 45, 47, 48–9
mystery religions, *see* religion
mystical hermeneutics 101, 113
 see also point-of-view, supernatural
mysticism 2, 5–6, 16, 29, 30, 48, 50, 58–60, 67, 92, 99, 101, 169, 179–80, 191–206
myth 18–19, 21–3, 25, 45, 174–5, 195, 208

natural law, *see* law
Nazism 2, 92, 110, 120, 140, 205
Nietzsche, Friedrich 21–2, 103
Noah 47–8
Numenius of Apamea 47

Origen 45
Osiris 2, 34
Otto, Rudolf 18

pacifism 5, 6, 116, 119, 140
paradox 75
Pascal, Blaise 49–52, 56, 60, 74, 75, 175
Passion 5, 43, 80, 108–9, 144, 149–50, 156, 162, 163, 174, 175
Paulhan, Jean 118–19
Paul VI, Pope 211
Péguy, Charles 11
Persephone 62, 179, 198
Perrin, Joseph-Marie Père 6, 7, 8, 13, 30, 35, 47, 58–9, 71, 111, 179
perspective, *see* point-of-view
pesanteur 40, 43, 67, 76, 86, 90, 100, 136
Pétrement, Simone 8, 13, 79
Plato 12, 14, 16–17, 23, 25, 45–6, 48–9, 70, 163
 Laws 94
 myth of the cave 29, 39, 63, 97
 Phaedrus 61, 64
 Republic 149, 156, 205

Plato (cont.)
  Symposium 64
  Timaeus 45, 66
point-of-view 35, 83–4, 89, 98–9
natural (also *raison d'état* or
  Realpolitik) 77–8, 83, 89, 100,
  102
supernatural 75, 78, 84, 99–100,
  102, 104, 134–5, 139, 140,
  152, 157, 164, 170, 203
Posternak, Jean 79, 117–18, 182
pre-Christian intuitions 17–20, 24,
  34, 44, 46, 166, 175, 208–9
prestige 39, 48, 53, 121, 127, 149–50
Prologue 179, 199–204
proofs for God's existence 54–5, 65–8
  from beauty 66
  from miracles 42–3
  from need 40–1, 57
  from prophecies 42, 44–9
  historical 41–2
  ontological 66–8
  teleological 66
propaganda 68, 134, 141, 205
Protagoras 33, 100, 141
Proust, Marcel 26
Pythagoras 46, 49

Rabelais 25
Racine, Jean 11, 14, 25, 79
reading 73, 214
religion 2, 4, 16, 18, 37–9, 42, 53, 55,
  92, 179, 201
  mystery religions 17, 46–7
Renaissance 33
Resistance 6, 111
responsibility of writers 68–70
resurrection 43–4
Retz, Jean-François-Paul de Gondi,
  cardinal de 25
Rimbaud, Arthur 26
Romains, Jules 26
Romans, the 98, 127
Romanticism 70, 150
Rousseau, Jean-Jacques 25

Saint-Exupéry, Antoine de 27
sanctity/saints 27, 40, 42, 43, 69, 138,
  172–3, 213–14
Sappho 26
Scève, Maurice 25
Scheler, Max 18

scholasticism 55–6
Schumann, Maurice 6, 9, 109, 144,
  158
science 4, 10, 18, 21, 42–3, 52–3
secularism 33, 39
Shakespeare, William 25, 26
  Hamlet 186
  King Lear 11, 110
sin 68–9, 76, 78–9, 91, 100, 106–8,
  115, 160–2, 188
  original sin 39, 156, 160
slaves/slavery 4, 122–6, 166
Socrates 23
Sophocles 22, 69, 75, 79, 82–3
  Ajax 15, 24
  Antigone 1, 11, 14, 15, 22, 26,
  77–114, 150
  Electra 1, 15, 79, 101, 178–206
  Philoctetes 15, 24
Souvarine, Boris 4
Stendhal (Marie-Henri Beyle) 26, 27
suffering, see *malheur*
supernatural 18, 33, 40, 54, 57, 75, 78,
  89, 96, 100, 101–2, 105, 113–14,
  164, 212–14
surrealists 26, 92
syncretism 45

Terence 15
Tertullian 148
theodicy 143–5, 158–173
Thibon, Gustave 6, 8, 111–12, 147,
  202
Thomism, see scholasticism
Thucydides 138
Tolstoy, Leo 26
tragedy, see Greek tragedy
truth 3, 13, 19, 35, 40, 41, 52, 53, 70,
  71, 72–3, 74, 110, 116, 163, 164,
  205, 210, 215

Upanishads 6, 15

Valéry, Paul 11, 26, 146
Vasto, Lanza del 26
Viau, Théophile de 25
Venise Sauvée 10, 11, 140, 146
Verhaeren, Émile 26
Verlaine, Paul 15, 26
Vernon, John 5
Vigny, Alfred de 25, 27, 166

Villon, François 25
Virgil 15, 24–5
vocation 71–3, 109

war 115–16, 119–21, 127–8, 131, 137–8, 140
World War I 119

World War II 29, 91, 140, 143, 176
Wilde, Oscar 26
wisdom 17, 75, 97, 152, 163–5
words 36, 74–6, 120–1
workers 36–7, 70, 80, 81–5, 181
works of art 62, 66, 69, 74, 171–3, 210, 213